"The most original and important contribution to the integration of Jungian psychology and physics since the original collaboration between Jung and Pauli."

Sean Kelly, Professor at the California Institute of Integral Studies and author of *Coming Home: The Birth and Transformation of the Planetary Era*

"Timothy Desmond's theory that the psyche is a gravitational singularity would drive both Isaac Newton and Sigmund Freud crazy. But any theory that doesn't is a waste of time. We are living in a break point of Western Civilization. In light of quantum physics and brain science, it is no longer viable to think of consciousness as a sideshow, but the pathway into an integral universe, which it is our true intellectual challenge to discover. Drawing upon his knowledge of string theory, the physics of black holes, the philosophy of science, and depth psychology, Desmond articulates a vision that just might be wild enough to take us home."

Brian Thomas Swimme, Professor at the California Institute of Integral Studies and author of *Journey of the Universe*

"*Psyche and Singularity* is one of the most profoundly significant books I've had the pleasure to read. Tracing striking parallels between string theory and Jungian thought, Desmond provides the most compelling explanation for how synchronicities work that I've encountered."

Grant Maxwell, Author of *The Dynamics of Transformation: Tracing an Emerging World View*

"From quantum physics to alchemical psychology, *Psyche and Singularity* takes the reader upon quite a ride as it alters one's view of consciousness. The first two chapters are, by themselves, worth the price of the book. Desmond dares to take the reader deep into the journey of the mathematics behind string theory and black holes, presenting such arcana as imaginary numbers and Riemann spheres in language that is quite accessible to the general reader.

As the subject unfolds, the discussion may sound like insane science fiction, but Desmond offers a refreshingly accurate picture, a synthesis of psyche and quantum physics that becomes the key to unlock a map of consciousness and synchronicity backed by the central ideas of Pauli, Susskind, and Jung."

Shelli Joye, Author of *Tuning the Mind: Holonomic Brain Theory and the Implicate Order*

PSYCHE AND SINGULARITY

PSYCHE AND SINGULARITY

JUNGIAN PSYCHOLOGY AND HOLOGRAPHIC STRING THEORY

$$\Psi = \odot$$

Timothy Desmond

PERSISTENT PRESS

est. 2012

To the eternal memory of the great Stephen Hawking, who gave birth to the black hole information paradox that led to this book, which was born the year he died.

Persistent Press
Nashville, Tennessee 37206
www.PersistentPress.com

ISBN 978-0-692-18501-8 (paperback)

CONTENTS

List of Figures

INTRODUCTION

It seemed to me as if behind the horizon of the cosmos a three-dimensional world had been artificially built up, in which each person sat by himself in a little box. . . . I had been so glad to shed it all, and now it had come about that I—along with everyone else—would again be hung up in a box by a thread.[1]

C.G. Jung, *Memories, Dreams, Reflections*

Psyche=highest intensity in the smallest space.[2]

C.G. Jung, February 29, 1952, the "Leap Day" letter

In 387 B.C.E. Plato opened a school in a park called Academia, where he perpetuated the Pythagorean hunt for the mathematical forms underlying the motions of the planets. He believed this quest could open the eye of the soul to eternal forms of knowledge that are imprinted on each psyche, including the psyche of the cosmos as a whole. According to Plato, the eternal ideas of the cosmic psyche project all of the temporary forms of matter we perceive out from the central point and in from the spherical circumference of the universe, to which each reincarnating psyche is tethered by a thread of destiny.[3] After the Enlightenment, Plato's theory was displaced by the mechanistic theory that the universe is like a machine made of material atoms that interact in empty space according to impersonal laws of nature, and that consciousness is an unintended byproduct of chance groupings of atoms. As a result, the study of the psyche and the study of matter are now segregated fields of thought. What most members of mainstream academia have yet to recognize, however, is that, throughout the twentieth century, Plato's cosmology gradually resurfaced. Aware of that historical trend, two academic superstars put their heads together to pave the way for a reunion of psychology and physics.

From the paramount positions of their respective fields, the psychologist Carl Jung (1875-1961) and the Nobel Prize-winning physicist Wolfgang Pauli (1900-1958) began constructing a conceptual bridge to span the academic abyss separating these two disciplines. Like laying out two parallel beams, they co-created a theory according to which the laws of psychology mirror the laws of microphysics because, they believed, mind and matter both radiate from the same transcendental source. Following the sixteenth-century alchemist, Gerhard Dorn, they called this source the *unus mundus*, or "one world" underlying both matter and mind.[4] Jung also refers to the *unus mundus* as the One, the God archetype, and the archetype of the Self.[5] Jung's analysis of Pauli's dreams in *Psychology and Alchemy* supported Jung's theory that the *unus mundus* spontaneously compensates a conscious mind being pulled between opposing demands by presenting itself to that conscious mind in the symbolic image of a mandala, a circle or sphere with a central point.[6] If the laws of physics and psychology mirror each other, and if the *unus mundus* presents itself as a mandala image to the psyche we each perceive inwardly, in what outwardly observable form, if any, does it demonstrate itself in the physical world?

In this book I extend Jung and Pauli's collaborative line of research by suggesting that physicist Leonard Susskind's holographic string theory description of black holes and the "inside-out black hole" universe perfectly conforms to the mandala image of the *unus mundus*, the archetype of oneness through the reconciliation of opposites that underlies and structures both cosmos and psyche.[7] Despite Susskind presenting his string theory as the ultimate atheistic alternative to "the illusion of intelligent design" (the subtitle of his 2006 book, *The Cosmic Landscape*), his interpretation of the black hole model of the cosmos (a perfect sphere encompassing a central singularity) clearly mirrors Jung's model of the psyche, apparently revealing the mandala image of the ultimate One in physical reality.

Susskind, Jung, and Pauli

Leonard Susskind is the Felix Block Professor of Theoretical Physics at Stanford University, and the author of several books, including: *The Cosmic Landscape: String Theory and the Illusion of Intelligent Design* (2006) and *The Black Hole War: My Battle with Stephen Hawking to Make the World Safe for Quantum Mechanics* (2008). As he explains in his books, at about the same time as physicists Yoichiro Nambu and Holger Nielsen, Susskind independently helped pioneer the original quantum theory of hadron-sized strings in the last two years of the 1960s.[8] Along with his partner, the Dutch Nobel laureate Gerard 't Hooft, Susskind then helped pioneer the holographic interpretation of the much tinier, fundamental strings in the first half of the 1990s.

According to string theory, quantum particles are made of even tinier strings of energy—so tiny that they cannot be empirically observed using any known technology available today. In fact, this is the greatest complaint critics of string theory have: if fundamental strings cannot be observed, they should not be included in the realm of physical science. Nevertheless, string theory mathematically unites the otherwise incompatible theories of general relativity (the physics of the force of gravity that governs nature at the largest scales) and quantum mechanics (the physics of the other three forces of nature—electromagnetic, strong, and weak—predominating at the smallest scales). String theory does this by describing how the various vibrations of a fundamental string manifest as all the different kinds of quantum particles (including theoretical gravitons that propagate the force of gravity), in the same way that an entire scale of musical notes can be drawn from a single violin string. Susskind's claim to fame is that he used a holographic interpretation of string theory to disprove Stephen Hawking's former (and ultimately recanted) claim that, according to the predictions derived from quantum mechanics and the general theory of relativity, information that falls into a black hole is permanently lost from our observable universe. Susskind realized, to his horror, that Hawking's seemingly solid reasoning violates the most fundamental principle of physics, even more basic than the conservation of mass and energy: namely, the principle of the conservation of information.

According to this principle, not only must the matter-energy content of the universe remain constant, but the information describing the trajectories of each particle must be capable, at least theoretically, of being retrieved and retraced so that each object and sequence of events is capable of being precisely reconstructed. For example, not only must all of the energy and mass of an exploding bomb remain in the universe, but the flight path and momentum of each fragment and particle of gas must remain traceable according to the principle of information conservation, although, practically speaking, the technology capable of tracing that much information is not available today. Susskind realized that if this edifice of physics were overturned, the entire field would collapse into a chasm of inconsistencies. He therefore rushed to its defense, and finally succeeded in defeating Hawking's claim.

On one hand, Susskind agreed with Hawking that, from the perspective of an observer who follows material as it falls past the event horizon of a black hole, all traces of that event would indeed be irretrievably lost from our observable universe. That observer would not be able to return from, or even send a signal traveling at the speed of light back out of the black hole, because the inward tidal flow of the fabric of space-time reaches the universal speed limit of light at the horizon, and achieves infinite speed at the central point, known as the gravitational singularity. On the other hand, Susskind argued that from the perspective of observers who remain outside the black hole, as material objects falling toward it reach the speed of light at the event horizon, the rapidly vibrating strings of which they are made would become slowed down and smeared all around that spherical boundary, as if on a holographic film. That information would then be released back into the observable universe with what is called Hawking radiation. Thus, the principle of the conservation of information would be preserved.

A similar situation would occur at the cosmic horizon, the inside-out event horizon of the universe, the spherical boundary where space-time appears to be expanding away from Earth in every direction at the speed of light. According to Susskind, from the perspective of an observer following material as it flows past the cosmic horizon, all information describing that event would be irretrievably lost from the universe. That observer would not be able to return to, or even transmit a signal back to our observable universe against the faster-than-light expansion of space-time beyond the cosmic horizon. However, from the perspective of an observer who stays within our universe and watches material flow toward the cosmic horizon, the vibrating strings of which each atom of that material is made would appear to slow down and become smeared all around the spherical boundary of the universe, from which they would be projected back into the universe with the cosmic microwave background radiation, the echo of the Big Bang. Again, Susskind saved the most fundamental principle of information conservation.

Given that I posit a mirror-symmetry between Jung's theory of a transcendental archetype of unity and Susskind's holographic string theory, it is especially pertinent to point out that Susskind presents himself as an atheist and devout Darwinian who rejects all spiritual world views. Like a defense lawyer, I emphasize the atheistic stance Susskind assumes in his books because it actually makes my case much stronger. Susskind's confrontational atheism renders his testimony especially trustworthy for my purpose because we can trust that he was not trying to twist his string theory in a way that could be mystically construed; on the contrary![9]

Carl Jung is the psychologist who, breaking from Sigmund Freud's materially reductionist psychology, pioneered instead the theory of a collective unconscious consisting of archetypal patterns underlying both experience and behavior. According to Jung, each member of a species automatically perceives the world through preprogrammed patterns of unconscious perception that are paired with instinctual patterns of behavior.[10] Jung's mission was to map the archetypal patterns of perception and behavior experienced by the human species. This quest gained tremendous practical support from his working assumption that the outer world and the inner world mirror each other because both emerge from the ultimate archetype of the One, so that the laws of physics provide a kind of map of the laws of psychology: we can infer unknown laws of psychology by looking at the parallel laws of physics, and vice-versa.

From 1909 to 1913, Albert Einstein periodically met with Jung in Zurich, Switzerland. Einstein had already published his special theory of relativity in 1905 and was working on his general theory to explain the force of gravity, which he published in 1915. Over several dinner conversations, he explained his basic ideas to Jung and other psychiatrists, thereby inspiring Jung to think more scientifically about "a possible relativity of time as well as space, and their psychic conditionality."[11] Then, from 1932 until Pauli's death in 1958, Jung worked intimately with the physicist to delineate a mirror-symmetry between psychology and quantum theory.[12] String theory, which Susskind helped to develop beginning in 1968, is an attempt to reconcile the warring paradigms of general relativity and quantum theory. My comparison of Susskind's string theory and Jung's psychology is thus a continuation of Jung's collaboration with Einstein and especially Pauli.

The most salient point for this book is that, according to Susskind, each cubic volume of our three-dimensional universe is like a holographic movie projected by one-dimensional strings that stretch all the way out to the two-dimensional horizon of the cosmos, upon which the past, present, and future are interwoven. That cosmology is almost identical to Jung's recollection of his near-death experience in 1944:

> It seemed to me as if behind the horizon of the cosmos a three-dimensional world had been artificially built up, in which each person sat by himself in a little box. . . . I had been so glad to shed it all, and now it had come about that I—along with everyone else—would again be hung up in a box by a thread.[13]

Referring to his near-death experience of the threads stretching out to the cosmic horizon, and the nightly visions he had for three weeks afterward, Jung goes on to say:

> We shy away from the word 'eternal,' but I can describe the experience only as the ecstasy of a non-temporal state in which the present, past, and future are one. . . . One is interwoven into an indescribable whole and yet observes it with complete objectivity.[14]

Given the clear parallels between them, it is not unreasonable to suggest that Jung's out-of-body encounter with the cosmic horizon provides unconventional empirical evidence for Susskind's holographic string theory, while Susskind's mathematically consistent cosmology supports Jung's outlandish account. That symbiotic similarity furthermore sheds light on Jung's psychological adaptation of Einstein's famous equation, $e = mc^2$.

Starting with Einstein's assumption that energy is equivalent to mass, and further assuming that psyche has energy, Jung theorized that psychic energy is not empirically measurable because it is equivalent to the greatest concentration of mass imaginable in the smallest space possible: "Psyche=highest intensity in the smallest space."[15] Jung's definition of psyche is equivalent to the gravitational singularity described by Einstein's general theory of relativity: a point of infinite density and zero volume. There is no intensity of mass higher than infinite density, and there is no space smaller than zero volume, which means Jung's equation can be restated as Psyche = Singularity.

The seventeenth-century mathematician and theologian Gottfried Wilhelm Leibnitz (who independently discovered the mathematical language of calculus at about the same time as Newton) put forth a postulate known as the identity of indiscernibles, which states that if no difference can be discerned between two objects, they must be identical. According to that postulate, there is a list of reasons why the singularity of the Big Bang and the surrounding horizon of the cosmos is identical to the innumerable singularities and event horizons of black holes located within the cosmos.[16] For one thing, the Big Bang universe and every black hole within it are structurally identical: a dimensionless point surrounded by a two-dimensional sphere (the surface of a three-dimensional ball). Moreover, even though black holes appear at different points in space and time within the universe, because the singularity and its horizon are places where space and time stop, they cannot be differentiated according to spatial or temporal references.

In fact, the singularity of the Big Bang from which space-time expands is present at each point of space-time. No matter where an individual observer is in the universe, that observer will perceive himself or herself as the central point away from which the fabric of space-time is expanding in every direction at an accelerating rate, culminating in the speed of light at the cosmic horizon. However, observers on a planet located at what we perceive to be the cosmic horizon would perceive themselves to be at the center of the expanding universe and Earth at the cosmic horizon. Even from our perspective on Earth, the omnicentric singularity of the Big Bang is present at each point of the cosmic horizon in the sense that the Big Bang echoes back from each point of that enclosing sphere in the form of cosmic microwave background radiation. Finally, from the perspective of quantum mechanics, a singularity at the center of a miniature black hole exists at each point of the infinitely dense quantum vacuum that underlies every point of three-dimensional space.

Thus, according to Leibnitz' principle of the identity of indiscernibles, the gravitational singularity is an omnipresent yet indivisible point that stands outside space-time by virtue of being its ultimate beginning and end. Therefore, the equation Psyche = Singularity indicates that every individual psyche is also somehow simultaneously an omnipresent point that gives birth to and consumes the fabric of space-time. More specifically, as we shall see, the equation Psyche = Singularity indicates that the conscious pole of the psyche is identified with the omnicentric singularity, while the unconscious pole of the psyche is identified with the holographic horizon of the cosmos.

That proposition corroborates and is corroborated by Jung's account of his near-death experience of the cosmic horizon and the threads stretching from it to form the cubic illusion of three-dimensional space. It should be kept in mind, however, that the two opposite poles of the psyche (conscious-unconscious) are complementary perspectives of the same entity, as are the two opposite poles of the cosmos (singularity-horizon), in the sense that people on a planet at what we perceive to be the cosmic horizon would see themselves at the center of the expanding universe and us at the horizon, while each of our inner thoughts at the center of our consciousness is at the unconscious boundary for other people. Thus, the ultimate archetype of the Self, defined as the union of all pairs of opposites, can be further defined by breaking each side of the ultimate equation of opposites, Psyche = Singularity, into its own constituent pair of opposites: Self = Conscious-Unconscious = Singularity-Horizon. The overall implication of the parallels between Jung's and Susskind's theories is that the conscious aspect of the archetype of the Self is the central singularity of the universe, while the unconscious aspect of the Self is the surrounding horizon. Each of us derivative selves participates in that overarching archetype of the universal Self. This proposed oneness of the Self with the central singularity and surrounding horizon of the cosmos conforms to Jung and Pauli's central claim that the ultimate archetype of oneness through the union of all opposites, the Self, manifests itself empirically in the form of a mandala.

In both of his books, Susskind offers special respect to Pauli's key contributions to physics, which include, among other things, the Pauli Exclusion Principle, which explains the structure and quantum mechanics of the interacting atoms on the Periodic Chart of chemical elements, and Pauli's successful prediction of the neutrino, which was later discovered to be responsible for spreading extremely rare elemental atoms out of and away from supernovas before those exploding stars collapse into neutron stars or black holes, thereby seeding the galaxies with otherwise unobtainable elements.[17] Scientists like Susskind who theoretically reduce consciousness to random chemical interactions may not be aware that the one physicist most responsible for discovering what chemicals are, how they interact, and how they are distributed throughout the universe, explicitly rejected materialistic reductionism. In fact, Pauli overtly questioned the legitimacy of the standard version of Darwinism, arguing instead that the supposedly random "process of evolution is directed toward the goal of completeness," as evidenced, for example, by meaningful coincidences, or synchronicities, which imply the idea of a *unus mundus* that unites the material world of physical events and the psychic world of perceived meanings.[18] Indeed, the entire evolution of the universe is constantly expanding away from the absolute wholeness of the omnicentric singularity toward the absolute wholeness of the cosmic horizon, each point of which contains all space-time. I argue that those two opposite poles of the cosmos combine to form the universal mandala of the archetype of the Self, which is the ultimate goal of completeness to which Pauli was referring. One wonders if Susskind knew that Pauli worked with Jung for over twenty-five years in the quest to synthesize spiritual psychology and microphysics specifically around the concept of the *unus mundus*.

There is written testimony from most of the major pioneers of relativity theory and quantum theory (Heisenberg, Schrödinger,

Einstein, De Broglie, Jeans, Planck, Pauli, and Eddington) who interpret those sciences spiritually, although not necessarily theistically.[19] Evidently unaware of that history, Susskind explains in the introduction to *The Cosmic Landscape* that his book is about a debate between two camps. After explicitly excluding "Biblical literalists," Susskind uses apparently conciliatory language to create a false dichotomy between intelligent people who see the fine-tuning of nature required for human beings to exist as a benevolent result of intelligent design in the universe, and "hard-nosed, scientific types" who see the world as the byproduct of random, purposeless forces.[20] Susskind fails to mention that the pioneers of relativity and quantum theory, who are surely every bit as "hard-nosed" and "scientific" as Susskind, nevertheless rejected the philosophical materialism he advocates in favor of variations of the Platonic-Jungian theory that the cosmos is organized by eternal, mathematically intelligible, archetypal forms. In his books, Susskind respectfully mentions those same giants of physics, and humbly acknowledges his specific debts to most of them, but he never mentions the fact that they philosophically interpreted their theories in precisely the way he rejects.

Perhaps Susskind's greatest scholarly oversight is his failure even to mention, let alone give credit to David Bohm (1917-1992), the physicist and associate of Einstein who first appealed to the science of holography in an attempt to reconcile general relativity and quantum mechanics.[21] Considering Susskind's otherwise careful summary of the history of twentieth-century physics, and his generous habit of acknowledging his specific debts to particular pioneers of that field, there is no plausible excuse for his failure to mention the one physicist who pioneered precisely the fusion of quantum mechanics, general relativity, and holography on which Susskind stakes his claim to fame. The most likely reason for Susskind's glaring omission seems to be his reluctance to have his overtly anti-spiritual interpretation of the holographic principle associated with Bohm's panpsychic interpretation of that same basic idea, which Bohm proposed over a decade earlier.

The word panpsychism refers to the theory that consciousness permeates the fabric of space-time. Bohm was the first prominent physicist to suggest a connection between the panpsychic theory and holography. He noticed that every bit of information describing a three-dimensional holographic image is interwoven at every point of the two-dimensional film from which it is projected, so that if you shatter a holographic film and shine a laser through one of the fragments the whole three-dimensional image still appears, though with less resolution. That technology gave Bohm the idea that mind and matter might be similarly interwoven at every point of a more fundamental level that he called the "implicate order," from which the universe is projected into what he called the "explicate order."[22] Thus, it is not unprecedented to interpret the holographic principle of physics in a way that indicates a synthesis of cosmos and psyche; on the contrary, that was the original intention articulated by the founder of holographic cosmology, David Bohm.[23]

As Susskind's holographic interpretation of string theory mathematically united the opposing theories of general relativity and quantum mechanics within the field of physics, so too may it offer an indispensable tool for bridging the even broader gap between physics and psychology by providing a plausible explanation for how mind and matter meet in the central singularity and surrounding horizon of the cosmos. Indeed, when we compare Susskind's string theory and Jung's psychology, those complex and apparently opposite world views merge neatly into a more comprehensive and comprehensible whole. Ironically, although Susskind was trying to explain why our extremely finely-tuned universe requires no organizing psyche, his string theory seems tailor made for Jung's universal archetype of the Self: the mandala-emanating archetype in which cosmos and psyche are united, and from which they unfold.

Keeping in mind Jung and Pauli's theory that physics and psychology mirror each other, Part I of this book begins by tracing out the basic history of modern physics, from Newton's theory of gravity to Susskind's string theory of holographic information conservation at the cosmic horizon. Keeping Susskind's string theory in mind, Part II begins by tracing out the basic history of the philosophical and cosmological concept of a Self, from the Vedanta philosophy of ancient India through Plato to Jung. With the historical context of Susskind's physics and Jung's psychology in place, I then explain how Susskind's holographic string theory corroborates four aspects of Jung's archetypal psychology: (1) his equation relating psychic energy to mass, "Psyche=highest intensity in the smallest space," which can be translated as Psyche = Singularity;[24] (2) his near-death experience, during which he perceived that each individual psyche in the universe is imprisoned in a separate little box of three-dimensional space, each of which is hung up by a thread to the illusion-producing horizon of the cosmos where the past, present, and future are experienced simultaneously; (3) his theory that psychic mandala images spontaneously emerge from the Self—the ultimate archetype of wholeness through the union of opposites—during dreams and fantasies to compensate an ego that is pulled between opposing demands; and, finally, (4) his theory of synchronicity.

Part I
Physics from Newton to Susskind

Chapter 1
The History of the Concept of a Gravitational Singularity

Based on Sir Isaac Newton's assumption that light consists of tiny massive particles, two late eighteenth-century physicists, the English cleric John Michell and the more famous Frenchman Pierre-Simon de Laplace, both theorized that there could be stars so dense that not even light could escape their gravitational pull, rendering them completely dark and therefore invisible.[25] Newton's theory of gravity does not describe conditions that would cause massive bodies to collapse indefinitely down to a point of infinite density as Einstein's general theory of relativity does. Thus, unlike the current concept of black holes, the "dark stars" imagined by Michell and Laplace do not contain singularities. The path that led from the Newtonian dark stars to the black holes of general relativity began with the discovery of the electromagnetic force.

The Absolute Speed of Light and Special Relativity

In 1862, the French physicist Leon Foucault—using an ingenious experiment involving a rapidly rotating mirror reflecting light off of a more distant mirror—measured the speed of light to be 299,796 kilometers per second. This speed is just four kilometers per second faster than the current measurement of 299,792, which is equivalent to 186,282 miles per second, or about 670 million miles per hour.[26] Referencing Foucault's measurements in the mid-1860s, James Clerk Maxwell discovered not only that electricity and magnetism are actually one electromagnetic force, but that the oscillating electric and magnetic waves travel at the same speed as light, indicating that the electromagnetic force *is* light.[27] However, in none of the four equations Maxwell developed to describe the electromagnetic force did he include a reference frame in comparison to which the speed of light is measured.

According to Brian Greene, a prominent string theorist from Columbia University and one of Susskind's greatest supporters, "it was as if someone gave the location for a party as 22 miles north without specifying the reference location, without specifying north of *what*."[28] Greene goes on to explain that, as sound waves travel with a specific speed in relation to the still air through which they move, it was assumed by many physicists of Maxwell's and Einstein's day that electromagnetic waves must also travel through some as-yet-undetected medium:

> To give this unseen light-carrying stuff due respect, it was given a name: the *luminiferous aether*, or the *aether* for short, the latter being an ancient term that Aristotle used to describe the magical catchall substance of which heavenly bodies were imagined to be made.[29]

Contrary to this theory, though, the absence of a light-carrying aether permeating space was apparently confirmed about twenty years after Maxwell's discovery. As Greene explains: "In 1887, however, when Albert Michelson and Edward Morley measured the speed of light, time and time again they found exactly the same speed of 670 million miles per hour *regardless of their motion or that of the light's source*."[30] The assumption prior to Einstein's special theory of relativity in 1905 was that, in the same way that swimming with or against the current of a river increases or decreases one's speed relative to the river bank, so too should accelerating a measured light source in various directions cause the light waves to flow with or against the unseen flow of the underlying aether, resulting in faster and slower measurements of the speed of light. Therefore, when Michelson and Morley repeatedly measured the speed of light to be exactly the same, regardless of the relative speeds of the light source and detector, the implication was that there is no luminiferous aether, and that the speed of light is absolute. In 1887, two hundred years after Newton formulated his fundamental principles of physics in *Philosophiæ Naturalis Principia Mathematica* (1687), Michelson and Morley experimentally demonstrated the absolute speed of light, which inspired Einstein's discovery of the elastic nature of space-time in 1905.

Einstein reasoned that if velocity equals the distance traveled divided by the time spent traveling ($v = d/t$), and if the velocity of light is always measured to be the same, then distance (space) and time must be malleable. Therefore, to uphold the absolute speed of light implied by Maxwell's equations in the mid-1860s, and confirmed by the Michelson-Morley experiments in 1887, Einstein rejected Newton's long-revered concept of the absolute nature of space and time: the idea that space consists of three rigid dimensions of unchanging emptiness (up-down, left-right, back-forth) while time flows forward everywhere at the same rate regardless of the relative velocities of different observers.[31] In the special theory of relativity (which is special as opposed to general because it applies only to bodies moving in uniform, as opposed to accelerating, motion), Einstein reasoned that light is always measured to be moving at the exact same speed because the length of each observer's measuring rod contracts in the direction of acceleration. Similarly, each observer's clock slows down with the increase in speed in just the right proportion so that, no matter how fast or slow different observers are moving relative to one another, their measuring rods and clocks always measure the same light wave as moving at exactly the same absolute speed.[32]

Greene provides an analogy from everyday experience to help us understand the relationship between space-time and motion. He begins by explaining that, according to special relativity, all objects in the universe are always moving at light speed through space-time: "We are presently talking about an object's combined speed through all four dimensions—three space and one time—and it is the object's speed in this generalized sense that is equal to that of light."[33] Because time is interwoven with space, if we are not moving through any of the space dimensions, all of our generalized speed through space-time is spent through time: time travels most swiftly (the speed of light in a generalized sense) for stationary observers. Conversely, the faster we travel through any of the space dimensions, the slower we travel through time: time stops for anything traveling through space at light speed, while space contracts to zero in the direction of travel, which is why a photon does not experience either time or space. According to David Bohm, from light's perspective, "you would find that the two ends of the light ray would have no time between them and no distance, so they would represent immediate contact."[34] It is important to keep in mind, however, that with the exception of light, any object that seems to be stationary from one perspective can be interpreted as moving from another perspective, just as people on a train may perceive the station platform to be moving backward as the train begins to pull away.

According to special relativity, if you could see a clock on a train as it speeds away at close to the speed of light, you would see the second hand moving very slowly, and the train would seem to contract dramatically in the direction of travel. However, if you were on the train, you would see your clock moving at normal speed, while clocks on the platform would appear to be moving very slowly (and the platform would appear to be contracted in the direction of its apparent travel *away* from the train). But if the movement of time is relative to the observer's speed through space, so are the concepts of past, present, and future.

Relativity of Simultaneity

In one of his famous thought experiments, Einstein imagined that observers standing at the midpoint of a railway platform see themselves aligned with the midpoint of a passing train as lightning strikes the tracks at both of its ends simultaneously. It takes an equal amount of time for the light to travel equal distances from either side of the train to their eyes, so they conclude that the strikes happened simultaneously. However, from the perspective of observers sitting in the middle of the moving train, the front strike hits first because they are moving toward it and away from the rear strike, the light of which has to travel farther to catch up to them. Who is correct, the observers on the platform who saw the lightning strikes hit simultaneously, or the observers on the train who saw the front strike first and the rear strike after? According to Einstein's interpretation of special relativity, both observers are correct from the relative perspective of their own reference frames.[35] Moreover, according to Greene,

> Once we know that your now can be what I consider the past, or your now can be what I consider the future, and your now is every bit as valid as my now, then we learn that the past must be real, the future must be real. They could be your now. . . . With this bold insight, Einstein shattered one of the most basic concepts of how we experience time. "The distinction between past, present, and future," he once said, "is only an illusion, however persistent."[36]

According to special relativity, as the space in front of us and the space behind us both continue to exist whether we walk forward, backward, or stand still, so do past and future coexist in the time dimension despite our being situated in what we perceive to be the present. Einstein interpreted his theory in a deterministic way, resulting in the idea of a "block universe," like a block of ice or a loaf of bread. As philosopher of science J. B. Kennedy explains: "The series of such three-dimensional 'slices'—past, present, and future—together make up the whole four-dimensional block."[37] This idea of a block universe led Einstein to reject the standard theory of evolution:

> Since there exist in this four-dimensional structure [space-time] no longer any sections which represent 'now' objectively, the concepts of happening and becoming are indeed not completely suspended, but yet complicated. It appears therefore more natural to think of physical reality as a four-dimensional existence, instead of, as hitherto, the *evolution* of a three-dimensional existence.[38]

Like Plato, Einstein suggests that reality is more accurately understood as a four-dimensional, space-time continuum (knowable through higher mathematics), whose deceptive shadows appear to us as the evolution of bits of matter through three dimensions of space and one of time.[39]

A few months after his discovery of a physical explanation for the absolute speed of light (length contraction and time dilation), and his related discovery that the past and future coexist with the present (relativity of simultaneity), Einstein noticed yet another strange consequence of his new theory: energy and mass are equivalent terms described with different units of measurement.[40] To translate units of energy into units of mass, Einstein multiplied the units of mass by the speed of light squared, $e = mc^2$.[41] Based on his assumption of the equivalence of energy and mass, Einstein realized that no massive object can travel at the absolute speed of an inherently massless photon because the faster massive things travel through space, the more kinetic energy they accumulate, which gives them more mass. According to a law of diminishing returns, ever more energy is required to accelerate an increasingly heavy object. As an object approaches light speed, its mass approaches infinity, as does the amount of energy required to accelerate it further. If we assume, as Einstein did, that there is no infinite energy supply, we must conclude that it is impossible to accelerate a massive object to the absolute speed of a massless photon. Indeed, Einstein believed that nothing at all can travel faster than light. He realized, however, that according to Newton's theory, the force of gravity travels infinitely fast, in that it acts instantaneously between distant objects. He therefore set about rendering the speed of the gravitational force consistent with the absolute speed of the electromagnetic force.

General Relativity and the Infinite Gravity of Black Holes

Einstein's first insight into how gravity can be made consistent with the speed limit of light came while he was sitting at his humble patent-clerk desk in Bern one day in 1907. At that moment, he had what he would describe as his "happiest thought": gravity and accelerated motion are equivalent.[42] Einstein, watching workers on a roof, realized that if someone were to step off of a high building and drop a ball at the same time on a windless day, the ball would remain right next to the falling person, as if the force of gravity in the person's local reference frame had been neutralized by the force of acceleration. Similarly, an elevator accelerating upward creates the same force as gravity pulling downward. Einstein understood that the cryptic force of gravity seems much less mysterious if we can equate it with the everyday experience of accelerated motion, which led him finally to realize a link between gravity and the curvature of space and time.

To demonstrate the difference between Newton's theory of gravity and Einstein's general theory of relativity, Greene uses the example of the vaporized Sun.[43] According to Newton's theory, if the Sun were to suddenly disappear, the gravitational tether connecting it to the orbiting planets would disappear, causing them to *instantaneously* career out of their orbits, which indicates that the force of gravity travels infinitely fast. However, Greene explains, "gravity, according to Einstein, *is* the warping of space and time."[44]

According to general relativity, the mass of the Sun creates an indentation in the *three-dimensional surface* of the four-dimensional fabric of space-time, in the same way that a bowling ball creates an indentation on the two-dimensional surface of a three-dimensional trampoline. The planets are held in orbit around the much more massive Sun (which is a million times more massive than Earth) because of the much deeper indentation it creates in the fabric of space-time, in the same way that billiard balls rolling across the surface of a trampoline would wind up revolving around the indentation created by a much more massive bowling ball. If the Sun suddenly disappeared, the indentation would rebound, creating an outward-radiating ripple in every direction of space-time, like a ripple on the elastic surface of the trampoline. According to general relativity, that outward-radiating gravitational wave would travel at exactly the same speed as an electromagnetic wave, so that each of the planets would remain in orbit around the point where the Sun used to be for as long as it took for the last photon shining from the Sun to reach them (about 8 minutes for Earth). Einstein had finally provided a clearly defined mechanism to account for Newton's ghostly force of gravity, for which the general theory of relativity was hailed as a triumph around the world. The gravitational waves Einstein predicted were detected for the first time a century later, on September 14, 2015, marking the birth of a new era of astronomy.[45]

However, there are deeply troubling implications in Einstein's equations, which the string theorist Michio Kaku compares to a "Trojan horse," a gift which at first appears acceptable, but later turns out to be filled with fatal trouble:

> Inside lurk all sorts of strange demons and goblins which allow for the possibility of interstellar travel through wormholes and time travel. The price we had to pay for peering into the darkest secrets of the universe was the potential downfall of some of our most commonly held beliefs about our world—that its space is simply connected and its history is unalterable.[46]

24

The darkest secrets of the universe revealed by general relativity are black holes, out of which an unexpected swarm of paradigm-sacking paradoxes emerged. The unintended trade-off Einstein had to make for solving the contradiction between special relativity (which says that nothing can travel faster than light) and the infinite speed of gravity predicted by Newton's theory was the equally disturbing idea of the *infinite gravity of the singularity* inside black holes and at the origin of the Big Bang. If gravity is equivalent to acceleration, infinite gravity is equivalent to infinite acceleration, which leads us right back to Newton's concept of the infinite speed of gravity.

On December 22, 1915, Carl Schwarzschild wrote a letter to Einstein that provided the first precise mathematical solution to the gravitational field equations of general relativity—Einstein's original paper provided only an approximate solution. Einstein was pleased with Schwarzschild's work and helped him publish it in January 1916. However, Einstein was not pleased with the second paper Schwarzschild published a month later.[47] According to that paper, when enough mass is condensed into a sufficiently small space (the mass-to-radius ratio now known as the Schwarzschild radius), it collapses down to an infinitely dense point that creates a spherical border around itself where the inward tidal flow of space-time reaches light speed, so that not even a photon can escape its gravitational pull. Einstein believed that nothing can travel through space faster than light, but Schwarzschild showed that the tidal flow of space-time itself surpasses light speed behind the event horizon of a black hole, and becomes infinite at the central point, later called the gravitational singularity, which Susskind defines as "the infinitely dense point at the center of a black hole where tidal forces become infinite."[48]

Although Einstein was appalled by the idea of a singularity, the gravitational effects of black holes have been empirically observed in the center of so many galaxies that it seems likely that all galaxies contain supermassive black holes at their centers, with smaller black holes strewn throughout their volumes.[49] Even if we ignore black holes, however, general relativity contains yet another avenue to a gravitational singularity: the concept that space-time is expanding so that, in the distant past, it must have been contracted in a single point.

The Big Bang Theory

French astrophysicist Jean-Pierre Luminet argues that Georges Lemaître, a Jesuit priest from Belgium, is too often overlooked as the first theorist to propose both the exponentially expanding space-time theory, and the related theory of the Big Bang from a singularity, which Lemaître called the "primeval atom."[50] Einstein, who believed the universe was static, realized that without antigravity to counteract the attractive force of all matter, the universe would be contracting. The "cosmological constant," symbolized by the Greek letter Lambda (λ), is the repulsive force of antigravity Einstein therefore inserted into his general relativity equations in 1917. However, a similar repulsive force can be explained by Lemaître's theory that the universe exploded from a single point. In 1927, Einstein originally rejected Lemaître's theory of an expanding space-time fabric and the related theory of the Big Bang, telling Lemaître: "Your mathematics are correct, but your physics is abominable."[51] Einstein also rejected the Russian mathematician and meteorologist Alexander Friedman's similar solutions to Einstein's equations in 1922, which describe an expanding fabric of space-time.

In Einstein's opinion, Friedman's and Lemaître's mathematical literalism was parochial: just because the mathematics of general relativity imply something incredible, like the birth of an expanding universe from a point of infinite density, this does not mean it necessarily happened. Einstein believed that there are certain physical limitations which prevent the fabric of space-time from undergoing the infinite contractions predicted by his own theory. Nevertheless, in 1929 Edwin Hubble used the 100-inch mirror in the largest telescope of his day at the Mount Wilson Observatory in Pasadena, California, to observe that what were then believed to be stellar nebulae are actually independent galaxies, and that those galaxies are accelerating away from Earth at an increasing rate proportionate to their distance. This observation indicates that the universe is indeed expanding from a gravitational singularity.[52] As Greene explains: "Lemaître and Friedman were vindicated. Friedman received credit for being the first to explore the expanding universe solutions, and Lemaître for independently developing them into robust cosmological scenarios."[53]

When Hubble independently confirmed Friedman's and Lemaître's theories of the expanding universe in 1929, Einstein reportedly called his previous insertion of the cosmological constant into his general relativity equations "the biggest blunder of his life."[54] However, as we will see later in this chapter, Einstein's cosmological constant—which he created in 1917, and then rejected in 1929—has subsequently been reincarnated as the "dark energy" of the quantum vacuum: the anti-gravitational repulsive force produced by the constant creation and annihilation of virtual particle-antiparticle pairs.[55] In light of Hubble's evidence, Einstein eventually embraced Lemaître's theory that the universe is expanding from a primeval atom, though he steadfastly rejected the idea that the original atom had infinite gravity (i.e., that it was a singularity), and he furthermore rejected the quantum theory of the atom that emerged that same year, 1927.

The Double-Slit Experiment and the Dice-Playing God

The quantum theory of the atom was inspired by the attempt to describe the wave-particle paradox revealed by the famous double-slit experiment. The experiment involves two narrow slits aligned very closely next to each other on a wall with a detector screen behind it. When electrons, photons, or any quantum particles are directed through the slits, they behave as either particles or waves, depending on which experimental conditions are used to measure them. The particles are always detected by the detector screen as particles. However, on one hand, if we use an electron microscope to detect which slit the particles pass through, they accumulate on the detector screen directly behind the slits in two narrow bands, just like little bullets would have done had they passed through the two slits. On the other hand, if we do not attempt to determine which slit the particles go through, the distribution pattern of individual hits on the detector screen gradually takes on the exact pattern one would see if a liquid wave had gone through the two slits all at once, splitting itself into two waves, which then collide as they spread forward, creating a ripple-like interference pattern of bright and dark bands spread across the whole detector screen. The dark bands correspond to those places where the waves cancel out, the bright bands to where the waves amplify each other. In 1926, Erwin Schrödinger discovered the equation, subsequently named after him, that mathematically describes the shape of the quantum waves. Initially, he believed the wave function describes how an electron actually smears out to form a physical wave. However, Max Born, another Nobel Laurette in physics, provided a rather different interpretation.[56]

According to Born, the quantum wave function described by the Schrödinger equation is not a physical wave. Rather, it represents the probability of finding a particle at any given point on the waveform. More specifically, Born discovered that if we square the mathematical wave function described by the Schrödinger equation, it reveals parabolas of statistical probabilities for where a particle might manifest if it were observed—most likely at the highest peaks or lowest valleys. Whether we square the positive amplitude of the peak of a wave, or the negative amplitude of a valley, both of those amplitudes become positive numbers (known technically as the intensity), which represent the probability that the wave will collapse into an actual particle at that point if it is observed.[57]

Werner Heisenberg, who developed equations using matrix mathematics to describe electron waves before Schrödinger introduced his more popular equation, subsequently discovered that his own matrix equations reveal what came to be called the Heisenberg Uncertainty Principle, which provides the mathematical explanation for why certain pairs of physical properties of a particle, such as its position (particle nature) and its momentum (wave nature), cannot both be known simultaneously with precision.[58] As the physicist Heinz R. Pagels explains, Niels Bohr's complementarity concept completes Heisenberg's Uncertainty Principle:

> Particle and wave are what Bohr called complementary concepts, meaning they exclude one another. . . . Bohr's principle of complementarity asserts that there exist complementary properties of the same object of knowledge, one of which if known will exclude knowledge of the other.
>
> We may therefore describe an object like an electron in ways which are mutually exclusive—e.g., as wave or particle—without logical contradiction provided we also realize that the experimental arrangements that determine these descriptions are similarly mutually exclusive. Which experiment—and hence which description one chooses—is purely a matter of human choice.[59]

Bohr realized that the more one knows about the position of the particle (which slit it passes through), the less one knows about its momentum, or movement through space as a wave.

Considering Jung's partnership with Pauli in the mission to synthesize physics and psychology, it is particularly pertinent to note Pauli's historical role in inspiring the Copenhagen interpretation of quantum mechanics. As Pagels explains:

> By February of 1927, Niels Bohr, Werner Heisenberg, and Wolfgang Pauli had exhausted themselves trying to figure out whether the electron is a particle or a wave. Bohr took a vacation while Pauli stayed in Copenhagen, lashing Heisenberg with constructive criticism. It was then that Heisenberg and Bohr each had independent insights into the wave-particle paradox. Heisenberg had discovered the uncertainty principle, and Bohr had discovered the principle of complementarity. Together these two principles

constituted what became known as the "Copenhagen interpretation" of quantum mechanics—an interpretation that convinced most physicists of the correctness of the new quantum theory. The Copenhagen interpretation magnificently revealed the internal consistency of the quantum theory, a consistency which was purchased at the price of renouncing the determinism and objectivity of the natural world.[60]

The concept that human choice determines whether the smallest physical entities will behave like particles or waves brings up the additional issue of determinism and the fact that, according to quantum mechanics, it is impossible to predict the future, or determine the past, with precision because it is impossible to know both the position and momentum of the particles that make up the present.

As discussed above, Pierre-Simon Laplace used Newton's theory in the late eighteenth century to mathematically imagine stars so dense that not even light could resist their gravity, thereby presaging the black holes of general relativity. It is interesting to note that in 1814, Laplace again used Newton's mechanistic cosmology to support the same kind of determinism later implied by special and general relativity. He theorized that if there was an intelligence vast enough to know the position and velocity of each particle in the universe at any given moment, that superhuman entity could extrapolate the exact position of each particle in the past and the future: "For it, nothing would be uncertain and the future, as the past, would be present to its eyes."[61] Einstein's special theory of relativity agrees that the past, present, and future of three-dimensional space are fixed and simultaneously existing in the block universe. However, to Einstein's dismay, it seemed that determinism was overthrown by the Copenhagen interpretation of quantum mechanics, which says that we cannot know the past and future positions and velocities of particles with precision because the more we know about one of those properties, the less we can know about the other. According to the Copenhagen interpretation, the best even a cosmic intelligence can do is make a probable prediction about the past and future of the universe based on knowledge of waves of probabilities. As Susskind explains: "Einstein pompously declared, 'God does not play dice.' Niels Bohr's response was sharp: 'Einstein,' Bohr scolded, 'don't tell God what to do.'"[62]

Quantum Entanglement and the Singularity

In 1935, Einstein and two colleagues, Boris Podolsky and Nathan Rosen, wrote a paper dealing with what became acronymically known as the EPR paradox. The EPR paper explains that, according to the standard Copenhagen interpretation of quantum mechanics, any two particles that have ever interacted will always remain in immediate contact, in such a way that what you do to one particle is *instantaneously* correlated with the partner particle in a predictable way, which seems to be a violation of the absolute speed limit of light because it implies that a signal is sent from one particle to the other at an infinite speed. Einstein developed his general theory of relativity explicitly to refute the infinite speed of gravity implied by Newton's theory, so he thought that if he could demonstrate how the same kind of "spooky action at a distance" is implied by quantum theory,[63] he would invalidate it and, along with it, the determinism-denying Copenhagen interpretation, which states that it is impossible simultaneously to measure the position and momentum of a particle.

Ironically, although Einstein suggested the idea of quantum entanglement to refute quantum theory, he thereby inspired the experiments that empirically confirmed it. Thirty years after the EPR paper, in 1965, John Bell, an Irish physicist working at CERN, conceived of a way to test the EPR prediction experimentally.[64] That experiment was successfully conducted many times in the following years, the first report coming from the University of California, Berkeley in 1972,[65] and the most definitive report coming in the summer of 1982 from the University of Paris, South. Alain Aspect, who led that team, concluded that there is in fact nonlocal action at a distance between particles that previously interacted.[66]

When we observe one partner of a pair of previously entangled particles, this observation seems to determine the quantum state of the other instantaneously. For example, if we rotate the quantum spin state of one particle, the spin of the other particle immediately rotates in the opposite direction, whether it is across a room or across the universe. In light of the Aspect experiment, physicist John Gribbin explains that "theorists such as d'Espagnat and David Bohm argue that we must accept that, literally, everything is connected to everything else, and only a holistic approach to the universe is likely to explain phenomena such as human consciousness."[67] Tying this holistic insight back to the history of the concept of a gravitational singularity, a few pages later Gribbin concludes that "if everything that ever interacted in the Big Bang maintains its connection with everything it interacted with, then every particle in every star and galaxy that we can see 'knows' about the existence of every other particle."[68] The empirically verified concept of quantum entanglement indicates that, because the entire universe was condensed in a single point at the Big Bang, every particle in the universe has always maintained an immediate connection to every other particle, regardless of their relative positions in space-time.

Uniting Relativity Theory with Quantum Mechanics, and the Infinite Problem of the Quantum Vacuum

After the Copenhagen interpretation's establishment, the next logical step toward unifying our understanding of the four known forces of nature was to unite quantum mechanics (which describes the electromagnetic, the strong nuclear, and the weak nuclear forces) with special relativity (which describes the absolute speed of light) and general relativity (which describes the gravitational force). Although general relativity and quantum mechanics remain unreconciled (because string theory remains experimentally and observationally unconfirmed), *special* relativity and quantum mechanics were at least tentatively synthesized in the early 1930s with the invention of "quantum field theory."[69] In a nutshell, quantum field theory describes the forces of the quantum realm as the emission and absorption of particles. One form of quantum field theory, quantum electrodynamics, describes the electromagnetic field of force as the photons that are rapidly passed between the orbiting electrons of an atom and its nucleus. As Susskind puts it: "Photons are the ropes that tether the electrons to the nucleus."[70] Similarly, quantum chromodynamics describes the strong and weak nuclear forces that hold the nucleons inside the nucleus of an atom together, "with a quark replacing the electron and a gluon taking the place of the photon."[71]

Most physicists believe that all particles create their own antiparticles in what is known as the quantum vacuum, and that the constant creation and immediate annihilation of those virtual particle-antiparticle pairs produces what is known as vacuum energy. According to Susskind, the fluctuations of the quantum vacuum are created by the fact that "all possible paths contribute to the probability for the particle to go from a to b," a result of the Heisenberg Uncertainty Principle.[72] There are infinite paths describing possible particle trajectories in an atom, some of which include electrons moving backward in time to create antielectrons, also known as positrons.[73] After astrophysicist Saul Perlmutter's shocking discovery in 1998 that the expansion rate of the universe is accelerating, physicists speculated that this expansion is caused by the quantum vacuum energy, which came to be called dark energy, discussed in more detail below. For now, though, it is important to note that ever since its discovery in the 1930s, there has been controversy among top physicists about how much energy virtual particle collisions create in the quantum vacuum.

Susskind recalls walking in on a conversation among eminent physicists during his first day as a physics professor in 1967, including Roger Penrose, Dave Finkelstein, and Paul Dirac, who helped formulate quantum field theory in the 1930s: "Dave was arguing that the vacuum is full of zero-point energy and that this energy ought to affect the gravitational field. Dirac didn't like vacuum energy because whenever physicists tried to calculate its magnitude, the answer would come out infinite."[74] To tame the calculation-paralyzing infinities mathematically derived from the quantum vacuum energy, physicists came up with the process of "renormalization" in the 1950s.[75] According to Pagels: "If someone could actually put on an infinite amount of weight and then reset the scale by an infinite amount to give a finite weight, then one gets an idea of the amount of cheating or renormalization required in the calculational procedures of quantum field theories."[76] Although the "cheating" process of renormalization works when special relativity and quantum mechanics are combined, when it comes to combining quantum mechanics and general relativity, renormalization fails catastrophically.[77] According to Kaku: "You get an infinite sequence of infinities. Infinitely worse than the divergences of Einstein's original theory. This is a nightmare beyond comprehension."[78]

To say that there is an infinite amount of energy at every point of the quantum vacuum is tantamount to saying that the vacuum is made of singularities or, in other words, tiny black holes. Relating quantum field theory to the concept of a gravitational singularity, Gribbin concludes that "empty space may be made up of black holes the size of the Planck length, packed tightly together."[79] Similarly, according to Susskind: "The world at the Planck scale is a very unfamiliar place, where geometry is changing, space and time are barely recognizable, and high-energy virtual particles are perpetually colliding and forming tiny black holes that last no longer than a single Planck time."[80]

After the infinite energy of the quantum vacuum was discovered in the thirties, Einstein submitted a paper on May 10, 1939 in which he argues that it is physically impossible to create a gravitational singularity: "There arises the question of whether it is possible to build up a field containing such singularities with the help of actual gravitating masses, or whether such regions . . . do not exist in cases which have physical reality."[81] Einstein's article was not published until October of that same year. On September 1, 1939, the very day World War II began, Robert Oppenheimer and his graduate student provided the first mathematical description of how a star could actually burn through its nuclear fuel, causing it to gravitationally contract indefinitely into a point of infinite density, which Oppenheimer was the first to call a "singularity."[82]

Susskind explains that when a star burns through its nuclear fuel, the outward pressure caused by the heat diminishes, allowing gravity to contract the star to a tiny fraction of its former size. For example, when the Sun of our solar system burns out, it will collapse into what is called a *white dwarf*, whose radius is approximately the same as that of the Earth (a million times smaller than the Sun). If our Sun were about fifty percent heavier, it would collapse even further, forcing the electrons orbiting the atoms to be pushed into the nucleus, so that the positively charged protons and the negatively charged electrons would cancel out, leaving only "an incredibly dense ball of neutrons."[83] If the Sun were about five times its size, then after its nuclear fuel is spent, "it would be crushed to a *singularity*—a point of almost infinite density and destructive power."[84]

But how can a finite quantity be *almost* infinite? Almost infinite can be defined as the finite mass-to-volume ratio that is just shy of the Schwarzschild radius, at which point gravity becomes infinite. For example, a neutron star is almost infinite in the sense that compressing just a little more mass within that collapsed star's sphere will trigger an indefinite gravitational collapse, creating a black hole with a singularity in the center. Nevertheless, the density of the singularity is, by definition, infinite. Therefore, by calling the gravitational force of the singularity "almost infinite," Susskind is evidently trying to hedge his bets on the single most controversial issue in cosmology today—the problem of infinite energy.[85] Two pages later, he more clearly claims that, despite the fact that Einstein detested the idea of a singularity in a black hole, "nothing can survive its infinitely powerful forces. . . . Nothing can withstand the overwhelming pull toward the center."[86]

As discussed above, before Oppenheimer explained the physics of how stars collapse into black holes in 1939, other quantum physicists theorized the existence of an infinite amount of energy underlying every point of three-dimensional space in the quantum vacuum, formed by the constant creation and annihilation of virtual particle-antiparticle pairs. Then in 1948, the Dutch physicist Hendrik Casimir discovered a way to detect experimentally the theoretical vacuum energy.[87] Casimir argued that the quantum fluctuations should cause two metal plates placed very close together to be pushed all the way together because there would be less vacuum energy between them and more vacuum energy pushing on the outside of each plate. The experiment that proved the existence of the Casimir effect was conducted about a decade later, with increasingly precise reproductions of the experiment occurring ever since.[88] Thus, the quantum vacuum energy is an experimentally verified physical reality, which lends credence to the equations indicating that the vacuum may consist of tiny black holes tightly packed at the Planck length.

Einstein and others initially rejected the wormholes and mirror universes predicted by Schwarzschild's original solution to the field equations of general relativity in 1916. However, in 1963 Roy Kerr discovered another exact solution to Einstein's field equations based on the assumption that a star collapsing into a black hole would be rotating at the time, causing it to contract into a ring-shaped singularity instead of a point. The ring-singularity is still infinitely dense, but, according to Micho Kaku, the opening in its center provides a potential portal to another universe.[89]

Throughout these pages, I have been referring to the singularity as a *point* of infinite gravity. It turns out, however, that a two-dimensional circle is the more physically relevant model of a singularity inside spinning black holes, which appears to be most, if not all of them. The infinite density of a two-dimensional ring singularity is still contained in the smallest three-dimensional space possible—it still has zero volume—despite the fact that it potentially provides something like a tunnel to another universe. The

Schwarzschild solution to the field equations of general relativity is mathematically easier to work with than the ring singularity described by the Kerr solution, which is why physicists usually explain the properties of black holes to the public using the Schwarzschild model of a point singularity. For the same purpose of pedagogical simplicity, I will continue to refer to the singularity as a point of infinite density.

Kerr produced his exact solution to Einstein's equations in 1963. Another powerful piece of evidence for the existence of a gravitational singularity came in 1964 when two radio-astronomers—and subsequent Nobel Prize winners—Arno Penzias and Robert Wilson accidentally discovered the cosmic microwave background radiation left over from the Big Bang.[90] The next year, despite physicists fearing the concept of a gravitational singularity as a pathological nightmare that spelled the breakdown of physics, Roger Penrose and Stephen Hawking used Einstein's general theory of relativity to prove mathematically that singularities must exist in certain types of collapsed stars *and* at the origin of the Big Bang. Penrose proved Oppenheimer's earlier claim that a star of sufficient mass must necessarily collapse into a singularity when it burns through its nuclear fuel. Hawking reversed the direction of Penrose's time dimension for a black hole to create a model of the Big Bang.[91] John Wheeler was subsequently given credit for coining the term "black hole" in 1967.[92]

A point of infinite gravity is a paradoxical union of opposite terms: a space-timeless "place" where space-time begins at the Big Bang and ends in a black hole (and at each point of the cosmic horizon), which means that the laws of physics do not apply to the singularity, although the laws of physics indicate that it must exist. The idea of an unlimited limit to science causes some physicists, such as Einstein and Kaku, to reject the whole idea of a singularity. In fact, Hawking was sometimes among that camp. As he explains in *A Brief History of Time*: "It is perhaps ironic that, having changed my mind, I am now trying to convince other physicists that there was in fact no singularity at the beginning of the universe—as we shall see later, it can disappear once quantum effects are taken into account."[93]

Hawking goes on to explain: "In 1981 my interest in questions about the origin and fate of the universe was reawakened when I attended a conference on cosmology organized by the Jesuits at the Vatican."[94]

After the Vatican conference, Hawking rejected his former belief in the infinite gravity of the singularity, which general relativity predicts, by appealing to quantum theory: at the quantum scale, the so-called point of infinite gravity would actually be a wave of probability (the wave function of the universe). However, in exchange for a point of infinite gravity, Hawking gains an infinite set of parallel universes: one for each point in the original wave of probability. Like the heads of a hydra, it appears that whenever physicists succeed in cutting off infinity in one corner of space-time, it regenerates itself by an exponent of itself elsewhere. For example, in the process of refuting Newton's theory of the infinite speed of gravity, Einstein created the concept of the equivalence of gravity and acceleration (general relativity), which led to a point of infinite gravity described by the Schwarzschild solution, which is equivalent to infinite acceleration, which leads right back to the problem Einstein was trying to solve. Similarly, in the process of trying to refute quantum theory, Einstein revealed what he thought was its fatal flaw: it predicts the infinite speed of quantum entanglement (spooky action at a distance), which has been experimentally confirmed many times. Finally, as we saw Kaku explain above, when physicists try to combine quantum theory with general relativity they get "an infinite sequence of infinities," which is "infinitely worse" than the infinite amount of energy predicted to be in the quantum vacuum according to the synthesis of quantum theory and special relativity.[95]

Physicist Hugh Everett III developed the first quantum theory of parallel universes in 1957. He argued that it is consistent with quantum theory to assume that when an observation causes a wave function to collapse into a single point somewhere within it (most likely at the peaks or valleys), all of the other points in that same wave manifest in parallel universes, the only difference between them being the position of that one point in that one wave of probability.

Comparing Hawking's wave function of the universe to Hugh Everett's many-worlds theory, Kaku explains that Hawking's theory describes wormholes connecting the parallel universes.[96] Even without those Einstein-Rosen bridges connecting the parallel universes, however, the effect of quantum entanglement—which was definitively confirmed by experiment in 1982—indicates that every particle in each of the infinity of parallel universes must always be in immediate contact, as they were all superimposed in the original wave function of the universe.[97]

In his book *Hegel: The Logic of Self-consciousness and the Legacy of Subjective Freedom*, Robert Bruce Ware consolidates the quantum relativistic implications of the omnipresent singularity examined thus far.[98] He explains that the singularity of the Big Bang pervades all space-time because space-time continues to expand in every direction from every point, and because the Big Bang is echoing back from every point of the encompassing horizon of the cosmos. He also points to the singularity at every point of the quantum vacuum. Finally, Ware explains that, according to Leibnitz's principle of the identity of indiscernibles, because they are all outside space-time, the seemingly different singularities and surrounding horizons of each black hole, and each inside-out black hole universe, cannot be differentiated according to spatial or temporal concepts, which means they are indiscernible, and therefore functionally as well as structurally identical.

Jean Eisenstaedt, emeritus Research Director at the Paris Observatory, explains that,

> for essentially mathematical reasons (they are after all mathematical objects!), black holes cannot have any properties other than mass, charge, and angular momentum, and these can only manifest themselves through their gravitational field. . . . Therefore, all black holes are alike and they are extremely simple objects (if we may say so . . .), at least from a physical standpoint.[99]

According to Eisenstaedt, a black hole is not a physical thing; it is a *mathematical* object, a two-dimensional sphere encompassing a literal point of infinite gravity. If all black holes are the same from a structural standpoint, and if their apparently different locations in different points of space-time are obviated by their being outside of space-time, then the singularity and horizon of every black hole is one with the omnicentric singularity and surrounding horizon of the universe: their differences are only apparent.

It is probably more accurate to say that every black hole, including the dense carpet of black holes forming the foam of the quantum vacuum, is simultaneously one with and different from the inside-out black hole universe. Ware further indicates that, according to the empirically verified effect of quantum entanglement, if the Big Bang exploded from a universal wave function, as Hawking suggests, and if everything was originally united in that wave function, then not only does each particle in this universe remain in some kind of immediate contact with every other particle, but so must each particle in each parallel universe in the megaverse remain in immediate contact, thereby connecting our fate with that of every parallel version of us branching out from our universe at each instant.

Chapter 2
Holographic String Theory

The last milestone on the timeline of the concept of a gravitational singularity that I will examine is Susskind and 't Hooft's holographic string theory. According to their newest and strangest idea at the pinnacle of contemporary academic physics, the three-dimensional universe is like a holographic movie projected by one-dimensional strings from the two-dimensional horizon of the cosmos, the spherical border where the fabric of space-time is receding away from us in every direction at the speed of light, and where every bit of information describing the past, present, and future of our universe is interwoven and conserved.[100] However, there appears to be a logical flaw in calling the cosmic horizon two-dimensional merely because it is perfectly flat, considering that it contains all space and time. The holographic cosmic horizon Susskind describes is more accurately described as a higher dimension, in that it simultaneously contains the entire temporal trajectory of three-dimensional space. Nevertheless, according to Susskind our experience of three-dimensional space is an illusion projected by fundamental strings. Reality is encoded on what he calls a two-dimensional holographic film at the cosmic horizon.

Unobservable Strings

In *The Cosmic Landscape*, Susskind offers a practical example to explain the limits involved with experimentally verifying string theory. He explains that, as a consequence of basic physical principles, such as the constancy of the speed of light, and the related fact that it takes increasingly more energy to generate the ever-smaller wavelengths of electromagnetic energy required to measure ever-smaller structures in space, we would need an accelerator the size of the galaxy, and a trillion barrels of oil per second to fuel it, to observe anything as small as a fundamental string or the compactified dimensions of space around which they are theoretically wound.[101] Nevertheless, despite a total dearth of empirical evidence, the mathematics of Susskind and 't Hooft's holographic interpretation of string theory are evidently elegant enough for many of the other top physicists in contemporary academia, including Brian Greene and the late Stephen Hawking, to accept it as one of the most likely candidates for reconciling the otherwise irreconcilable theories of general relativity and quantum mechanics. As Susskind observes: "That is not a small thing, given the way the two giants—gravity and quantum mechanics—have been at war with each other for most of the twentieth century."[102]

Susskind's theoretical fundamental strings are *one-dimensional*, though they stretch across the exponentially expanding cosmos to the *two-dimensional* horizon where space is receding, from our point of view on Earth, at the speed of light, vibrating along the way through one dimension of time, and *nine dimensions of space*. According to this theory, six of these dimensions are curled up, or "compactified," at every point of three-dimensional space in twisted, non-Euclidean geometrical shapes called "Calabi-Yau manifolds," which are six-dimensional special cases of the more general class of Calabi-Yau spaces.[103] Although our macroscopic-sized bodies are too large to move in, or even directly detect, these extra six dimensions of space, the elastic strings, which are also theorized to be too narrow to measure (the Planck length),[104] can be mathematically wound around those compactified geometrical shapes of space in such a way that almost miraculously accounts for the internal machinery and corresponding quantum mechanics of the fundamental particles, such as electrons, protons, neutrons, photons, and theoretical "gravitons."[105]

Susskind goes on to explain that, as a result of the extremely energetic creation and destruction of virtual particle-antiparticle pairs constantly occurring in the quantum vacuum (which cause the exponential expansion of space), the one-dimensional strings get stretched all the way out to a two-dimensional film at the horizon of the cosmos (about fifteen billion light years away from Earth in every direction), where all of the information of the past, present, and future of the universe is timelessly recorded. It is important to note, however, that hypothetical people on a planet at what we perceive to be the cosmic horizon would see themselves at the center of the expanding universe, and Earth at the horizon. To use a common analogy, the same effect can be demonstrated by gluing pennies to a balloon: as the elastic material of the balloon expands, tiny people inhabiting each penny would perceive their penny as a fixed center, away from which all of the other pennies would seem to accelerate at a speed that increases in proportion to their distance (for galaxies, the distance-to-speed ratio is called the Hubble constant).

A crucial detail of Susskind's version of string theory is that information is always located at the boundary of *any* given volume of three-dimensional space (the ceiling, walls, and floor of a room, the atmosphere of Earth, the heliosphere of the solar system, the galactic halo, etc.).[106] However, when we approach the boundary, the information seems always to recede out to the next concentric boundary of our exponentially expanding universe, until it reaches the terminal speed of light at the holographic horizon of the cosmos, on which the information is timelessly recorded, and is simultaneously projected back inward with the cosmic microwave background radiation.[107]

Information Conservation

Basing his reasoning on the predictions of Einstein's general theory of relativity, Hawking previously claimed that because nothing, not even light, can escape the gravity of the event horizon of a black hole (where the fabric of space-time is contracting toward the central singularity at the speed of light), anything that falls past that horizon is permanently removed from the observable universe. If that were true, Susskind realized, it would violate the most basic physical principle, even more fundamental than energy conservation, of *information conservation*, which he describes as follows: "Information conservation implies that if you know the present with perfect precision, you can predict the future for all time. But that's only half of it. It also says that if you know the present, you can be absolutely sure of the past. It goes in both directions."[108] The principle of information conservation is at the heart of the concept of determinism, according to which the future is just as fixed as the present and the past. Hawking rejected the principle of information conservation and, therefore, the concept of determinism by saying that we cannot know the details of the past inside a black hole, because it destroys all of the information by which we could retrace the events that unfolded within it.

In agreement with Laplace's deterministic interpretation of Newtonian physics, Einstein interpreted his special and general theories of relativity in a deterministic way, resulting in the idea of a "block universe" in which each event in the four-dimensional space-time continuum continues to exist simultaneously. He therefore rejected quantum theory, which indicates that it is impossible to determine the past and future of the universe because it is impossible to measure simultaneously the position and momentum of a quantum particle. On one hand, the experimentally confirmed theories of special and general relativity indicate that the past, present, and future coexist while, on the other hand, the experimentally confirmed Copenhagen interpretation of quantum mechanics indicates that it is impossible to determine the past and future positions of any of the particles. Nevertheless, despite the apparent impossibility of simultaneously measuring the precise position and momentum of quantum particles, Susskind asks: "Does the randomness of Quantum Mechanics ruin the conservation of information? The answer is weird: it all depends on whether or not we look at the photon."[109] According to Susskind's complex explanation, although we cannot simultaneously know the position and momentum of particles in the present, and therefore cannot predict the future or recall the past with perfect precision, the information describing the future and the past is nevertheless timelessly conserved. In short, according to Susskind's interpretation of quantum mechanics, the future is determined, but we can never determine what it is.

Susskind and 't Hooft claim to have saved the principle of information conservation from Hawking's assault by using string theory to explain how every bit of information in any *volume* of space is actually stored by strings on the holographic *surface area*, a general principle which also applies to black holes. On one hand, because the information never occupies the volume of the black hole, it never passes the event horizon, and is therefore not erased from the universe. On the other hand, Susskind and 't Hoof admit that, from the perspective of someone who actually follows a bit of information past the event horizon in order to observe what happens, that bit of information *and* the observer would indeed be irretrievably lost from our observable universe. Susskind makes sense of his string theory, which conserves information at the event horizon, by an appeal to the "holographic principle," calling the theory that information is nevertheless simultaneously lost inside a black hole "black hole complementarity." He extends this theory to "cosmic complementarity," which is the inside-out version of "black hole complementarity," with the cosmic horizon of the universe serving the same role as the event horizon of a black hole. However, before explaining the details of Susskind's solution to the black hole paradox of information conservation, it is helpful first to establish a working definition of the most basic term of all, a bit of information.

What is a Bit of Information?

In a footnote in his first book, Susskind writes that "a bit is a technical term for an indivisible unit of information—a yes-no answer to a question."[110] Susskind defines the most basic term of his atheistic cosmology in a way that overtly implies a dialogue between an original cosmic questioner and a corresponding answerer. Who asked the original question required to bring the original bit of information into existence? And who answered it? Terrence Deacon, a professor of biological anthropology and neuroscience at the University of California, Berkeley, compares the anthropomorphic causative principles that reductionists typically slip into their ostensibly explanatory theories to a "homunculus." The homunculus was a small, artificial humanoid supposedly created by alchemists in the Middle-Ages. According to Deacon, the term "has also come to mean the misuse of teleological [goal directed] assumptions: the unacknowledged gap-fillers that stand behind, outside, or within processes involving apparent teleological processes, such as many features of life and mind, and pretend to be explanations of their function."[111] Susskind's homunculi are the questioner and answerer implicit in his definition of a bit of information as "a yes-no answer to a question."[112] Evidently also an atheist, unlike Susskind, Deacon attempts the difficult task of defining information and other apparently non-existent entities (which he calls "absential phenomena") as being simultaneously materially emergent and yet, somehow, not reducible to matter.[113] He explicitly rejects spiritual interpretations of quantum mechanics and the singularity of the Big Bang (theories he dismisses as "panpsychism"), and he never mentions string theory directly.[114] Nevertheless, Deacon's attempt to reunite the sciences and humanities with his theory of absential phenomena demonstrates a trend away from Susskind's entirely reductionist interpretation of string theory and toward Jung and Pauli's panpsychic cosmology.[115]

In his second book, Susskind calls information "the data that distinguishes one state of affairs from another. Measured in bits."[116] If we accept that everything is made of fundamental strings, then a bit of information can ultimately be defined as the yes-no answer to a question about the twists and turns of a string. As Susskind explains: "Imagine moving along the string as it turns and twists. Each turn and twist is a few bits of information."[117] Susskind writes that everything is made of bits of information: "Smaller than an atom, smaller than a quark, smaller even than a neutrino, the single bit may be the most fundamental building block. Without any structure, the bit is just there, or not there."[118]

Black Hole Complementarity, Cosmic Complementarity

To explain his new concepts of black hole complementarity and cosmic complementarity, Susskind developed a thought experiment starring Bob and Alice the astronauts.[119] As Bob, in a spaceship a safe distance from a black hole, watches Alice fly a propeller airplane toward the event horizon, he sees the rapidly vibrating strings of which her constituent particles are made gradually slow down and unravel under the influence of the intensifying gravity, in an analogous way to that in which the propellers of an airplane whirling invisibly around the central hub gradually become visible as they slow down. The quantum string propellers of Susskind's thought experiment each have propellers on their ends, which have propellers on their ends, and so on. Eventually Bob would see all of the information of which Alice is made smeared out onto a two-dimensional film that covers and wraps around, but never passes, the event horizon. Alice, on the other hand, would notice nothing unusual as she flies freely through the event horizon, although she would eventually feel herself being ripped apart by the infinite gravity of the central singularity. Two different perspectives of the same event result in two different events: in Alice's reference frame, information is irretrievably lost from our universe after it passes the unnoticed event horizon; in Bob's reference frame, though, information never makes it past the event horizon. Susskind calls this "black hole complementarity."[120]

Black hole complementarity explains how information is simultaneously lost and conserved in a black hole. But how is it released back into our observable universe? According to Susskind, all of the information smeared out just above the event horizon will be projected back out into the observable universe with "Hawking radiation." As discussed above, underlying each point of three-dimensional space is a field of infinite energy called the quantum vacuum seething with quantum fluctuations. As Susskind explains: "Quantum fluctuations are due to virtual photon pairs, which are created, then quickly absorbed back into the vacuum."[121] Hawking radiation, proposed by Stephen Hawking, is theoretically created when a virtual particle-antiparticle pair appears spontaneously from the quantum vacuum right on the razor's edge of the event horizon, so that the antiparticle gets absorbed into the black hole, while the particle escapes into the universe (giving the illusion that the black hole is radiating internal heat, and with it, entropic information). Susskind uses string theory to argue that, while the Hawking radiation is not scrambled information from inside the black hole, it does carry the scrambled bits of information frozen in time just above the event horizon back out into the observable universe, like a letter carrier. The same thing happens in reverse at the cosmic horizon.

An astronaut floating past what appears to us on Earth as the cosmic horizon—which is about fifteen billion light-years away—would notice nothing unusual, while people back on Earth, if we had a telescope that could see that far, would see the astronaut's fundamental-string structure slowed down and smeared all around the *infinitely hot* sphere of the cosmic horizon, where space-time is expanding away from Earth in every direction at the speed of light. Susskind's mathematics indicate that the information of anything that is smeared around the cosmic horizon—be it an astronaut or a galaxy—is projected back in by the cosmic microwave background radiation, the echoing afterglow of the Big Bang, which is equivalent to inside-out Hawking radiation. The implication is that the three-dimensional volume of the universe filled with galaxies is actually a holographic movie projected by one-dimensional strings from the "two-dimensional" film at the cosmic horizon. Susskind calls this inside-out version of black hole complementarity the "principle of cosmic complementarity."[122]

Megaverse of Universes

Discussion of the wave-particle paradox leads naturally to Hugh Everett's many-worlds interpretation of quantum mechanics, which Susskind equates with his own string theory: "I believe the two versions are complementary versions of exactly the same thing."[123] As discussed above, Everett put forth the theory in 1957 that, although a quantum wave of probability seems to collapse into a single point when it is observed (most likely at the peak or valley of the wave), the wave never really collapses; rather, each point in every wave of probability bubbles into a separate, parallel universe. The only difference between them, according to Everett, is the position of that one point in that one wave. The accumulated effect of such microcosmic differences results in an infinite variety of alternate universes, leading Susskind to ask, for example, "What if Germany had won World War II?"[124]

Susskind's string theory indicates that, although our future, present, and past fate in this universe are eternally conserved, and therefore determined at the cosmic horizon, each alternative we never choose is chosen by some parallel version of us branching off into the infinity of parallel universes. Susskind describes a "virtually infinite collection of 'pocket universes,'"[125] and admits that limiting the number of universes to 1 x 10 to the power of 500 "may not be enough to count the possibilities."[126] In an interview, Susskind points out an important distinction: "The number 10 to the 500 gets bandied about a lot. Not 10 to the 500 little pocket universes, but 10 to the 500 types of them, each one being repeated over and over again."[127]

If a singularity really does have infinite gravity, and therefore infinite energy (as Penrose, Susskind, and, sometimes, Hawking believe), it makes sense that there would be no limit to the number of universes bubbling out of it. However, according to Susskind's interpretation of quantum mechanics, although the future of each universe is determined, it is impossible to predict precisely which point in each wave of probability will manifest in which universe. It seems, therefore, that combining the opposite extremes of general relativity (infinite gravity) and quantum mechanics (infinitesimal size) results in a string theory that unites determinism and indeterminism. This unification can be interpreted in the following paradoxical maxim, which I will explain below: At each moment we are forced by the flow of fate to choose freely from an infinity of fixed futures frozen in time by the infinite temperature at the horizon of each alternative universe.

According to Susskind, owing to the exponential expansion of space, if people on Earth attach a thermometer to a long cable and let the cable unspool, "as things approach the cosmic horizon, we would discover that the temperature increases, eventually approaching the infinite temperature at the horizon of a black hole."[128] However, owing to the principle of cosmic complementarity, people on a planet being swept outward with the expansion of space at what we perceive to be the cosmic horizon would notice nothing unusual, and would instead see people on Earth roasting in the infinite temperature of the cosmic horizon, where space is expanding at the speed of light. They would then see each bit of information formerly describing planet Earth radiating back from the horizon as photons (cosmic microwave background radiation).

The infinite temperature caused by the light-speed expansion of space accounts for the timelessness of the cosmic horizon, as infinite heat is equivalent to infinite energy which, according to Einstein's $e = mc^2$, is equivalent to infinite mass, and therefore infinite gravity. Susskind explains that, according to general relativity, as with acceleration at the speed of light, so does the gravity of a black hole stop time: "The closer the clock is to the black hole horizon, the slower it seems to tick. Right at the horizon, time comes to a complete standstill for clocks that remain outside the black hole."[129] The cosmic horizon is an inside-out event horizon so that, from the perspective of someone remaining inside the universe, time stops at the cosmic horizon where, according to Susskind, every bit of information describing the past, present, and future of our universe is simultaneously conserved on an infinitely hot holographic film. Thus, it seems that at each moment, each of us is absolutely free to choose from an infinite array of pre-determined futures, while all of the alternatives we do not choose will nevertheless be chosen by some other version of us corresponding to the parallel universe in which "we" make that choice.

The subtitle of Susskind's first book, *The Cosmic Landscape: String Theory and the Illusion of Intelligent Design,* seems to acknowledge that it is too statistically unlikely that our universe would spontaneously erupt from the original singularity at the Big Bang, with all of the physical parameters required for life (especially the "cosmological constant" that determines the expansion rate of space) perfectly fine-tuned the way they are, *if ours is the only universe.* String theory, however, mathematically requires not only that higher dimensions of space be "curled up" in each point of our three-dimensional space, but that our entire universe of three-dimensional space is only one bubble in an infinite ocean of bubble universes. According to Susskind, even if there is a finite number of universes (after using mathematical tricks to eliminate the infinities that naturally emerge), there are still 1×10 to the 500 *types* of universes, each type being repeated again and again. Given that preposterously large number, the outrageously improbable chance that some of the universes will have the constants of nature (especially the cosmological constant) perfectly balanced for life becomes almost inevitable. He relates this idea to the "anthropic principle," a term coined by Steven Weinberg in the mid-1980s, which Susskind defines as "the principle that requires the laws of nature to be consistent with the existence of intelligent life."[130] *The Cosmic Landscape* is Susskind's atheistic explanation of the anthropic principle which, he says, was forced upon scientists by the need to account for the exquisitely fine-tuned ratio that describes the expansion rate of space, known alternately as the cosmological constant, vacuum energy, and dark energy.

Anthropic Principle and the Cosmological Constant

Einstein, who initially believed the universe is static, realized that the gravitational attraction of all matter for all other matter should be causing the universe to collapse into itself, unless there were some kind of anti-gravitational force, which he therefore inserted into his equations for general relativity, calling it the cosmological constant. When Hubble independently confirmed Lemaître's and Friedman's independent theories about the expanding fabric of space-time in 1929 (which bolstered the Big Bang theory), Einstein called his previous insertion of the cosmological constant into his general relativity equations his "greatest blunder."[131] However, referring to Einstein's cosmological constant, Susskind writes: "Pandora's box, once opened, could not be closed so easily."[132] Einstein's cosmological constant—which he created in 1917, and then rejected in 1929—has subsequently been reincarnated as the "dark energy" of the quantum vacuum: the anti-gravitational, repulsive force produced by the constant creation and annihilation of particle-antiparticle pairs.[133] The cosmological constant, Einstein's rejected stone, has become the cornerstone of current cosmology.

Although Hubble realized that galaxies appear to expand away from one another at a rate that increases with their distance (like pennies glued to an inflating balloon), he did not know that the overall expansion rate of the universe is actually increasing, rather than decreasing, over time. To their great surprise, Saul Perlmutter in 1998, and Adam G. Riess and Brian Schmidt in 1999, led independent teams of physicists who unexpectedly discovered that the expansion rate of the universe is increasing.[134] They were studying type 1A supernovas (which serve as "standard candles" of luminosity) in different galaxies in an attempt to measure the expansion rate of the universe, which they mistakenly assumed would be gradually slowing down under the influence of its own gravity. Instead, they discovered that the expansion rate accelerates, as if one were to throw a ball into the air and it continued to accelerate upward faster and faster. This epochal discovery was confirmed by photographs of the cosmic microwave background radiation taken by the WMAP satellite, which was launched on June 30, 2001.[135]

The WMAP pictures of the CMB radiation indicate that there is dark energy emanating from the quantum vacuum, which consists of a sea of virtual particle-antiparticle pairs that emerge momentarily and then destroy one another. As Susskind explains, according to quantum field theory, the quantum vacuum should have an infinite amount of energy:

> There are so many high-energy virtual particles that the total energy comes out infinite. Infinity is a senseless answer. It's what made Dirac skeptical of vacuum energy. But as Dirac's contemporary Wolfgang Pauli quipped, "Just because something is infinite doesn't mean it's zero." . . . Ultimately we reach a value of the energy so large that if two particles with that much energy collide, they create a black hole.[136]

Pauli, who was at the forefront of this debate about the quantum vacuum, criticized physicists who use tricks to try to ignore the infinite energy associated with miniature black holes in the vacuum. Susskind continues:

> We call it cutting off the divergences or regulating the theory. . . . It's a very unsatisfactory situation, but once we do this we can estimate the vacuum energy stored in electrons, photons, gravitons, and all the other known particles. The result is no longer infinite, but it is also not small. . . . The estimate that quantum field theory gives is so

big that it requires a 1 with 116 zeros after it: 10 to the 116th power![137]

Susskind frankly admits that it is inadequate simply to ignore the effects of very high-energy virtual particles which we know exist, but which we do not yet understand. After expediently ignoring the higher-energy virtual particle-antiparticle pairs that would produce black holes upon colliding in the quantum vacuum, the positive and negative charges of the remaining kinds of virtual particle-antiparticle pairs *almost* perfectly cancel out to zero. Neither quantum theory nor string theory has been able to explain why so many enormous sets of numbers should cancel each other out to such a precisely miniscule, but non-zero number. As Susskind observes: "It truly is the mother of all physics problems."[138] The ultra-extreme precision of interacting forces required to account for the extraordinarily tiny cosmological constant forced Susskind to confront the anthropic principle, for "if a reason could be found why a slightly larger cosmological constant would prevent life, then the Anthropic Principle would have to be taken seriously."[139]

Susskind admits that the existence of intelligent, biological life requires that the cosmological constant be precisely what it is, no bigger and no smaller, and he further admits that the exceedingly precise fine-tuning of the cosmological constant makes it seem plausible at first to suspect that it may have been the work of some intelligent designer. His explanation for the anthropic principle, however, appeals to the theory of the megaverse of parallel universes: a theory that is already inherent in general relativity, quantum theory, and string theory. In other words, according to Susskind, the megaverse theory was not artificially concocted just to counter the intelligent design interpretation of the anthropic principle, although it does provide an atheistic explanation for it: given enough universes randomly erupting from the quantum vacuum, the extremely remote chance that some of them will have their physical constants perfectly balanced for intelligent life becomes inevitable.

In a 2004 debate between Susskind and Lee Smolin, a fellow Perimeter Institute physicist, Smolin argues against Susskind's string theory interpretation of the anthropic principle by saying that the "Anthropic Principle cannot yield any falsifiable predictions, and therefore cannot be a part of science."[140] However, Smolin's and Susskind's opinions about why the universe appears to be intelligently designed to facilitate the evolution of intelligent life are not fundamentally different: both account for the fine-tuning required for intelligent life by first dismissing the possibility of intelligent design and, second, by assuming some random Darwinian process involving a staggeringly large number of universes, resulting in a series of lucky accidents required for intelligent life to evolve. In *The Cosmic Landscape*, Susskind summarizes Smolin's viewpoint by saying that, according to Smolin, baby universes are born inside black holes, the creation of which coincidentally requires the same physical conditions required for human life so that, in the end, "the universe is not tuned for life. It is tuned to make black holes."[141] The irony about Smolin's theory is that if Psyche = Singularity, and if the universe is tuned to make black holes, then our inside-out black hole universe is not only tuned for life, it is itself a living being, which would bring the history of academic cosmology full-circle back to Plato.

PART II
SYNTHESIZING
SUSSKIND AND JUNG

In Part I we reviewed the basic history of modern physics, from Newton through Einstein to the founders of quantum mechanics. Then we saw how Susskind used string theory to reconcile the previously incompatible theories of general relativity and quantum mechanics. According to Susskind's holographic interpretation of string theory, quantum particles are made of even tinier strings of energy that are wrapped around six dimensions of space that are compactified at each point of three-dimensional space in geometrical shapes called Calabi-Yau manifolds. These fundamental strings and the compactified dimensions of space around which they are wound are too small to be measured by current measuring devices, though the mathematics of Susskind's theory indicate that these incredibly thin strings stretch out to, and are projected in from, the horizon of the cosmos. According to Susskind, the universe expands from the gravitational singularity at the Big Bang, and simultaneously projects in from something like a holographic film at the cosmic horizon, at each point of which all of the information from the past, present, and future of three-dimensional space is interwoven.

So as not to lose a vision of the forest for the trees, in the first chapter of Part II I explain how the proposed Jung-Susskind synthesis is presaged by the ancient cosmologies presented in the Vedic Dialogues of India and in Plato's Greek Dialogues. Those broad comparisons provide a comprehensive world view within which the more detailed comparisons of Jung and Susskind that follow should fall more easily into place, in the same way that looking at the whole picture of a jig-saw puzzle on the box helps us connect the pieces properly. In the first chapter of Part II I also examine how Plato's cosmology permeated the Christian world view in the West throughout the entire medieval era, from St. Augustine to Dante. I then briefly outline the history of modern Western philosophy, beginning with Rene Descartes, one of the founders of the Scientific Revolution, and namesake of both the geometrical coordinate system called the Cartesian grid, and the philosophical "Cartesian split" between mind and matter. I examine how David Hume provided the ultimate empiricist response to Descartes' rationalist philosophy of the immaterial self, and how Immanuel Kant responded to Hume by developing his philosophy of the inborn, *a priori* categories of thought (especially space, time, and causality).

With that basic history of philosophy in place, I discuss several passages in which Jung and Pauli identify their theory of the archetypes of the collective unconscious with Plato's original theory of eternal ideas. I then compare Jung's theory of the collective unconscious to Susskind's opinions about the nature of consciousness, especially his assumption that we are "hardwired" by Darwinian evolution to perceive the world through the Newtonian concepts of three-dimensional space and linear time.[142] In the remaining chapters of Part II I compare the details of Susskind's holographic string theory to four aspects of Jung's psychology: 1) his equation, "Psyche=highest intensity in the smallest space," which I translate as Psyche = Singularity; 2) his near-death experience of the cosmic horizon; 3) his theory that the mandala is the psychic image of the ultimate archetype of the Self; and 4) his theory of synchronicity.

Chapter 3
Philosophical Precedents for the Jung-Susskind Synthesis

According to Jung, the great works of religion, philosophy, art, and science that have flowered periodically throughout world history all rose into the conscious minds of their disparate creators from archetypes that remain the same beneath the changing currents of the cultures they inspire.[143] Susskind's holographic string theory certainly seems to qualify as an important idea in the history of physics, so it must possess some historical antecedents if Jung's theory of the archetypes is correct. Moreover, if the synthesis of Susskind's cosmology and Jung's psychology presented here is valid, then it too must have some prototypes from the past. And indeed, the Jung-Susskind synthesis does seem to be clearly presaged by the psycho-physical cosmologies presented in the two respective pillars of Eastern and Western philosophy: the Vedanta philosophy of India and Plato's Greek philosophy.

Vaishnava Vedanta Cosmology

In the Vaishnava, or Vishnu-centric school of Vedanta philosophy (which is based on the authority of the Vedic Dialogues), the supreme God is called Vishnu, each of whose innumerable but equally potent forms are eternally paired with a corresponding form of the supreme Goddess called Lakshmi.[144] Each Lakshmi-Vishnu couple (such as Radha-Krishna and Sita-Rama) eternally presides over a separate spiritual planet (Vaikuntha-loka), each of which is populated by an ecosystem of spiritual species, the form of each member of which is made of eternal knowledge and bliss.[145] The self-effulgent radiation of all of the spiritual planets creates the spiritual sky-ocean known as the *brahmajyoti*, or Brahman.[146] According to A. C. Bhaktivedanta Swami Prabhupada:

> In the Fifteenth Chapter of the *Bhagavad-gītā,* the real picture of the material world is given. . . . "The Supreme Lord said: There is a banyan tree which has its roots upward and its branches down, and the Vedic hymns are its leaves. One who knows this tree is the knower of the *Vedas.*". . . We have experience of a tree whose roots are upward: if one stands on the bank of a river or any reservoir of water, he can see that the trees reflected in the water are upside down. The branches go downward and the roots upward. Similarly, this material world is a reflection of the spiritual world. The material world is but a shadow of reality.[147]

If the material world is the inverted reflection of the spiritual world, there should be a mirror-symmetry between the laws of physics that govern matter and the psychological laws that govern psyche. In agreement with that line of thinking, the Vaishnava Vedanta philosophers explain that the material world is the inverted, shadowy reflection of the spiritual world because the material world is Vishnu's dream, which indicates, from a Jungian perspective, that the material world is the unconscious mind of God, the dynamics of which are mathematically modeled by physics.[148]

According to this Vaishnava cosmology, an eternal Vishnu Avatar called Karanodakashayi-Vishnu (also known as Maha-Vishnu) occasionally descends from the spiritual world and falls asleep on the waves of the Causal Ocean (a kind of temporary coagulation of the infinite expanse of Brahman). From the pores of his skin, the sleeping form of Maha-Vishnu exhales and inhales a megaverse (*mahat-tattva*) of bubble universes (*brahmandas*), each of which manifests his dreaming potency (*yoga-nidra*).[149] Each universe bubbling into Maha-Vishnu's dream is centered around another Vishnu Avatar (Garbhodakashayi-Vishnu), who further expands into an omnipresent particle of infinite intelligence (Kshirodakashayi-Vishnu, or Paramatma, the Supersoul) located in the center of every material and spiritual atom in all of the material universes.[150] Paramatma is simultaneously all of the waves in the infinite ocean of pure potentiality (Brahman) underlying all manifest reality—including the Causal Ocean of material energy. According to the Gaudiya Vaishnava school of Vedanta, each form of Vishnu is "inconceivably, simultaneously one with and different from" all other material and spiritual atoms, a fundamental tenet summarized in the slogan, *achintya bedha-bedha-tattva*.[151] That same basic doctrine is expressed in the phrase "atman is brahman,"[152] which means that the infinitely powerful point of personal consciousness is one with the impersonal waves of precognitive bliss, which is structurally similar to the particle-wave paradox of quantum mechanics.[153]

In the Vaishnava philosophy, individual souls, known as *jivas* or *atmas*, are infinitesimal atoms of eternal, personal consciousness, each of whom has all of the qualities of the supreme Atman from whom they expand, which means, moreover, that each soul is also merged with the impersonal waves of Brahman. Occasionally, some souls abuse their free will in the spiritual world, and thus fall into Maha-Vishnu's tempestuous dream, from which they must struggle their way back up to their original spiritual form by suffering through the egregious cycle of physical reincarnation (*samsara*), with its fourfold miseries of birth, death, old age, and disease.[154]

Each material universe in the Vaishnava model consists of eight concentric spheres of increasingly subtle material elements (earth, water, fire, air, ether, mind, intelligence, and false-ego).[155] The ether element, known as *akasha*, is the intermediary sphere between, on one side, the grosser elements terminating with the innermost sphere of the earth element and, on the other side, the subtler elements ending at the outermost sphere of false-ego. The earth element is not planet Earth; it is the innermost sphere encompassing a hollow area in the middle of the universe, which is half-filled with water. Garbhodakashayi-Vishnu reclines in the middle of the surface of that water on the belly of an enormous spiritual serpent, Ananta Shesha, or Seshanaga (yet another form of Vishnu), while a form of Lakshmi massages his legs. A cosmic lotus plant then stems from Garbhodakashayi's naval, and the first demigod, Brahma, is born in the blossom. Brahma then creates all of the planetary systems in the cosmic lotus stalk.[156]

According to Srimad-Bhagavatam, also known as the Bhagavata Purana, each of the five gross elements is coupled with one of the five sense perceptions, so that earth is paired with smell, water with taste, fire with sight, air with touch, and, finally, ether with sound.[157] Furthermore, as discussed above, there are three super-etheric shells of subtle material energy surrounding each universe, composed of mind, intelligence, and false ego.[158] There seems to be a correlation between what current cosmologists describe as the exponential expansion rate of the fabric of space-time, culminating at the space-timeless speed of light at the cosmic horizon, and the eight increasingly subtle, elemental coverings of the universe described in Srimad-Bhagavatam, each of which is ten times thicker, and therefore farther out in space, than the preceding sphere.[159]

Krishna, the most famous form of Vishnu, describes the same Vaishnava cosmology in the Bhagavad-gita, where he also declares himself to be the Supreme Self and, importantly, a spiritual string on which all the cosmos is strung: "Everything rests upon Me, as pearls are strung on a thread. . . . I am the sound in ether and ability in man."[160] Later in the Bhagavad-gita, Krishna says: "I am the Self, O Gudakesha, seated in the hearts of all creatures. I am the beginning, the middle and the end of all beings."[161] In both the Bhagavad-gita and the Srimad-Bhagavatam, Krishna claims to be, and is described by others as the ultimate Self, the original Vishnu whose omnicentric Purusha Avatars—Maha-Vishnu, Garbhodakashayi-Vishnu, and Kshirodakashayi-Vishnu (Paramatma)—carry on the business of manifesting the bubbling cloud of material universes. In the Bhagavad-gita, Krishna furthermore describes himself as the string that threads each of these other Vishnu manifestations together, like pearls on a thread, after which he describes himself as the sound of ether (*akasha*) and the syllable *om*, which could imply that Krishna, as the all-uniting cosmic thread, is creating the sound of the ether by vibrating.[162]

In the Brihadaranyaka Upanishad, another text from the Vaishnava Vedanta tradition, Uddalaka Aruni asks Patancala Kapya: "Do you know the string on which this world and the next, as well as all beings, are strung together?" He then asks: "Do you know the inner controller of this world and the next, as well as of all beings, who controls them from within?" Concluding, he says: "If a man knows what that string is and who that inner controller is—he knows *brahman*; he knows the worlds; he knows the gods; he knows the Vedas; he knows the spirits; he knows the self; he knows all."[163] The conversation about this ultimate string is later picked up by the sage Yajnavalkya, who refers to the threaded layer of information contained at the cosmic horizon as *akasha*, which is translated as "space," although it is sometimes also translated as "ether." He describes *akasha* as: "The things above the sky, the things below the earth, and the things between the earth and the sky, as well as all those things people here refer to as past, present, and future—on space, Gargi, are all these woven back and forth."[164]

When Gargi asks in whom the timeless, spaceless *akasha* is woven, warp and woof, Yajnavalkya replies:

'Pitiful is the man, Gargi, who departs from this world without knowing this imperishable [Akshara, a name for the personified *akasha*]. . . . Besides this imperishable, there is no one that sees, no one that hears, no one that thinks, and no one that perceives.

'On this very imperishable, Gargi, space [*akasha*] is woven back and forth.'[165]

The three forms of Vishnu (known collectively as the Purusha Avatars) responsible for creating the megaverse of universes have all of the characteristics of the gravitational singularity in Susskind's cosmology: the omnipotent, omnisicient (information conserving), omnicentric source and all-consuming boundary of the megaverse of universes. Importantly for the comparison with Susskind's string theory traced below, we further see in the Bhagavad-gita and the Brihadaranyaka Upanishad that the idea of an all-knowing God takes the form of a string that interweaves the past, present, and future together specifically at the spherical horizon of the gross physical cosmos, the ether sphere (beyond which there are three more subtle material spheres).

Plato's *Timaeus*

Although Plato does not mention a megaverse of bubble universes, in all other respects his descriptions of our universe are very similar to the Vaishnava interpretation of the Vedanta school of Vedic cosmology. Because Susskind's academic achievement stems directly from the Platonic tradition, I examine Plato's Dialogues more extensively than the Vedic Dialogues.

As depicted in Plato's Dialogues the *Apology* and the *Phaedo*, in 399 B.C.E. his beloved teacher Socrates was ordered to drink a lethal dose of hemlock in an Athenian prison cell after being convicted by a slim majority of the democratic Assembly on charges of corrupting the youth and believing in gods of his own invention instead of the gods of the state.[166] In response to that catastrophe, Plato resurrected his martyred master in the literary masterpieces of his Dialogues. Socrates is the star of almost all of Plato's Dialogues, with a notable exception in the *Timaeus*, which features the Pythagorean philosopher and astronomer Timaeus explaining to Socrates and two others that, "on this wise, using the language of probability, we may say that the world came into being—a living creature truly endowed with soul and intelligence by the providence of God."[167] Timaeus describes the soul of our spherical universe as radiating out in every direction from the central point to the circumference:

> Such was the whole plan of the eternal God about the god [the cosmos] that was to be; he made it smooth and even, having a surface in every direction equidistant from the center, a body entire and perfect, and formed out of perfect bodies. And in the center he put the soul, which he diffused throughout the body, making it also to be the exterior environment of it, and he made the universe a circle moving in a circle.[168]

Like the central soul of the universe in Timaeus' vision, so does the omnicentric singularity of the Big Bang, as described by Susskind, diffuse throughout the spherical body of the universe, while at the same time occupying each point of the exterior horizon, from which it echoes inward on threads that produce the holographic illusion of the corporeal world.

Timaeus, who does not explicitly mention cosmic threads, nevertheless goes on to provide what can be interpreted as more parallels with Big Bang cosmology:

> Now when the creator had framed the soul according to his will, he formed within her the corporeal universe, and brought the two together and united them center to center. The soul, interfused everywhere from the center to the circumference of heaven, of which also she is the external envelopment, herself turning in herself, began a divine beginning of never-ceasing and rational life enduring throughout all time.[169]

Timaeus reaffirms that the soul of the universe is interfused everywhere, specifically from the center to the circumference of the universe. He also says that the creator God first framed the soul of the universe in the shape of a sphere with a point in the middle (in other words a spherical mandala), and then formed the corporeal universe within that shape, specifically by uniting them "center to center," which provides a Platonic precedent for the superimposition of the central point of Susskind's black hole model of the universe on the central point of Jung's mandala model of the Self. It is also important to note that, like Plato's cosmology in the *Timaeus*, Susskind's cosmology of the cosmic horizon is inherently geocentric. As discussed above, one effect of the expanding nature of space-time is that observers occupying any point of space necessarily perceive themselves as the central point away from which the rest of the universe is expanding at an exponentially accelerating rate, terminating at the speed of light at the cosmic horizon. Susskind, residing on planet Earth, therefore naturally defines the cosmic horizon as the spherical border of the universe from a geocentric perspective.

After describing the central point of the universe as the location of its soul, which permeates the volume of space and envelops the spherical horizon, Timaeus later says that the outermost sphere actually has no shape at all, this "mother and receptacle of all created and visible and in any way sensible things . . . an invisible and formless being which receives all things and in some mysterious way partakes of the intelligible, and is most incomprehensible."[170] Timaeus' seemingly contradictory claims that the cosmic horizon is both a sphere and formless, and his additional claim that it is like a mother and an incomprehensible receptacle that partakes mysteriously of the intelligible realm of eternal forms, make more sense in light of Susskind's new principles: cosmic complementarity, according to which the cosmic horizon simultaneously does and does not exist, depending on the observer's relative reference frame; and the holographic principle, according to which the information describing any three-dimensional volume of space is recorded on and projected from each point of its two-dimensional surface area (culminating at the cosmic horizon). Timaeus goes on to say that this "mother substance" becomes the four material elements (fire, water, earth, and air) "in so far as she receives the impressions of them."[171]

That the outermost perimeter of the cosmos receives all things within the universe like a mother also indicates that she gives birth to all things. Timaeus' related claim that the cosmic horizon partakes of the intelligible realm of eternal ideas further indicates that the visible world is projected from the cosmic horizon because, as he goes on to explain, the visible world of temporary forms is like a shadow of the invisible but intelligible world of eternal forms.

Timaeus asks the group: "Is there any self-existent fire, and do all those things which we call self-existent exist, or are only those things which we see or in some way perceive through the bodily organs truly existent?"[172] Using fire as an example, Timaeus asks his group of friends, including Socrates, to choose between two opposing philosophical positions, which academics now call: *rationalism*, the belief that there are physically imperceptible but rationally perceivable, eternal forms of knowledge that structure the physical world and the human mind; and *empiricism*, the belief that only things that are perceivable by the five bodily sense organs (or their instrumental extensions) truly exist. Based on the assumption that everything in the visible world is made of a mixture of four material elements—fire, air, water, earth—Timaeus asks: Is there an eternal *idea* of fire, one unchanging, perfect, *conceptual essence* of fire that all temporary instances of visible fire imperfectly reflect? Or are the particular instances of visible fire—as well as the other things we can see, hear, touch, taste, and smell—all that really exist?

Timaeus assumes that the group agrees with him that there are eternal, self-existent forms, but he goes on to question how the ideal forms can be related to temporary, imperfect, material forms. How do spiritual forms interface with matter? To help explain this relationship, Timaeus divides existence into three, instead of two worlds: being, space, and generation.[173] Being is the unchanging world of eternal forms that are physically intangible but accessible to reason; generation is the always-changing world of temporary forms that are empirically perceivable by physical sense organs; while space is the intermediary world that partakes of the eternal forms and gives birth to their temporary shadows. According to Timaeus, there is a third nature, which is space and is eternal, and admits not of destruction and provides a home for all created things, and is apprehended, when all sense is absent, by a kind of spurious reason, and is hardly real—which we, beholding as in a dream, say of all existence that it must of necessity be in some place and occupy a space, but that what is neither in heaven nor in earth has no existence. . . . For an image, since the reality after which it is modeled does not belong to it, and it exists ever as the fleeting shadow of some other, must be inferred to be in another, or it could not be at all.[174]

The apparently empty space that contains our bodies, and separates them from all other physical objects, does not make a physical impression on any one of our five sense organs: we cannot see space, hear it, touch it, taste it, or smell it. Space is therefore not an empirically observable, material object. However, according to Timaeus, though it is eternal and indestructible, space is not quite the same as the eternal forms either because it is formless or, rather, filled with temporary forms. It is evident that space is another word for what Timaeus calls the "mother substance" located specifically at the spherical boundary of the universe, separating and, at the same time, connecting the spiritual world of eternal forms (being) and the temporary world of material forms (generation).[175] Space, occupying its own category, is the infinitely impressionable intermediatrix between the material and spiritual worlds. Notice that Timaeus does not give the Newtonian definition of space as the three-dimensional volume of emptiness that immediately surrounds our material bodies; rather, like Susskind, Timaeus locates space at the cosmic horizon, which simultaneously absorbs and projects the world of temporary forms.

According to Timaeus, all empirically observable things in the universe are absorbed within the cosmic horizon, from which they are cast into the visible world like grains from a winnowing machine: "In this manner, the four kinds of elements [earth, water, fire, air] were then shaken by the receiving vessel, which, moving like a winnowing machine, scattered far away from one another the elements most unlike, and forced the most similar elements into close contact."[176] Timaeus later equates the receiving vessel that projects the four elements with the fifth element, ether,[177] which agrees with the Vedanta cosmology, according to which the past, present, and future of the four material elements that create the visible world are projected from the ether element (*akasha*) at the outermost sphere of gross matter, into which is interwoven the universal thread soul of Vishnu known as Sutratman and Akshara.[178]

Shing-Tung Yau Compares String Theory to Plato's *Timaeus*

Earlier we saw Susskind explain that vibrating strings form the different types of quantum particles by wrapping around the six higher dimensions of space that are compactified in each point of three-dimensional space in geometrical shapes called "Calabi Yau manifolds."[179] Shing-Tung Yau, the Harvard mathematician who co-discovered these geometrical shapes, begins and ends his book *The Shape of Inner Space: String Theory and the Geometry of the Universe's Hidden Dimensions* by relating his discoveries to Plato's *Timaeus*, in which Plato depicts the talented astronomer explaining that the five fundamental elements of nature are made of corresponding atoms which are constructed of fundamental triangles that combine to form the five regular convex polyhedra—cube (earth), icosahedron (water), octahedron (air), tetrahedron (fire), dodecahedron (ether)—which came to be called the Platonic solids because of their appearance in Plato's *Timaeus*. Ether is the fifth element that Timaeus identifies with the outer shape of the universe as a whole, which he further identifies with the fifth Platonic solid, the dodecahedron,[180] which means, finally, that Timaeus describes the cosmic horizon alternately as spherical, dodecahedral, and shapeless.[181]

In his commentary on the *Timaeus*, Tau explains:

> In basing his cosmology on these shapes [the Platonic solids], Plato correctly surmised that symmetry ought to lie at the heart of any credible description of nature. For if we are ever to produce a real theory of everything—in which all the forces are unified and all the constituents obey a handful (or two) of rules—we'll need to uncover the underlying symmetry, the simplifying principle from which everything else springs.[182]

Yau, like Jung and Pauli, acknowledges that Plato provided the basic scientific precedent of using the eternal truths of geometry to discover the unifying symmetries underlying nature. However, unlike Jung and Pauli, Yau does not take the next logical step, which indicates that there might be a mirror-symmetry between the quantitative laws of physics and the qualitative laws of psychology. Using Yau's words, I suggest that the ultimate "underlying symmetry, the simplifying principle from which everything else springs," may be found in the mirror-symmetry between Susskind's black hole model of the universe and Jung's mandala model of the Self, which can be distilled into the formula Psyche = Singularity.

Susskind would have us believe that "hard-nosed, scientific types" do not fall for naïve theories about an intelligently designed universe,[183] yet his whole string theory is literally wrapped around the compactified shapes of inner space that Yau co-discovered, while Yau places that accomplishment squarely in the tradition of Plato's *Timaeus*, which clearly describes the intelligent universe as the creation of an intelligent designer.[184] In fact, during an interview, Susskind personally told Yau that the Calabi-Yau manifolds are "the DNA of string theory."[185] That the co-discoverer of what Susskind calls the DNA of string theory very closely compared that discovery to Plato's *Timaeus* supports the project of correlating Susskind's string theory with the archetypal cosmology described by Plato and, subsequently, Jung and Pauli.

That support is reiterated in the conclusion of Yau's book, where he writes:

Let us end where we began, looking to the past in the hopes of gleaning hints about the road ahead. The year was 387 B.C. or thereabouts, when . . . Plato established his Academy, which is sometimes referred to as the world's first major university. . . . Even though the particulars of Plato's "theory of everything," as outlined in the *Timaeus*, strike the modern sensibility as absurd (if not borderline psychotic), there are many parallels between his picture of the universe and that embodied in string theory. . . . Plato was on the right track in many ways, identifying some of the key pieces of the puzzle—such as symmetry, duality, and the general principle of geometrization—that we now believe any workable attempt to explain it all ought to include.[186]

Although Yau sees "many parallels" between Plato's cosmology and the equally bizarre string theory cosmology, he does not mention the most blatant parallel between Susskind's string theory of the holographic horizon of the cosmos and Timaeus' description of the cosmic horizon as the eternal mother from which the temporary world of three-dimensional forms is projected like a shadowy dream. Yau hopes to glean hints from Plato about the road ahead for string theory, so it should not surprise him that another prominent string theorist, Brian Greene, did notice the striking parallel between Susskind's theory and Plato's cosmology, specifically as presented in the famous cave allegory of the *Republic*.[187]

Brian Greene, Susskind, and Plato's Cave

In the *Republic*, Plato depicts his mentor Socrates recounting a conversation he had the day before with Plato's brothers, Glaucon and Adimantus, and a few others. In the text of the *Republic*, Plato never reveals who Socrates is recalling the previous day's events to, but in the preface to the *Timaeus*, Plato presents Socrates indicating that he spoke the *Republic* the day before, and now expects Timaeus to return the favor by telling a story of his own. The point is that while writing the *Timaeus*, Plato evidently intended us to see it as a continuation of the conversation of the *Republic*, which warrants a comparison of the cosmologies in those two Dialogues, which presents us, finally, with a model of the universe that is unmistakably similar to Susskind's model.

In the cave allegory of the *Republic*, the most famous part of what is now Plato's most famous Dialogue, Socrates asks his interlocutors to imagine prisoners who are chained, head to foot, in the back of a subterranean cave immediately after birth.[188] These unfortunates are forced by their chains to face away from the entrance of the cave, above which a blazing fire burns, so that all they ever see are shadows cast on the back wall facing them. They can see their own shadows, as well as the shadows cast by a parade of puppets behind them, each of which simulates some natural object from outside the cave. Guards carry these shadow-puppets up on sticks just above a partition spanning the width of the cave, which conceals the guards' shadows as they pace back and forth in front of the fire. According to Socrates, the prisoners, never having seen their own bodies or any of the bodies beside or behind them, naturally assume that the shadows on the wall in front of them, and the echoes they hear bouncing off the wall, are the totality of reality.

Socrates then describes the arduous and mortally dangerous process of releasing a reluctant prisoner from the cave and showing him, ultimately, the blindingly bright disc of the Sun (which he perceives indirectly at first, in mirror-reflections on puddles of water). After the prisoner has seen the Sun directly, he is directed to descend back into the cave to return the favor of his release by releasing other prisoners. However, because his eyes are no longer adapted to the dark, he can no longer compete in the daily activity on which the prisoners pride themselves—predicting which shadows will pass by in which order—so that those whom he is trying to release to the upper world would rather kill him than allow him to make them as blind and mad as he apparently is.

Socrates then correlates each part of the cave allegory to the soul's embodied imprisonment in the material world, which is like a shadow or dream of the spiritual world. As the two-dimensional shadows that are projected by the fire onto the back wall of the cave are in relation to the three-dimensional objects we see on Earth and in the sky (people, animals, trees, planets), all of which are created and illuminated by the visible Sun, so too are the three-dimensional forms on Earth and in the sky (including the visible Sun) like dream-shadows of eternal forms that radiate from the invisible but intelligible Sun, also called the "*idea* of the good." Socrates describes this archetype of archetypes: "In the visible it gave birth to light and its sovereign [the Sun]; in the intelligible, itself sovereign, it provided truth and intelligence—and the man who is going to act prudently in private or in public must see it."[189]

Socrates defines the idea of the Good as the source of cosmos (visible light) and psyche (intelligible light), which is equivalent to Jung's archetype of the Self. Moreover, if the idea of the Good is the source of visible light, and if all visible light emerges ultimately from the singularity at the Big Bang then, extrapolating from Socrates' reasoning, the idea of the Good is the singularity, which would therefore also be the source of psyche. A tentative equation of the idea of the Good with the central singularity (which is present at each point of the cosmic horizon) could possibly shed light on a point of confusion regarding a parallel between Susskind's string theory and Plato's cave allegory. In *The Fabric of the Cosmos*, Brian Greene points to this parallel:

> Whereas Plato envisioned common perceptions as revealing a mere shadow of reality, the holographic principle concurs, but turns the metaphor on its head. The shadows—the things that are flattened out and hence live on a lower-dimensional surface—are real, while what seem to be the more richly structured, higher-dimensional entities (us; the world around us) are evanescent projections of the shadows. . . . While it is a fantastically strange idea, and one whose

role in the final understanding of spacetime is far from clear, 't Hooft and Susskind's so-called holographic principle is well motivated.[190]

Greene gives an even stronger endorsement of Susskind and 't Hooft's holographic string theory a few pages later: "Of all the theories discussed here, I'd pick the holographic principle as the one most likely to play a dominant role in future research."[191]

In *The Hidden Reality*, Greene again compares Susskind's holographic principle to Plato's cave allegory:

> Two millennia later, it seems that Plato's cave may be more than a metaphor. To turn his suggestion on its head, reality—not its mere shadow—may take place on a distant boundary surface, while everything we witness in the three common spatial dimensions is a projection of that faraway unfolding. Reality, that is, may be akin to a hologram. Or, really, a holographic movie.[192]

Greene goes on to explain that, according to the holographic principle, "if we could understand the laws that govern physics on that distant surface, and the way phenomena there link to experience here, we would grasp all there is to know about reality."[193] Similarly, according to Plato's cave allegory, if we turn the eye of the soul inward to see how the idea of the Good contains all of the other eternal ideas that project this temporary shadow-world of three-dimensional forms into existence, then we would know everything. This same claim is made in the Upanishad cited above: "If a man knows what that string is and who that inner controller is—he knows *brahman*; he knows the worlds; he knows the gods; he knows the Vedas; he knows the spirits; he knows the self; he knows all."[194]

After losing the Black Hole War, Hawking deferred to Susskind's holographic principle in his book *The Grand Design* where he also makes an allusion to the apparent connection with Plato's cave allegory: "If a theory called the holographic principle proves correct, we and our four-dimensional world may be shadows on the boundary of a larger, five-dimensional space-time."[195] In his book *The Fourth Dimension*, mathematics professor Rudy Rucker explains that, according to Plato's cave allegory, the two-dimensional shadows are cast from three-dimensional objects, the puppets and the bodies of the prisoners themselves, which "suggests the idea that a person is really some higher-dimensional soul that influences and watches this 'shadow world' of three-dimensional objects."[196] As Greene points out, though, according to Susskind and 't Hooft's holographic string theory, our three-dimensional bodies are like holographic movie projections radiating from a *two*-dimensional film at the cosmic horizon, which seems to reverse the direction of the dimensional analogy of Plato's cave allegory. However, there is an obvious flaw in calling Susskind's description of the holographic horizon two-dimensional merely because it is perfectly flat, considering all space (including the six dimensions of space compactified in each point of three-dimensional space) and all time is said to be interwoven into each point of it. Moreover, as discussed above, people living at what we perceive as the cosmic horizon would see themselves as the center of the expanding universe, and us at the two-dimensional horizon, so that the singularity and surrounding horizon are actually mutually exclusive perspectives of the same entity. The point is that a standard two-dimensional surface, like the wall of a cave, does not function in the same way that the cosmic horizon does.

On one hand, therefore, the cosmic horizon is two-dimensional, which means, in effect, that it has only one side, a perfectly flat surface with no back side. Indeed, it is impossible to observe the back side of the cosmic horizon, which recedes as we physically approach it. On the other hand, the two-dimensional horizon is more deeply understood as a higher-dimensional region containing all lower dimensions of space and the time dimension. Susskind asserts that every region of three-dimensional space "has a boundary—not physical walls, but an imaginary mathematical shell—that contains everything within it."[197] According to Susskind, ultimately, we all live in an imaginary mathematical shell surrounding the cosmos, into which is interwoven every bit of information describing all of the three-dimensional events in the universe that ever have or ever will unravel from it via cosmic threads. This is very similar to Plato's cave allegory, especially when we factor in the threads of destiny mentioned in the near-death experience account known as the "myth of Er" at the end of the *Republic*, which we will discuss in a moment.

Before leaving the cave allegory, however, it seems that on closer inspection Susskind's holographic string theory does not turn it on its head; on the contrary, it helps us perform the internal rotation of the "eye of the soul" required to understand Plato's allegory more precisely. As Socrates explains:

> Even so this organ of knowledge must be turned around from the world of becoming together with the entire soul . . . until the soul is able to endure the contemplation of essence and the brightest region of being. And this, we say, is the good, do we not?[198]

Socrates says that we cannot see the source of all light, the idea of the Good, with physical eyes. Similarly, despite the fact that it is an infinitely bright concentration of light, we cannot see the singularity inside a black hole (because the inward tidal flow of space-time reaches the speed of light at the event horizon), or at any point of the cosmic horizon (where the outward tidal flow of space-time reaches the speed of light), from each point of which the Big Bang echoes inward. According to Socrates, however, because the idea of the Good is the essence of each of our souls, we can see it if we learn how to turn the eye of the soul inward.[199] A synthesis of Susskind's string theory and Jung's psychology indicates that to escape from the cave of shadows described by Plato in the *Republic*, we must perceive how each of us eternally participates with the idea of the Good as it projects the three-dimensional volume of the universe into existence over time from our original, eternal position in the omnicentric singularity and its holographic horizon, which also correlates to the "mother substance" described in the *Timaeus*.[200]

String Theory and the Myth of Er

Considering the surprising precision of the parallels between Jung's near-death experience of the cosmic horizon and Susskind's holographic string theory, and considering that Plato's cosmology provides a clear historical precedent for the fusion of Susskind and Jung, it is especially noteworthy that Plato concludes the *Republic* with the near-death experience account of a solider named Er. According to Plato, Er's disembodied psyche rose above the cosmos (which he saw as a series of eight nested hemispheres, or upward-facing bowls), from where he was able to see how the moral habits each psyche develops on Earth influence the fate it chooses for the next life, which becomes the "threads of its destiny."[201] These threads are woven by three sister goddesses, the Fates (representing past, present, and future), first into the rim of the outermost hemisphere (the celestial sphere of fixed stars), and then into the rim of each concentric hemisphere (the orbits of the planets visible to the naked eye: Saturn, Jupiter, Mars, Mercury, Venus, Sun, Moon) centering on Earth. The Fates sing while they spin the eight hemispheres and sew the threads of destiny into each rim, on each of which a Siren sits and sings a single note as she goes around, forming a complete harmonic octave, so that each of us is pictured as a kind of karmic-marionette dancing to the siren-songs of fate.[202] The image of the universe as a series of nested-hemispheres in the *Republic*, as opposed to the spherical universe presented in the *Timaues*, is probably meant to help us picture the inner structure of a sphere, like geological maps depicting the concentric layers of the interior of the Earth. The parallel between Susskind's holographic principle and Plato's cave allegory gains the missing ingredient of cosmic strings when we join it with the myth of Er.[203]

That Plato really did picture the realm beyond the cosmic horizon as the world of eternal forms that souls can perceive between material incarnations is clearly confirmed in another Dialogue, the *Phaedrus*, where Socrates explains that reincarnating souls follow the procession of one or the other of eleven different demigods.

Occasionally the gods go to feast, at which point "they move up the steep to the top of the vault of heaven."[204] The mortals who follow the gods have a difficult time, and few of them reach the topmost destination where the gods "stand upon the outside of heaven . . . and behold the things beyond."[205] Those fortunate souls who do reach the outside of heaven go around with the revolution of that outer sphere, from which they perceive "justice, and temperance, and knowledge absolute," as well as "the other true existences," after which they come back down to "the interior of the heavens and return home."[206]

When we combine the cosmologies of Plato's different Dialogues, especially the *Timaeus* and the *Republic*, we find clear prototypes of the essential conceptual ingredients that make up Susskind's holographic string theory. The most notable gap in the parallels is Plato's failure to mention the megaverse.[207] Nevertheless, it still seems to be the case that Susskind provides a precise mathematical description of Plato's cosmology of eternal ideas in a universal Mind at the cosmic horizon, from which the three-dimensional illusion of matter unfolding over time is projected by strings. The irony is that Susskind uses his essentially Platonic cosmology to support his own Newtonian-Darwinian version of Plato's contemporary Democritus' materialistic reductionism, according to which human life and all order in the universe result from an infinity of inert atoms randomly interacting in an infinite void over an infinite amount of time.[208]

The Original Academic Curriculum in the *Republic*: Astronomy and Music

The cave allegory in Book VII of the *Republic* is an elaboration of the analogy of the divided line, which Socrates presents at the end of Book VI. There Socrates imagines the whole of existence as a line divided into two unequal parts, the larger segment representing the invisible but intelligible world of eternal forms, the smaller segment representing the visible world of temporary forms. Each segment is again divided in the same proportion. If we imagine the four sections of the divided line standing vertically, the smallest, bottom segment (which we can call the first level) represents two-dimensional mirror-reflections and shadows of visible, three-dimensional objects, which occupy the second level up on the divided line. Visible, three-dimensional objects are in turn like shadows and reflections of the third level, which represents the bottom segment of the invisible but intelligible world. This third level contains the eternal, mathematically demonstrable forms that describe the laws of physical nature, which, finally, are like shadows and reflections of the intelligible forms that occupy the fourth level up on the divided line, the highest, largest segment of the intelligible realm. In Book VII of the *Republic*, Socrates correlates each aspect of the cave allegory with one of the four segments on the divided line so that, ultimately, the Sun, which is the highest source of the visible world, is described as the shadow of the limitlessly luminous and numinous idea of the Good, which is the highest source of the intelligible world, from which the visible world is projected. Anything good about any other eternal or temporary form derives its goodness, including the goodness of existence itself, from the ultimate idea of the Good.

Following in the footsteps of Pythagoras, after the cave allegory Plato depicts Socrates planning out the ideal curriculum for teaching students of an ideal state how to escape from the cave of shadows by turning the eye of the soul inward toward a supremely brilliant vision of the idea of the Good. In the same way that the prisoner who was freed from the cave observed the blinding Sun at first only indirectly by observing its reflections in puddles of water, Socrates' assumption is that we can gradually prepare our benighted eye of the soul for the initially disorienting epiphany of the idea of the Good by studying its dimmer reflections in the intelligible, mathematical forms underlying the visible, natural forms. With that spiritual goal in mind, Socrates sets up a step-by-step mathematical study of the ascending dimensions of nature:[209] from an introduction to the dimensionless concept of individual numbers, beginning with number one (like the ABCs of the alphabet); to the study of how to add, subtract, multiply, and divide those numbers (all of which can be conceived as laying on a one-dimensional number line);[210] to the study of two-dimensional plane geometry; then three-dimensional solid geometry; then the fourth-dimensional geometry of time as manifest in the periodic movements of three-dimensional solids, specifically the orbits of the planets and stars (astronomy) and the vibrations of musical instruments (music).[211] The fifth and final step of knowledge Socrates prescribes is to discover how the previous four steps (representing the four dimensions of space-time) are related to each other and the idea of the Good from which they originate.[212] When that most brilliant form is perceived with the eye of the soul, only then can a person be just in private and public life.

Socrates specifically says that a twofold study of astronomy and music provides the capstone of the mathematical curriculum designed to teach students how to perceive the idea of the Good: "We may venture to suppose, I said, that as the eyes are framed for astronomy so the ears are framed for the movements of harmony, and these are in some sort kindred sciences, as the Pythagoreans affirm and we admit."[213] According to Michio Kaku, a co-founder of string theory, "the laws of physics can be compared to the laws of harmony allowed on the string. The universe itself, composed of countless vibrating strings, would then be comparable to a symphony."[214] By that definition, Susskind's string theory is a fusion of astronomy and music, and it does seem ideally suited to prepare students for the spiritual vision of the idea of the Good that Socrates describes in the cave allegory which, when combined with the threads of destiny in the myth of Er and the cosmology of the *Timaeus*, reveals a Platonic cosmology that is functionally and structurally similar to the universe formed by the central singularity and holographic horizon that Susskind describes.

As discussed in Part I, string theory mathematically unifies the recalcitrant force of gravity (described by general relativity as the curvature of space-time) with the other three forces of nature (electromagnetic, strong nuclear, and weak nuclear) that are described by quantum mechanics.[215] Similarly, in the *Republic*, after prescribing the mathematical study of the four ascending dimensions of space-time, culminating with the twin studies of time as measured by astronomy and music, Socrates says that the ultimate goal is to see how those fields of study are united with each other:

> And what is more, I said, I take it that if the investigation of all these studies goes far enough to bring out their community and kinship with one another, and to infer their affinities, then to busy ourselves with them contributes to our desired end, and the labor taken is not lost, but otherwise it is vain.[216]

String theory shows how the four forces of nature are mathematically commensurable (they can each be described by a force-carrying particle, including the theoretical graviton), and how, furthermore, all physical forces and points of space-time may be united in the infinite temperature of the gravitational singularity that is simultaneously present in the center of the universe and at each point of its encompassing sphere.[217]

It is fitting, therefore, that Susskind's string theory version of Big Bang cosmology correlates to the central soul of the spherical universe and the space-time-projecting "mother substance" of the cosmic horizon in Plato's *Timaeus*,[218] and the related idea of the Good in the cave allegory in the *Republic*,[219] a vision of which the mathematical study of the four ascending dimensions of nature is intended to initiate. As Socrates explains: "It is literally true that when the eye of the soul is sunk in the barbaric slough of the Orphic myth, dialectic gently draws it forth and leads it up, employing the sciences which we enumerated."[220] I will discuss the Orphic myth in a moment. As for dialectic, it is the method of discovering the eternal ideas inscribed on each of our souls, culminating with the idea of the Good. According to Socrates in the *Republic*, knowledge of the mathematical forms underlying the four dimensions of space-time provides the proper framework for a dialectical conversation in search of the absolute source of everything: as each side presents evidence that contradicts the other, both parties gradually narrow their search down to a common first principle. The Black Hole War between Hawking and Susskind is an excellent example of Socrates' dialectical method although, ironically, neither of the interlocutors in that modern dialogue believes in the idea of the Good, or the soul for that matter. Rather, it seems that by faithfully following the academic procedure Socrates initiated two dozen centuries ago, Susskind accidentally arrived at the goal Socrates proposed.

Returning to Socrates' mention "of the Orphic myth," in the original Greek Plato did not actually write the word Orphic, but, according to philosophy professor Robert McGahey, "both the vision and the logic of the passage are Orphic, in the sense that there is a necessary connection between the things of Tartarus and the things of the Beyond: a connection whose thread the soul may follow if dialectic would gently draw her up."[221] McGahey's thread metaphor is especially apt considering the "threads of destiny" mentioned in the myth of Er at the end of the *Republic* link each reincarnating soul in "the barbaric slough" back to the cosmic horizon, which is the border between the material world and the spiritual world of eternal forms. It seems all the more likely that Plato really did intend to link Socrates' mention of the "barbaric slough" in the *Republic* to the Orphic myth because, as Plato describes in the *Phaedo*, on the day Socrates died in an Athenian prison cell, he defended the "mystery-rites" (an allusion to the Orphic mystery religion) to his friends, saying, "Where by 'Bacchants' I understand them to mean simply those who have pursued philosophy aright; to be numbered amongst whom I have bent all the effort of a lifetime, leaving nothing undone that was within my power."[222] The Bacchants are the female devotees of Dionysus, the central god of the Orphic mystery religion, so that Socrates, on his last day on Earth, said that he had spent his entire life trying to be like the ultimate devotees of the Orphic god.

There is also a possible link between the Orphic myth about Dionysus and the "winnowing machine" that Plato depicts Timaeus comparing to the mother substance of the cosmic horizon that spreads the four elements (air, fire, water, earth) into the universe, as we saw above.[223] Anthropologist James Frazer explains this link in his classic *The Golden Bough*, where he writes: "The god is traditionally said to have been placed at birth in a winnowing-fan as in a cradle."[224] According to the Orphic myth, as a baby, the god Dionysus, who slept in a winnowing-fan (an open-faced basket), was lured away by the Titans, torn to pieces, and devoured, after which Dionysus' enraged father, Zeus, struck the Titans with a lightning bolt, thereby disseminating the ingredients of the universe, so that the tiny particles of Dionysus (the plethora of reincarnating souls) are miserably mixed with and imprisoned by the titanic impulses of the material body.

In *The Birth of Tragedy Out of the Spirit of Music*, the philosopher Friedrich Nietzsche comments on the Orphic myth in a way that supports the hypothesis that Plato's comparison of the cosmic horizon to a winnowing machine is an allusion to the Orphic Dionysus: "Thus it is intimated that this dismemberment, the properly Dionysian *suffering*, is like a transformation into air, water, earth, and fire, that we are therefore to regard the state of individuation as the origin and primal cause of all suffering, as something objectionable in itself."[225] It is important to note that Nietzsche's use of the word "individuation" is the opposite of Jung's. Nietzsche uses the word to refer to the separation of individual ego consciousness (which he identifies with the god Apollo) from the undivided oneness of the underlying will of the universe (which he identifies with the god Dionysus). According to Jung, however, individuation is the union of these two opposite sides of the psyche: after the conscious ego has successfully separated itself from the collective unconscious archetypes, it achieves individuation by reuniting with the ultimate archetype of the Self.[226]

Similarly, according to Nietzsche in *The Birth of Tragedy*, the reunion of the Apollonian and Dionysian artistic impulses of nature is the highest goal of culture, which was achieved in ancient Athens in the musically choreographed tragic plays performed each spring for Dionysus. Nietzsche argues that Socrates destroyed that pinnacle of cultural achievement—which could put whole throngs of people in immediate, ecstatic touch with the divine core of the universal will—by replacing it with the love of science, which can only ever reveal the superficial surface of the phenomenal world (the world of space, time, and causality, which Nietzsche also equates with the Hindu concept of Maya). Indeed, as Nietzsche points out, Socrates overtly bans tragic plays from his ideal city in the *Republic*, but the mathematical-musical curriculum for the leaders of that same city is slyly spliced with allusions to the Orphic god who is, after all, the trickster god of theatrical masks.

A combination of Socrates' allusion to the Orphic myth while describing the acme of the academic curriculum in the *Republic*, and Timaeus' apparent allusion to the Orphic myth about the winnowing machine provides a more comprehensive understanding of both. The implication is that to rise out of the cave of shadows (the material illusion of the three-dimensional world unfolding over time), we must learn to turn the eye of the soul away from the "barbaric slough" of bodily desire by studying the mathematical formulas that describe the four ascending dimensions of space-time. The goal is to realize how all of the broken fragments of the material universe are projected constantly by threads of destiny from the idea of the Good, which exists simultaneously in the center of the spherical universe, and at the mother substance of the cosmic horizon, where spirit and matter are interwoven everlastingly with the body of the ever-dying-and-resurrecting god.

Furthermore, that Plato linked the Pythagorean study of astronomy and music to the Orphic myth may imply that we can acquire a kind of concord with the cosmic strings tethering each of us to the eternal horizon of the cosmos by dancing in unison while singing in harmony about that ultimate archetype of the union of all opposites. This aspect of the Orphic myth is captured in Euripides' tragic play *The Bacchae*, wherein the chorus sings: "Blessed is he who hallows his life in the worship of god, / he whom the spirit of god possesseth, who is one / with those who belong to the holy body of god."[227] In Plato's late Dialogue the *Laws*, he depicts the Athenian stranger explaining how the brother gods, Apollo and Dionysus, bolster the neglected education of humans by presiding over the annual cycle of religious festivals featuring song and dance in honor of the gods: "They string us together on a thread of song and dance, and have named our choirs so after the delight they naturally afford."[228]

St. Augustine and the Heaven of Heaven

If ancient Greece is the cradle of Western civilization, then Plato's Dialogues are its genetic code, which was subsequently spliced with the Bible. According to T. Z. Lavine: "For two thousand years, when Christians thought of God they envisioned the divided line and the ascent out of the cave through the power of reason and the power of love to Plato's Idea of the Good."[229] Cultural historian Richard Tarnas explains that many early Christian sages considered Plato's philosophy to be "a divinely prearranged matrix for the rational explication of the Christian faith."[230] Indeed, "so enthusiastic was the Christian integration of the Greek spirit that Socrates and Plato were frequently regarded as divinely inspired pre-Christian saints. . . 'Christians before Christ,' as Justin Martyr claimed."[231] For present purposes, it is particularly pertinent that the early Christian Platonist St. Augustine (354-430) identified God with Plato's ultimate idea of the Good, and described Christ as living eternally with the cosmic mother and Spouse of God specifically at the outermost sphere of the universe.[232] According to Tarnas: "It was Augustine's formulation of Christian Platonism that was to permeate virtually all of medieval Christian thought in the West."[233]

Following Catholic dogma, Augustine believed in the triune God, consisting of God the Father, God the Son (Jesus Christ), and God the Holy Spirit. According to Augustine's Platonic interpretation of the Biblical Jesus Christ, he is the walking incarnation of all of the eternal ideas of God the Father's creative mind, and is referred to in the first verse of the Gospel of St. John as the Logos, translated as the "Word": "In the beginning was the

Word, and the Word was with God, and the Word was God."[234] The Logos, as Augustine interprets it, is equivalent to Plato's idea of the Good which, as shown above, has all of the qualities of the gravitational singularity: an omniscient and omnipresent point of infinite power that creates and structures the cosmos by conserving and projecting each bit of information of which it is made. If the singularity were self-aware, it would very closely conform to Augustine's idea of God.

Augustine interspersed his theological autobiography, *Confessions*, with italicized quotes from the Bible. Explaining why no specific day of creation is assigned to the heaven and the earth of the first verse of Genesis, just the indefinite concept of "the beginning," Augustine writes: "I assume that it is because by 'heaven' is meant *heaven of heaven*, the intellectual heaven, where it is given to the intellect to know in one act, and not part by part . . . not to know now one thing, now another but, as has been said, to know in one act without any succession of time."[235] According to Augustine, Jesus is the personified beginning of all creation, the Logos, in whom God the Father created the timeless *heaven of heaven* and the formless earth from which the visible, temporal heaven and Earth were subsequently created. In the *heaven of heaven* knowledge is not experienced piecemeal as a succession of events on a timeline, but, rather, all at once. Augustine writes: "Clearly the *heaven of heaven* which You made *in the beginning* [and not on any numbered day] is in some way an intellectual creature; although in no way co-eternal with You, the Trinity, it is yet a partaker in your eternity."[236] Augustine equates God with Plato's idea of the Good, while his concept of the *heaven of heaven* is very similar to the cosmic horizon which Plato describes in the *Timaeus* as the "mother and receptacle of all created and visible and in any way sensible things."[237] In fact, like Plato, Augustine goes on to describe the *heaven of heaven* as our mother: "There was then a created wisdom created before all things, the reasonable and intellectual mind of Your pure City, *our mother, which is above and is free and eternal in heaven.*"[238]

According to Augustine, the forms of reason, the ideas of God's rational mind, are found specifically in the outermost sphere of the cosmos, the timeless *heaven of heaven*, our mutual mother, in each point of which God, the idea of the Good, is housed: "with You ever indwelling and illuminating it . . . a pure mind united in perfect harmony in a binding union of peace with those holy spirits, the citizens of Your City which is in heaven far above the heavens we see."[239] The "holy spirits" in the City of God, the *heaven of heaven* above the sphere of fixed stars, seem to be fused with Augustine's Biblical interpretation of Plato's concept of the eternal ideas that are united in the ultimate idea of the Good. As the idea of the Good is a personal God for Augustine, and as God is absolute, so that each part has all of the qualities of the whole, each idea in God's mind must also be a complete personality.

In, the following passage, Augustine compares the *heaven of heaven* to divine Scripture, which God spread over the cosmos like a "firmament of authority."[240] He explains that the "super-celestial hosts" of God's angels have no need to read the Bible, "for their book is Yourself and You eternally are: because You have established them above the firmament which You have established above the infirmity of the peoples below: and there they may look up and know Your mercy."[241] The angels do not have to read the Bible because God is manifest to them directly in the timeless firmament above the firmament of stars. Like Augustine's eternal God who occupies each point of the *heaven of heaven*, the infinitely dense and therefore space-timeless singularity exists in each point of the cosmic horizon, thereby rendering it a timeless domain where all of the information of the past, present, and future of the universe is present at each point, which is exactly what Jung said he experienced during his near-death experience. Augustine's Platonic-Christian cosmology held sway over the Western mind for over a thousand years, culminating in the cultural imagination with the poetry of Dante Alighieri (1265-1321).

Dante, Descartes, Hume, and Kant

According to Tarnas: "Dante realized in his epic poem *La Divina Commedia* what was in effect the moral, religious, and cosmological paradigm of the medieval era."[242] In Dante's cosmology, Earth is the center of the universe, while the omnipresent God's throne rests in an omniscient and omnipotent point of light at the outermost sphere. Robert Osserman—who earned his Ph.D. in mathematics from Harvard, and formerly served as chair of the Department of Mathematics at Susskind's own Stanford University—explains that "the big bang occupies the position where Dante placed a point of light radiating with great intensity."[243] Describing his prolonged vision of this "Eternal Light," Dante says: "In its depths I saw that it contained, bound by love in one volume, that which is scattered in leaves through the universe."[244] He goes on to say that once one gazes at this eternal point of light it is impossible to look away willingly, "for the good which is the object of the will is all gathered in it."[245] From Plato through the entire span of the medieval era, the intellectual class imagined the universe as a series of concentric spheres with Earth at the center and the eternal ideas of God's creative mind condensed in an infinitely dense point of light that somehow encompasses the circumference of space-time, from which the visible, temporal world is born. However, Kepler, Galileo, and Newton each successively vindicated Copernicus' mid-sixteenth-century theory that the Earth and the other planets revolve around the central Sun.

Though these pioneers of modern science saw their mission as the culmination of the Christian quest to know the eternal ideas of God's creative mind, in light of their mathematically formulated and empirically verified discoveries, the Platonic-Christian myth about the intercessory sphere at the edge of the universe diffusing God's grace to the central Earth eventually collapsed.[246] The colorful splinters of that fallen world view—like an overarching stained-glass dome filigreed with angels and saints—were swept from mainstream academia to the fringes of society, along with astrology. And when the Platonic-Christian cosmology collapsed, the corresponding theology fell deeply into doubt. Renè Descartes (1596-1650), a Catholic contemporary of Kepler and Galileo, therefore set about reestablishing a belief in the soul and God based on the power of skeptical human reason.

Descartes is credited with (and accused of) initiating the Scientific Revolution by clearly defining the two worlds of his strictly dualistic world view: the unthinking world of material substance extended in space (*res extensa*); and the spatially unextended world of thinking substance (*res cogitans)* found in humans and God alone.[247] This sharply dualistic world view is the infamous Cartesian split. Descartes further defines God as the only infinite substance, in addition to being the omnipotent and omniscient creator of everything: "By the name of God I understand an infinite substance, eternal, immutable, independent, omniscient, omnipotent, and by which I and all the other things which exist (if it be true that any such exist) have been created and produced."[248]

According to Descartes, irrational objects in the material world (including animals and plants) have no soul, but they do have an enduring extension in space that can be precisely measured in a way that allows reason to discern mathematically expressible connections between them. Knowledge of these mathematically certain relationships allows humans to manipulate the material world for our own needs. In a way that combines the opposing principles of Democritus and Plato, Descartes describes the universe created by God as a marvelously designed machine made of interacting atoms of soulless matter, like a great clock, the inner workings of which are ordered by impersonal mechanical forces that lend themselves to mathematically precise descriptions, the truths of which are certified by the fact that the perfectly honest God created the correlations between nature and the rational laws of mathematics.

Plato's theory of the predictive power of the mathematical forms underlying nature was practically deified by scientists after Newton, but Plato's related geocentric theory of an eternal spiritual order shining in from the cosmic horizon on threads of destiny was discarded.[249] Similarly, Descartes' vision of a concerted scientific search for the mathematical formulas that predictively describe the interacting movements of soulless atoms stayed constant through the subsequent centuries of scientific advancement, but his related belief in the mind of God and the human soul was rejected by most mainstream scientists and empiricist philosophers, such as David Hume (1711-1776).

Hume rejected Descartes' rationalism, according to which the self is an immaterial thinking substance stamped by God with innate forms of knowledge that reason can behold. Instead, Hume argues that individual sense impressions (i.e. empirical observations, which he calls "matters of fact") are the only true source of knowledge, and that subsequently we imagine relationships (which he calls "relations of ideas") between these fundamentally unconnected sights, sounds, smells, tastes, and touches.[250] Hume argues that it is not unreasonable to assume that Newton's laws could stop predicting the future at any moment, because those laws are not based on eternal forms of reason; rather, they are based on the false assumption that the sequence in which "matters of fact" unfolded in the past must necessarily continue in the future. In other words, according to Hume, the very notions of space, time, causality, and mathematics—the fundamental principles of Newtonian physics—are merely "relations of ideas" invented by humans for our convenience; as vitally useful as they are, they are not eternal ideas of God's universal mind that must necessarily hold true for all time, nor are they "matters of fact," because we do not perceive space, time, causal connections, or numbers with any of our five physical sense organs.[251] Similarly, we do not have a sense impression of a self.

As Hume explains, if each of us is the same self from one moment to the next, and if the self is an empirically real entity, then it must manifest as one continuous, unchanging sense impression, though that does not appear to be the case.[252] Hume argues that the "inconceivable rapidity" of the flux of individual sense impressions deceives us into the false opinion that they are one uninterrupted stream of consciousness forming what we call a self.[253] He goes on to explain that "as memory alone acquaints us with the continuance and extent of this succession of perceptions, it is to be considered, upon that account chiefly, as the source of personal identity."[254] The indivisible simplicity and invariable constancy of the self that Hume demands is supplied, at least in theory, by the equation of the psyche with the gravitational singularity and the holographic horizon of the cosmos, which serves as the eternal memory bank of the universe whereupon all sense impressions from the past, present, and future are interwoven at each point. That cosmic memory bank fulfills Hume's definition of what a self must be, and it is precisely what Jung said he encountered during his near-death experience.

In the late-eighteenth century, Immanuel Kant (1724-1804) credited Hume with waking him from his "dogmatic slumber."[255] On the one hand, he recognized the logical consistency of Hume's empiricist philosophy, yet, on the other hand, he recognized that Newton's laws do seem to reveal unchanging, infallible forms of reason that structure the material world. Kant responded to Hume by showing that the empirically unobservable concepts like space, time, causality, and mathematics (on which Newton based his laws of physics) are not fictions humans create to help us explain the empirical world; rather, they are the innate, *a priori* categories of thought through which the unknowable *thing-in-itself* is unconsciously presented to our conscious mind.[256]

Kant synthesizes Descartes' rationalism and Hume's empiricism by arguing that we *can* be absolutely certain that Newton's laws will continue to work everywhere in the universe throughout all time, not because they describe the eternal ideas of God's creative mind, but because wherever humans go we will automatically interpret our sense impressions of the unknowable thing-in-itself through the same unchanging *a priori* categories of thought—space, time, causality— on which Newtonian science is based. Although Plato clearly portrayed Socrates prescribing the empirical sciences of astronomy and music as the penultimate step toward the inner vision of the idea of the Good in the *Republic*, Kant still criticizes him for ostensibly "abandoning the world of sense."[257] He compares Plato to a dove who imagines she could fly even faster were it not for the drag of the air that carries her; similarly, according to Kant, Plato imagined that he could escape from the mental drag of sense-perceptions by relying only on eternal ideas that exist in "the void space of pure intellect."[258]

Nevertheless, despite his criticism, Kant associates the mind upon which the *a priori* categories are imprinted with the old Platonic image of the intelligent, outermost sphere of the cosmos encompassing the inner spheres of matter: "And just in this transcendental or supersensible sphere, where [empirical] experience affords us neither instruction nor guidance, lie the investigations of reason, which, on account of their importance, we consider far preferable to, and as having a far more elevated aim than, all that the understanding can achieve within the sphere of sensuous phenomena."[259] This passage is similar to Plato's description in the *Timaeus* of the cosmic horizon as the supersensible sphere that mediates between the eternal ideas and the inner spheres of matter, which inspired Augustine's description of the supercelestial *heaven of heaven* wherein resides Christ, the universal Logos embodying all of God's eternal ideas.[260] Jung, similarly drawing on Plato's theory of ideal forms in a supercelestial place, called Kant's *a priori* categories *archetypes* of the *collective unconscious*.

Jung, Pauli, and Plato

Susskind repeatedly offers special respect to Pauli's contributions to physics,[261] though he seems unaware of, or perhaps unwilling to admit to, Pauli's prolonged collaboration with Jung (which lasted for over twenty-five years, from 1932 to 1958, the year Pauli died). In the following passage, Pauli explains that each law of physical nature should have a psychological counterpart because both emerge from the same archetypes, which he relates to Plato's theory of ideas:

> *The ordering and regulating factors must be placed beyond the distinction of "physical" and "psychic"—as Plato's "ideas"*

94

share the notion of a concept and of a force of nature (they create actions out of themselves). I am very much in favor of referring to the "ordering" and "regulating" factors in terms of "archetypes"; but then it would be impermissible to *define* them as contents of the *psyche*. The mentioned inner images ("dominant features of the collective unconscious" after Jung) are rather *psychic* manifestations of the archetypes which, *however*, would *also* have to put forth, create, condition anything lawlike in the behavior of the corporeal world. The laws of this world would then be the *physical manifestations of the archetypes.* . . . Each law of nature should then have an inner correspondence and vice versa, even though this is not always directly visible today.[262]

Following Jung and Pauli, and drawing from Susskind, it seems clear that the empirically observable gravitational effects of black holes, including the inside-out black hole universe, are the physical counterparts of the psychic mandala images rising from the archetype of the Self so that, ultimately, Susskind's holographic string theory of the universe and Jung's archetypal psychology of the Self mirror each other.

Pauli and Jung both saw their theory of archetypes as an elaboration of Plato's original theory of ideas. According to Jung:

"Archetype" is an explanatory paraphrase of the Platonic *eidos*. For our purposes this term is apposite and helpful, because it tells us that so far as the collective unconscious contents are concerned we are dealing with . . . universal images that have existed since the remotest times.[263]

In the following passage, Jung links his theory of archetypes to Plato's *eidos* again, and mentions the "supracelestial place" where they are "stored up," which is similar to the holographic horizon of the cosmos:

> Take, for instance, the word "idea." It goes back to the *eidos* concept of Plato, and the eternal ideas are primordial images stored up . . . (in a supracelestial place) as eternal, transcendent forms. The eye of the seer perceives them as "imagines et lares," or as images in dreams and revelatory visions. . . . It is sufficient to know that there is not a single important idea or view that does not possess historical antecedents. Ultimately they are all founded on primordial archetypal forms.[264]

If we grant that there are fundamental parallels between Susskind's cosmology and Jung's archetypal psychology, and if we consider that Jung and Pauli both acknowledged that Plato's theory of eternal ideas is the historical antecedent of their own theory of the archetypes, and if we take into account, finally, that Plato nested his theory of ideas within a well-defined cosmology, then it makes sense to suspect that Plato's cosmology also provides the closest historical precursor of the synthesis of Jung and Susskind outlined here. After all, like Jung's theory of archetypes, the whole academic project of theoretical physics in which Susskind is engaged can be traced directly back to Plato, who founded the first Academy in 387 B.C.E., just north of the wall surrounding Athens, in the sacred olive grove named after the mythical hero Academus, and dedicated to the goddess Athena. Susskind, despite repudiating his Platonic ancestry, currently carries the Promethean torch that has been passed down through the centuries from the original fire of Plato's Dialogues, which continue to promulgate the Pythagorean-Socratic quest to know the divine intelligence permeating the cosmos—and, thus, to know oneself—by discovering how the geometrical forms that describe the movements of the planets and stars relate to the ratios that describe the music of vibrating strings.[265]

Susskind's and Jung's Reflections on the A Priori Categories of Thought

Susskind describes himself as a reductionist who believes that life emerged from, and can be reduced to, material interactions. Nevertheless, he begins *The Black Hole War* by explaining that the "classical" Newtonian physics concept of three-dimensional space is not necessarily inherent to the cosmos. We perceive the world in three dimensions, he argues, because "all complex life-forms have built-in, instinctive physics concepts that have been hardwired into their nervous systems by evolution."[266] However, in regard to the "wholesale breakdown of intuition" that accompanied twentieth-century physics, Susskind goes on to say that "there is no way that evolutionary pressure could have created an instinctive comprehension of these radically different worlds."[267] Immediately after describing his near-death experience of the cosmic horizon in *Memories, Dreams, Reflections*, Jung admits: "We cannot visualize another world ruled by quite other laws, the reason being that we live in a specific world which has helped to shape our minds and establish our basic psychic conditions."[268] Jung agrees with Susskind's basic claim that nature helps to form the human species' psychic structure, which is adapted to perceive things instinctively in three-dimensional space and linear time, but Jung also argues that the space-timeless archetypes form nature, so that our psychic structure is formed ultimately by the eternal archetypes.

The first unfounded assumption Susskind makes is that humans *do not* have an "instinctive comprehension" of the higher-dimensional worlds revealed by twentieth-century physicists, which ignores the striking parallels between their mathematical models of the universe and cosmologies of the ancient past, such as the Vedic and Platonic cosmologies examined above. Similar parallels were pointed out by the founders of relativity theory and quantum theory themselves.[269] That the basic concepts of twentieth-century mathematical physics were anticipated by ancient religious world views indicates that humans do indeed have what Susskind refers to as an "instinctive comprehension" of those "radically different worlds."[270]

The second erroneous assumption Susskind makes results from the logical fallacy of circular reasoning. He assumes that an instinctive comprehension of classical Newtonian physics concepts has been hardwired into our nervous system by Darwinian evolution, but the Darwinian theory of evolution is based on the assumed validity of Newton's theory that the universe consists of solid bits of matter enduring through one dimension of forward flowing time and three rigid dimensions of empty space. Over enormous amounts of time, bits of matter interacting in myriads of ways eventually, and quite accidentally, combine in just the right formations to produce self-replicating life, which is modified subsequently into the entire spectrum of species by the constant process of random mutation and natural selection. Therefore, by saying that Darwinian evolution *caused* us to perceive the world through a Newtonian worldview that does not reflect material reality at quantum-relativistic scales, Susskind illogically places the supposed effect (Newtonian physics concepts hardwired into the human nervous system) *before* the ostensible cause (Darwinian evolution).

In other words, according to Susskind's materialist theory of the origin of consciousness, in order for the first living being to evolve from matter hardwired to instinctively perceive the world through the classical Newtonian physics concepts (objectively and continuously existing bits of insentient matter moving through three dimensions of absolute space along one dimension of linear time flowing forward everywhere in the universe at a constant rate), those illusory but evolutionarily valuable concepts must paradoxically have been in effect eons earlier, or there would never have been a *temporal process* of *material evolution* to begin with. After all, how could the evolutionarily expedient concepts of three-dimensional space, linear time, and solid bits of matter have gradually evolved if those fundamentally fictitious physics concepts were not already factually in effect? Susskind pulls the Newtonian rug of classical physics out from under Darwin's feet, yet assumes that the standard interpretation of the neo-Darwinian theory of the origin and essence of consciousness still stands.

According to general relativity, all points in space-time coexist, like slices of bread in a single loaf, which begs the question: How can bits of matter evolve randomly from one point on the Darwinian timeline to the next if all points on that timeline—past, present, and future—coexist? Earlier we saw Einstein say:

> Since there exist in this four-dimensional structure [space-time] no longer any sections which represent 'now' objectively, the concepts of happening and becoming are indeed not completely suspended, but yet complicated. It appears therefore more natural to think of physical reality as a four-dimensional existence, instead of, as hitherto, the *evolution* of a three-dimensional existence.[271]

Roger Penrose—who developed the mathematics of a star collapsing into a black hole that Hawking time-reversed into a model of the Big Bang—made the same observation about evolution that Einstein made: "The idea that the history of the universe should be viewed, physically, as a *four*-dimensional spacetime, rather than as a three dimensional space evolving with time is indeed fundamental to modern physics."[272] Similarly, according to Susskind's own holographic principle—which unites general relativity and quantum mechanics—each event on the Darwinian timeline of the universe is timelessly interwoven at each point of the cosmic horizon, in from which they are projected by threads to form the holographic movie of natural history. Despite what Terrance Deacon argued above, from the perspective of general relativity and Susskind's string theory, it is logical to say that the developmental pattern of life on Earth *is* aimed teleologically toward some future goal, in the same way that the sequence of scenes in a movie unfolds toward some predetermined conclusion. After all, if Susskind is correct, then, like a motion picture, so too is the biological history of Earth prerecorded on and projected from a two-dimensional film. Nevertheless, as discussed above, the determinism inherent in the holographic principle is united with the free will implied by the related theory of parallel universes, according to which each of us is forced to choose freely from an infinity of fixed futures at each moment, though each choice we do not make is made by some parallel version of us.

Although Susskind assumes that each species has an "instinctive comprehension" of classical Newtonian physics concepts, he never mentions the unconscious mind in which instinctive comprehension must necessarily take place, a typical oversight which Jung addresses directly: "A discussion of the problem of instinct without reference to the concept of the unconscious would be incomplete because it is just the instinctive processes which make the supplementary concept of the unconscious necessary." Jung goes on to distinguish between the personal unconscious consisting of the repressed biographical material that is unique to each of us, and a deeper level, the "collective unconscious" consisting of the instincts and their corresponding archetypes that all humans inherit. According to Jung: "Just as his instincts compel man to a specifically human mode of existence, so the archetypes force his ways of perception and apprehension into specifically human patterns."[273]

What Susskind calls "instinctive comprehension," Jung calls archetypes of the collective unconscious. In his early work, Jung developed a quasi-Freudian-Kantian-Darwinian theory according to which the archetypes are merely human thought structures accumulated over the generations through the process of material evolution. That early phase of Jung's theory is much more in line with Susskind's perspective. After his near-death experience in 1944 and his subsequent collaboration with Pauli on the theory of synchronicity, Jung changed his opinion.[274] Picking up where Kant left off, Jung and Pauli brought the tradition of Western philosophy full circle back to Plato's original theory of eternal ideas imprinted on each soul, and the soul of the cosmos as a whole located specifically in the central point and spherical perimeter. On the assumption that mind and matter both emerge from the ultimate archetype of the

Self, Jung and Pauli posited that each law of psychology should mirror and be mirrored by a corresponding law of physics.

The uncanny compatibility of Susskind's string theory with a panpsychic cosmology he scorns predictably conforms to two of Jung's theories: his theory of a parallel between psychology and physics, and his theory about the psychological process that results from being too one-sided in our world view:

> I use the term *enantiodrama* to describe the emergence of the unconscious opposites, with particular relation to its chronological sequence. This characteristic phenomenon occurs almost universally wherever an extreme one-sided tendency dominates the conscious life; for this involves the gradual development of an equally strong, unconscious counterposition.[275]

While Susskind was consciously framing his string theory as an attack on "the illusion of intelligent design," he was unconsciously articulating a cosmology that seems to provide precisely the structure and physical mechanisms required to explain how the intelligent archetypes of our collective unconscious, culminating with the archetype of the Self, might actually form and help us co-create the "cinematic hologram" of the three-dimensional universe apparently evolving over time.[276]

In *The Tao of Physics*—one of the first and perhaps the most famous book to popularize the attempt to discern parallels between twentieth-century physics and ancient philosophy—physicist and philosopher Fritjof Capra says: "It is fascinating to see that twentieth-century science, which originated in the Cartesian split and in the mechanistic world view, and which indeed only became possible because of such a view, now overcomes this fragmentation and leads back to the idea of unity expressed in the early Greek and Eastern philosophies."[277] It is also fascinating to see that Susskind, with the explicit intention of furthering the mechanistic worldview—which started with Descartes' definition of the absolute split between mind and matter—should provide instead what appears to be a mathematically precise description of the idea of unity expressed in the ancient Hindu and Platonic cosmologies. The gravitational singularity is the ultimate idea of unity in the field of physics and, as seen above, it has many of the characteristics of the Purusha Avatars of Vishnu, and of Plato's idea of the Good, in which all mind and matter are one. Fatefully, Descartes, who initiated the Cartesian split by defining matter as unthinking substance extended in space, and mind as unextended, thinking substance, also defined God in a way that is very similar to the singularity: "By the name of God I understand an infinite substance, eternal, immutable, independent, omniscient, omnipotent, and by which I and all the other things which exist (if it be true that any such exist) have been created and produced."[278] Like Descartes' idea of God, so is the gravitational singularity a spatially unextended, infinitely powerful point that creates everything at the ongoing Big Bang, and omnisciently contains every bit of information from the past, present, and future at each point of the cosmic horizon. Thus, it seems that the Cartesian split between mind and matter may be healed if Psyche = Singularity.

CHAPTER 4
PSYCHE = SINGULARITY

On February 29, 1952 Jung wrote a letter to J.R. Smythies. In the final sentence of that letter—which I will call the Leap Day letter—Jung compresses his speculations about the equivalence of psychic energy and mass into a single equation: "Psyche=highest intensity in the smallest space."[279] The highest intensity of mass imaginable is infinite density, while the smallest space is zero volume, which is the precise definition of a gravitational singularity, both at the origin of the Big Bang and in black holes. This equivalence allows us to restate Jung's equation as: Psyche = Singularity. If it is correct, this formula could serve as a pivot upon which point-for-point correspondences between physics and psychology may be mapped, providing the truly unified field theory which Jung and Pauli sought.

I have not found any direct evidence demonstrating that Jung was specifically aware of the concept of a gravitational singularity, which unexpectedly emerged from Karl Schwarzschild's "exact solution" to Einstein's "field equations" for the general theory of relativity in 1916.[280] We know for certain, however, that the entire context of the Leap Day letter is based on Jung's knowledge of the general theory of relativity, so that his equation of psychic energy with an infinitely dense point of mass leads, in his letter, to the same transcendence of space and time that was revealed by the Schwarzschild solution. Jung's partner Pauli was directly engaged in disputes about the infinite gravity of the quantum vacuum, so it is possible that Pauli discussed the concept of a gravitational singularity with Jung. At any rate, whatever the sources of Jung's knowledge of the general theory of relativity may have been, we know for certain that he learned about Einstein's special theory of relativity from Einstein himself, as Jung explains in a letter he wrote to Carl Seelig on February 25, 1953:

> Professor Einstein was my guest on several occasions at dinner. . . . These were very early days when Einstein was developing his first theory of relativity. It was Einstein who first started me off thinking about a possible relativity of time as well as space, and their psychic conditionality. More than thirty years later, this stimulus led to my relation with the physicist Professor W. Pauli and to my thesis of psychic synchronicity.[281]

Jung's reference to Einstein's "first theory of relativity" shows that he was aware of the second, or general theory of relativity as well, which is confirmed by the fact that, one year earlier when he wrote the Leap Day letter in 1952, he was thinking in the context of general relativity when he came up with the equation "Psyche=highest intensity in the smallest space."[282] Interpreting this equation in terms of general relativity, as the context of the letter requires, points unambiguously to the concept of a gravitational singularity, whether Jung was aware of this inherently ambiguous concept or not.

On the Nature of the Psyche

In 1946, two years after his near-death experience, Jung published *On the Nature of the Psyche*, which he significantly revised and republished in 1954. Although Jung does not mention his out-of-body encounter with the cosmic horizon, where he felt himself interwoven with all space and time, his speculations about the relationship between psyche and matter in *On the Nature of the Psyche* were made soon after his NDE and the nightly visions that followed, which he described as "the most tremendous things I have ever experienced."[283] Erwin Schrödinger—one of the discoverers of quantum mechanics—cites a passage from Jung's book (first published as a paper) in his own book *Mind and Matter*, after explaining why the human mind has been excluded from the realm of physical science in the Western world.[284] In the passage quoted by Schrödinger, Jung writes:

> The psyche is the greatest of all cosmic wonders and the *sine qua non* of the world as an object. It is in the highest degree odd that Western man, with but very few—and ever fewer—exceptions, apparently pays so little regard to this fact. Swamped by the knowledge of external objects, the subject of all knowledge has been temporarily eclipsed to the point of seeming nonexistence.[285]

Jung's mention of Western man is evidently a reference to the post-Cartesian, late modern Western mind, in comparison with which, in Jung's opinion, Eastern people do not generally suffer from the same schizophrenic split between mind and matter.[286] As Schrödinger writes:

> Mind has erected the objective outside world of the natural philosopher out of its own stuff. Mind could not cope with this gigantic task otherwise than by the simplifying device of excluding itself—withdrawing from its conceptual creation. Hence the latter does not contain its creator.[287]

As the source of vision, the eye does not see itself in its field of view. Similarly, according to Jung and Schrödinger, the psyche, as the source of consciousness, does not observe itself in the objective world it projects. The implication, however, is that we should be able to find the psyche if we trace space-time back to its source.

In *On the Nature of the Psyche*, Jung suggests that the frontiers of physics and psychology both extend into an unknowable zone, in which he postulates a point where psyche and matter meet: "Our present knowledge does not allow us to do much more than compare the relation of the psychic to the material world with two cones, whose apices, in a point without extension—a real zero point—touch and do not touch."[288] The gravitational singularity is perfectly suited to fulfill Jung's idea of a real zero point without extension where the psychic and material worlds touch and do not touch. A few pages later, Jung writes: "The psyche is the world's pivot: not only is it the one great condition for the existence of a world at all, it is also an intervention in the existing natural order, and no one can say with certainty where this intervention will finally end."[289] As with the psyche, so is the singularity at the Big Bang the pivotal point, and one great condition, for the existence of a world at all, which is exactly what we would expect if Psyche = Singularity. Moreover, as discussed above, the singularity is also an intervention in the existing natural order, in the sense that it stands outside space-time, and therefore marks a point where the laws of physics as they are currently understood totally break down. There is no telling where this intervention will finally end, because it does not end if the psyche is indeed an omnicentric point of infinite gravity.

Jung describes the need for an "Archimedean point," a hypothetical vantage point outside the psyche from which to gain objective knowledge of the psyche: "If we are to engage in fundamental reflections about the nature of the psychic, we need an Archimedean point, which alone makes a judgment possible. This can only be nonpsychic, for, as a living phenomenon, the psychic lies embedded in something that appears to be of a nonpsychic nature."[290] The equation Psyche = Singularity seems to be precluded if the singularity is the Archimedean point *outside* of the psyche, from which alone an objective judgment about the psyche becomes possible. Therefore, using Plato's terminology (which is especially appropriate in Jung's case), we can make a distinction between the archetypal Psyche (which Jung calls the Self) and the individual psyches that participate in it, the individual selves. Just as all particles of matter emanate from the singularity, which can therefore be understood as the archetype of matter, so too can we assume theoretically that all particular psyches emanate from the universal Self. We can furthermore speculate that the archetype of psyches, the Self, is equivalent to the archetype of matter, the singularity. In that case, neither the singularity nor the Self is either purely psychic *or* purely physical, as they are one and the same origin *and* end point of both matter *and* psyche. Jung explains that he coined a new meaning for an older term "psychoid" to denote that which transcends matter and psyche by being the unknowable limit of both.[291] If the omnicentric singularity is equivalent to the archetypal Psyche, also known as the Self, then it is the epitome of the psychoid: a real Archimedean zero point with an absolutely objective point of view, gained by virtue of being each subjective point of space-time simultaneously.

Jung goes on to explain that his simplifying strategy for constructing a formula that can bridge the descriptive gap between matter and psyche is to assume that psychic processes, being energetic, are therefore equivalent, though not reducible, to mass. He further explains that the main practical problem this strategy must confront is that the mass associated with psychic energy does not seem to be physically measurable:

The formula for kinetic energy, $E = mv^2 / 2$, contains the factors m (mass) and v (velocity), and these would appear to be incommensurable with the nature of the empirical psyche. If psychology nevertheless insists on employing its own concept of energy for the purpose of expressing the activity (*energia*) of the psyche, it is not of course being used as a mathematical formula, but only as its analogy. But note: this analogy is itself an older intuitive idea from which the concept of physical energy originally developed. The latter rests on earlier applications of an *energeia* not mathematically defined, which can be traced back to the

primitive or archaic idea of the "extraordinarily potent.". . .
In psychology the exact measurement of quantities is
replaced by an approximate determination of [qualitative]
intensities, for which purpose, in strict contrast to physics,
we enlist the function of *feeling* (valuation). The latter takes
the place, in psychology, of concrete measurement in
physics.[292]

Jung contrasts the exact *quantities* of physical energy concretely
measured in physics with the *qualitative intensities* of psychic energy
(feelings) measured to an approximate degree in psychology.
However, if Psyche = Singularity (and therefore also Singularity =
Psyche), the implication is that quantity becomes quality when
multiplied by infinity and compacted into a point. In other words, an
infinite quantity of energy-mass has the subjective quality of the
psyche when it is compacted into a region of zero volume.

Like the more ancient concept of *energeia*, the infinitely dense
singularity upon which modern cosmology is based is also not
mathematically defined (infinite is not definite, and so cannot be
defined), which is why physicists such as Einstein, Kaku, and,
sometimes, Hawking reject it as a highly repugnant concept. The
space-timeless singularity appears to be the archetypal idea of the
"extraordinarily potent" from which, according to Jung, the
mathematically defined concept of energy originated. In line with this
interpretation, physical energy is calculated by general relativists to
have originated from the indefinable singularity at the origin of the
Big Bang. In other words, the infinite energy of the singularity
indicates that it is an archetypal form that gives birth to matter.

Jung's Letters Equating Psychic Energy and Mass

In a letter to Gebhard Frei dated January 17, 1949, after referring to
a truncated version of Einstein's iconic equation, e = mc², Jung makes

the simplifying assumption that psychic energy, like all energy, must be equivalent to mass:

> Dear Professor Frei,
>
> Many thanks for kindly sending me your recent paper on magic. The question of the 'subtle body' interests me too. I try, as my custom is, to approach the problem from the scientific angle. I start with the formula: E = M, energy equals mass. Energy is not mere quantity, it is always a quantity of something. If we consider the psychic process as an energetic one, we give it mass. This mass must be very small, otherwise it could be demonstrated physically.[293]

Considering the letter was written in 1949, Jung's notion of a "subtle body" is perhaps influenced by his near-death experience five years earlier. The implication—which becomes more obvious in light of the Leap Day letter—is that gross matter, subtle matter, and psyche are all various frequencies of a more fundamental source of infinite energy.[294]

In Jung's letter, he starts by applying the equation E = M to psychic energy. As Susskind explains the meaning of Einstein's equation $e = mc^2$: "Mass and energy are really the same thing. They are just expressed in different units: to convert from mass to energy, you multiply by the square of the speed of light."[295] In the 1949 letter, Jung does not mention how the speed of light relates to the equivalence of psychic energy and mass, and he assumes that the mass associated with psychic energy cannot be measured because it is too small.

However, Jung amends those aspects of his argument in the Leap Day letter of 1952, which ends with the equation that can be translated as Psyche = Singularity:

> The question is, in short: shouldn't we give up the time-space categories altogether when we are dealing with psychic existence? It might be that psyche should be understood as

unextended intensity and not as a body moving with time. One might assume the psyche gradually rising from minute extensity to infinite intensity, transcending for instance the velocity of light and thus irrealizing the body. That would account for the 'elasticity' of space under ESP conditions. If there is no body moving in space, there can be no time either and that would account for the 'elasticity' of time.

You will certainly object to the paradox of 'unextended intensity' as being a *contradictio in adiecto*. I quite agree. Energy is mass and mass is extended. At all events, a body with a speed higher than that of light vanishes from sight and one may have all sorts of doubts about what would happen to such a body otherwise. Surely there would be no means to make sure of its whereabouts or of its existence at all. Its time would be unobservable likewise.

All this is certainly highly speculative, in fact unwarrantably adventurous. But Ψ-phenomena [Psi, a Greek letter, refers to parapsychology] are equally disconcerting and lay claim to an unusually high jump. Yet any hypothesis is warrantable inasmuch as it explains observable facts and is consistent in itself. In light of this view the brain might be a transformer station, in which the relatively infinite tension or intensity of the psyche proper is transformed into perceptible frequencies or 'extensions'. Conversely, the fading of introspective perception of the body explains itself as due to a gradual 'psychification', i.e., intensification at the expense of extension. Psyche=highest intensity in the smallest space.[296]

Although he does not directly mention it, Jung's speculations clearly assume the validity of Einstein's general theory of relativity, which defines gravity as the "elasticity" of space-time. According to general relativity, the singularity arises as the last "minute extensity" of a dying star collapses into itself to become a point of infinite density, thereby "transcending the velocity of light." For if gravity is equivalent to accelerated motion, as general relativity indicates, then a point of infinite gravity is equivalent to a point traveling infinitely fast.[297] As a point of zero volume, the singularity transcends space; as a point of infinite density, and therefore infinite gravity, it transcends time, which seems to render the singularity equivalent to Jung's concept of the psyche. After all, Jung defines the term "psychification" as "intensification at the expense of extension." By that definition, we could say that the collapse of a star into a singularity is a process of psychification, as is the process of matter merging into the event horizon of a black hole or the cosmic horizon.[298] Thus, the Leap Day letter's culminating equation, "Psyche=highest intensity in the smallest space," can be translated as Psyche = Singularity.

Just as Jung, in the Leap Day letter, acknowledges the apparent contradiction inherent in his concept of the psyche as "unextended intensity," so too do physicists acknowledge the apparent contradiction inherent in their concept of the singularity as a point of zero volume and infinite density. Nevertheless, it seems poetically appropriate that Jung's proposed cure to the Cartesian split between mind and matter is the purest expression of it: per Descartes' demand, Jung's definition of the psyche (*res cogitans*) is indeed an unextended thinking substance; not, however, because it is separate from the extended substance of matter, but because it is an infinite concentration of matter.

Contradictio in Adiecto

In the Leap Day letter Jung admits that his description of the psyche as an unextended intensity of infinite energy is "highly speculative, and in fact unwarrantably adventurous." That is the same opinion some of the top physicists, including Einstein, have had about the idea of the infinite gravity in a singularity. Near the end of *Memories, Dreams, Reflections*, after recalling his near-death experience of the cosmic horizon, Jung suggests that, "The decisive question for man is:

Is he related to something infinite or not?"[299] In *The Black Hole War*, Susskind writes: "I suspect that infinity has been a prime cause of insanity among mathematicians."[300] For example, after calling the concept of a gravitational singularity a "monstrosity" that "means the collapse of everything we know about the physical universe," Michio Kaku points out his agreement with Einstein, and concludes that, despite the mathematical anomaly found in the Schwarzschild solution to the field equations of general relativity, "in the real world, there's no such thing as infinity."[301] However, as Susskind approvingly quotes Wolfgang Pauli: "Just because something is infinite doesn't mean it's zero."[302]

Ironically, in opposition to Pauli's quip, the infinitely dense singularity is a point of zero volume so, in that sense, for something to be infinite actually does mean it is zero. Nevertheless, despite his close relationship with Jung, and despite his belief in the *unus mundus* (the infinite source of cosmos and psyche), Pauli believed that singularities should be eliminated in a final theory of quantum gravity as of his Nobel Prize acceptance speech of 1946:

> At the end of this lecture I may express my critical opinion, that a correct theory [of quantum gravity] should neither lead to infinite zero-point energies nor to infinite zero charges, that it should not use mathematical tricks to subtract infinities or singularities, nor should it invent a "hypothetical world" which is only a mathematical fiction before it is able to formulate the correct interpretation of the actual world of physics.[303]

At least as late as 1946, Pauli seemed to have the kind of mindset that would have dismissed Susskind and 't Hooft's hypothetical world consisting of an empirically unobservable megaverse of universes made of empirically unobservable strings. Indeed, Pauli seems to have been in agreement with Einstein, who also rejected the notion that singularities had physical reality. Still, Pauli said mathematical tricks, such as renormalization, should not be used to subtract infinities or singularities from a valid theory of quantum gravity. Although renormalization works to combine quantum mechanics and special relativity, it fails miserably when physicists combine quantum mechanics with general relativity. As Kaku explains: "In fact, you get an infinite sequence of infinities. Infinitely worse than the divergences of Einstein's original theory. This is a nightmare beyond comprehension."[304]

Physicists admit that the gravitational singularity is a conundrum of contradictions that could conceivably spell the end of physics—that is what Kaku means when he calls it a nightmare beyond comprehension. Denis Sciama served as a graduate advisor for Roger Penrose and Stephen Hawking at Oxford University while his two students were solving the riddles of singularities inside black holes and at the Big Bang. Referring to the infinite gravity of a singularity, he says: "The theory of relativity contains in itself the seeds of its own decay." Nevertheless, he acknowledges that in 1965 Penrose proved that a star of sufficient mass would collapse into "this self-contradictory state of infinite density. So the whole space-time has gone pathological." Later that year Sciama accepted Hawking's dissertation proposal to reverse the time dimension of Penrose's equation for the collapse of a star in order to create a mathematical model of the Big Bang exploding from, rather than contracting into, a singularity. According to Hawking, he was awarded his PhD for showing that "both the Big Bang and black holes would contain singularities, places where space and time come to an end, and the laws of physics break down."[305] Hawking pioneered the concept of the singularity of the Big Bang in 1965, but later rejected the idea at a Vatican conference in 1981.[306]

In *Two Essays on Analytical Psychology*, Jung's description of the unfathomable "self," which he also calls the "God within us," closely parallels the various definitions of a singularity we have seen thus far:

This "something" is strange to us and yet so near, wholly ourselves and yet unknowable, a virtual centre of so mysterious a constitution that it can claim anything—

kinship with beasts and gods, with crystals and stars—without moving us to wonder, without even exciting our disapprobation. This "something" claims all that and more, and having nothing in our hands that could fairly be opposed to these claims, it is surely wiser to listen to this voice.

I have called this centre the *self*. Intellectually the self is no more than a psychological concept, a construct that serves to express an unknowable essence which we cannot grasp as such, since by definition it transcends our powers of comprehension. It might equally well be called "God within us." The beginnings of our whole psychic life seem to be inextricably rooted in this point, and all our highest and ultimate purposes seem to be striving towards it. This paradox is unavoidable, as always, when we try to define something that lies beyond the bourn of our understanding.[307]

If Psyche = Singularity, then Jung's description of our instinctive human response to the psychological concept of the "virtual center," the "God within us," explains the unconscious motivation behind the fact that the highest and ultimate purposes of academic physicists today converge in their common quest to reconcile general relativity and quantum mechanics in a way that can describe the point of infinite gravity in which the whole cosmos seems to be inextricably rooted.

As discussed above, according to Leibnitz's principle of the identity of indiscernibles, each singularity is identical to every other in the sense that all of them are points of infinite density that stand outside space-time, so we cannot discern any spatial or temporal differences between them (although we can assume there are psychic differences between them if Psyche = Singularity).[308] With this in mind, recall that, according to general relativity, any observer in any part of space-time necessarily sees himself or herself as the center away from which space is expanding at an exponential rate, so that it is as if each of us is the singularity of the Big Bang. Moreover, according to the experimentally confirmed concept of quantum entanglement, if Psyche = Singularity, then each psyche must be in immediate contact with every other psyche and every particle in the universe, because all of them were originally compacted in the singularity at the Big Bang. There furthermore seems to be a singularity at every point of the quantum vacuum underlying all space-time.

In his book *Coming Home: The Birth and Transformation of the Planetary Era*, philosopher Sean Kelly cites cosmologist Brian Swimme to argue that the "original Singularity" at what Swimme calls the "primal flaring forth" of the Big Bang necessarily "contains" and so unifies each point of space-time expanding from it, which accounts for the "non-locality" of this cosmological model.[309] On the same page, Kelly quotes Swimme saying that the "central archetypal pattern for understanding the nature of the universe's birth and development is omnicentricity," and "the consciousness that learns it is at the origin point of the universe is itself an origin of the universe."[310] This reasoning becomes all the more appropriate if we assume that Psyche = Singularity. Moreover, the cosmic horizon is the perspectival inversion of the omnicentric singularity from which the cosmos continuously radiates, so people on a planet we perceive to be at the horizon would perceive us to be at the horizon and themselves in the center of the expanding universe. Therefore, the equation Psyche = Singularity is equivalent to the claim that there is a communion of cosmos and psyche at the cosmic horizon as well, which Jung directly encountered during his near-death experience.

CHAPTER 5
NEAR-DEATH EXPERIENCES AT THE COSMIC HORIZON

Jung's Near-Death Experience

In 1944, Carl Jung suffered a heart attack. Immediately after the episode, lying in a Swiss hospital, he felt his consciousness rise out of his body, above planet Earth, specifically above the island of Ceylon (now Sri Lanka), so that he was overlooking India.[311] He felt that he was on the point of leaving Earth forever. Recalling his "glorious" view of the various continents, he later calculated how high up in space he must have been as "approximately a thousand miles!"[312] It was at that point that he noticed, also floating in space, a brilliantly lit temple hollowed out from a huge, house-sized dark stone, like the ones Jung had seen on the coast of the "Gulf of Bengal."[313] "To the right of the entrance," he recalls, "a black Hindu sat silently in lotus posture upon a stone bench. He wore a white robe, and I knew that he expected me."[314] Approaching the temple gave Jung the feeling that "the whole phantasmagoria of earthly existence . . . fell away or was stripped from me—an extremely painful process."[315] As soon as he lost everything, however, he gained it all blissfully back, and became one with his entire earthly biography simultaneously: "I consisted of my own history."[316] Drawn by a powerful attraction to an illuminated room in the back of the black rock temple, Jung felt certain that he would meet there "all those people to whom I belong in reality," who would teach him everything about how his earthly biography related to "what had been before and what would come after."[317] To his dismay, however, he was prevented from entering the temple by the "primal form," rising up from Europe, of his physician, "Dr. H.," who "had been delegated by the earth" to call him back, at which point the vision ended.[318]

Jung describes his thoughts upon returning to his physical body:

> Disappointed, I thought, "Now I must return to the 'box system' again." For it seemed to me as if behind the horizon of the cosmos a three-dimensional world had been artificially built up, in which each person sat by himself in a little box. And now I should have to convince myself all over again that this was important! Life and the whole world struck me as a prison, and it bothered me beyond measure that I should be finding all that quite in order. I had been so glad to shed it all, and now it had come about that I—along with everyone else—would again be hung up in a box by a thread.[319]

Jung's NDE recollection seems like a synthesis of Susskind's string theory and the cosmology of Plato's *Republic* as presented in the cave allegory and the myth of Er.

Recalling his near-death experience, and the related visions that followed each night for the next three weeks, Jung writes:

> It was not a product of imagination. The visions and experiences were utterly real; there was nothing subjective about them; they all had a quality of absolute objectivity.
>
> We shy away from the word 'eternal,' but I can describe the experience only as the ecstasy of a non-temporal state in which the present, past, and future are one. . . . One is interwoven into an indescribable whole and yet observes it with complete objectivity.[320]

Jung's use of the word "interwoven" to describe his experience of being eternally merged with the past, present, and future of the "whole" during the nightly visions is consistent with the realization he had during the near-death experience that triggered them, and is strikingly similar to Susskind's holographic string theory.[321]

In apparent accord with Jung's account, Susskind describes each cubic volume of three-dimensional space as an illusion created by one-dimensional strings that stretch out to, and are projected in from, a two-dimensional holographic film at the horizon: "It seems that the solid three-dimensional world is an illusion of a sort, the real thing taking place out at the boundaries of space."[322] Similarly, Susskind's use of the word "voxelated" (the three-dimensional analogue of pixelated) in another passage to describe the illusion of three-dimensional space resonates with Jung's use of the image of the "box system" of "little boxes."[323] As shocking and counterintuitive as it may seem, Susskind explains, "the world is not voxelated; it is pixelated, and all information is stored on the boundary of space. But what boundary and what space?"[324]

Susskind gives the example that, from the perspective of someone inside Grant's Tomb, the information describing that room is recorded on the boundary of that space, meaning the inner walls, floor, and ceiling. However, if we approach that inner boundary of Grant's Tomb we find that the information we are trying to observe recedes out to the next concentric boundary of space, the outer atmosphere of Earth, and so on, from the boundary of the Solar System, to the halo surrounding the Milky Way galaxy, to the horizon of the universe.[325] According to this same principle, it is consistent to assume that the living history of planet Earth is recorded on, and projected from the outer edge of Earth's atmosphere, which is in fact where Jung had the experience of becoming one with his entire earthly biography simultaneously during his NDE.[326] By itself, this aspect of Jung's experience suggests some kind of timeless collective consciousness at the boundary of Earth's atmosphere.[327]

Susskind openly admits that his holographic principle is contingent on the assumed existence of fundamental strings, six compactified spatial dimensions, and a megaverse of other universes, all of which are currently, and perhaps permanently outside the scope of empirical measuring devices. However, if we "think outside the box," so to speak, it becomes apparent that the fundamental details of Susskind's string theory seem to find direct experiential confirmation in Jung's memory of his NDE which, in return, gains a plausible scientific explanation. It is, of course, ironic that Susskind, who explicitly presents his string theory as the scientific remedy to "the illusion of intelligent design," inadvertently corroborates Jung's experiential account of the illusion-designing horizon of the cosmos, while Jung's out-of-body, "eye-witness" testimony of his near-death experience seems to supply Susskind's string theory with precisely the kind of empirical evidence it so scandalously lacks.

Because Jung had his NDE in 1944, which he recalls in *Memories, Dreams, Reflections* (published in 1961, the year he died) his memory of his NDE could not have been influenced by holographic string theory, which Susskind developed with Gerard 't Hooft in the early 1990s. There is also no reason to suppose that Susskind might have drawn inspiration from Jung. Nevertheless, their intellectually independent and theologically antithetical accounts of our tethered connection to the cosmic horizon agree to a degree of detail that suggests both might be true.

Stanislav Grof on LSD and Near-death Experiences

According to Richard Tarnas: "The most epistemologically significant development in the recent history of depth psychology, and indeed the most important advance in the field as a whole since Freud and Jung themselves, has been the work of Stanislav Grof."[328] Grof's contribution to NDE research is especially pertinent to the comparison of Jung's NDE and Susskind's holographic principle for several reasons. First, as one of Jung's most prominent successors, Grof has arguably extended the logic of Jung's depth psychology deeper than anyone else. Second, Grof places his analysis of NDEs explicitly within the holographic paradigm as it was originally formulated by David Bohm, and only later developed by Susskind. And last, but not least, Grof, like Jung, personally went through an out-of-body experience (OBE) of the cosmic horizon, although his psychic journey was induced by a clinical experiment with LSD and stroboscopic light, rather than a heart-stopping brush with death.

In 1957, after receiving his MD in psychiatry in Prague, Grof volunteered for a clinical psychiatric experiment designed to determine whether beaming a strobe light at the optic nerves of someone under the influence of LSD could "entrain" the brainwaves to the same frequency as the light.[329] After the third hour into his first trip, when the drug normally achieves peak potency, the enormous light was fixed to his head and turned on. As he recalls in a video recording of a casual interview, even with his eyes closed the light was more intense than anything he could have imagined. He compares it to "mystical literature" where they talk about a "light that was like millions of suns," which he further compared to the atomic bomb being dropped on Hiroshima. Those comparison are allusions to the famous quotes from Robert J. Oppenheimer, chief scientist of the Manhattan Project that created the bombs that were dropped on Hiroshima and Nagasaki in 1945.

While witnessing the very first atomic explosion—the test bomb detonated on July 16, 1945 at the Trinity Site in New Mexico—Oppenheimer recalled two verses from the Bhagavad-gita. Grof recalls the most famous of those quotes later in *Psychology of the Future*: "Robert Oppenheimer thought of Krishna's words to Arjuna in the Bhagavad Gita: 'I am become Death, the Shatterer of Worlds.'"[330] The two quotes from the Bhagavad-gita that Oppenheimer cited at the Trinity detonation are specifically references to Krishna's "universal form" (*virat rupa*), the all-devouring flames of the outermost etheric shell of the universe, where space, time, and causality originate.[331] Continuing Grof's interview about his first LSD trip: "My consciousness was catapulted out of my body, and I lost connection with the research assistant, with the clinic, with Prague, with the planet, and I had this amazing experience of my consciousness just embracing everything." Most pertinently to the comparison with Jung's NDE and Susskind's cosmology about the cosmic horizon, Grof concludes his interview by saying "I actually . . . became the physical universe somehow. I had the feeling I had been back to [the] Big Bang."[332]

As Susskind explains, going out in space in our exponentially expanding universe is the same as going back in time, so that going out to the cosmic horizon is in fact going back to the Big Bang, which could also account for Grof's experience of a "light that was like millions of suns":

> Think of the universe as a series of concentric shells with us at the center. . . . By looking deeper and deeper, we are, in effect, running the movie of the universe backward. . . . Now let us travel backward in time and outward in space to the last visible shell, where the conditions are similar to the sun's surface. . . . Astronomers call it the *surface of last scattering*. Sadly, looking through the conducting plasma to an even earlier and more distant shell is no more possible than looking through the sun.[333]

Judging by his testimony, it appears that Grof's first experiment with a "consciousness expanding" drug compelled him to experience his consciousness literally expand with the fabric of space-time, through concentric boundaries, until he encompassed the whole cosmos. Grof's experiential description of the awesome light of the Big Bang at the cosmic horizon is consistent with Susskind's description of the cosmic horizon in the passage above, as well as in the following passage: "That light does not seem to be coming from a boundary of space; rather, it seems to come from a boundary of time—from what appears to be a Big Bang taking place in the past."[334] That the intense light focused on Grof's optic nerve triggered such an unusually intense LSD trip, making him feel as if he had become one with the entire biography of the universe at the cosmic horizon, seems to imply that the sentient spectrum of the psyche and the electromagnetic spectrum of light are united at the cosmic horizon and, therefore, at the singularity from which it radiates.

What would a physicist expect to see if he or she were somehow one with the light of which the universe is made? We know from special relativity that the hands of a clock rotate more slowly the faster the clock travels through space, which means time moves more slowly for fast moving objects. Time stops for objects moving at light speed. Photons are light, so they do not experience time, which means that, from a photon's perspective, it takes no time to travel from one end of the universe to another. That is the same as saying that, from a photon's perspective, each point in the universe is in immediate contact with every other point. According to physicist John Gribbin: "The mystics and popularizers who seek to equate Eastern philosophy with modern physics seem to have missed this point, which tells us that everything in the universe, past, present, and future, is connected to everything else, by a web of electromagnetic radiation that 'sees' everything at once."[335]

Jung and Grof both describe experiences during which they felt as if they were merged with the entire temporal trajectory of the universe at the cosmic horizon, which is consistent with the physics of the photons of which the cosmic horizon consists. Contrary to Gribbin's assumption, both Fritjof Capra and David Bohm realized that the experimentally confirmed phenomenon of space contraction and time dilation associated with the speed of light corroborates certain strains of Eastern philosophy (and much of Western philosophy as well). Specifically addressing near-death experiences, Bohm has suggested that the mystical feeling of eternal unity with the cosmos is a physical reality from the perspective of light, of which everything is made. He explains that matter is merely light bouncing back and forth within an overall pattern that moves slower than light, so that matter is included in the spaceless and timeless unity of light. According to Bohm, from light's perspective, "you would find that the two ends of the light ray would have no time between them and no distance, so they would represent immediate contact."[336]

According to Susskind's theory, from our Earth-bound perspective, the fundamental strings of which everything is made stretch all the way out to the cosmic horizon, about fifteen billion light-years away from Earth in every direction. From the perspective of those fundamental threads of energy, however, there is no spatial distance between the center of the universe and the spherical horizon, and no temporal separation between now and the Big Bang, which still exists at the horizon. From the theoretical perspective of the strings that stretch across the cosmos, each point in space-time is in immediate spaceless and timeless contact. The distinguishing feature of Susskind's string theory is that all of the information of which light consists is ultimately located at each point of the cosmic horizon, which seems to corroborate Jung's and Grof's accounts of experiencing the eternal perspective of light specifically at the cosmic horizon.

After Grof's first LSD trip, he conducted clinical analyses of thousands of patients under the influence of psychedelic drugs, mainly LSD-25, "first in Czechoslovakia in the Psychiatric Research Institute in Prague, and then in the United States, at the Maryland Psychiatric Research Center in Baltimore, where I participated in the last surviving American psychedelic research program."[337] Grof coined the word *holotropic*—which means "moving in the direction of wholeness"[338]—to describe the state of mind prompted by psychedelic drugs and other factors, such as breathing techniques and NDEs. He reports that all of these experiences tend to open the conscious ego to a direct experience of the holographic nature of the cosmos, in which each part contains all of the information of the whole. Applying Grof's holotropic theory of cosmic consciousness to Susskind's holographic principle is therefore a logical continuation of Grof's own research. In fact, inscribed right above the title on the hard cover edition of Susskind's book *The Black Hole War* is a quote from the *New York Times Book Review*: "This is your universe on acid." Indeed, in *The Cosmic Landscape*, Susskind admits to experimenting with LSD while at the University of California in Berkeley in the 1960s, which makes it all the more pertinent to compare his theories to Grof's.[339] Confirming this apparent link between psychedelics, NDEs, and black hole cosmology, Michio Kaku says: "A trip to a black hole would be fantastic, almost psychedelic. It's like having a near-death experience."[340]

Grof specifically cites Susskind's unacknowledged predecessor, David Bohm, as well as neurologist Karl Pribram and philosopher of science Ervin Laszlo, all of whom support the theory that consciousness is interwoven with matter through the same holographic process that enfolds all points of space-time into one another.[341] Although Susskind conspicuously neglects to give him credit in his books, Bohm, an American protégé of Einstein's, was the first physicist to attempt to reconcile general relativity and quantum mechanics within a holographic paradigm.

According to Bohm, when we see how the information describing three-dimensional objects is recorded on a two-dimensional holographic film in such a way that "each part contains information about the *whole object*,"[342] it makes it easier for us to imagine how consciousness is similarly enfolded with matter: "Thus we could come to the germ of a new notion of unbroken wholeness, in which consciousness is no longer to be fundamentally separated from matter."[343] Whereas for Bohm, the key feature of the holographic film plate is that each part contains all of the information of the whole, for Susskind the key feature is that a three-dimensional image radiates out from a two-dimensional surface, which enabled him to save the principle of information conservation from Stephen Hawking's former claim that information is swallowed by black holes. If the information is located on the surface area, Susskind reasons, then it never enters the volume of a black hole (at least from the perspective of someone observing from outside the black hole), which means it never passes the event horizon, and is therefore not lost from the observable universe.

Susskind demonstrates his string-theory version of the holographic principle by contrasting a holographic camera with a digital camera, which transfers images of three-dimensional objects to a "two-dimensional 'retina' of light-sensitive area-cells called *pixels.*"[344] Although the images produced by a digital camera look realistic, we cannot walk around them and see the original three-dimensional objects from all sides. It seems logical to suppose, therefore, that in order to faithfully reproduce the image of a three-dimensional object we would need to replace the two-dimensional pixels with three-dimensional "voxels" to create a point-for-point correspondence between the object and a scale model made of light.[345] However, there is one kind of two-dimensional surface that can faithfully capture the information of three-dimensional objects—a hologram—a realization of which led Susskind and 't Hooft to develop their holographic interpretation of string theory: "This new law of physics, known as the Holographic Principle, asserts that everything inside a region of space can be described by bits of information restricted to the boundary."[346]

According to the holographic principle, information is always recorded at the holographic surface area of any given volume of space, though if we approach the boundary to examine the information, it always recedes out to the next concentric boundary, until it reaches the cosmic horizon. Although Susskind calls this principle a "new law of physics," it is very similar to the ancient Hindu concept of the *akashic* shell of the universe, discussed above.[347] Grof also discusses the *akasha* element in relation to Ervin Laszlo in *The Ultimate Journey: Consciousness and the Mystery of Death*.[348] In that passage, Grof differentiates between the world of information and the world of matter. Information is, of course, the fundamental term in Susskind's string theory of holographic information conservation, according to which the world of matter is the illusion of three-dimensional space, while the world of information is the holographic film at the cosmic horizon. However, despite these similarities, Laszlo dismisses Susskind's theory as "science fable."[349] Laszlo overlooks two essential correlations between Susskind's holographic principle and the Hindu concept of the *akashic* field: the idea of eternal information conservation at the cosmic horizon, and the idea that the illusion of three-dimensional space is projected inward from the cosmic horizon by fundamental threads. Failing to see those correspondences, Laszlo concludes his dismissal of Susskind's theory by pointing out that Susskind's own partner, 't Hooft, now criticizes the idea.

Behind the Blinding Veil

According to Laszlo:

> The holographic principle may make string theory's calculations easier, but it makes fabulous assumptions about the nature of the world. Even Gerard 't Hooft, who was one of the originators of this principle, changed his mind about its cogency. Rather than a "principle," he said, in this context holography is actually a "problem." Perhaps, he speculated, quantum gravity could be derived from a deeper principle that does not obey quantum mechanics.[350]

The deeper principle required to make Susskind and 't Hooft's holographic string theory cogent may perhaps be found in the primordial being hidden from our view in Susskind's definition of his most fundamental term: a bit of information. As discussed above, Susskind defines a bit of information as a yes-no answer to a question about the twists and turns of one-dimensional strings.[351] But who, it might be asked, poses the yes-no question about a string that brought forth the first bit of information at the Big Bang?

With this question in mind I turn to the concluding passage of Susskind's first book, his ostensible antidote to "the illusion of intelligent design":

> If there was a moment of creation, it is obscured from our eyes and our telescopes by the veil of explosive Inflation that took place during the prehistory of the Big Bang. If there is a God, she has taken great pains to make herself irrelevant.

Let me then close this book with the words of Pierre-Simon de Laplace that opened it: "I have no need of this hypothesis."[352]

Susskind uses exactly the same argument against the idea of a creator God who existed before the Big Bang that his own opponents use against his string theory of a megaverse of universes: it is scientifically irrelevant because it is empirically unobservable as a result of the faster-than-light recession of space-time outside the cosmic horizon. Susskind ridicules this short-sighted argument by comparing it to behaviorism in the field of psychology in the 1950s, writing: "Perhaps we should simply accept worlds beyond the horizon in the same way that we accept that other people have an impenetrable interior life."[353] Susskind's analogy is especially fitting if the cosmic horizon is the border between consciousness and the collective unconscious archetype of the Self dwelling within all of us.

Despite his plea that we all accept the existence of empirically unobservable worlds beyond the horizon, at the end of his first book Susskind says he has no need of the hypothesis of an empirically unobservable creator God working from the pre-Big Bang era behind the cosmic horizon. However, given his definition of a bit of information as a yes-no answer to a question, he does apparently need the hypothesis of an unobservable speaker behind the cosmic horizon in order to ask and answer the first yes-no question about a string required to bring the first bit of information into being at the Big Bang. Rather than cutting off the search for God because we are blinded by the veil of explosive inflation that shields us from seeing the other side of the cosmic horizon, the devotee who wrote Sri Isopanishad simply prays that the veil be removed: "O my Lord, sustainer of all that lives, Your real face is covered by your dazzling effulgence. Kindly remove that covering and exhibit Yourself to Your pure devotee."[354]

Grof's Cartography of Consciousness

Informed by his extensive research and personal experience, Grof writes: "The universe is imbued with creative intelligence and consciousness is inextricably woven into its fabric."[355] Although Grof does not appear to make the connection explicitly, if consciousness is woven into the holographic fabric of space-time, as his pharmaceutically amplified research indicates, then consciousness must experience the effects of exponential expansion outward in space and backward in time, which is exactly what Grof experienced during his LSD-induced out-of-body experience in 1957. Grof's "cartography of the unconscious," in addition to the usual *biographical* level, contains two transbiographical realms: *the perinatal domain*, related to the trauma of biological birth; and *the transpersonal domain*, which accounts for such phenomena as experiential identification with other people, animals, plants, and other aspects of nature.[356] According to Grof, the latter realm is also the source of ancestral, racial, phylogenetic, and karmic memories, as well as visions of archetypal beings and mythological regions. The most extreme experiences in this category are identification with the Universal Mind and with the Supracosmic and Metacosmic void. In accordance with Jung's criteria for labeling psychic phenomena as archetypal, perinatal and transpersonal phenomena have been described throughout the ages in the religious, mystical, and occult literature of various countries of the world.[357] Grof further explains that "the perinatal domain of the psyche also represents an important gateway to the collective unconscious in the Jungian sense."[358]

However, Grof does not underscore the correspondence between what he sees as the three successively deeper layers of the unconscious—biographical, perinatal, and transpersonal—and the physics of expanding space-time. In this model, going deeper in space is equivalent to going backward in time, literally through the moments of our own earthly lives (biographical), past the point of our own biological birth and gestation in the womb (perinatal), until finally reaching the birth of the universe itself, the Big Bang, at the cosmic horizon (transpersonal—also known as the Supracosmic and Metacosmic void). In light of Susskind's theory, Grof's research seems to indicate that going deep into the unconscious is equivalent to going deep into space, and therefore backward in time. This progression can continue until one reaches the deepest realm, the collective unconscious, at the birth of the universe at the cosmic horizon, from where the eternal archetypal forms (including the Kantian *a priori* categories of space, time, and causality) project the holographic illusion of our material world.

The psyche is a union of the conscious and unconscious; similarly, the cosmos is a union of the omnicentric singularity and the holographic horizon. If the cosmic horizon correlates with the collective unconscious, the implication is that the singularity correlates with individual ego-consciousness. In this view, the two poles of the psyche are united by the same complementarity that describes the two poles of the cosmos. People we see at the cosmic horizon would see themselves in the center of the expanding universe, and us at the horizon, in the same way that each of us sees our own inner thoughts as the center of consciousness, and everyone else's inner thoughts as the unconscious periphery.

Near-Death Experiences and LSD

Grof's research into the perinatal realm of the unconscious is intimately connected to his research into near-death experiences, which frequently involve a sense of expanding away from the body and a corresponding life-review, culminating with a sense of being reborn into a state of cosmic unity specifically at the border of the cosmos, the point of no return. Grof describes terminal cancer patients he worked with who had out-of-body, cosmic experiences under the influence of LSD (during psychotherapy to help them prepare for death), and then again during actual NDEs caused by heart failure:

The similarity between these two categories of experiences hardly supports a simple chemical explanation for NDEs. . . . If consciousness were nothing else but a product of neurophysiological processes in the brain, it could not possibly detach itself from the body and from the brain, become autonomous, and be able to perceive the environment without mediation of the senses.[359]

Given the eye-witness testimonies from respected scholars and physicians—including Grof himself—it is plausible to suggest that, like NDEs, LSD and other psychedelic compounds affect the chemistry of the brain in a way that temporarily inactivates the cosmological filtering function it normally serves, allowing the psyche to directly experience its innate oneness with the expanding fabric of space-time.

From the Ceiling to the Point of No Return

As Grof explains:

Many accounts of NDEs refer to what appears to be a "point of no return." This threshold may take a concrete form—a fence, body of water, cliff, or some other type of barrier—or involve simply a strong sense of an invisible but nevertheless compelling obstruction. Reaching this limit is associated with a convincing feeling that continuing beyond this point would mean physical death and would make return into one's body impossible.[360]

The psychic "point of no return" experienced during NDEs seems to correlate with the cosmic horizon, where exponentially expanding space-time is receding from the singularity of the Big Bang at the speed of light, rendering it a physical point of no return as well as a border zone between space-time and space-timelessness. Although in one sense the cosmic horizon is the extreme opposite of the singularity from which it is receding, in another sense the singularity is present at every point of the infinitely hot cosmic horizon, from where the Big Bang is continuously echoing inward. From this perspective, if we accept the equation Psyche = Singularity, then the point of light at the end of the dark tunnel often perceived during NDEs is the point of no return, understood as the singularity from which the cosmos is expanding and toward which it is constantly returning. The singularity is the beginning and ending of space-time, which resonates precisely with what Christ claims in the Apocalypse,[361] and what Krishna says about himself in the Bhagavad-gita.[362]

In the context of Jung's and Grof's work, it is plausible to suggest that the cosmic horizon described by Susskind is indistinguishable from the collective unconscious, the space-timeless realm from which the archetypes project what we consciously experience as the temporary world of three-dimensional forms. The cosmic horizon seems, moreover, to be the geometrical expression of the archetype of the principle of limit in particular, which tends to invoke symbolically related images of the limiting principle, such as a pearly gate, river, door, wall, or waterfall, in disembodied psyches who approach it during NDEs. And as indicated by Jung's and many other NDE accounts, the cosmic horizon is evidently filled with archetypal beings when perceived from the inside. In other words, what appears from Earth as the mundane source of the cosmic microwave background radiation (the echo of the Big Bang), appears from the timeless consciousness suspended there during an NDE as an eternal ecosystem of beings formed of omniscient radiance, fully equipped with all of the subtleties of human consciousness, each of which is amplified to archetypal acuteness.

In *Synchronicity: An Acausal Connecting Principle,* Jung describes the NDE of a former patient of his, a woman who suffered a heart attack during a caesarean childbirth. Her NDE demonstrates most of the commonly documented motifs of those experiences: "The remarkable thing was that it was not an immediate perception of the situation through indirect or unconscious observation, but she saw the whole situation from *above*, as though 'her eyes were in the ceiling,' as she put it."[363] That the patient's vision occurred from the perspective of the ceiling of her hospital room is especially reminiscent of Susskind's holographic principle, according to which each bit of information that appears to be contained in any three-dimensional volume of space is actually conserved on its two-dimensional surface area. As Susskind writes, all of the information describing each object in a room "is precisely coded in Planckian bits, far too small to see but densely covering the walls of the room."[364] That people who return from death frequently recall looking down at their dead bodies from the perspective of the ceiling is a vital clue pointing to a correspondence with Susskind's holographic principle.

Jung's patient described how, after observing the doctor panic over her dead body from above, her disembodied psyche left the hospital room and approached a beautiful landscape. She intuitively knew that the feeling of attraction for the idyllic landscape behind her, leading up a sloping green meadow past a wrought-iron gate, would have been too powerful to resist had she turned to look at it. That strong force of psychological attraction for the point of no return seems to correlate with the repulsive force of expanding space-time (the cosmological constant) as it approaches the speed of light at the cosmic horizon.

Returning to Grof, he describes what he refers to as "veridical" out-of-body experiences had by blind people. The veracity of many of these visions has been confirmed by consensual validation. Various aspects of the environment accurately perceived by the disembodied consciousness of the blind subjects ranged from details of electrical fixtures on the ceiling of the operating room to the surroundings of the hospital observed from a bird's eye view.[365] Mundane but verifiable details perceived by congenitally blind people during NDEs serve as strong evidence in favor of the theory that psyche is interwoven with the fundamental strings that conserve information at every holographic boundary of three-dimensional space. If out-of-body experiences during NDEs have been verified, as Grof and others report, this same evidence provides powerful support for Susskind's holographic string theory, while turning his materialist interpretation on its head. If Jung's and Grof's OBEs of the cosmic horizon were real events, as they both adamantly insist, and not merely delusions, it is reasonable to assume that many other people's NDE accounts are also true.

Pim van Lommel

Dr. Pim van Lommel is a cardiologist who personally dealt with patients who had near-death experiences after suffering a heart attack. In his book *Consciousness Beyond Life: The Science of the Near-Death Experience*, he discusses documented cases of veridical out-of-body experiences from people who had NDEs while their brains were being monitored for electrical activity. As van Lommel writes: "There are only a few known cases in which this loss of [brain] function has been carefully monitored."[366] In the case of Pamela Reynolds, "because she had her NDE during brain surgery, when the activity of the cerebral cortex and brain stem were constantly monitored, hers is a good example of an NDE during carefully documented loss of brain function."[367] Van Lommel reports that Reynolds' blood had been cooled and then drained from the artery in her leg to deflate a brain aneurism, which was being removed to save her life. Her eyes were smeared with lubricant and taped shut, while ear plugs, which made a constant clicking sound, had been placed in her ears to help monitor the hearing reflex and, thus, the overall electrical activity of her brain. Even if her brain had been electrically active, which it was not at all, she was physically blinded and deafened.

The moment her heart was intentionally stopped, she felt her consciousness "pop out" of the top of her head, after which she watched the doctor operating on her, as if she was "sitting on Dr. Spetzler's shoulder."[368] Her doctors and nurses confirmed the accuracy of her observations of the operation, while her brain was completely inactive. In her account, after describing the view of her dead body from above, Reynolds describes the other typical experiences of most NDE survivors, including being pulled extremely quickly through a "tunnel" toward an incredibly attractive "pinpoint of light," then not being allowed to go further lest she be unable to return to her body.[369]

Similarly, van Lommel cites Monique Hennequin's account of her two NDEs following a caesarian childbirth. She felt herself "picking up speed" as she traveled from her own hospital room to the adjacent room, where she felt the nurses' panic when they heard the alarm on her heart-monitoring machine,[370] an experience which seems especially pertinent to the theory of the psyche's unity with exponentially expanding space-time. She felt herself picking up more speed as she passed through every room of the hospital, which made her feel as if she had merged with "the past, present, and future of everything that whizzed past me."[371] Hennequin's account continues in a way that is especially consistent with Grof's theory of the perinatal level of the psyche, as well as Susskind's holographic principle of information conservation at every concentric boundary of space:

> I felt dizzy, and I seemed to be experiencing birth at different levels and in different dimensions. . . . I sensed a hierarchy of the regions or atmospheres I literally and figuratively went through. Every "layer" had its own atmosphere with distinct boundaries and restrictions. . . . Gradually, the notion of "enlightenment" began to take shape in me. I had never thought about spirituality, and to my embarrassment I had been known to make fun of it.[372]

Hennequin goes on to compare the outermost boundary of the cosmos to "God," and the "Akasha field," and recalls how she felt as if it were a point of no return:

> This is where I belonged! This was no longer the dimension of earth or other spheres, this was more! This was the

beginning and the end, this was the source. . . . And I would know and understand everything as soon as I had become one with this whole. Everything! I hesitated at the prospect of becoming one because I knew that once I decided to do so I would never be in a body again. The force of attraction was incredibly strong, but at the same time I realized that if I connected there would be no way back.[373]

It is easy to see a correlation between Hennequin's description of the outermost shell of the cosmos, containing all of the information describing all points of space-time, and Susskind's description of holographic information conservation at the cosmic horizon, especially when she mentions the incredibly strong "force of attraction" she felt for that peripheral sphere, which seems to be the psychological correlate of the cosmological constant, the force of exponentially expanding space-time.

Van Lommel posits a strong connection between NDEs and the holographic paradigm, citing Susskind's partner, Gerard 't Hooft, and directly linking holographic string theory to the concept of the ether, and to Laszlo's related interpretation of the *akashic* field as a "quantum vacuum or 'cosmic plenum.'" As Van Lommel writes:

> This absolute vacuum, this nonlocal space, could be a basis or foundation for consciousness. I support the interpretation . . . that this nonlocal space is more than a mathematical description; it is also a metaphysical space in which consciousness can exert influence because it has phenomenal properties.[374]

If Psyche = Singularity, as Jung posits in the Leap Day letter, and if the quantum vacuum is made of miniature black holes, then the vacuum could perhaps be described as a rapidly flashing firmament of sentient mandalas. Moreover, if the quantum vacuum is a plenum of tiny black holes (some of which inflate to become universes), then the equation Psyche = Singularity is equivalent to Bohm's, Laszlo's, and van Lommel's theory that the quantum vacuum is the source of consciousness.[375] Furthermore, if each psyche is woven into the exponentially expanding fabric of space-time, and if we become aware of that fundamental fact during out-of-body NDEs when our awareness of our psyches is no longer localized in material bodies, then we should expect NDE accounts to recount what the special and general theories of relativity predict a sentient being would see if it were accelerating toward the speed of light at an exponentially expanding rate, or if it were enduring the equivalent gravitational tidal force near the event horizon of a black hole. In fact, this is precisely what we find when we compare the typical tunnel vision of an NDE to relativistic tunnel-vision descriptions.[376]

Tunnel Vision

In *The Ultimate Journey*, Grof describes some of the common experiences reported in NDE literature:

> Many of the accounts included descriptions of passage through a dark enclosed space, referred to as a funnel, cave, tunnel . . . followed by encounters with divine light. . . . Out-of-body phenomena were some of the most common characteristics of near-death experiences. . . . Many dying individuals mentioned in [Dr. Raymond] Moody's study reported encounters with other beings, such as dead relatives or friends, "guardian spirits," or spirit guides. Visions of the "Being of Light" were especially common. . . . Some accounts spoke of reaching some absolute border or limit, where the decision had to be made as to whether to return or to continue the journey to the Beyond. . . . The first few moments after death were often characterized by a desperate desire to get back into the body and regrets over one's demise. This attitude typically changed into unwillingness

to return after a certain depth had been reached and especially after the encounter with the Being of Light.[377]

Regarding Grof's comments on the "absolute border" people experience during NDEs, earlier we saw him refer to it as the "point of no return," which seems to be a perception of the cosmic horizon of the universe, which is the inside-out event horizon where, from our reference frame on Earth, the exponentially expanding fabric of space-time is receding at the speed of light.[378] If the psyche is spiritual light, then it makes sense that it would interpret the point where the outward flow of space-time reaches the speed of light as a point of no return. Moreover, considering the light of the Big Bang is echoing back from every point of the cosmic horizon with the CMB radiation, it is reasonable to equate the point of light at the end of the dark tunnel perceived during an NDE with the omnicentric singularity conserved at every point of the holographic cosmic horizon, which would indicate that at the end of embodied life, each psyche rushes back to the point of no return from which everything flares forth. Finally, NDE accounts of what people perceived as they rapidly accelerated through a tunnel toward a brilliant point of infinitely loving light are unmistakably similar to the tunnel vision associated with near-light-speed travel (an effect known as aberration, which is predicted by special relativity), and the tunnel vision associated with the gravitational lensing effect near a black hole, which is predicted by general relativity.[379]

The encounter with divine light at the end of a dark tunnel is probably the most famous aspect of near-death experience accounts. According to special relativity, any observer who accelerates toward the speed of light would see all of the light in the universe, even the light directly behind the observer, gradually wrap into a circle tightening into a point at the end of a dark tunnel in the forward field of vision (aberration), which is equivalent to what general relativity tells us an observer would see from just in front of, but looking away from, the event horizon of a black hole as a result of the near-light-speed of the inward tidal flow of space-time (gravitational lensing). We can see a distant galaxy even if it is directly behind a closer galaxy in our line of view, because the light from the more distant galaxy will be gravitationally bent around the closer galaxy, surrounding it with what is known as an Einstein ring (although usually galaxies are not perfectly aligned, so that a perfect ring is not usually perceived).

Another important term associated with the lensing effect predicted by general relativity is "tidal force," which Susskind defines as "the distorting forces caused by variations in the strength and direction of gravity."[380] In the Glossary of *The Black Hole War* Susskind defines the term singularity as "the infinitely dense point at the center of a black hole where tidal forces become infinite."[381] To say that the tidal forces become infinite at the singularity in a black hole is to say that the gravitational lensing effect also becomes infinite. At the event horizon, however, the lensing effect is still finite. In other words, the inward rushing tidal force of the fabric of space-time reaches the speed of light at the event horizon of a black hole, and presumably surpasses that speed on the inside of a black hole, reaching "infinite speed" at the singularity. The tunnel vision experienced during an NDE can thus be correlated with the tunnel vision produced by the gravitational lensing effect associated with the tidal force of a black hole *and* the equivalent "g-force" associated with accelerating through space toward light speed (aberration).

Astronomer Karen Masters explains that, if we were inside a black hole looking away from the central singularity, and if we could see light which has "an infinite blue shift," we would be able to see "the whole universe in one small patch of our sky—even the stuff that is actually behind the singularity!"[382] The gravitational field inside the black hole would be so strong that it would pull the light beaming in from behind us all the way around to a small patch of light in our forward field of vision. Masters also explains that time would appear to be running so much faster outside of the black hole that "we would be able to see the evolution of the universe 'flash' before our eyes."[383] Without further comment, Masters simply puts the word "flash" in quotation marks, apparently confident that everyone will immediately know that she is drawing a parallel with popular NDE accounts, during which people typically recall their "whole lives flashing before their eyes" while hurtling through a dark tunnel toward a point of supernatural light.

Finally, Masters mentions the need to be able to see "the light which has an infinite blue shift" in order to perceive the gravitational lensing effect from inside a black hole. Blue shift is a reference to the more general phenomenon of a Doppler shift.[384] In galaxies that are farther away and therefore receding faster, the light from those standardized stars gets stretched out, or shifted, toward the longer, redder wavelengths of the electromagnetic spectrum on the way to Earth; the effect is known as red shifting. Similarly, the light that emanates from the galaxies closer to Earth is less stretched out, and is therefore relatively blue shifted toward the shorter, higher frequency wavelengths. Inside a black hole, the light from *all* of the stars of the universe is rushing in faster than the speed of light, reaching infinite speed, and therefore undergoing what Masters refers to as an "infinite blue shift" at the singularity.

Strikingly, two NDE accounts cited in van Lommel's book combine the usual tunnel-vision effect with the related blue shifting of light:

> As I peered into the dark, the color changed from black to deep blue, not dark, but an intense cobalt blue that leaves you speechless. . . . Soon I found myself in a dark space, a kind of tunnel. . . . [A] glimmer of light appeared at the end, and after a real struggle I stood, or found myself in, this absolute light, which seemed to envelop me.[385]

> I entered an extremely dark, long, and spiral-shaped tunnel. . . . I soared through this spiral-shaped funnel, and the further or the higher I got, the lighter it became. The intensity of the light changed to a deep purple/violet. "Above" me I saw an extremely bright, radiant white light. I whirled, floated, toward it.[386]

Both of these NDE accounts depict a disembodied psyche accelerating through a tunnel in space while perceiving a blue shift of light that condenses into a single, all-consuming point, which resembles what general relativity predicts a person would see from inside a black hole if he or she could hypothetically survive the tidal force and was looking away from the central singularity. Considering Einstein's discovery that gravity is equivalent to accelerated motion, a body enduring the tidal force of space-time (gravity) inside a black hole is equivalent to that same body accelerating *through* space-time outside a black hole. In both cases relativity theory (special and general) predicts that we would see the entire temporal trajectory of all of the light of the universe blue shifted and condensed into a single point at the end of a dark tunnel through which we would appear to be traveling very fast, which clearly correlates to the typical tunnel visions associated with NDEs.

Astronomer Sara Slater explains that "everyone inside the event horizon is a psychic." If you are inside a black hole looking away from the center "you see two images of everything—one from T hours in the past and one from T hours in the future." For example, "if both you and Tolstoy were in a black hole and were separated by 3 light years, you could be watching him start and finish War and Peace at once."[387] NDE accounts of traveling incredibly fast through a dark tunnel toward an all-embracing light, while undergoing a life review and a life preview, find point-for-point correspondences with what astronomers say we would see from inside a black hole, looking out. However, if the event horizon is a point of no return then, by definition, NDE survivors do not go past the event horizon.

Clifford A. Pickover's educational work of fiction *Black Holes: A Traveler's Guide* features two astronauts, the captain on the spaceship (with whom the reader is identified), and his assistant, Mr. Plex (a very durable creature made of diamonds), who is lowered down to 1.01 times the radius of the event horizon of a black hole. After describing the "weird colors," Mr. Plex describes what he sees while looking away from the black hole: "The starry sky got smaller and smaller, as though I had tunnel vision, as though all the stars were being squeezed into a disk the size of a Frisbee. I felt as though I were trapped in a dark pipe."[388] This passage about looking up at the starry sky while hovering just above the event horizon of a black hole parallels the standard NDE tunnel experience: "weird colors" are caused by the Doppler shifting of all of the light of the universe, which is bent inward from all directions and condensed into a small disk at the end of a dark tunnel.

Pickover gives the mathematical formula that describes the exact diameter of the disk of universal light relative to the size of the black hole, and goes on to describe the effect of gravitational time dilation as perceived from just above the event horizon: "During one second of your time near the hole, millions of years could have flown past our ship."[389] Again, Pickover provides the formula that describes exactly how long each second near a black hole of a given size lasts relative to time outside of the black hole's gravitational influence. It is precisely that kind of mathematically descriptive precision that NDE accounts of cosmic tunnel vision lack, although, in turn, NDE accounts appear to provide the ultimate requirement of science: empirical confirmation. It is plausible to suggest that by combining the two types of tunnel-vision descriptions (relativistic and NDE) we could be able to arrive at a truly unified field theory describing both cosmos and psyche.

With that in mind, I turn now to astronomer Alexis Brandeker, who describes the perspective of traveling through outer space at close to the speed of light, which, though equivalent to hovering near the event horizon of a black hole, is even more similar to the typical NDE accounts of the psyche rising above the body, into outer space, and then zooming through a tunnel toward a point of supernatural light. Describing a hypothetical astronaut named Celesta, he explains that at relativistic speeds she would see how the "whole field of view seems to shrink in the direction of travel. Even photons from stars that Celesta knows are behind, come in from the forward direction. This is the effect of aberration." He goes on to explain that the faster the traveler's speed, the more constellations of stars converge in the forward field of view, so that all of the constellations converge in a single point just prior to the speed of light. Someone travelling at "0.9999999999999994c, or (1 − 6×10−16)c" would see all of the radiation of the universe "emanate from a single point in the direction of travel, and all radiation, even the cosmic background, would be Doppler shifted out to gamma ray wavelengths or far radio, with next to nothing in between."[390] As discussed above, Jung and Pauli argue that evidence for their theory that cosmos and psyche emerge from and are ordered by the same "psychoid" archetypes comes from the empirically observable mirror-symmetries between the laws of psychology and physics.[391] That theory is powerfully supported by the straightforward correlations between descriptions of the NDE tunnel experience and descriptions of the relativistic tunnel vision associated with traveling at close to light speed or enduring the equivalent tidal flow of gravity close to a black hole.

Regarding the validity of NDE testimonies, we can assume that the vast majority of those people were not aware of the relativistic descriptions of tunnel vision, and were not therefore bending their testimonies to conform to that scientific paradigm. Certainly, Plato was not trying to imitate the tunnel vision predicted by Einstein's theories when he concluded his most famous Dialogue, the *Republic*, with the NDE account known as the myth of Er, which includes not only a musical string theory of information conservation at the cosmic horizon (as discussed above), but also a description of cosmic tunnels that seem to suck psyches through space-time to their allotted fates. In the myth of Er, Plato depicts Socrates describing a soldier named Er recalling his NDE, during which his disembodied psyche traveled to "a mysterious region where there were two openings side by side in the earth, and above and over against them in the heaven two others."[392] In the myth, good souls are directed to exit to their new lives through one of the upward openings in the heaven (which seems to indicate the sky), while bad souls are forced to exit through one of the downward openings on the ground; similarly, after their allotted time, good souls come back down to the ground from the other opening in the heaven, while bad souls return up from the other opening on the earth after "a long journey."[393] The implication is that the mysterious openings are connected to long tunnels, which calls to mind the steep opening leading down to and up from the subterranean cave in the allegory of Book VII of the *Republic*.

The following NDE account from van Lommel's book is reminiscent of the reincarnation tunnels of Plato's *Republic*. It is also an excellent summary of all of the correlations between NDE tunnel-vision descriptions and relativistic descriptions of tunnel vision discussed so far.

> I felt that I was letting go of my body and rising up. Through the roof. Over the hospital. Everything became smaller, and I began to accelerate. Everything around me was dark, with the exception of several stars that hurled toward me and I noticed their different colors. . . . Then I realized that I wasn't alone because a flow of translucent beings was heading the same way as me and another flow was moving in the opposite direction. When I thought about reincarnation, it later dawned on me that it could well be this flow. . . . An overwhelming feeling of love came over me, not the earthly feeling I was quite familiar with, but something I can't describe. Above me I saw a bright light, and on my way there I heard beautiful music and I saw colors I'd never seen before.[394]

One main aspect of the typical NDE tunnel-vision account that does not seem to have a direct correspondence with the relativistic descriptions of tunnel vision is the overpowering conviction that the omniscient and omnipotent point of light at the end of the tunnel is also all-loving.[395] Nevertheless, in the context of Jung and Pauli's theory that each law of physics is mirrored by a corresponding law of psychology because cosmos and psyche both emanate from the same "psychoid" archetypes, we can interpret cosmologist Brian Swimme's equation, "Gravity is Love," to mean that the physical force of gravity reflects the psychological force of love.[396] Moreover, if Gravity = Love, then a point of infinite gravity (the singularity) equals a point of infinite love, which unfolds a deeper meaning from the equation, Psyche = Singularity. In short, Swimme's equation, Gravity = Love, completes the correlations between the NDE tunnel experience and relativistic descriptions of tunnel vision: the point of light at the end of the tunnel, in which the entire temporal evolution of the universe is contained, is the singularity, which is experienced as an infinitely attractive point of infinitely intense love.[397]

Another possible explanation for why the singularity is experienced as a point of infinitely intense love at the end of a dark tunnel during NDEs stems from a combination of Leibnitz's principle of the identity of indiscernibles and the instinct of self-love. According to Leibnitz's principle, despite being situated at different points in space-time, each singularity is identical to every other because they are all indistinguishable points of infinite density which stand outside space-time by virtue of being its source and its boundary. Thus, when a singularity, which is (theoretically) a psyche, experiences its oneness with the singularity at the end of the dark tunnel during an NDE, the instinctive self-love of that psyche automatically encompasses the whole cosmos. In other words, when a psyche is localized in a material body, it tends to feel isolated and alienated from every other psyche, and the cosmos as a whole, though when a psyche, which is another word for a singularity, is disembodied during a near-death experience, it experiences its inherent union with every other singularity, and thus the entire cosmos, as it approaches the singularity at the end of the relativistic tunnel.

A similar explanation for the feeling of infinite love associated with the point of light at the end of the NDE tunnel comes from a Kantian perspective. According to Kant, space and time are not empirically observed by any of our five sense organs; rather, they are *a priori* categories of thought imprinted on our minds. Our minds, in other words, *are* space-time. As embodied psyches, we project these inborn concepts of space and time out of ourselves, thereby creating the self-alienating illusion of three-dimensional space and linear time, though, when we are disembodied during a near-death experience, it

145

seems that we recapture the holographic projection of space-time, reabsorb and reincorporate it so that our instinct of self-love suddenly embraces all the cosmos. In short, during a near-death experience, our disembodied minds, which are the essence of space-time, therefore experience exponentially accelerating expansion, resulting in a relativist vision of a dark tunnel with an all-embracing, infinitely attractive point of omni-benevolent light at the end.

Eben Alexander

In 2012, Eben Alexander published *Proof of Heaven: A Neurosurgeon's Near-Death Experience and Journey into the Afterlife*, preceded by a front-page story in the October 8, 2012 edition of *Newsweek* magazine, in which Alexander explains that:

> As a neurosurgeon, I did not believe in the phenomenon of near-death experiences. I grew up in a scientific world, the son of a neurosurgeon. I followed my father's path and became an academic neurosurgeon, teaching at Harvard Medical School and other universities.[398]

Although Alexander, an eminent brain surgeon, formerly accepted the standard academic tenet that consciousness is a byproduct of the brain, his own NDE convinced him that a divine consciousness permeates a megaverse of universes, and "that love lay at the center of them all."[399] If Gravity is Love, as Brian Swimme says, and if love lay at the center of every universe in the megaverse, as Alexander says, then the singularity at the center of each universe is a point of infinite love.

Alexander explains that in 2008 he was afflicted with a rare case of meningitis caused by *E coli* bacteria, which completely paralyzed his brain stem, leading him later to conclude that "I was encountering the reality of a world of consciousness that existed *completely free of the limitations of my physical brain.*"[400] Considering the documented severity of his brain disease, the intensity of his NDE, and his decades of experience in both teaching and practicing neurosurgery, Alexander considers his "a perfect storm of near-death experiences,"[401] rendering him uniquely qualified to comment on the implications of his experience, which he considers to be "tremendous beyond description." First of all, he realized that "the death of the body and the brain are not the end of consciousness." More importantly, in his opinion, he learned that human consciousness "continues under the gaze of a God who loves and cares about each one of us and about where the universe itself and all the beings within it are ultimately going."[402]

Like Grof and van Lommel, Alexander refers to Einstein's relativity theory, and cites the pioneers of quantum physics, including Werner Heisenberg and Wolfgang Pauli, who both claimed that consciousness is interwoven with the fabric of the cosmos.[403] Alexander furthermore argues that there is as yet "no unified theory of everything that can combine the laws of quantum mechanics with those of relativity theory in a way that begins to incorporate consciousness."[404] To fill the gap between the current level of academic knowledge and the unified field theory pointed out by Alexander, it is important to note that string theory is the attempt to combine the laws of quantum mechanics with those of general relativity (specifically by describing the quantum particle that transmits the force of gravity, the theoretical graviton), while Susskind's holographic string theory seems ready-made to incorporate NDE accounts like Alexander's and Jung's, despite Susskind's atheistic-materialist presentation of his own theory.

Although Alexander does not mention string theory, he does emphasize the proven fact of nonlocal quantum entanglement, which he claims to have experienced directly during his NDE.[405] Moreover, although he does not mention the holographic principle, he does relate his NDE to the megaverse theory that is implicit in string theory. In a way that resembles Grof's description of the perinatal level of the unconscious as a gateway to the "Metacosmic void" of the transpersonal realm,[406] as well as Susskind's theory of the holographic

147

horizon of the cosmos, Alexander describes his experience at the outer edge of the cosmos:

> I continued moving forward and found myself entering an immense void, completely dark, infinite in size, yet also infinitely comforting. Pitch black as it was, it was also brimming over with light: a light that seemed to come from a brilliant orb that I now sensed near me.[407]

Alexander goes on to describe his situation at the edge of the cosmos as being similar to a "fetus in a womb," with God as the mother, creator, and source of the universe. He remembers hearing the sound "Om" associated with that "omniscient, omnipotent, and unconditionally loving God." Moreover, "through the Orb, Om told me that there is not one universe but many—in fact, more than I could conceive—but that love lay at the center of them all."[408]

Susskind's description of the holographic horizon of the cosmos provides a plausible explanation for the "deep but dazzling darkness" Alexander associates with God, understood as the enveloping cosmic womb.[409] According to Susskind, from our vantage point on Earth, the mathematics of string theory indicate that the infinitely hot holographic film in front of the cosmic horizon absorbs all of the light of the universe, and radiates it back inward with the cosmic microwave background radiation, although the horizon itself (which is an inside-out event horizon) technically radiates no light, which could account for Alexander's description of God: "Pitch black as it was, it was also brimming over with light."[410]

The cosmology revealed to Alexander in his near-death experience, featuring a megaverse with God as the center and surrounding womb of each universe, is structurally consistent with Susskind's string theory of a megaverse of universes, each with a central singularity surrounded by a holographic horizon, although the theological interpretation is precisely opposite. The cosmology Alexander describes also agrees with the Hindu cosmology featuring a Vishnu Avatar (Garbhodakashayi Vishnu) in the center of every bubble universe (*brahmanda*) in the cloud of universes (*mahat-tattva*) exhaling from, and inhaling back into Maha-Vishnu while he sleeps and dreams the universes into being. In the Bhagavad-gita, Krishna identifies himself as the ultimate example of every category of being, including the forms of Vishnu.[411] Directly pertinent to Alexander's experience of God as the sound Om, Krishna declares that, "of vibrations I am the transcendental syllable om."[412] Moreover, as discussed above, after describing the eight concentric shells of material elements surrounding each spherical universe, and after declaring that "everything rests upon Me, as pearls are strung on a thread," Krishna claims to be "the syllable om in the Vedic mantras; I am the sound in ether and ability in man."[413] Om is the spiritual sound associated with the etheric shell of the universe, where the past, present, and future are interwoven, and from which the grosser elements successively radiate inward, which correlates with what Alexander perceived as the all-loving and omniscient womb of our universe, which also exists as the central point of all universes.

Like the Hindu cosmology formed by concentric spheres of increasingly subtle elements—earth, water, fire, air, ether—Alexander experienced the cosmos as consisting of three ascending levels, the lowest of which he describes as the "realm of the Earthworm's-Eye View,"[414] followed by a brilliant green meadow sloping up to a "Gateway," which leads up to "the Core." Alexander alludes to a correlation between the Core and the cosmic horizon though, he is careful to note, "that doesn't mean that I saw anything like the whole universe."[415] However, although he never saw the whole universe, at times Alexander felt as if he had become the universe itself.[416] He recalls rising up from the inchoate consciousness of the Earthworm layer of the cosmos, through an idyllic ecosystem including colorful choruses of singing clouds and telepathic flocks of butterflies, until he ascended past a brilliant green meadow to an archetypal Gateway, where he saw and heard a spinning orb of light radiating a beautiful melody. As he explains, he traversed the various levels of the cosmos, from the lowest to highest realm, "any number of times."[417] Asserting that we have an eternal connection to the "idyllic realm" he perceived, Alexander writes: "We just forget that we do, because during the brain-based, physical portion of our existence, our brain blocks out, or veils, that larger cosmic background, just as the sun's light blocks the universe from view each morning."[418] Alexander equates the idyllic Core with the "larger cosmic background," which seems to correlate with the cosmic horizon as described by Susskind and Jung. He also describes his experience in the realms above the lowest Earthworm level.

He noticed that in those higher levels of the afterlife he would become one with anything he looked at or listened to.[419] The correlation between Alexander's experience and the ancient Hindu theory of the eight concentric spheres of increasingly subtle elements becomes especially pronounced by his recollection of a warm, "divine breeze" that shifted the world around him into a "higher octave" of vibration (an octave is a series of eight notes),[420] which perhaps indicates a shift from the earth and water elements to the air element. Alexander's NDE account also resembles the eight concentric hemispheres of the cosmos, each with a singing Siren sitting on its edge, in the myth of Er in Plato's *Republic*. Alexander recalls posing wordless questions to the divine breeze, and receiving telepathic answers: "Thoughts entered me directly. . . . These thoughts were solid and immediate—hotter than fire and wetter than water."[421]

According to Hindu cosmology, the gross material elements are contained in the subtler elements, so that the archetype of the earth element is contained in the elemental water sphere, which is contained in the larger fire sphere, and so on through the concentric spheres of air, ether, mind, intelligence, and false ego. Alexander equates the idea of solid thought forms specifically with divine, or archetypal, fire and water, which seems to support the correlation between his experience and the Hindu cosmology. From the Earthworm's-eye view through the spheres of water, fire, and air (the divine breeze), the next sphere we should expect him to encounter is the ether. Although Alexander does not explicitly mention the ether, he does identify the outermost sphere of the universe with God, whom he calls "Om" while, as discussed above, in the Bhagavad-gita

Krishna describes himself as God and the transcendental syllable om,[422] the sound of the ether. Alexander writes:

> Just as my awareness was both individual yet at the same time completely unified with the universe, so also did the boundaries of what I experienced as my "self" at times contract, and at other times expand to include all that exists throughout eternity. The blurring of the boundary between my awareness and the realm around me went so far at times that I *became* the entire universe.[423]

He goes on to say that it seemed to him as if the outer edge of the cosmos was like a hen's egg, and that "the creative, primordial (prime mover) aspect of God was the shell around the egg's contents."[424]

Alexander's parenthetical mention of the "prime mover" is a reference to Aristotle's and Aquinas' theological cosmologies (inherited from Plato), according to which God is the original source of motion who exists eternally as an infinitely powerful and all-attractive point encompassing the outermost sphere of the cosmos. This model of the cosmos found its most popular expression in Dante's *Paradiso*. Alexander explains that when he arrived at that outermost realm, his consciousness became one with the universe, which is consistent with Jung's and Grof's independent experiences of becoming one with the past, present, and future of the universe at the cosmic horizon, which is consistent, finally, with Susskind's holographic string theory. According to Alexander: "The place I went was real. Real in a way that makes the life we're living here and now completely dreamlike by comparison."[425] Jung is similarly adamant about the objective reality of his experience, to which I now return.

Jung's Near-Death Experience of the Cosmic Horizon

Even without any reference to string theory and the holographic principle, if we accept Jung's testimony of his near-death experience at face value, his initial claim that his disembodied psyche floated a thousand miles above the surface of Earth clearly violates the materialist paradigm that reduces consciousness to a chemical reaction in the brain. Referring to Jung's experience, van Lommel writes: "His description of the earth from a great height is remarkable because it is quite consistent with what images from outer space taught us only . . . decades after Jung's experience."[426] Jung claims that, although he could not see the whole Earth, "the global shape was plainly distinguishable," as was the "deep blue sea and the continents," which gave off a "silvery gleam" mixed with a "blue light," except for the "reddish-yellow desert of Arabia."[427] Jung recalls that, while floating above Earth, he saw a large block of dark stone, the size of his house, hollowed out into a temple: "To the right of the entrance, a black Hindu sat silently in lotus posture upon a stone bench. He wore a white robe, and I knew that he expected me."[428] As Jung approached the temple, however, he felt as if "the whole phantasmagoria of earthly existence, fell away or was stripped from me—an extremely painful process."[429] The way in which Jung's earthly biography was stripped away, like a layer of skin, is reminiscent of the powerful gravity of the event horizon of a black hole, which would seem to correlate the singularity inside a black hole with the black Hindu inside the black rock temple.

Immediately after Jung felt his earthly life stripped from him, his entire biography was given back to him all at once, so that, in Jung's words, "I consisted of my own history."[430] In the context of Susskind's holographic principle (and the theories of thinkers such as Rupert Sheldrake, Michael Persinger, Ray Kurzweil, and, as we have seen, Ervin Laszlo), Jung's claim that he became his entire earthly history simultaneously a thousand miles above Earth points to the possibility of an Earth consciousness, traditionally referred to as the *anima mundi,* which includes the collective memory of all the creatures who have ever lived on Earth.[431] Susskind says that the information describing any three-dimensional volume of space is actually stored at the two-dimensional surface area, which means that the history, as well as the future, of Earth is stored holographically at the outermost atmosphere.

Jung says he became each point of his history simultaneously at the periphery of Earth's atmosphere, while furthermore gaining intense intimations of his future by looking inside a brilliantly lit room inside the temple, in which he believed he would meet "all those people to whom I belong in reality. There I would meet the people who knew the answer to my question about what had been before and what would come after."[432] According to Susskind, reality is ultimately located at the cosmic horizon, from which the holographic illusion of the interior universe is projected. If his theory is true, the people to whom Jung felt that he belonged "in reality" inside the illuminated room in the back of the black rock temple would have to somehow exist simultaneously at the cosmic horizon. However, before Jung could enter the temple and learn about his entire chain of existence stretching into the infinite past and future—of which his earthly biography appeared to be one isolated link—he was retrieved by the "primal form" of his doctor, who floated up from Europe, having been "delegated by the earth to deliver a message to me, to tell me that there was a protest against my going away. I had no right to leave the earth and must return."[433] Immediately after the encounter with Dr. H., Jung's near-death experience ended.

While convalescing in his hospital bed, Jung felt severely depressed by the realization that:

> Now I must return to the "box system" again. For it seemed to me as if behind the horizon of the cosmos a three-dimensional world had been artificially built up, in which each person sat by himself in a little box. . . . I had been so glad to shed it all, and now it had come about that I—along

with everyone else—would again be hung up in a box by a thread.[434]

It does not take any stretch of the imagination to see the succinct correlation between Jung's NDE account of the threads stretching from each little box of three-dimensional space to the illusion-producing horizon of the cosmos and Susskind's holographic string theory. The implication of that precise parallel is that Psyche = Singularity, which is present at each point of the cosmic horizon. In contrast to the gloomy realization of his cosmic imprisonment in the box system of the three-dimensional world that Jung felt each day after his NDE, each night for the next three weeks he fell into a pattern of sleeping until midnight, then waking into an ecstatic trance for about an hour before falling asleep again: "I felt as though I were floating in space, as though I were safe in the womb of the universe—in a tremendous void, but filled with the highest possible feeling of happiness."[435] As discussed above, Alexander uses similar words to describe his blissful NDE encounter with God as the enveloping Mother of the cosmos.[436] And just as Jung's vision of the cosmic womb was initially opened to him by the black Hindu in the black rock temple, so too was Alexander's vision of God—whom he identified with the syllable Om—mediated by the black Orb, which could indicate that the black rock temple and the black Orb are both black holes perceived differently by different psyches.

It seems as if Jung's initial encounter with the black Hindu gave him repeated access to the eternal horizon of the cosmos for about an hour after midnight each night for the next three weeks, though the blissful visions were followed each dawn by the depressing return of what Jung calls "the gray world with its boxes! . . . Although my belief in the world returned to me, I have never since entirely freed myself of the impression that this life is a segment of existence which is enacted in a three-dimensional boxlike universe especially set up for it."[437] As after his initial heart attack, each morning after his nightly visions, Jung bemoaned his plight as a prisoner in the three-dimensional boxlike illusion, artificially created behind, and projected in from, the cosmic horizon. That belief lived with him to the day he died. Jung's realization that three-dimensional space is a "boxlike" illusion hung up to the cosmic horizon by threads is structurally identical with Susskind's holographic cosmos, and it is the continuous thread that weaves Jung's various near-death-experience-related visions together.

In light of Susskind's work, and recalling Robert Bruce Ware's interpretation of Leibnitz's principle of the identity of indiscernibles, the black rock temple Jung encountered during his NDE appears to be functionally equivalent to a black hole, while the event horizon and singularity of all black holes are identical to the singularity and cosmic horizon of the inside-out black hole universe. Though black holes appear in different parts of space and at different periods of time, and though each black hole appears to be different from the universe in which it is situated, black holes and the universe as a whole cannot be distinguished from each other based on spatio-temporal differences because each of them stands outside of space-time by virtue of being its origin and end: a perfect point encompassed by a perfect sphere where all of space-time is holographically conserved. In other words, the space-timeless interior of each black hole is identical to the space-timeless horizon of all of them, including the cosmic horizon of our inside-out black hole universe. This indicates that the people Jung felt he belonged to "in reality" inside the black rock temple would also have to exist in the true reality of the cosmic horizon, from which the boxlike illusion of three-dimensional space is projected by threads. It is as if the black rock temple, as a black hole, offered Jung a window to the cosmic horizon. Indeed, if the temple Jung encountered one thousand miles above Earth was his psychic interpretation of a black hole, it would explain several crucial aspects of his near-death experience.

As mentioned above, the painful feeling of having his earthly biography stripped away from him as he approached the temple, as well as the nearly irresistible attraction he subsequently felt for the people in the illuminated room in the temple, would both be accounted for by the tremendous gravitational pull associated with an event horizon (a point of no return). One problem with this hypothesis is that light cannot escape from inside a black hole, while Jung saw light radiating out of the temple. One possible solution to this problem is to correlate the light Jung saw coming out of the temple with Hawking radiation, which is produced when the antiphoton of a virtual pair of particles emerges from the quantum vacuum just inside the event horizon of a black hole, allowing the photon, which emerges just outside, to carry bits of information conserved on the holographic event horizon back out into the universe.

Another possible solution is to correlate the light apparently coming out of the black rock temple with the relativistic effect of gravitational lensing near the event horizon of a black hole. As discussed earlier, general relativity predicts that someone hovering just above and looking away from the event horizon would see the entire temporal evolution of the universe condensed into a single point at the end of a dark tunnel, which is equivalent to the singularity conserved at each point of the cosmic horizon. However, that correlation seems less plausible because Jung did not mention a tunnel experience, and he was not looking away from the black hole. Nevertheless, he did see the black Hindu sitting inside the temple, who can be equated with the omnicentric singularity, and also perhaps with Jung's concept of the Self.

Immediately after Jung's cosmic insight mediated by the black Hindu, the personified planet Earth called him back with an urgent demand via the delegate of Dr. H., whose primal form floated up to Jung from the direction of Europe. It was as if, having had the universal vision of the fundamental strings stretching out to the eternal horizon, Jung was duty bound to describe it to people back on Earth, as if to stave off some impending, planetary emergency. However, it seemed to Jung that the price which had to be paid for that delegated message was the mortal life of Dr. H., who took to his death bed, Jung noticed, on the very day Jung rose from his, April 4, 1944.[438] The gravity of that life and death synchronicity, combined with the series of four fours in that date   04-04-44—indicated to

Jung a symbolic, archetypal completeness to the whole experience for, as Jung explains: "The necessary statement of the number four, therefore, is that, among other things, it is an apex and simultaneously the end of a preceding ascent."[439] Earth's urgent plea to Jung in the middle of the universal vision could perhaps be meaningfully related to the fact that, the following year, Oppenheimer—who first mathematically described how a star would burn through its nuclear fuel to collapse into a "singularity" on the first day of WWII[440]—quoted two verses from the Bhagavad-gita, describing the universal form of the ultimate black Hindu, Krishna, to christen the first atomic explosion (at the Trinity site in New Mexico), and thus the birth of the age with the potential for the annihilation of every creature on the face of Earth.

Concluding this chapter, and preparing for the next, according to Jung, whenever an individual, or society as a whole, is confronted with seemingly insurmountable crises, like the threat of nuclear war-induced mass extinctions, the archetype of the Self compensates us with mandala images.[441] The year before Earth first entered the prolonged near-death experience presented by the continuing threat of nuclear war, Jung became one with the spherical mandala of the cosmos during his own NDE, at the end of which, it seemed to Jung, Earth called him back, as if to fulfill some duty that he had no right to abandon. The precise correlations between Jung's NDE account and Susskind's string theory of the holographic horizon of the cosmos, and the equally succinct correlations between NDE and relativistic tunnel-vision descriptions, provide a bottomless well of compensatory insight to people confronted with the constant possibility of personal and planetary death. These correlations imply that we are all timelessly one with every living being from the past, present, and future of our planet at the outer edge of Earth's atmosphere, and that we are ultimately one with the entire expanse of space-time at the cosmic horizon. In other words, the parallels between NDE accounts and twentieth-century physics indicate that the end of our embodied lives in space-time entails a return to the origin of space-time (the gravitational singularity of the Big Bang), which is reminiscent of the proclamation of Christ at his return in the *end times*, as prophesied in the final book of the Bible, the Apocalypse, as follows: "I am the Alpha and Omega; the beginning and the end, saith the Lord God, who is, and who was, and who is to come, the Almighty."[442] Similarly, in the Bhagavad-gita, Krishna proclaims: "I am the Self, O Gudakesha, seated in the hearts of all creatures. I am the beginning, the middle and the end of all beings."[443] Krishna and Christ have all of the characteristics of what Jung and Pauli call the *unus mundus*, the ultimate archetype of the Self, the psychic mandala images of which are perfectly mirrored by the mandala-model of our inside-out black hole universe—the omnicentric singularity and holographic horizon of the cosmos.

CHAPTER 6
BLACK HOLE AS UNIVERSAL MANDALA

Empirical observation usually means receiving physical impressions from outward objects through at least one of our five bodily sense organs, with which we see, hear, feel, taste, and smell. However, Jung expands the category of empirical observation to include the psychic images and scenarios we experience vividly in our dreams and spontaneous fantasies, despite their lacking the capacity for mutual verification: no one else can see our dreams or reveries. Nevertheless, we can all agree that we do each privately "sense" things in our dreams, as if we were actually experiencing a concrete world of bodily forms with our bodily sense organs.

Jung theorized that the same basic types of psychic symbols and scenarios spontaneously emerge in the conscious minds of people all around the world, throughout all recorded time, because they are rooted in timeless archetypes in our collective unconscious. These perennial images and situations can be inwardly witnessed by each of us, and can be even more widely surveyed in the global gallery of religions, philosophies, art forms, and sciences. Gathering this vast historical archive of what he defined as empirical evidence, Jung theorized that mandalas are the empirically observable psychic images of the unperceivable archetype of the Self.

According to Jung and Pauli, the archetype of the Self—also known as *unus mundus*, God, and the One—is the ultimate archetype from which all other archetypes emerge and toward which they converge. Its unlimited energy is fueled by the tension between all of the archetypal pairs of opposites radiating from and returning to it.[444] After years of psychoanalyzing himself and others, Jung realized that psychic mandala images spontaneously emerge from the collective unconscious archetype of the Self during dreams and fantasies to compensate an ego that is being painfully pulled between opposing demands.[445] In *Memories, Dreams, Reflections*, near the end of his life, Jung writes: "I knew that in finding the mandala as an expression of the self I had attained what was for me the ultimate. Perhaps someone else knows more, but not I."[446] If there is a mirror-symmetry between the laws of psychology and the laws of physics, as Jung and Pauli theorized, then the empirically observable mandala images that emerge in the psyche from the Self must have some empirically observable counterparts in the cosmos. This chapter discusses the hypothesis that the empirically observable gravitational effects of invisible black holes—including the inside-out black hole universe— are the cosmic correlates of psychic mandala images. This proposed correlation is especially clear in Jung's description of Tantric mandalas.

Jung explains that "the Sanskrit word *mandala* means 'circle.' It is the Indian term for the circles drawn in religious rituals."[447] In the Tantric school of Hindu thought the god Shiva as world-creator is usually depicted in the center of mandalas. Each part of Jung's description of Tantric mandalas below is similar to the cosmic mandala formed by the singularity at the Big Bang:

> Shiva, according to Tantric doctrine, is the One Existent, the Timeless in its perfect state. Creation begins when this unextended point—known as *Shiva-bindu*—appears in the eternal embrace of its feminine side, the Shakti. . . . From Shakti comes Maya, the building material of all individual things. . . . Creation therefore begins with an act of division of the opposites that are united in the deity. From their

160

splitting arises, in a gigantic explosion of energy, the multiplicity of the world.[448]

Jung's description of the *Shiva-bindu* as an "unextended point" from which all energy emerges in a gigantic explosion resembles the singularity of the Big Bang, and recalls Jung's Leap Day letter from 1952, culminating with his equation, "Psyche=highest intensity in the smallest space."[449] If we combine Jung's description of Tantric mandalas with the logic of his Leap Day letter, then the *Shiva-bindu* can be understood as a timeless, infinitely dense, unextended point, which is equivalent to the psyche and the singularity, which, like the *Shiva-bindu*, splits from the building material of all individual things (space-time/Maya) in a "gigantic explosion of energy" at the ongoing Big Bang.

Continuing in the same passage about Tantric mandalas, Jung provides a check-list of their typical attributes, which describes a kind of map of the concentric structure of the Self archetype expanding out in every direction from a central point symbolizing consciousness, through the personal unconscious to the indefinitely deep boundary of the collective unconscious. I will analyze each sentence of this crucial passage below:

> There are innumerable variants of the motif shown here, but they are all based on the squaring of the circle. Their basic motif is the premonition of a centre of personality, a kind of central point within the psyche, to which everything is related, by which everything is arranged, and which is itself a source of energy. The energy of the central point is manifested in the almost irresistible compulsion and urge to *become what one is*. . . . The centre is not felt or thought of as the ego but, if one may so express it, as the self. Although the centre is represented by the innermost point, it is surrounded by a periphery containing everything that belongs to the self—the paired opposites that make up the total personality. This totality comprises consciousness first

of all, then the personal unconscious, and finally an indefinitely large segment of the collective unconscious whose archetypes are common to all mankind.[450]

If Psyche = Singularity, then the almost irresistible tidal flow of space-time contracting toward the singularity of a black hole, or expanding toward the singularity at each point of the cosmic horizon, correlates to Jung's claim that "the energy of the central point is manifested in the almost irresistible compulsion and urge to *become what one is.*" Everything in the universe emerges from the singularity at the Big Bang, the central point "to which everything is related, by which everything is arranged, and which is itself a source of energy." Most importantly for a comparison with Susskind's theory, like the central point of a mandala representing the Self, so too is the singularity "surrounded by a periphery containing everything that belongs to" it: the holographic horizon of the cosmos toward which all space-time is expanding, at each point of which every bit of information describing each point of space-time is conserved, and from which, finally, they are all projected by threads back inward as the holographic movie of three-dimensional space.

The totality of the archetype of the Self includes the central point of consciousness first of all, which can be equated with the central singularity, then the personal unconscious, which can be equated with the holographic illusion of the interior volume of the cosmos that is simultaneously expanding toward and echoing back from the cosmic horizon, which, finally, Jung calls "the periphery that contains everything that belongs to the self," and which he furthermore equates with "an indefinitely large segment of the collective unconscious." Evidence and explanations for these correlations come from near-death experience accounts.

Lemaître was the first person to reason that, according to Einstein's general theory of relativity, the universe is expanding, which indicates two things: the universe may have been contracted in a single point at some point in the distant past; and the farther we look out in space, the farther we look back in time. During a near-death experience, people typically recall their individual ego-consciousness (which necessarily sees itself as the center of an expanding universe) rising out of its material body into outer space, through which it accelerates at an exponential rate, while reliving each instant of its earthly life in a vivid flash of detail, which indicates that the interior volume of expanding space-time is a kind of unconscious memory bank for our personal biographies.[451]

Eventually psyches feel themselves humming along so swiftly through space and backward through time that they perceive exactly what special relativity predicts people would see if they could travel at almost the speed of light. All of space and time would appear to be condensed in an infinitely bright point of light at the end of a dark tunnel, which correlates to the Big Bang radiating back from each point of the holographic horizon of the cosmos. This horizon is equivalent to the collective unconscious, as opposed to the personal unconscious, in as much as the past, present, and future of the entire cosmos are conserved at each point of the cosmic horizon, from which they glow back inward as the three-dimensional holographic movie of universal history. Jung equated the periphery of the mandala of the self with "the paired opposites that make up the total personality," which refer to the archetypes, each of which is united with its opposite in the central point and surrounding periphery of the cosmos.

The Self Mandala as a Complementary Union of All Archetypal Pairs of Opposites

In his essay "The Religious and Psychological Problem of Alchemy," Jung writes: "The self is a union of opposites *par excellence*."[452] According to Jung, each archetype is connected to an opposing archetype in such a way that all psychic *and* physical energy is produced by the tension between those fundamental polarities.[453] If Psyche = Singularity, then all of the archetypal pairs of opposites that manifest in the realm of space-time are united in the singularity, which exists at the center and at each point of the surrounding sphere of the cosmos. Jung also states that "the self is by definition the centre and the circumference of the conscious and unconscious systems."[454] Each pair of archetypal opposites can be classified as either psychological (e.g., happy-sad, excited-bored) or physical (e.g., up-down, hot-cold). By that reasoning, all archetypal pairs of opposites are contained conceptually in the overall opposition between psyche and cosmos, which means that the Self, defined as a union of all opposites, can be summarized by the equation Psyche = Singularity. This equation unfolds into the more complex equation of two opposing pairs of archetypal opposites: Conscious-Unconscious = Singularity-Horizon. Thus, it seems consistent with Jung's reasoning about the symbolic meaning of mandalas to equate the circumference of the cosmos with the archetypal source of the unconscious system of the Self, and the center of the cosmos with the archetypal source of the conscious system of the Self. In other words, the supreme archetype of wholeness, which involves the union of all archetypal pairs of opposites, can be expressed by equating the two opposite but complementary poles of the cosmos (singularity-horizon) with the two opposite but complementary poles of the psyche (conscious-unconscious), resulting in the following equation: Self = Conscious-Unconscious = Singularity-Horizon.

In a footnote in *On the Nature of the Psyche*, Jung quotes Pauli, who writes: "The physicist would expect a psychological correspondence at this point, because the epistemological situation with regard to the concepts 'conscious' and 'unconscious' seems to offer a pretty close analogy to the undermentioned 'complementarity' situation in physics."[455] Jung and Pauli compare the complementarity of the conscious and unconscious systems of the psyche to the complementarity of the particle and wave duality of the quantum world revealed by the two-slit experiment. If we shoot quantum particles such as electrons or photons through two narrow slits in a wall that is placed in front of a detector screen, and set up a measuring device to observe which slit a quantum particle goes through, it behaves just like a normal particle passing through either one or the other slit, after which it hits the detector screen directly behind that slit, like a bullet would have done, thereby creating two narrow bands on the detector screen. However, if we do not observe which slit the particle goes through, it apparently goes through both slits like a wave, creating two new waves radiating forward from each slit, which interfere with each other before collapsing at some specific point on the detector screen that is not necessarily in line with either slit. The detector screen always detects single particle hits, whether the particles are observed as they pass through the two slits or not, though when the particles are not observed passing through the slits, the accumulating particle hits on the detector screen gradually reveal the same rippling interference pattern that a single wave would have caused had it gone through both slits at once. This experiment reveals that, at the quantum level, matter behaves in two mutually exclusive but complementary ways: as particles when it is observed, and as waves when it is not observed.

One way to think about the parallel between particle-wave and conscious-unconscious complementarity is to think of an idea, such as the number 3, and then think of another number, such as 7. When we think of 7, 3 disappears, though we can instantly draw 3 back up from the unconscious by thinking about it, at which point 7 sinks back into the unconsciousness, where it presumably merges with all other potential ideas about which we are not currently thinking. Ideas in our mind act like particular concepts when we observe them, though they merge into some unconscious memory bank when we stop thinking about them, like a drop of water falling back into the ocean. On a wider scale, to the degree that we consciously observe our continuous stream of thoughts and actions we tend to act like individual, more-or-less morally autonomous egos (particles), though to the degree that we do not monitor ourselves, we tend to get carried away on fantasy streams of collective unconscious, archetypal imagery and corresponding patterns of instinctual behavior. The transformation of a morally autonomous, conscious ego into an unleashed automaton of the unconscious is most prominent when we dream, or when we enter a dream-like state through intoxication. If

Jung and Pauli were correct about the parallels between the conscious-unconscious complementarity of the mind and the particle-wave complementarity of matter, then it is reasonable to suspect that there might also be parallels with Susskind's twin concepts of black hole complementarity and cosmic complementarity.

According to Susskind, someone traveling freely past the event horizon of a black hole or the cosmic horizon of our universe will notice nothing unusual at that terminal boundary, though from the perspective of someone watching from the proper distance (which is roughly fifteen billion light-years for the cosmic horizon), the rapidly vibrating strings constituting the body of the person approaching the infinitely hot horizon will appear to slow down, stretch out, and smear all around the two-dimensional surface of the spherical boundary of space-time (which is like a holographic film), from which the scrambled bits of information will radiate back into the observable universe with either the Hawking radiation of an event horizon or the cosmic microwave background radiation of the cosmic horizon.[456] Responding to skeptics who disregard theories about the empirically unobservable realm beyond the cosmic horizon, Susskind writes: "Perhaps we should simply accept worlds beyond the horizon in the same way that we accept that other people have an impenetrable interior life."[457] Susskind directly compares unobservable universes beyond the cosmic horizon of our own universe to the interior life of other human beings, thereby relating the cosmic horizon to the psychic horizon which separates our inner thoughts from the outer world, which harmonizes with Jung and Pauli's theory that the laws of physics mirror the laws of psychology. If the cosmic horizon Susskind describes is equivalent to the collective unconscious mind Jung describes, then the interior of the universe, consisting of matter interacting in three-dimensional space and linear time, is a projection from the eternal archetypes of the collective unconscious, all of which (including the archetypes of space and time) are interwoven with each other at each point of the universal mandala formed by the central singularity and holographic horizon.[458]

If Psyche = Singularity, then the psychological mandala formed by the union of the conscious and unconscious systems in the Self archetype is mirrored by the cosmic mandala formed by the central singularity and surrounding horizon of the cosmos (which contains the singularity at each point), so that consciousness and the unconscious are interchangeable terms depending on the relative positions of the observers, as are the central singularity and cosmic horizon. The principle of complementarity applies to Susskind's theory of the cosmic horizon that separates our universe from all others, and to Jung's theory of the psychic horizon that separates the inner thoughts of each ego from all others, and from the collective unconscious. That parallel supports the possibility that the cosmic horizon and the psychic horizon separating each ego-consciousness from the collective unconscious are one and the same. In this view, the underlying identity of the Self and the Singularity (which also includes a horizon) can be inferred from the unintentional mirror-symmetry between Susskind's black hole string theory and Jung's theory of the mandala images of the Self. This hypothesis is entirely consistent with the line of reasoning Jung developed with Pauli.

Pauli, Individuation, and Mandala Dreams

The extent of Pauli's participation in the development of Jung's mandala theory is evidenced by Jung's essay "Individual Dream Symbolism in Relation to Alchemy," in which Jung develops his claim that mandalas are the psychic images of the Self by analyzing a selection of over a thousand of Pauli's carefully recorded dreams. To protect Pauli's scientific reputation, Jung describes him only as "a young man of excellent scientific education."[459] The essay opens with the following paragraph:

The symbols of the process of individuation that appear in dreams are images of an archetypal nature which depict the centralizing process or the production of a new centre of personality. . . . The self is not only the centre, but also the whole circumference which embraces both conscious and unconscious; it is the centre of this totality, just as the ego is the centre of consciousness.[460]

Jung goes on to explain that he is not currently examining the symbolic images that are concerned with all of the phases of the individuation process; his exclusive focus is on the psychic images that emerge in relation "to the new centre as it comes into consciousness. These images," he writes, "belong to a definite category which I call mandala symbolism."[461]

In the passage above Jung mentions three concepts: individuation; the self as the common center of the conscious ego and the unconscious; and psychic mandala symbolism. According to Jung, after a person adapts to at least the minimum level of collective social standards, he or she must then assume the new goal of individuation, or becoming a complete person by gradually differentiating the ego from the collective consciousness of society, and the collective unconscious of the species as a whole, after which the differentiated ego must reintegrate itself with those two opposing poles by recognizing its relationship to the archetype of the union of all opposites, the Self.[462] Individuation, in other words, is the life-long process of self-realization, toward which the Self guides the struggling ego with mandala imagery. The tortuously twisting road narrowing down to the point of individuation culminates with an ego's mortifying-yet-revitalizing realization that it is merely one among countless other absolute iotas of the ineffable Self, understood most generally as the common center and circumference of both cosmos and psyche.[463]

According to Jung, the ego is the center of the conscious field of the psyche, while the Self is the center of the whole psyche, the complete union of consciousness *and* the unconscious, so that the

Self is also the center of each ego.[464] In *Memories, Dreams, Reflections* Jung writes that "our basis is ego-consciousness, our world the field of light centered upon the focal point of the ego."[465] If the realm of ego-consciousness is the field of light centered on each ego (because each ego necessarily sees itself as the center away from which the universe is expanding in every direction at an exponential rate), then it is reasonable to suspect that the perimeter of ego-consciousness, the border between consciousness and the collective unconscious, is the outermost perimeter of the field of light, also known as the cosmic horizon, where according to Jung's near-death experience account, the past, present, and future of the three-dimensional universe, as well as each conscious experience of it, are eternally interwoven, and from which each cubic volume of space-time is projected by a thread. According to Jung, when our consciousness is confined to a material body, we are imprisoned in an illusory box of space-time that is hung up to and projected from the illusion-producing horizon by a thread. Jung says the Self is the common center of the unconscious and the conscious ego, the latter of which is the center of the field of light, but the Self is also the perimeter of the field of light, which is consistent with the equation of the Self with the central singularity and surrounding horizon of the cosmos, as well as with Jung's other definition of the Self as "the centre and the circumference of the conscious and unconscious systems."[466]

Each ego is the center of its own field of light, or, in other words, its own universe, because the perimeter of the universe is relative to the position of each observer. Each observer unavoidably perceives itself as the central point of the universe, away from which space-time is exponentially expanding in every direction, as if each of us is the singularity of the Big Bang.[467] This is what Susskind means when he writes: "It is as if we all live in our own private inside-out black hole."[468] In the same passage from *The Black Hole War* Susskind admits that we may never be able to observe the cosmic horizon, which is fifteen billion light-years away from each of us, or any of the information that exists beyond it. He then addresses the accusation that if something is "unobservable in principle—it is not part of science . . . it belongs to the realm of metaphysical speculation, together with astrology and spiritualism."[469] According to Jung, however, the cosmic horizon actually is empirically observable during an out-of-body, near-death experience.[470]

Despite the fact that Schrödinger, Heisenberg, and especially Pauli all embraced Jung's theory of the archetypes, Susskind would probably dismiss any correlation between his black hole theory and Jung's mandala theory as superstitious speculation. However, whereas the presence of the singularity inside black holes has been repeatedly inferred from its gravitational effects on visible matter, the most basic building blocks of Susskind's holographic string theory—fundamental strings, extra-dimensions of space, and parallel universes—have neither been directly observed through microscopes or telescopes, nor even been indirectly inferred to exist by any observation of their effects on measurable matter. It is only by the compelling force of its mathematical consistency, and by its ability to reconcile the opposition between general relativity and quantum mechanics that Susskind and 't Hooft's holographic string theory is respected by some of the other most respected physicists today, such as the late Stephen Hawking, Brian Greene, Edward Witten, and Michio Kaku. Thus, Susskind's presumed dismissal of an archetypal interpretation of his black hole theory on the basis that it is empirically ungrounded is not only inaccurate; it is belied by the fact that Susskind's own string theory is entirely bereft of the traditional, academically acceptable forms of empirical confirmation.

In the same way that Susskind's string theory of information conservation at the cosmic horizon unexpectedly corroborates, and is therefore corroborated by Jung's recollection of his near-death experience of the cosmic horizon, so too does it parallel Jung's related theory of the mandala images of the Self, thereby validating what Jung calls his ultimate theory, while providing Susskind's string theory with yet another avenue toward what it requires most: empirical confirmation.[471] If precise parallels between Susskind's holographic string theory of black holes and Jung's compensatory mandala theory are observable, the ultimate implication is that both theories are describing the organizing influence of the same underlying archetype of the Self.

Jung developed his mandala theory with the enthusiastic cooperation of Pauli, whose contributions to quantum physics Susskind repeatedly praises, calling him "one of history's greatest theoretical physicists,"[472] and giving him credit for inventing what Susskind describes as the mathematical basis of the Standard Model of quantum mechanics. The fact that Susskind so profoundly respects Pauli's foundational contributions to his own field of theoretical physics should incline him, and other skeptics, to accept Pauli and Jung's theory that the laws of physics and the laws of psychology mirror each other because both emerge from the same transcendental source, the *unus mundus*, which they also refer to as the archetype of the Self. After all, if there are mutually corroborating correlations between Jung's near-death experience, his theory of psychic mandala images of the Self, and Susskind's string theory, it would place Susskind squarely in the historical lineage of Pauli, whom he so clearly admires.

Black Hole as Magic Circle

In his essay "Individual Dream Symbolism," Jung writes: "'Mandala' (Sanskrit) means 'circle,' also 'magic circle.' Its symbolism includes— to mention only the most important forms—all concentrically arranged figures, round or square patterns with a centre, and radial or spherical arrangements."[473] A black hole is a geometrically perfect mandala, which unites two geometrically opposite shapes: the shape with the greatest volume per given surface area (a two-dimensional *sphere* at the horizon), and the shape with no volume at all (a *central point* of infinite gravity).

A black hole is not a physical thing. Moreover, Jung says that the Sanskrit word mandala means "magic circle," which is exactly what a black hole was originally called by many in the physics community. Eisenstaedt writes: "The expression 'magic circle,' due to [Sir Arthur]

Eddington, was used at the time by many authors, as well as 'limit circle' and 'singular sphere.'"[474] Eddington was the first astronomer to observationally verify Einstein's general theory of relativity by photographing the bent pathways of starlight caused by the gravity of the sun during the total solar eclipse of 1919. However, as Eisenstaeadt continues, "nobody understood the meaning of that sudden turnabout of space and time, and because nobody understood it, there was an impasse. The peculiar character of that strange place was for them reason to stop there, on this singular sphere—on this *magic sphere*, as Eddington called it—where light seemed to come to a stop."[475]

The event horizon of a black hole is a "magic sphere" in the sense that it converts space and time into one another. Astronomer Sara Slater explains: "Inside the event horizon time and space change places."[476] Like the movement of time outside of a black hole, space inside a black hole becomes a linear dimension inexorably flowing forward toward the central singularity. Similarly, like movement through space outside of a black hole, movement through time inside a black hole is both forward and backward, so that the past and future can be seen simultaneously. According to Slater, someone inside a black hole looking away from the center would see "two images of everything, one from T hours in the past, and one from T hours in the future."[477]

Like the "magic circle" of the event horizon, the central singularity is also magic, not only because it generates the horizon, but because it does so by miraculously uniting the opposite extremes of infinite gravity and infinitesimal size. Using string theory to reconcile the opposition between general relativity and quantum mechanics, Susskind and 't Hooft introduce three new "magic" principles of physics to describe black holes: the holographic principle, black hole complementarity, and cosmic complementarity. If Jung and Pauli were correct, each of these physical principles should have a psychological correlate, which it is the aim of this chapter to reveal.

The Pleroma as the Origin of Jung's Mandala Theory

Jung discovered that mandalas are spontaneously arising images of the Self when he was undergoing a mid-life crisis, which occurred throughout the duration of World War I. In *Memories, Dreams, Reflections* he explains that he felt pulled between two irreconcilable demands. On the one hand, Jung yearned to retreat from his professional responsibilities in order to finish forging his new psychology of the unconscious. On the other hand, as a family man, he desired the economic security provided by his teaching career at the University of Zurich, despite his doubts about the fundamental principles of the subject he taught, psychiatry.[478] He goes on to explain how a confrontation with a woman (an anima figure) during several active imagination sessions and, more importantly, the writing of the *Seven Sermons to the Dead* in 1916, led him to paint his first mandala later that same year, after which his theory that mandalas are the psychic images of the Self gradually developed.[479] 1916 is also the year Schwarzschild first discovered the concept of a black hole implied in Einstein's general theory of relativity.

In her prefatory comments to the English translation of *Septem Sermones ad Mortuos, Seven Sermons to the Dead*, Aniela Jaffe explains that, although he gave copies to friends, Jung never published *Seven Sermons* separately as a book for the general public. He later regretted the work "as a sin of his youth," and only agreed to have it published with his memoir "for the sake of honesty."[480] Nevertheless, this relatively youthful work contains the seeds of most of his mature ideas.[481]

In *Seven Sermons*, Jung plays the role of the Egyptian Gnostic Basilides preaching to the dead who have returned, theologically unsatisfied, from Jerusalem:

Hear Ye: I begin with nothing. . . . That which is endless and eternal has no qualities, because it has all qualities.

The Nothing, or fullness, is called by us the PLEROMA. . . .

> The Pleroma is the beginning and end of the created world. . . . The Pleroma is the nothingness which is everywhere complete and without end. . . . We, also, are the total Pleroma; for figuratively the Pleroma is an exceedingly small, hypothetical, even non-existent point within us, and also it is the limitless firmament of the cosmos about us.[482]

Like the Pleroma, so is the singularity "an exceedingly small, hypothetical, even non-existent point within us, and also it is the limitless firmament of the cosmos about us," the holographic horizon of the cosmos. Similarly, like Jung's Pleroma, so is the singularity "the beginning and end of the created world," which began from the singularity at the Big Bang and ends when it encounters the singularity inside black holes, or the singularity echoing back from each point of the spherical horizon of the cosmos. By that same reasoning, the realm of the created world (which Jung calls creatura) corresponds to what Susskind describes as the holographic illusion of three-dimensional space and forward-flowing linear time, each cubic volume of which is projected inward from the eternal horizon of the cosmos by infinitely elastic, fundamental strings of energy, which Jung seems to have encountered during his NDE. These correspondences seem to suggest that the Pleroma, which manifests as the cosmic mandala formed by the central-most point (singularity) and the surrounding firmament (cosmic horizon), is therefore synonymous with the Self. As Jung suggests, the naturally arising psychic image of the Self is the mandala, which means that the mandala is also the psychic image of the Pleroma.

According to Jung, all of the energy of the psychic and physical worlds arises from the tension between archetypal pairs of opposites, all of which are contained in the overarching opposition between mind and matter, which are, finally, united in the ultimate archetype of the Self.[483] The same quality of uniting all archetypal pairs of opposites is inherent in the Pleroma, as Jung describes it in the *Seven Sermons*: "The pairs of opposites are the qualities of the Pleroma: they are also in reality non-existent because they cancel each other out. Since we ourselves are the Pleroma, we also have these qualities present within us."[484] Like the Pleroma, so too does the mathematical model of the quantum vacuum indicate that it does and does not exist, in the sense that it consists of tightly packed, miniature black holes generated by the constant creation and annihilation of virtual particle-antiparticle pairs, which cancel each other out immediately after they come into existence. The energy created by the constant creation and annihilation of virtual particle-pairs is called dark energy, which fuels the expansion of space-time, just as the creation and annihilation of archetypal pairs of opposites is the energetic manifestation of the Pleroma.

The exception to the rule of virtual particle-pair annihilation takes place at the event horizons of black holes and the horizon of the cosmos, when an antiparticle appears from the vacuum just beyond the gravitational point of no return, and its virtual particle partner appears just in front, thereby saving it from an annihilating reunion with its antiparticle, while allowing it to carry the bits of information holographically stored on the horizon back into the observable universe, either in the form of Hawking radiation or cosmic microwave background radiation.[485] Susskind calls this concept the holographic principle, which correlates to Jung's concept of the creation of creatura from the Pleroma. Moreover, according to Leibnitz's principle of the identity of indiscernibles, each miniature black hole in the quantum vacuum is equivalent to the inside-out black hole formed by the cosmic horizon and the omnicentric singularity, which means that each point of the quantum vacuum also corresponds with the Pleroma, from which the three-dimensional illusion of creatura is projected.

Physicist and philosopher F. David Peat asserts this correspondence in *Synchronicity: The Bridge Between Mind and Matter*.[486] Although Peat does not mention miniature black holes in the quantum vacuum, in the following passage (which he concludes with a quote from the *Seven Sermons*), he does point out that each point of the infinitely energetic vacuum contains the whole universe, which is equivalent to saying that the vacuum is an omnicentric singularity: "Like the vacuum state of physics, the pleroma is at once both empty and perfectly full, and as in Bohm's implicate order, a universe is enfolded within each of its points, for 'Even in the smallest point is the PLEROMA endless.'"[487] Not only does the quantum vacuum house the creation and destruction of all of the fundamental polarities of the physical world (particle-antiparticle pairs), it produces an infinite sea of miniature black holes in the process, thereby redoubling the correlation between the vacuum and the mandala-manifesting archetype of wholeness through the union of opposites. As discussed above, Pim van Lommel also associates the quantum vacuum with Jung's concept of the collective unconscious.[488] Similarly, cosmologist Brian Swimme, after equating the vacuum with Bohm's concept of the implicate order, states that: "The universe is all one vast display that's flaring forth out of the unmanifest or the quantum vacuum. It's incessant vibration in and out. These are ancient spiritual ideas now resurfacing within science."[489]

In *On the Nature of the Psyche*, Jung applies the same concepts he used to describe the Pleroma in the *Seven Sermons* to Nicholas of Cusa's definition of God as the "*complexio oppositorum.*"[490] Using the analogy of positive and negative electricity, he suggests that the psychological opposites are also ultimately commensurable with each other: "Opposites are extreme qualities in any state, by virtue of which that state is perceived to be real, for they form a potential. The psyche is made up of processes whose energy springs from the equilibration of all kinds of opposites."[491] Even more fundamental than negative and positive electricity are the particle-antiparticle pairs of the quantum vacuum, the plenum of pure potentiality which is the source of all physical and, extrapolating from Jung, psychic energy. The quantum vacuum corresponds with Jung's concept of the Pleroma, which is equivalent to his concept of the archetype of the Self, which he also calls the God archetype understood as the *complexio oppositorum*, which can be equated with the complementary relationship between the singularity and the cosmic horizon.

In "Archetypes of the Collective Unconscious," Jung explains that every archetype has its opposite, and that all oppositions are included in the overall opposition between "spirit and matter," which "are very real opposites that are part of the energetic structure of the physical and of the psychic world, and without them no existence of any kind could be established." After stating that "there is no position without its negation," Jung concludes that "matter therefore would contain the seed of spirit and spirit the seed of matter."[492] Matter contains the seed of spirit and spirit the seed of matter if the gravitational singularity is the seed of both. Moreover, if Psyche = Singularity, then the singularity of the Big Bang forms the "energetic structure of the physical and of the psychic world" by expanding outward in every direction as the fabric of space-time, terminating at the holographic horizon manifesting all of the qualities of the cosmic mandala that Jung calls the Pleroma.

In Jung's 1952 essay *Answer to Job*, he describes the relation between Christ and the Pleroma: "Although the birth of Christ is an event that occurred but once in history, it has always existed in eternity."[493] He explains that, though difficult for the layperson to understand, the eternality of the birth of Christ is possible because "'time' is a relative concept and needs to be complemented by that of the 'simultaneous' existence, in the Bardo or pleroma, of all historical processes."[494] Though he does not mention it, Jung had first-hand experience of this simultaneity of all historical processes in the Pleroma during his near-death experience. He goes on to explain that, "when Yahweh created the world from his *prima materia*, the 'Void,' he could not help breathing his own mystery into the Creation which is himself in every part, as every reasonable theology has long been convinced."[495] The Void mentioned by Jung, God's *prima materia*, fulfills the same function as the quantum vacuum in Susskind's cosmology: the breath of Yahweh is similar to the expansion of space-time caused by the creation and destruction of particle-antiparticle pairs (dark energy), while the presence of the singularity in every point of the infinitely dense vacuum is similar to the concept of God's presence in every part of his Creation, from which, Jung says, "comes the belief that it is possible to know God from his Creation."[496] Following Jung and Pauli, I suggest that it is possible to know the God archetype (the Self) by studying the mirror-symmetry between "every reasonable theology" of the past and Susskind's string theory.

Continuing the passage under analysis, Jung qualifies his previous claim that Yahweh could not help breathing his own mystery into his Creation: "When I say that he could not help doing this, I do not imply any limitation of his omnipotence; on the contrary, it is an acknowledgement that all possibilities are contained in him."[497] Jung concludes by reaffirming that God is all Creation, which reaches to the "remotest stellar galaxies," which directly links the God archetype, or Pleroma, with the cosmic horizon, where the most distant galaxies appear to be receding from us at the speed of light.[498] According to Jung's interpretation of the Biblical God, he is the omnipotent source of Creation, in each point of which he is fully present in such a way that he contains all possibilities. That definition of God is indistinguishable from the definition of the singularity that is present in each point of the quantum vacuum, which is, from one perspective, an infinite sea of waves of probability containing all possible particle-antiparticle pairs, while, from another perspective it is a boundless plenum of tightly-packed, Planck-length black holes, some of which expand into an infinite, bubbling cloud of parallel universes, throughout which, incredibly, all possible historical scenarios necessarily unfold.[499]

Considering Jung's claim that "every reasonable theology" has long perceived the basic understanding of God's omnipotent omnipresence, his specific description of the relationship between the Pleroma and the historical appearance of Christ is basically the same as St. Augustine's various descriptions of Christ's eternal relationship to the supercelestial sphere that Augustine called the *heaven of heaven*, as well as the Spouse of God, the City of God, and Jerusalem, as discussed earlier. Augustine's Christian cosmology is furthermore based on Plato's archetypal cosmology. The image of Yahweh breathing his own mystery into the Void is also very similar to the

Vaishnava branch of Hinduism, the cosmology of which features the three nested Purusha Avatars of Vishnu. Finally, the "Void" mentioned by Jung appears to correlate with the Hindu concept of the impersonal Brahman effulgence (the complementary opposite of the individual Atman).

If we combine Jung's various descriptions of the Pleroma with his NDE account we see an unmistakable resemblance to Susskind's description of the singularity and surrounding horizon of the cosmos. From *Seven Sermons* in 1916 to *Answer to Job* in 1952 and beyond, Jung maintained a lifelong meditation on the Gnostic concept of the Pleroma. In 1952, the year Jung published his first version of *Answer to Job*, he also penned his Leap Day equation, "Psyche=highest intensity in the smallest space."[500] Thus, Jung's postulation of the equation that can be translated as Psyche = Singularity coincided with a return to his long-running meditation on the Pleroma, which perhaps indicates a connection in his mind between the two concepts. If there is an infinite amount of energy at each point of the quantum vacuum, then each point of the vacuum is by definition a singularity in the center of a black hole, which means that the quantum vacuum can be defined as a boiling sea of geometrically perfect mandalas, which are the images that Jung noticed emerging from the archetype of the Self, also known as the *unus mundus*, the One, the God archetype, and the Pleroma.

Immediately after writing the *Seven Sermons* in 1916, Jung painted his first mandala, two years after which he developed his key psychological theory—which he calls the "ultimate" discovery of his life—that the mandala is the psychic image of the Self.[501] As he explains in *Memories, Dreams, Reflections*: "It became increasingly plain to me that the mandala is the center. It is the exponent of all paths. It is the path to the center, to individuation. . . . There is no linear evolution, there is only a circumambulation of the Self."[502] Although he denies linear evolution in the passage above, in other essays Jung specifically mentions a "spiraling" path of development toward the Self.[503] The figure of the spiral combines linear evolution with an endless circling of the Self, which seems to be a more appropriate process of development for the archetype of the union of all opposites.

Jung's Method of Identifying Mandalas as Images of the Self

In *Memories, Dreams, Reflections*, Jung explains that his theory of mandalas as psychic images of the Self needed to be verified by some "historical prefiguration."[504] In *On the Nature of the Psyche*, Jung describes the same need for comparative historical analysis.[505] He posits a three-stage method by which to demonstrate that a mental concept or image is actually emerging into our consciousness from a collective unconscious archetype. First, we perceive the image or idea spontaneously emerge into our own consciousness, especially during dreams and fantasies. Then we confirm that our contemporaries have the same spontaneous experiences. Finally, we demonstrate that the collectively recurring psychic images or ideas of our contemporaries are present in the historical records of people from other epochs and places. Jung cites the mandala as the foremost example of a psychic image that has met all three criteria required to be categorized as a genuine archetypal image. He also makes a point of specifically rejecting accusations that his theory about the psychic mandala image is an artificial imposition of Indian or Chinese philosophy into what is assumed to be a nondenominational, collective unconscious. He responds by saying that the mandala is in fact a genuine psychic image of the archetype of the Self, the central and most primary ordering principle of the cosmos *and* the psyche, which "introspective" people in every age and culture inevitably discover on their own, evidenced by the fact that mandalas repeatedly crop up as the symbol of the ultimate ordering principle in the literature and art of most civilizations, not only ancient India and China, but Egypt, Greece, and Medieval Europe, to name only a few. We have already seen two examples of the mandala symbol in ancient India: the Vaishnava cosmology of bubble universes, each with an *akashic* periphery and a Vishnu avatar in the center; and the Tantric mandala paintings featuring the Shiva-bindu in the center. To substantiate Jung's claim that mandala images do indeed emerge around the central-most concept of the ultimate union of all opposites as it manifests in the philosophies and religions of nearly every nation and age, we move now to examples from ancient China.

Cosmological Mandalas in Confucian and Taoist Texts

In *The Doctrine of the Mean*, the most famous text attributed to Confucius, he defines the ultimate virtue of *cheng*, which is usually translated as "sincerity," but is also sometimes translated as "wholeness," and seems to be synonymous with Jung's concept of individuation, the psychological process that leads the ego to a reunion with the ultimate archetype of wholeness, the Self. Sincerity, as Confucius describes it, is not only the path to the Self, it has all of the qualities of Jung's concept of the Self *and* Susskind's concept of the Big Bang singularity that is present at each point of the cosmic horizon.

> Sincerity is that whereby self-completion is effected, and its way is that by which man must direct himself. Sincerity is the end and beginning of things . . . the most excellent thing. . . . With this quality he [the sincere man] completes other men and things also. . . . This is the way by which a union is effected of the external and internal. . . . Hence to entire sincerity there belongs ceaselessness. Not ceasing, it continues long. Continuing long, it evidences itself. Evidencing itself, it reaches far. Reaching far, it becomes large and substantial. Large and substantial, it becomes high and brilliant. . . . The Heaven now before us is only this bright shining spot; but when viewed in its inexhaustible extent, the sun, moon, stars, and constellations of the

zodiac, are suspended in it, and all things are overspread by it. . . . Therefore, the superior man honors his virtuous nature, and maintains constant inquiry and study, seeking to carry it out to its breadth and greatness, so as to omit none of the more exquisite and minute points which it embraces, and to raise it to its greatest height and brilliancy, so as to pursue the course of the Mean.[506]

To realize how one ceaseless point of light can reach far out in space to become the encompassing sphere of the constellations of the zodiac emanating from it is to gain the ultimate Confucian virtue of sincerity, which empowers a person to unite the internal and the external in such a way that promotes completion in one's self, others, and even nature.

In the previous chapter, we compared the typical near-death experience account of seeing a profoundly brilliant point of light at the end of the dark tunnel to the aberration effect predicted by special relativity, according to which someone traveling at almost exactly the speed of light would see all of the constellations of the zodiac condense into a single point of light at the end of a dark tunnel in the forward field of vision. The singularity is a single point in which all of the stars of the universe are condensed, which indicates that the sincere person Confucius describes perceives the universe from the same light-speed perspective people experience at the brink of death. In a way that is very similar to Confucius' description of the one bright shining spot that encompasses the zodiac, in Sermon VII of *Seven Sermons to the Dead* Jung describes the dead being taught that "man" is a gateway between the outer world of the gods and souls (the cosmic horizon) and the inner world (creatura), so that the dead have passed through man to "endless space, in the smallest or innermost infinity. At immeasurable distance standeth one single Star in the zenith. This is the one god of this one man. This is his world, his pleroma, his divinity. . . . Toward him goeth the long journey of the soul after death." [507] Confucius' concept of self-completion through sincerity is also equivalent to Jung's concept of individuation, the process of uniting the conscious mind with the unconscious archetype of the Self, the spontaneously emerging psychic image of which is a mandala. Finally, Confucius' advice that the virtuous ruler should meticulously study the brilliant point of light from which mind (the inner) and matter (the outer) emerge, and in which they are contained, is reminiscent of the curriculum Socrates prescribes for the philosopher-king in the *Republic*, culminating with an initially blinding vision of the ultimate idea of the Good.

From Confucius' key concept of sincerity we move to what Lao Tzu describes in the *Tao Te Ching* as the inherently unspeakable concept represented by the Chinese word Tao (pronounced Dao).[508] In the following passage notice the similarity between the Tao (referred to here as the "great" and the "original point") and the Big Bang mandala formed by the singularity and cosmic horizon: "Being great implies reaching out in space, reaching out in space implies far-reaching, far-reaching implies reversion to the original point."[509] The gravitational singularity from which the Big Bang continuously flares forth does indeed reach out in space as far as possible, all the way to the horizon of the cosmos, where the fabric of space-time is expanding at the speed of light in such a way that each point of that encompassing sphere reverts back into the original point of infinite density from which it exploded. According to Lao Tzu, when we see our identity with the Tao, understood as the original point into which far-reaching space reverts, then only do we embody the harmony of all pairs of opposites: "When the Mystic Virtue becomes clear, far-reaching, and things revert back (to their source) then and then only emerges the Grand Harmony."[510]

In accord with this Grand Harmony, near-death experience survivors typically recall their psyches rising out of their bodies, then traveling faster and faster out to the farthest reaches of space, back through the entire history of their lives, beyond the trauma of their own biological birth to the brilliant birth point of the cosmos itself, where every event from the past, present, and future of the universe is constantly occurring. That original point of light is often perceived as the point of no return at the end of a dark tunnel, which is what relativity theory predicts people would see if they could travel at close to light speed. What relativity theory does not predict, however, is the psychological experience of overwhelming love associated with that farthest and brightest point at the horizon of the cosmos, which inflicts many psyches who witness it with a burning conviction of their eternal union with everyone and everything that ever was or will be. It is as if the embodied psyche's miserly instinct of self-love abruptly expands to encompass the whole cosmos when a psyche rises out of the body and reunites with the original point at the outer limit of space. According to Lao Tzu, a sage ruler endowed with Mystic Virtue can tune all of the rancorous tones of discord down on Earth to the one Grand Harmony of the farthest sphere where all opposing pairs of perspectives are interwoven at each point.[511]

The second most famous Taoist text is known as *The Writings of Chuang Tzu*. In the following passage, Chuang Tzu explains how the Tao, as the union of all opposites, is able to harmonize opposing moral opinions (the parenthetical remarks are the translator's):

> This view is the same as that, and that view is the same as this. But that view involves both a right and a wrong; and this view involves also a right and a wrong:— are there indeed, or are there not the two views, that and this? They have not found their point of correspondency which is called the pivot of the Tao. As soon as one finds this pivot, he stands in the centre of the ring (of thought), where he can respond without end to the changing views;— without end to those affirming, and without end to those denying. Therefore I said, 'There is nothing like the proper light (of the mind).'[512]

If the "ring of thought" is equated with the cosmic horizon where near-death experience survivors claim to have become conscious of all of the information from the past, present, and future of the entire universe, then the singularity of the Big Bang is "the pivot of the

Tao," the center of the ring of thought where all archetypal pairs of opposites originate. The implication is that we can understand the mirror-symmetry that reveals how each side of a pair of opposites corresponds to the other side when we trace them both back to their source. For example, we can understand point-for-point correlations between the opposing paradigms of Susskind's physics and Jung's psychology when we see the identity of the first principle of each, which Susskind calls the singularity and which Jung calls the archetype of the Self. By realizing our identity with that central "point of correspondency" (which also exists at each point of its encompassing sphere), we automatically realize our union with all opposing philosophies unfolding through three-dimensional history on Earth, thereby enabling us to identify with and effectively answer questions from both sides of every issue.

In modern Europe, the Taoist idea that each opposing philosophical perspective contains and is therefore in some sense the same as its opposite was most famously expressed by Georg Wilhelm Friedrich Hegel (1770-1831). In fact, Hegel's theory of the union of opposites through a dialectical process of a thesis being contradicted by its antithesis, only to be united in a new synthesis, is directly related to his theory of gravity, which plainly foreshadows the black hole mandala predicted by Einstein's theory of gravity, as we shall see.

Hegel's Mandala of the Idea

In the following passage Hegel distinguishes between matter and spirit—the ultimate pair of polar opposites within which all other polarities are contained—by saying that matter seeks a center outside itself, while spirit seeks the center that *is* itself.

> Just as gravity is the substance of matter, so also can it be said that freedom is the substance of spirit. . . . Matter possesses gravity in so far as it is impelled to move towards a central point; it is essentially composite, and consists

185

entirely of discrete parts which all tend toward a centre; thus matter has no unity. . . . Spirit, on the other hand, is such that its centre is within itself; it too strives towards its centre, but it has its centre within itself. . . . Matter has its substance outside itself; spirit, on the other hand, is self-sufficient being, which is the same thing as freedom.[513]

If Psyche = Singularity, that would confirm Hegel's claim that spirit (psyche) strives toward the center that is itself (singularity), because the singularity is a point in which space-time is contracting into itself at an infinite speed.

From a Newtonian perspective (which is inaccurate at the scales of space-time described by relativity theory and quantum theory), every atom of matter is gravitationally pulled toward some central point outside itself. For example, according to Newton's theory, the atoms that make up an apple are pulled toward the center of the apple, which is pulled toward the center of the Earth, which is pulled toward the center of the solar system in the center of the Sun. However, interpreting Hegel's philosophy through the lens of general relativity tells us that matter and spirit are ultimately compelled toward the same center, the omnicentric singularity, in the sense that spirit *is* the singularity which is contracting into itself, while every particle of matter that is issuing forth in every direction from the singularity at the ongoing Big Bang is being constantly swept back toward the singularity at each point of the cosmic horizon by the exponentially accelerating expansion of space-time (which is the reverse scenario of being pulled by the contraction of space-time toward the singularity of a black hole).

Hegel says gravity is the substance of matter, while freedom is the substance of spirit, but if spirit is a point of infinite gravity, it would seem that when we intensify gravity, the material force of contraction, to an infinite degree it reverts into its opposite, freedom. In other words, although according to Hegel, gravity is the substance of matter, if we compress enough matter into a small enough space, it eventually collapses indefinitely into a point of zero volume and infinite density, at which point it qualifies as spirit, the substance of which is freedom.[514] This interpretation of Hegel agrees with Jung's Leap Day equation, "Psyche=highest intensity in the smallest space."[515] It also resonates with Jung's claim that, "mandala symbolism shows a marked tendency to concentrate all the archetypes on a common centre, comparable to the relationship of all conscious contents to the ego."[516]

Hegel refers to the ultimate source of matter and spirit as the Idea, which is also equivalent to the archetype Jung calls the Self: "The Idea is the central point, which is also the periphery, the source of light, which in all its expansion does not come without itself, but remains present and immanent within itself. Thus it is both the system of necessity and its own necessity, which also constitutes its freedom."[517] Robert Bruce Ware does an excellent job of explaining the correlations between Hegel's Idea in this passage and the omnicentric singularity described by general relativity and quantum mechanics.[518] Hegel's description of the Idea is indistinguishable from the singularity associated with the Big Bang, the central point and original source of light, which is contained within, and radiates back from each point of its periphery. Moreover, using the same language he applies to spirit, Hegel identifies the Idea with freedom, in the sense that it is the author of the universal system of necessity, and is thus free from all necessary actions save those of its own design: to be one's own enforcer is to be free.[519]

From the perspective of modern physics, which describes the system of necessary physical interactions in the universe, the four fundamental forces of nature (gravity, electromagnetism, strong nuclear, and weak nuclear) emerge from and are reunited in the singularity, which breaks the laws of physics. According to Hawking: "Both the Big Bang and black holes would contain singularities, places where space and time come to an end, and the laws of physics break down."[520] If the laws of physics do not apply to the singularity from which the forces of nature emerge, then the ubiquitous singularity obeys no law other than itself, and is in that sense totally free, just like Hegel's concept of spirit and the absolute Idea. Jung made a similar connection between freedom and his near-death experience of the cosmic horizon, which he contrasted to the three-dimensional, boxlike prison-cell of space-time projected from the horizon by a thread.[521] As with Hegel, so too with Jung do we find the idea that the essence of freedom is spiritual, and that it is associated specifically with the periphery of the material cosmos, which is understood to be the source and boundary of matter and its deterministic laws.

Given all of the evidence accumulated thus far, it seems reasonable to suggest that we can equate the singularity and its horizon with any archetypal concept we want (Sincerity, Freedom, Love), and also the opposite concepts, because it is the uniting source of *all* archetypes. The gravitational effects of black holes and the Big Bang universe form the physical correlates of the psychic mandala images emerging from the Self. By this reasoning, we should find parallels between the physics of the Big Bang theory and the philosophies of the previous manifestations of the same mandala-producing archetype. Confirming that prediction, Hegel uses the same mandala imagery of a central point of light expanding through spherical space only to revert into itself at the horizon that was used to describe the union of all opposites in ancient India, China, Greece, medieval Europe, and elsewhere. What separates Hegel from philosophers before him is that he adds the cosmological concept of gravity to his mandala imagery, making it that much easier to see the startling correlation with modern cosmology, which was born in 1854 from the mathematical mandala known as the Riemann sphere.

Riemann's Mathematical Mandala of the One

The mandala structure of the universe described by general relativity is conspicuously similar to the mandala structure of the mathematical framework Einstein used to develop his theory: the unit circle of the complex number plane, which expands to a point at infinity in what is known as the Riemann sphere, named after its discoverer, the mathematician Georg Friedrich Bernhard Riemann (1826-1866). Jung says that "the psyche of a people is only a somewhat more complex structure than the psyche of an individual."[522] If what happens in the individual psyche also happens in a collective psyche, then whenever an academic field of thought is pulled painfully between opposing principles, we should see mandala images emerging in the minds of people in that field to lead it toward a union of the opposing principles. There is no purer example of the mandala-manifesting tendency of the *unus mundus* than the unit circle, which mathematicians developed in the eighteenth and nineteenth centuries to reconcile "real" and "imaginary" numbers (square roots of negative numbers) on the complex number plane, from which twentieth-century physics was born. Pauli was especially enthralled with the power of the unit circle (which he called the "ring i") to provide a conceptual bridge between mind and matter.

To appreciate the significance of the unit circle as supporting evidence for Jung and Pauli's mandala theory, first we need to appreciate their more basic theory that numbers are the most fundamental common ground between psyche and matter. In *Pauli and Jung: The Meeting of Two Great Minds*, Paul Lindorff examines Jung's claim that the archetype of number is the most fundamental common ground between psyche and matter, which is consistent with Jung's ultimate claim that the *unus mundus*, also known as the One, is the ultimate archetype of unity through the union of opposites.[523] In particular, Jung notes that whole numbers, especially one through four, relate to both matter and psyche: to the former mathematically, to the latter symbolically. The most notable example of this theory is Jung's claim that the stages of the psychological process of individuation were intimated by the alchemists in the axiom of Maria: "The problem that runs like a red thread through the speculations of alchemists for fifteen hundred years thus repeats and solves itself, the so-called axiom of Maria the Jewess (or Copt): 'Out of the Third comes the One as the Fourth.'"[524]

Individuation culminates with an ego's realization of its relationship with the archetypal One, the Self, understood as the common center and circumference of both cosmos and psyche.[525] If the mathematical expression of the One mirrors its psychological expression, then we should expect the four-phased psychological process of individuation that leads an ego toward a realization of the union of all opposites in the mandala-projecting archetype of the One to be mirrored by some equivalent mathematical process. Pauli believed that the unit circle—formed by raising the square roots of -1 (denoted as i and $-i$) on the complex number plane through four successive powers (i, i^2, i^3, i^4; or, conversely, $-i$, $-i^2$, $-i^3$, $-i^4$)—is the most perfect mathematical expression of the One. To understand why, it helps to know the history of imaginary numbers.

In his 1930 classic, *Number: The Language of Science*, which Einstein admired, the University of Maryland mathematician Tobias Dantzig explains that the Indians are credited with inventing the number 0 and the concept of negative numbers in the first centuries after Christ.[526] The Italians are credited with inventing the square roots of negative numbers, which came to be called imaginary numbers, in the sixteenth century.[527] The problem, of course, is that when any number is multiplied by itself, be it negative or positive, the result will always be positive: 2 x 2 = 4, but so does -2 x -2. In other words, the square root of 4 is both 2 and -2. It is therefore impossible to find the square root of a negative number, unless we simply imagine we can. Dantzig explains that the ancient Hindu and Arab mathematicians had resisted the temptation "to write x = $\sqrt{-1}$ as a solution" to a particular equation, because they knew there was no way to concretely apply the concept of the square roots of negative numbers.[528] He goes on to say that "the glory of having discovered the *imaginary* goes to the Italians of the Renaissance. Cardan in 1545 was the first to dare to denote the meaningless by a symbol." The word "glory" seems appropriate in relation to the discovery of imaginary numbers, given that they provide the mathematical language required to model: the hypersphere, or Reimann sphere, upon which general relativity is based; and the fundamental wave-particle paradox of quantum mechanics. Dantzig admits that the square root of a negative number "was written with the reservation that it was *meaningless, sophisticated, impossible, fictitious, mystic, imaginary*. Yet, there is a great deal in a name, even if it be but a nickname or a term of abuse."[529] The √-1 was originally rejected with abuse, only to become the cornerstone of twentieth-century physics.

Later in his book Dantzig explains that, building on the work of Caspar Wessel and Jean-Robert Argand, in 1831 Carl Friedrich Gauss gave imaginary numbers a geometrical expression on the Cartesian number plane, formed by the perpendicular intersection of a vertical and a horizontal number line which meet at the common point, 0. Gauss replaced the vertical number line of positive (up) and negative (down) real numbers with the "imaginary" number line, the positive and negative square roots of negative numbers. According to Gauss' geometrical interpretation of imaginary numbers, multiplying 1 on the complex number plane by each of the four consecutive powers of the square root of -1 describes a circle (which came to be called the unit circle) consisting of four 90 degree counter-clockwise *rotations* around the axial point, 0. In other words, multiplying 1 times i, i^2, i^3, i^4 describes a circle rotating from 1 on the horizontal "real" number line straight up to i on the vertical imaginary number line, back down to -1 on the horizontal real number line, then straight down to –i on the imaginary number line, and ending, finally, all the way back up and around to 1. Multiplying 1 by –i raised by four consecutive powers ($-i$, $-i^2$, $-i^3$, $-i^4$) describes a circle rotating in the opposite direction. 0, the intersecting central point of the real and imaginary number lines, is the only number that is simultaneously "real" *and* "imaginary," while points on the circumference of the unit circle (except for the four cardinal points that are directly on the real or imaginary number lines) are called "complex," because they are described with a complex of numbers, one real, and one imaginary (thus we have the complex number plane).

Gauss furthermore described how to add, subtract, multiply, and divide complex numbers by tracing out lines connecting points on the complex plane. The process of adding and subtracting complex numbers involves connecting the two ends of two such lines to form a parallelogram (parallelogram law), while multiplying and dividing involves stretching or contracting two lines of a triangle (similar triangle law).

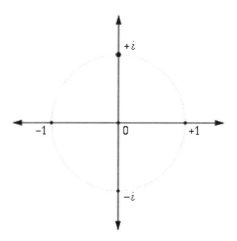

Figure 1 Unit Circle on the Complex Number Plane.[530]

The unit circle on the complex number plane is a geometrical expression of the number 1, which includes within itself the concept of its own negative, and the square roots of its negative. In line with Jung and Pauli's theory about the archetype of the One, the unit circle does indeed manifest as a geometrically perfect mandala that unifies the fundamental opposition between real and imaginary numbers, and it does progress through four-phases of development that fulfill the axiom of Maria, "Out of the Third comes the One as the Fourth."[531] From i^1 comes i^2, from i^2 comes i^3, from i^3 comes i^4 literally as the number 1. The fourfold squaring of the imaginary unit resulting in the unit circle also resembles the concept of "the squaring of the circle" that Jung identifies as a key attribute of mandalas.

Earlier we saw Jung comment on Tantric mandalas, which typically display a circle enclosed within a square. He explains that the many varieties of mandalas "are all based on the squaring of the circle," and that "their basic motif is the premonition of a centre of personality, a kind of central point within the psyche, to which everything is related, by which everything is arranged, and which is itself a source of energy."[532] This description of the central point of the mandala is very similar to the singularity of the Big Bang, while the process of squaring the circle is reminiscent of the unit circle which gave birth to the mathematics that describe the Big Bang. According to Jung:

> the squaring of the circle was a problem that greatly exercised medieval minds. It is a symbol of the *opus alchymicum*, since it breaks down the original chaotic unity into the four elements and then combines them again in a higher unity. Unity is represented by a circle and the four elements by a square. [533]

As discussed above, in Plato's *Timaeus* and the Hindu texts, the four elements—earth, water, fire, air—are seen as concentric spheres that merge in the higher unity of the fifth element, the ether sphere surrounding the universe, which Plato's Timaeus calls the "mother and receptacle of all created and visible and in any way sensible things . . . an invisible and formless being which receives all things and in some mysterious way partakes of the intelligible, and is most incomprehensible."[534] Considering that Jung calls Plato's *Timaeus* "the prime authority for Hermetic philosophy" in the medieval era,[535] it is reasonable to equate the circle of the mandala symbolizing the *opus alchymicum* with Plato's ether sphere, which finds a suitable mathematical expression in Susskind's model of the holographic horizon of the cosmos, which is based on Riemann's hypersphere (from which general relativity and quantum mechanics were born), which emerged, finally, from the unit circle.

In *Civilization in Transition*, Jung describes mandalas in a way that is especially reminiscent of the unit circle:

> Mandalas . . . usually appear in situations of psychic confusion and perplexity. The archetype thereby constellated represents a pattern of order which, like a

psychological 'view-finder' marked with a cross or circle divided into four, is superimposed on the psychic chaos so that each content falls into place and the weltering confusion is held together by the protective circle. . . . At the same time they are *yantras*, instruments with whose help the order is brought into being.[536]

Like a rifle scope, the unit circle on the complex plane is a circle divided into four sections by the perpendicular intersection of the imaginary number line and the real number line at the central point, 0, which form a protective circle with whose help the psychic chaos created by the discovery of imaginary numbers was brought to a higher level of order. There was, however, one major hole in Gauss' geometrical interpretation of imaginary numbers: the inability to divide complex numbers by 0, which causes one line of the representative triangle to stretch out to infinity, which has no representation on the complex plane.

Gauss served as Riemann's doctoral advisor at the University of Gottingen, awarding him a Ph.D. in mathematics for his 1854 lecture, "The Hypotheses Which Lie at the Foundation of Geometry," in which Riemann completed Gauss' work by explaining how it is possible to graphically represent the division of complex numbers by 0 by rolling the complex number plane into a sphere with the north pole representing a point at infinity.

The Riemann sphere derived from the unit circle on the complex number plane is not only the basic mathematical tool required to describe black holes and the Big Bang universe, it is also symbolically comparable to them: a central point that is both real and imaginary encompassed by a two-dimensional sphere that is one part real, and one part imaginary. The point at infinity represented by the north pole of the Riemann sphere furthermore resembles what special relativity predicts observers would see if they could travel through any direction of space at close to light speed, and what general relativity predicts observers inside a black hole would see by looking away from the central singularity: an all-embracing point of light at the end of a dark tunnel at the boundary of the universe, which is indeed what many people claim to see during near-death experiences.

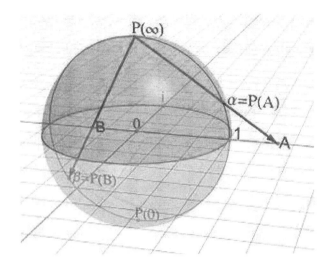

Figure 2 Riemann sphere B.[537]

Jung's theory that mandalas are the spontaneously emerging psychic images of the archetype of wholeness through the union of opposites (*unus mundus*, the Self, God, the One) is powerfully supported by the fact that the irreconcilability in the field of mathematics between real and imaginary numbers was finally resolved in the unit circle of the complex number plane, and the corresponding Riemann sphere. This mathematical object is not only a geometrically perfect mandala representing the number One, it also provides the mathematical formalism Einstein required to create the general theory of relativity that implies the reconciliation of opposites (infinite gravity and infinitesimal size, space and time, past and future) in the cosmic mandala of a black hole. In *Poetry of the Universe: A Mathematical Exploration of the Cosmos*, Robert Osserman (former chair of the Stanford Mathematics Department) says Riemann's 1854 Ph.D. defense is the moment that "we now see clearly in retrospect as marking the birth of modern cosmology."[538] Riemann's guiding purpose was to unite the mathematical descriptions of electricity, magnetism, light, and gravitation within one equation, which agrees with Jung's empirical observation that mandala images emerge in the psyche from the *unus mundus* with the purpose of unifying opposing forces. As Osserman notes, "the very notion that there might be a 'unified field theory' was so far ahead of its time that even a century later Einstein would be mocked for spending his latter years in a vain search for it."[539]

Referring to Reimann's lecture, in his book *Hyperspace*, Kaku writes: "On June 10, 1854, a new geometry was born."[540] In a way that strongly supports Jung's compensatory mandala theory, Kaku explains how Einstein encountered Riemann's mathematical mandala only after suffering through extreme exasperation while fruitlessly searching for the proper mathematical formalism for his theory that the force of gravity is actually caused by the curvature of the three-dimensional surface of four-dimensional space-time. From 1912 to 1915, Einstein frantically sought for a way to reconcile the conflict between Newton's theory of gravity (which implies that the gravitational force travels infinitely fast because it acts instantaneously between massive objects) and Maxwell's theory of the absolute speed limit of light. He pleaded to his mathematician friend Marcel Grossman for help: "Grossman, you must help me or else I'll go crazy."[541] It was then that Grossman "accidentally stumbled on the work of Riemann," meaning Riemann's 1854 lecture on the Riemann sphere. The chaos of Einstein's confusion was transformed into euphoria as each of his physical principles found what Kaku calls a "line for line" correlation with Riemann's mathematical mandala of the number One. In Kaku's words, "The physical reinterpretation of Riemann's famous 1854 lecture is now called *general relativity*, and Einstein's field equations rank among the most profound ideas in scientific history."[542]

In 1915 Einstein used the Riemann sphere to develop general relativity. In 1916 the German artillery officer Karl Schwarzschild discovered black holes implied within Einstein's theory. That same year Jung, a German-speaking Swiss, started painting mandalas and wrote about the mandala of the Pleroma in *Seven Sermons to the*

Dead. Thus far, we have seen the psychic mandala image representing the union of all opposites unfold in modern German thought from Hegel, to Riemann, to Einstein, to Schwarzschild, to Jung and Pauli. We saw Hegel say that "the Idea is the central point, which is also the periphery."[543] That is exactly the way general relativity describes the structure of the Big Bang universe originating from and ending in the gravitational singularity. It should not be surprising, therefore, that there appear to be detailed parallels between Hegel's philosophy and the geometry of complex numbers that culminated with the Riemann sphere twenty-three years after Hegel died. That Hegel's cosmology should so closely resemble the Riemann sphere and the physics of black holes and the Big Bang is evidence that his ideas emerged from the same mandala-manifesting archetype of the Self that gave birth to those latter manifestations.

Jung's Comments on Complex Numbers

Whether or not Jung was aware of the Riemann sphere and the idea of black holes and the Big Bang, he did comment on the connection between his mandala theory and the higher mathematics of imaginary numbers. In a passage in *Memories, Dreams, Reflections* where Jung discusses the possibility of life after death, he includes a reflection on his own near-death experience and a dream he had about his deceased wife. He goes on to make a connection between his inability to describe these experiences adequately and higher-dimensional mathematics. Using a metaphor from Plato's cave allegory, he explains that his descriptions of the afterworld are like the image of a three-dimensional body projected on a two-dimensional plane (like a shadow), or a four-dimensional object represented by a three-dimensional model. He says that in the same way that "mathematics goes to great pains" to create expressions for these higher-dimensional concepts, psychologists should develop ways to interpret higher-dimensional psychic experiences, which are represented to us empirically during near-death experiences and dreams. He then compares his own method of interpreting dreams about the afterlife to the symbolic significance of the numbers one through four:

> The method employed is what I have called "the method of the necessary statement." It represents the principle of *amplification* in the interpretation of dreams, but can most easily be demonstrated by the statements implicit in simple whole numbers.
>
> One, as the first numeral, is unity. But it is also "*the* unity," the One, All-Oneness, individuality and non-duality —not a numeral but a philosophical concept, an archetype and attribute of God, the monad. . . .
>
> The necessary statement of the number four, therefore, is that, among other things, it is an apex and simultaneously the end of a preceding ascent.[544]

In other essays, Jung explains that he borrowed the "principle of *amplification* in the interpretation of dreams" from Jerome Cardan, who also happens to be the first person to publish an answer to an algebraic equation using the square roots of negative numbers in 1545.[545] The claim that there are strong parallels between the unit circle and Jung's concept of the psychic mandala image of the Self that appears in dreams is supported by the fact that Jung borrowed his method of dream interpretation (the principle of amplification) from the father of imaginary numbers. Similarly, to amplify his understanding of four-dimensional space-time, Einstein, following Riemann, meditated on how the numbers 0, -1, and the square roots of -1 are implicit in the whole number 1 represented by the unit circle. In agreement with the axiom of Maria, and Jung's theory that the number four symbolizes an apex that is simultaneously the end of a preceding ascent, the four right angle rotations of i and $-i$ describe the unit circle of the complex number plane.

In *Two Essays on Analytical Psychology*, Jung relates the main ingredients of the mandala—the circle and the quaternity—to the psychological transcendent function, which he furthermore relates to the individuation process:

> The transcendent function does not proceed without aim and purpose, but leads to the revelation of the essential man. . . . The symbols used by the unconscious to this end are the same as those which mankind has always used to express wholeness, completeness, and perfection: symbols, as a rule, of the quaternity and the circle. For these reasons I have termed this the *individuation* process.[546]

If the collective consciousness of the academic field of mathematics goes through the same process of individuation as an individual ego, we should see a union of quaternity and circle symbols emerge as it approaches completeness through a union of opposing principles.[547] This is precisely what we see in the developmental history of mathematics, from the Cartesian grid centered at point zero to the geometrical expression of the union of real and imaginary numbers on the Riemann sphere, whose equator is the unit circle on the complex number plane. In fact, Jung refers to imaginary numbers earlier in the essay cited just above: "It has been named the 'transcendent function' because it represents a function based on real and 'imaginary,' or rational and irrational data, thus bridging the yawning gulf between conscious and unconscious."[548] In a footnote he comments that "I discovered only subsequently that the idea of the transcendent function also occurs in the higher mathematics, and is actually the name of the function of real and imaginary numbers."[549] Jung's comparison of the psychological transcendent function to the mathematical transcendent function of real and imaginary numbers supports the claim that there is a correlation between Jung's mandala theory and the mathematical mandala of the unit circle.

Jung discovered the mathematical concept of the transcendent function only after he devised his own psychological version of a similar function that leads an ego to realize how all conscious and unconscious contents of the psyche are united in the ultimate archetype of the Self, the spontaneously arising images of which are mandalas typically divided into four quadrants. Similarly, real and imaginary numbers are united in the mandala of the unit circle described by the fourfold rotations of the square roots of -1 around the cross-hairs of the complex number plane centered at point 0. And Jung relates the universal quaternity archetype to the horizon:

> The quaternity is an archetype of almost universal occurrence. It forms the logical basis for any whole judgment. If one wishes to pass such a judgment, it must have this fourfold aspect. For instance, if you want to describe the horizon as a whole, you name the four quarters of heaven.[550]

Riemann extended the unit circle to a point at infinity in the Riemann sphere, which Einstein used to model the universe according to general relativity, so that the four quarters of the unit circle are literally used to describe what Jung refers to above as the "horizon as a whole."

The Mathematical Mandala of the One and Quantum Mechanics

Riemann's geometrical explanation of the unit circle was equally influential in the development of quantum mechanics, so much so that Pauli dreamed and fantasized about it. In one particularly impressive active imagination exercise, which Pauli later wrote about in a paper titled "The Piano Lesson," Pauli describes his anima figure (a piano-playing Chinese lady who reminded him of his grandmother):

> At that moment the lady slipped a ring from her finger which I had not seen yet. She let it float in the air and

taught me: "I suppose you know the ring from your school of mathematics. It is the ring i."

I nodded and I spoke the words:

"The 'i' makes the void and the unit into a couple. At the same time it is the operation of rotating a quarter of the whole ring."

She: It makes the instinctive or impulsive, the intellectual or rational, the spiritual or supernatural, of which you spoke, into the unified or monadic whole that the numbers without the "i" cannot represent.

I: The ring with the i is the unity beyond particle and wave, and at the same time the operation that generates either of these.

She: It is the atom, the indivisible, in Latin.[551]

Pauli's anima figure taught him that the imaginary number provides a unifying understanding of the relationship between mind and matter, which is somehow related to the musical vibrations of the piano strings, which seems especially pertinent to string theory.[552] Susskind credits Pauli with inventing the mathematical "basis for the entire Standard Model" of quantum mechanics, while Pauli perceived the ring i as the basis, not only for a model of quantum mechanics, but for a model of the entire span of possible experience, both cosmic and psychic.[553] In the same way that the ring i creates and unites the fundamental pair of opposites in quantum mechanics (particle-wave), according to the anima figure in Pauli's imagination it also creates and unites the polarity between the conscious and unconscious.[554]

In his book *The Dreaming Universe*, the quantum physicist Fred Allan Wolf explains how Schrödinger and Heisenberg (with Pauli's help) used imaginary numbers on the unit circle to mathematically unify the opposition between the wave and particle interpretations of the quantum world, which resulted in the idea of a wave of probability that can be described as the union, or multiplication, of two counter-rotating circles, one moving forward through time and the other moving backward: "This idea that one multiplies two counterstreaming waves together, one coming from the present and one coming from the future, is called the transactional interpretation."[555] Continuing this line of reasoning, in *A Brief History of Time* Hawking describes how imaginary numbers lead to the concept of "imaginary time" which, despite sounding like "science fiction . . . is in fact a well-defined mathematical concept" that has "interesting effects on space-time: the distinction between time and space disappears completely."[556] Even without knowing any of the finer details of the mathematical physics that employ imaginary numbers, the basic outline provided by experts for the general audience is sufficient to demonstrate how they use the mandala of the unit circle to transform opposites into each other so as ultimately to unify them, which is exactly what Jung said mandala imagery does. If Jung and Pauli were correct, then the mathematical laws that describe physical processes mirror corresponding psychological processes.

Summarizing the history of the imaginary unit, Dantzig writes: "For centuries it figured as a sort of mystic bond between reason and imagination." He concludes with a quote from the mathematician-philosopher Leibnitz, who wrote that "the Divine Spirit found a sublime outlet in that wonder of analysis, that portent of the ideal world, that amphibian between being and not-being, which we call the imaginary root of negative unity."[557] Leibnitz uses the Platonic language of the Two Worlds theory depicted in the cave allegory of the *Republic*, for if the imaginary unit rotates between being and not-being, it serves as a bridge between the Two Worlds, which can lift us out of the cave of material illusion into the intelligible sunshine of the One. In other words, the imaginary unit can lift us out of the holographic illusion of three-dimensional space into the eternal light of the cosmic horizon where the central idea of the Good resides. The unit circle thus serves as a bridge between the physical world and the world of eternal forms because it enabled the mathematical physics that describe the space-timeless singularity and holographic horizon from which the three-dimensional world of temporary forms is projected, which significantly narrows the believability gap between modern skepticism and the archetypal cosmologies of the past. I equate this cosmic mandala with the archetype of the Self in which mind and matter are One. The unit circle is itself also a mathematical mandala image that independently emerged from that same archetype of wholeness through the union of opposites, thereby providing powerful empirical evidence in support of Jung and Pauli's unifying theory that the laws of physics and the laws of psychology mirror each other because cosmos and psyche emerge from the same archetype of the One.

The Sphere Whose Center Is Everywhere and Circumference Nowhere

According to Jung's method, to substantiate the claim that the mandala image described by Susskind's black hole string theory emerged from the archetype of the Self, there must be parallels between Susskind's black hole mandala and the mandalas described by thinkers from the past. The most pertinent detail in the parallels from the past that we have examined thus far is that the universe originates from a central point of light that somehow encompasses the outer sphere. This same basic idea has been expressed in the West in a phrase commonly repeated since St. Augustine, as Jung explains in *Psychology and Religion*: "God is an intellectual figure whose center is everywhere and the circumference nowhere."[558] This definition of God as the omnicentric point can be correlated with Susskind's black hole/Big Bang cosmology in several ways.

First, if Psyche = Singularity, then the center of the Self, also known as the God archetype, is everywhere in the sense that it is anywhere any observer might happen to be, in as much as each of us necessarily sees our self as the center of an expanding universe. Secondly, while within a material body, a psyche cannot physically experience either the event horizon of a black hole or the cosmic horizon of the universe (which recedes as we approach it), though, according to Susskind's concepts of black hole complementarity and cosmic complementarity, observers watching from the proper distance (fifteen billion light-years away for the cosmic horizon) would see a person traveling into the horizon approach an infinitely hot sphere around which all of the information making up that person's body would be smeared out as if on a holographic film. Though the sphere—whether the concave outside of an event horizon or the convex inside of the cosmic horizon—exists from certain perspectives, at the same time, even from those perspectives it could be said to be nowhere in the sense that it marks the point where space and time stop (because it marks the place where the fabric of space-time is either contracting or expanding at the speed of light).[559] Finally, the original light from the singularity of the Big Bang is echoing back from each point of the cosmic horizon as CMB radiation, which indicates that the circumference of the universe is nowhere in the sense that it is made of the central point that is everywhere.[560]

In *Psychology and Religion*, Jung goes on to explain that this omnicentric image of God dates back to Plato: "The image of the circle—regarded as the most perfect form since Plato's *Timaeus*, the prime authority for Hermetic philosophy—was assigned to the most perfect substance, to the gold, also to the *anima mundi* or *anima media natura*, and to the first created light."[561] Above we saw Plato's image of the universe as the sphere whose soul is the central point that also exists at each point of the cosmic horizon, where the past, present, and future are conserved, and from where they are projected inward on threads of destiny. Regarding the claim that God is the sphere whose center is everywhere and circumference nowhere, in the *Timaeus* Plato depicts the astronomer by that name describing the outermost sphere of the ether element as the "mother and receptacle of all created and visible and in any way sensible things . . . an invisible and formless being which receives all things and in some mysterious way partakes of the intelligible, and is most incomprehensible."[562] The mysterious circumference of the universe in the *Timaeus* is nowhere in the sense that it is invisible and formless, although it is at the same time the receptacle and mother of all sensible things, which is consistent with Susskind's theory of the cosmic horizon. After the study of Plato's cosmology above we saw how St. Augustine synthesized it with Christian theology, thereby forming the Western world view of the medieval era. We also saw that Jung and Pauli both openly acknowledged that they based their theory of the archetypes underlying mind and matter on Plato's theory of eternal ideas. Now we see Jung cite Plato as the origin of the famous phrase attributed to St. Augustine, and passed down by eminent philosophers from Nicholas of Cusa to Ralph Waldo Emerson, describing God as the sphere whose "center is everywhere and the circumference nowhere."[563]

If we equate the Self with the singularity at the center of the gravitational horizon of a black hole, then we might also equate the singularity with what Jung says medieval alchemists called the "Deity dormant and concealed in matter," which suggests that a black hole, including the inside-out black hole universe, is that alchemical "round thing . . . in possession of the magical key which unlocked the closed doors of matter."[564] This correlation seems to find independent confirmation from Harvard physicist Andrew Strominger, who explains that "black holes are the key to taking the next step, they're the doorway to our next step in understanding the basic laws of the universe around us."[565] If the mandala-manifesting Deity (the archetype of the Self) concealed in matter can be correlated with the singularity inside a black hole, or at the Big Bang, this realization would indeed serve as the key that unlocks the basic laws describing the ultimate unified field theory. In other words, if Psyche = Singularity, then any attempt at a unified field theory that does not take that equation into account is doomed to incompleteness.

In *The Masks of God*, Joseph Campbell writes that "the principle of relativity had been defined already in mythopoetic, moral, and metaphysical terms" by the medieval claim that "God is an intelligible sphere, whose center is everywhere and circumference nowhere."[566] He goes on to compile an historical list of Western thinkers who have revived that image over the centuries, one of whom is the seventeenth-century mathematician, scientist, and Catholic theologian Blaise Pascal, who combines mathematical logic and theology in a way that is surprisingly consistent with Susskind's black hole cosmology and Jung's mandala theory. As Pascal writes: "Nature is an infinite sphere whose centre is everywhere and circumference nowhere. In short it is the greatest perceptible mark of God's omnipotence that our imagination should lose itself in that thought."[567] According to Pascal, of all of the innumerable indicators of God's greatness, the greatest one of all is the fact that our imagination should lose itself in the idea of God's creation being an infinite sphere whose center is everywhere and circumference nowhere. Pascal's proclamation clearly concurs with Jung's claim that "I knew that in finding the mandala as an expression of the self I had attained what was for me the ultimate. Perhaps someone else knows more, but not I."[568]

In another passage, Pascal relates the idea of God as the sphere whose center is everywhere and circumference nowhere to the concept of an infinite regress of universes, the same basic structure of which, from the outermost "firmament" of stars to the tiniest "mites," repeats itself at endlessly smaller and greater scales.[569] This same idea of an infinity of parallel, mandala-shaped universes stretches back to the ancient Hindus, and forward to Susskind's string theory of the megaverse. In yet another aphorism, Pascal explains the apparent paradox of how an indivisible God can nevertheless be extended throughout infinite space by citing the example of "a point moving everywhere at an infinite speed."[570] According to Einstein, gravity is equivalent to accelerated motion, so that a point moving everywhere at an infinite speed is equivalent to a point of infinite gravity. Thinking of the singularity as a point moving everywhere infinitely fast gives new insight into the ancient idea of God as the sphere whose center is everywhere and circumference nowhere.

Thus, Susskind's atheistic cosmology is presaged by a religious thinker, Pascal, whose mathematical contributions include pioneering work in projective geometry, the physics of the vacuum, probability theory, and the invention of calculating machines.[571] Dantzig lists

Pascal as one of a trinity of mathematical forefathers of modern physics, calling them "the great triumvirate: Descartes, Pascal, Fermat."[572] Susskind's proposed pinnacle to the pyramid of mathematical physics, his holographic string theory of the megaverse of inside-out black hole universes, rests on the foundation of other mathematical geniuses who had similar ideas centuries earlier. From the Vaishnava megaverse to the megaverse described by Pascal, there is a great deal of historical precedent for the supposition that Susskind's mandala model of the megaverse emerged from the same archetype of the Self.[573]

Einstein based his theory that gravity is the curvature of the three-dimensional surface of a four-dimensional hypersphere on the Reimann sphere, which is the complex number plane rolled into a sphere with the north pole representing a point at infinity. Philosopher Rudy Rucker correlates Pascal's claim that "God is an intelligible sphere, whose center is everywhere and whose circumference is nowhere" with Riemann's hypersphere, which he furthermore correlates with Dante's cosmology of concentric spheres, about which he explains that beyond the outermost sphere of angels "lies a *point* called the Empyrean, which is the abode of God."[574] According to Rucker, the mental puzzle of how a single point at the outermost sphere of the universe can nevertheless encompasses all of spacetime "can be remedied if we take space to be hyperspherical!"[575] He explains that "if one lets a sphere expand in hyperspherical space, there comes a time when the circumference of the sphere turns into a point and disappears."[576]

Robert Osserman points to the same parallel between Dante's cosmology and Riemann's hypersphere, and explains that "the big bang occupies the position where Dante placed a point of light radiating with great intensity."[577] In keeping with Jung's theory that psychic mandala images emerge from the space-timeless archetype of the Self in people of all places and times on Earth, we find the same basic idea of God as the sphere whose center is everywhere and circumference nowhere in Dante's and Pascal's cosmologies, in the Riemann-Einstein hypersphere, and in Susskind's inside-out black hole cosmology. That Dante's and Pascal's images of the cosmos should so closely correlate with the mandala models of the cosmos described by Vyasadeva (author of Vedic texts), Plato, Lao Tzu, Chuang Tzu, Confucius, Hegel, Riemann, Einstein (via Lemaître), and Susskind provides the kind of historical evidence Jung suggests that we require in order to verify that a concept or image is rooted in an archetype. However, the first order of evidence we require, according to Jung, is spontaneously emerging images in our own minds, as in dreams.

Jung's Mandala Dreams: UFOs, the Dreaming Yogi, and the Black Hindu

In his essay "Flying Saucers: A Modern Myth of Things Seen in the Skies," which appears in *Civilization in Transition*, Jung suggests that some of the reported UFOs are probably physically real objects, though the notion that they are the vehicles of saviors from a highly advanced civilization is probably a collective projection of an unconscious wish for an archetypal savior. Jung suggests that this collective delusion has arisen because "a political, social, philosophical and religious conflict of unprecedented proportions has split the consciousness of our age."[578] Jung theorizes that flying saucers, which are mandala shaped, are perfectly suited for absorbing the projection of the "uniting symbol" unconsciously generated by the threatening tension of opposing demands on the collective consciousness of modern civilization, which includes the (then) emerging threat of nuclear war.[579]

It is not so surprising that Jung believes some UFOs are real physical objects embodying psychic projections of the Self archetype considering he observed a UFO containing an archetypal Self figure during his near-death experience in 1944. This "unidentified flying object" took the form of the black rock temple his disembodied psyche encountered while floating a thousand miles above the Earth, with the black Hindu who was waiting for him inside.[580]

Approaching the black rock temple impelled Jung's realization that our three-dimensional world is a boxlike prison system tethered to the illusion-projecting horizon of the cosmos by threads.

Later, in *Memories, Dreams, Reflections*, Jung discusses the relation between the Self and the ego in the context of Hindu philosophy and two dreams he had involving mandalas. The first dream he mentions involves UFOs in a way that is reminiscent of the supposition that our three-dimensional cosmos is actually a hologram projected from the horizon. Jung explains that in October of 1958, he dreamt about "gleaming disks" that flew toward him over the lake next to his house. The third disk, attached to a metal box that Jung calls a "magic lantern," pointed straight at him, causing him to ruminate: "We always think that the UFOs are projections of ours. Now it turns out that we are their projections."[581] Fourteen years before he had this dream, Jung had his near-death experience during which his encounter with a UFO (the black rock temple housing the black Hindu) made him realize that the three-dimensional world is an illusion projected from the horizon of the cosmos by threads. Although Jung does not compare the UFO to a mandala while he describes the UFO dream from 1958, in his description of the second dream (which occurred soon after his near-death experience in 1944) he refers to the later UFO dream and relates it to the mandala symbol.

Jung's near-death experience occurred in March of 1944. Later that year he had another dream about "the problem of the self and the ego."[582] In the dream, he was walking along a country road and noticed a small chapel. He was surprised to find no crucifix or statue of the Virgin Mary on the altar, although he did notice a beautiful arrangement of flowers there, in front of which sat a yogi in the lotus posture, deep in a trance. The yogi had Jung's own face, which caused Jung to awaken with a profoundly frightening thought: "He has a dream, and I am it."[583] The black Hindu from Jung's near-death experience and the yogi of Jung's dream that same year seem to be parallel figures: both are sitting in the lotus posture in a temple, and both seem to be the ultimate source of reality. By identifying the figure in his dream after his illness as the symbol of his Self, Jung indirectly draws the same conclusion about the black Hindu in the black rock temple. According to Jung, the meaning of the yogi dreaming him into existence is that the unconscious is the "generator of the empirical personality."[584] Similarly, during his near-death experience earlier that same year, Jung's encounter with the black Hindu sparked the realization that reality is projected from the horizon of the cosmos by threads. These observations seem to correlate the collective unconscious mind with the cosmic horizon, which Jung and Susskind both describe as the generator of the illusion of the three-dimensional world. After noting that he had this dream of the dreaming yogi soon after his near-death experience in 1944, Jung points out a parallel to the dream he had about the UFO in 1958: "Like the magic lantern, the yogi's meditation 'projects' my empirical reality."[585] He concludes the analysis of the two dreams by saying that they both resemble the "Oriental conception of Maya."[586] Considering Jung was following in the footsteps of previous German-speaking philosophers, it is pertinent to note that Nietzsche and Schopenhauer both identified the oriental concept of Maya with the Kantian *a priori* categories of space, time, and causality.[587]

If we identify the yogi with Jung's face (who was dreaming Jung into existence in his 1944 dream) with the black Hindu in the black rock temple from Jung's NDE earlier that same year, and if we link both of those experiences to the UFO projecting the world into existence from Jung's 1958 dream, and, finally, if we identify the illusion of three-dimensional space with Maya, as Jung does, then it is plausible to identify the black Hindu from Jung's NDE with Vishnu, who dreams Maya into existence, and who exists as the eternal string who interweaves past, present, and future into the *akashic* sphere surrounding the universe. According to Jung, the purpose of the two dreams—the dreaming yogi and the UFO with the magic lantern—was to "effect a reversal" of the relationship between his conscious world, which Jung defines as "the field of light centered upon the focal point of the ego," and the collective unconscious, which seems to correspond with the mandala-shaped boundary of the field of light formed by the cosmic horizon and central singularity.[588] After all, if the world of ego-consciousness manifests as the field of light centered on the ego, then the world of ego-consciousness ends where the field of light ends, which is the omnicentric singularity, the event horizon of every black hole and, ultimately, the cosmic horizon of our inside-out black hole universe. In short, it appears that the unifying aim of Jung's dreams was to help him realize that his conscious ego is projected from the archetype of the Self, which is the universal mandala formed by the all-encompassing horizon and omnicentric singularity.

Susskind's Reconciliation of General Relativity and Quantum Mechanics

In the same way that Susskind's black hole string theory corresponds to, and thereby corroborates Jung's near-death experience account of the cosmic horizon, so too does it corroborate Jung's closely related theory of the mandala images of the Self. Further evidence in favor of Jung's mandala theory (and, by extension, Susskind's black hole string theory) comes from the fact that Susskind's theory emerged historically in precisely the kind of extremely polarized situation from which Jung says compensatory mandala images typically emerge. We saw above how both general relativity and quantum theory use the mandala of the unit circle and the related Riemann sphere to transform opposites into each other so as ultimately to unify them (i.e., space and time, particle and wave). Nevertheless, despite conceptually reconciling pairs of opposites around the unit circle in their separate scales of the universe (the very big and the very small), those two fields of physics (general relativity and quantum mechanics) remain incommensurable with each other, unless, of course, we accept the empirically unverified (by conventional standards) but mathematically consistent claims that string theory is a genuine theory of quantum gravity.

Michio Kaku and writer Jennifer Trainer Thompson point out how the prestigious *Science* magazine compares the emergence of string theory to the discovery of imaginary numbers and the mythic idea of the "Holy Grail."[589] In the same way that Gauss and Riemann used the mandala of the unit circle to reconcile the opposition between imaginary and real numbers, Susskind used the mandala image of a black hole to resolve the opposition between the universal laws of general relativity (the theory of the very big and heavy) and quantum mechanics (the theory of the very small), which are forced to work together while describing a gravitational singularity because it is simultaneously the heaviest and smallest thing imaginable. More specifically, the conflict that seems to have activated the compensating mandala image in Susskind's mind was the apparent contradiction between the most fundamental physical principle of information conservation, upon which the consistency of quantum mechanics is especially dependent, and the information-swallowing gravity of a black hole as described by general relativity, and pointed out by Stephen Hawking.

There is reason to suspect that Susskind might be interested in this Jungian analysis of his great insight, considering he wrote that "the history of scientific ideas has always fascinated me. I am as interested in how the great masters came to their insights as I am in the ideas themselves."[590] Jung's analysis of the schizophrenic situation of modern civilization that accompanied widespread sightings of compensatory mandala images in the form of UFOs (beginning in 1945) also applies to the schizophrenia in the field of physics that triggered Susskind's healing image of the black hole mandala. In *Memories, Dreams, Reflections*, after describing his UFO dream and the related dream of the dreaming yogi, Jung again cites UFOs in the context of a more general summary of his theory that psychic mandala images emerge from the archetype of the Self to compensate an ego that is torn between opposing necessities. Jung explains that "the *complexio oppositorum* of the God-image thus enters into man, and not as unity, but as conflict, the dark half of the image coming into opposition with the accepted view that God is 'Light.'"[591] He goes on to equate "the ground of the psyche" with the God-image, whose cleavage in the modern mind triggers compensating mandala images, the ultimate symbol of the union of opposites, in the form of "worldwide rumors" of UFOs beginning in 1945.[592]

Jung explains that in 1918, he began realizing that a spontaneously arising mandala image "signifies the *wholeness of the self*," which is another way of expressing "the divinity incarnate in man."[593] According to Jung, that UFO sightings occur all over the world is evidence of the collective unconscious origin of those mandalic shapes in the sky.[594] He further explains how mandala images begin to emerge from the collective unconscious when the ego is confronted by some clash of principles:

> The clash, which is at first of a purely personal nature, is soon followed by the insight that the subjective conflict is only a single instance of the universal conflict of opposites. Our psyche is set up in accord with the structure of the universe and what happens in the macrocosm likewise happens in the infinitesimal and most subjective reaches of the psyche. For that reason the God-image is always a projection of the inner experience of a powerful *vis-à-vis* [face to face].[595]

We saw the image of seeing God "face to face" at the cosmic horizon earlier in Augustine's *Confessions*.[596] If "our psyche is set up in accord with the structure of the universe," and if the structure of the universe is the mandala formed by the complementary relationship between the central singularity and the holographic horizon of the cosmos, then our psyche must mirror that relationship. This correlation of cosmos and psyche can be summarized with the equation: Self = Conscious-Unconscious = Singularity-Horizon.

According to Jung, the psychic God-image of the mandala enters into us from the archetype of wholeness "not as unity, but as conflict." True to Jung's theory, the cosmic mandala of a black hole did indeed enter into Susskind's ego-consciousness as a personal

213

conflict with Stephen Hawking, which he describes in *The Black Hole War: My Battle with Stephen Hawking to Make the World Safe for Quantum Mechanics*. In exact agreement with Jung's description of the psychological situation from which mandala images typically emerge in the conscious psyche, Susskind's black hole string theory entered his mind after an initial conflict with Hawking over the most fundamental principle of information conservation (also known as reversibility). In this case, what Jung refers to as the "dark half" of the mandala (God-image) is represented by Hawking's former claim that black holes swallow information (light), while the opposing view that "God is 'Light'" is represented by Susskind's victorious claim that black holes ultimately conserve information, and release it with the outgoing Hawking radiation. By mathematically reversing the description of that physical process, Susskind describes how the information that escapes the observable universe after expanding past the cosmic horizon is simultaneously conserved there on a kind of holographic film and projected back by fundamental threads that form the cosmic microwave background radiation which manifests as the cinematic hologram of three-dimensional space.

Jung says that soon after the initial disagreement between personalities, the ego who is eventually compensated by a mandala image realizes that "the subjective conflict is only a single instance of the universal conflict of opposites." In line with Jung's diagnosis, Susskind explains how his personal clash with Hawking was almost immediately followed by the insight that their personal disagreement over the issue of information conservation in black holes represents a universal conflict between the two conflicting theories that describe the physical universe: general relativity and quantum mechanics. Susskind explains that the first time he heard Hawking present his theory that black holes devour information was in the attic of a mansion in San Francisco, which belonged to a motivational speaker, Werner Erhard, who used his wealth to host high-level theoretical physics conferences. The correlations with Jung's theory of the compensatory mandala images are manifest in certain key phrases Susskind uses to explain the aftermath of that meeting, during which he realized that Hawking had discovered "a clash of principles that rivaled the great paradoxes of the past."[597]

Hawking realized that the equivalence principle (i.e. information conservation)—upon which quantum mechanics' validity is especially dependent—is violated by the information-swallowing black holes predicted by general relativity. According to Susskind, "the paradox could bring down the whole structure, or reconciling the two could bring deep new insight into both."[598] Susskind explains that "the clash created an unbearable itch," and "that reconciling the principles of Quantum Mechanics with those of relativity was the great problem of our generation."[599] Convincing Hawking of this task became Susskind's "obsession," and he was certain that "the key was not to abandon Quantum Mechanics, but to reconcile it with the theory of black holes."[600] He found it "intellectually intolerable" to leave quantum mechanics and general relativity unreconciled.[601]

In profound agreement with Jung's compensating mandala theory, the decades-old conflict between the previously irreconcilable mathematics of general relativity and quantum mechanics was brought to an extreme impasse, and then arguably resolved within the developing mathematical descriptions of mandalic black holes. According to Jung, "we know from experience that the protective circle, the mandala, is the traditional antidote for chaotic states of mind."[602] The situation in the physics community is therefore ideal for invoking compensatory mandala imagery. In Michio Kaku's words, "physics is having a nervous breakdown" caused by tension between the opposing principles of general relativity and quantum mechanics, both of which are required to describe the singularity inside black holes and at the Big Bang.[603] The black hole mandala forces the irreconcilable languages of general relativity and quantum mechanics into a fatal confrontation that demands reconciliation, which is precisely what Susskind claims to have done using string theory.

As the developmental process of the psyche leads the conflicted ego toward a union of opposites in the mandala-manifesting archetype of the Self, so does the developmental process of mathematical physics lead to a union of opposites in the singularity surrounded by a spherical horizon. Thus, in both psychology and physics, the developmental process manifests as a compulsion toward wholeness through the unification of opposing principles in a space-timeless central point that encompasses the periphery of a sphere. That quest for unification is nicely summarized by physicist Steven Weinberg: "Unification is where it's at. Unification is what we're trying to accomplish. The whole aim of fundamental physics is to see more and more of the world's phenomena in terms of fewer and fewer and simpler and simpler principles."[604] Physicists seek unification, psychologists seek individuation, and both arrive at a mandala image of the One.

Echoing *Science* magazine, Michio Kaku even equates the quest for a unification of general relativity and quantum mechanics with the mythic quest for the Holy Grail: "A quantum theory of gravity that unites it with the other forces is the Holy Grail of physics."[605] In another book, he writes: "For ages, the holy grail of physics has been to search for unifying themes that can explain the complexities of the universe in the simplest, most coherent fashion."[606] Brian Greene employs the same mythic metaphor in *The Elegant Universe*, in which, referring to string theory, he writes that "today's physicists are in possession of what may well be the Holy Grail of modern science, but they can't unleash its full predictive power until they succeed in writing the full instruction manual."[607] In the context of Jung and Pauli's psychological theory, it is plausible to suggest that string theorists like Kaku, Greene, and Susskind are indeed in possession of the Holy Grail that unifies gravity and quantum mechanics in the form of Susskind and 't Hooft's black hole string theory, though they cannot unleash its full power until they acknowledge the mirror-symmetry with Jung's mandala theory. This acknowledgment could result in the kind of grand synthesis Pauli and Jung imagined. In Pauli's words, "I don't know whether and when this *coniunctio* will be realized, but I have no doubt that this would be the most beautiful destiny that could befall psychology and physics."[608] Perhaps this beautiful *coniunctio* of psychology and physics may be realized by narrowing the task down to a synthesis of the first principles of each field, represented by Jung's theory of the psychic mandala images of the Self and Susskind's black hole string theory.

CHAPTER 7
STRING THEORY AND SYNCHRONICITY

The *unus mundus* is the archetype of wholeness through the union of opposites. Mind and matter are the overarching pair of opposites: all other pairs of opposites are correlated with either one or the other of those two categories. Therefore, a union of mind and matter includes a union of all other pairs of opposites. Meaningful coincidences, which Jung calls synchronicities, point to the *unus mundus* because they indicate that our mental world of perceived meanings is united with the material world of empirical events.

Jung coined the term "psychoid" to describe the realm of the archetypes, which are beyond mind and matter by being the source and limit of both.[609] If Psyche = Singularity, then the singularity, which is present at each point of the quantum vacuum and the cosmic horizon, is the *unus mundus*, the unitary background to existence in which mind and matter are merged, and in which all of the psychoid archetypes are condensed. This infinitely dense point is not a part of the empirically observable "phenomenal" world—which, for Jung, includes the psychic images emerging from our unconscious—though its presence can be inferred from the empirically observable, organizing influence it has on physical objects and psychic images.

We saw above that, according to Jung and Pauli's theory of the "psychoid" archetypes, the presence of those transcendental ordering principles can be indirectly inferred from the empirically observable mirror-symmetries between the laws of physics and the laws of psychology.[610] The unintended parallels between Jung's synchronicity theory and Susskind's holographic string theory seem to indicate that they both emerge from, and converge on, the same underlying archetype of the Self, whose empirical manifestations are psychic mandala images on the one hand, and the gravitational effects of black holes on the other, including the inside-out black hole of our universe as a whole.

In *Mysterium Coniunctionis*, Jung draws a correlation between mandalas and synchronicities: "If mandala symbolism is the psychological equivalent of the *unus mundus*, then synchronicity is its parapsychological equivalent."[611] According to Jung, both spontaneously emerging psychic mandala images *and* synchronicities emerge from the ultimate archetype of wholeness because synchronicities indicate a meaningful union of the ultimate archetypal pair of opposites: cosmos and psyche. Therefore, if the empirically observable gravitational effects of black holes are the physical correlates of the psychological mandala images of the *unus mundus*, and if synchronicities are the parapsychological correlates of the mandala images, then synchronicities are necessarily the parapsychological correlates of the gravitational effects of black holes, including the inside-out black hole universe.

Susskind's holographic string theory is entirely bereft of the standard forms of empirical evidence physics has traditionally required, though strong empirical evidence for his theory is available if we believe Jung's near-death experiential account of the cosmic horizon, his theory of psychic mandala images, *and* his synchronicity theory. On one hand, synchronicities are empirically observable events (psychic events and symbolically related, but causally unconnected, physical events) that appear to indicate the existence of a cosmic domain where psychic and physical events are *meaningfully* connected. On the other hand, Susskind's empirically unsubstantiated, yet mathematically consistent string theory describes precisely the kind of uniting medium synchronicities seem to require. Jung's synchronicity theory and Susskind's ideologically opposed string theory each provide precisely what the other lacks, like two halves of a broken locket that converge on the ultimate archetype of the Self. This archetype of wholeness can be understood as the universal mandala formed by the holographic horizon, the omnicentric singularity, and the psychoid string that connects those two complementary poles.

Jung's Synchronicity Theory, his NDE, and Susskind's String Theory

Jung explains how his synchronicity theory is connected to his relationships with Albert Einstein and Wolfgang Pauli in a letter he wrote to Carl Seelig on February 25, 1953:

> Professor Einstein was my guest on several occasions at dinner. . . . These were very early days when Einstein was developing his first theory of relativity. It was Einstein who first started me off thinking about a possible relativity of time as well as space, and their psychic conditionality. More than thirty years later, this stimulus led to my relation with the physicist Professor W. Pauli and to my thesis of psychic synchronicity.[612]

Not only did his association with Einstein (between 1909 and 1913) and Pauli (between 1932 and 1958) help Jung shape his "thesis of psychic synchronicity," but Jung—accepting Pauli's invitation—co-published his first comprehensive explanation of that theory, titled *Synchronicity: An Acausal Connecting Principle*, in 1952, along with one of Pauli's essays about the influence of archetypes on Kepler.[613] Considering that Susskind hails Pauli as "one of history's greatest theoretical physicists,"[614] he should be sympathetic to the synchronicity theory which Pauli helped Jung express with scientific rigor. Whether Susskind accepts or rejects the theory of synchronicity, however, if his string theory really does reconcile quantum theory with general relativity, as it seems to, and if those two opposing branches of physics both help explain the occurrences of synchronicities, as Jung and Pauli suggest, then we should expect Susskind's string theory to shed new light on Jung's theory of synchronicity as well.

In an earlier version of *Synchronicity* titled "On Synchronicity," published in 1951, Jung says that synchronicities "have to do with spontaneous, meaningful coincidences of so high a degree of improbability as to appear flatly unbelievable."[615] As an example, Jung mentions one of his patients who was incapable of overcoming her overly dualistic, rationalistic, "Cartesian" attitude, and was therefore incapable of perceiving the influence of the collective unconscious mind. One night she dreamed that someone gave her a golden scarab beetle, a costly piece of jewelry. As she was telling Jung her dream the next day, a very similar looking beetle, which was not usually seen in that part of Switzerland, began persistently buzzing against the window, which was against the normal habit of insects, who usually try to go away from a dark place toward light. Jung opened the window, let the beetle fly in, caught it in his hands, then handed it to the patient, saying, "here is you scarab."[616] Even to the stubborn Cartesian intellect of his patient, the apparent meaningfulness of this coincidence seemed to result from something more than blind chance, which helped her overcome her ostensibly rational doubts about the reality of the organizing influence of archetypes underlying mind and matter.

In *Synchronicity*, which followed the next year, Jung explains that the beetle symbolizes the archetype of rebirth: "The ancient Egyptian Book of What Is in the Netherworld describes how the dead sun-god changes himself at the tenth station into Khepri, the scarab, and then, at the twelfth station, mounts the barge which carries the rejuvenated sun-god into the morning sky."[617] Jung's patient's psychic life had been "dead," but was rejuvenated by a synchronicity which convinced her of a meaningful connection between her inner psychic life and the natural world around her. Although the patient's particular synchronicity pointed specifically to the rebirth archetype symbolized by the scarab, all synchronicities ultimately point to the ultimate archetype of wholeness through the union of opposites, because all of them indicate a meaningful union of the overarching opposition between our mental life (psyche) and the physical world around us (cosmos).

The unitary dimension of existence (the *unus mundus*) with which Jung directly united during his near-death experience (and toward which he considered synchronicity to be pointing) is specifically the "horizon of the cosmos," where the past, present, and future are united at each point, and to which each cubic volume of psyche-imprisoning space-time is tethered by a thread.[618] Although Jung published his recollection of his near-death experience in *Memories, Dreams, Reflections* in 1961, he concealed that ultimate experience of his life ten years earlier while writing *Synchronicity*, perhaps because he suspected that his extraterrestrial tale might have discredited him among the scientific community he was hoping to persuade. Nevertheless, Jung's NDE provides the perfect mechanism to explain meaningful coincidences: all physical events and psychic experiences from the past, present, and future of the universe are interwoven at each point of the cosmic horizon, from where they are projected inward by threads to create the holographic movie of three-dimensional space.

In one passage in *Synchronicity*, following Einstein, Jung points out that "space and time, the conceptual co-ordinates of bodies in motion, are probably at bottom one and the same." Assuming the mask of a cautious skeptic, he goes on to say that "synchronicity in space can equally well be conceived as perception in time, but remarkably enough it is not so easy to understand synchronicity in time as spatial, for we cannot imagine any space in which future events are objectively present and could be experienced as such through a reduction of this spatial distance."[619] Jung does not have to imagine a space in which future events are objectively present because he directly experienced the past, present, and future simultaneously at the cosmic horizon during his near-death experience in 1944. Moreover, in response to Jung's claim that we cannot imagine a reduction of the spatial distance separating the present from the future, according to special relativity, the more closely an observer accelerates toward the absolute speed of light, the more compressed the entire cosmos (including galaxies directly behind the traveler) appears in the direction of travel (aberration), and the slower time seems to flow, so that, according to David Bohm, from light's perspective, "you would find that the two ends of the light ray would have no time between them and no distance, so they would represent immediate contact."[620] From the perspective of the photons radiating from the Big Bang and echoing back from the cosmic horizon, all points of space and time unfolding as the holographic movie of cosmic history are in immediate contact. Jung's NDE convinced him that each psyche is imprisoned in a separate little box of three-dimensional space, each of which is tethered by a thread to the illusion-producing horizon of the cosmos.[621] It is specifically from "behind the horizon of the cosmos" that Jung suspected the illusion of the three-dimensional world is "artificially built up." If the illusory projection of three-dimensional space unfolding through time is recorded on and projected from the cosmic horizon, then synchronicities must also be coordinated there.

For three weeks after his initial heart attack, Jung had hour-long ecstasies beginning each night around midnight, although he dreaded the dawn which brought the return of "the gray world with its boxes!" "Although my belief in the world returned to me," he writes, "I have never since entirely freed myself of the impression that this life is a segment of existence which is enacted in a three-dimensional boxlike universe especially set up for it."[622] In both places where Jung mentions his experiential realization of the boxlike illusion of cubic space, he also mentions his suspicion that the whole prison system has been "artificially" and "especially" set up for us. The implication is that there is an Artist, or community of artists living behind the horizon of the cosmos who construct the illusion of our three-dimensional world. That being, or beings behind the horizon would therefore also be responsible for orchestrating synchronicities. The most likely culprit is the archetype of the Self, the universal mandala whose periphery is the cosmic horizon.

Describing his initial out-of-body experience and the nightly visions that followed for three weeks, Jung writes that "one is interwoven into an indescribable whole and yet observes it with complete objectivity."[623] It seems plausible, therefore, that as absolute particles of the archetype of the Self, each subsidiary self somehow participates in artificially setting up our own three-dimensional box of illusion from our eternal position at the cosmic horizon. In the aftermath of his blissful near-death experience, Jung, like Plato and the Gnostics before him, derided the three-dimensional interior of the universe as a prison for the soul. A less derogatory way of explaining the same basic idea is to say that we creatures in the holographic movie of three-dimensional space are the *dreams* of our own true selves slumbering at the cosmic horizon, where all points of space-time are experienced concurrently. This simultaneous awareness of all of the quantifiable points in space-time manifests as the qualitative experience of infinite bliss.

At the climax of Jung's near-death experience, just as he was about to enter the black rock temple floating in space, and learn about his past, present, and future from the black Hindu and the other people to whom he belonged "in reality," he was stopped by the "primal form" of his physician, Dr. H, who "had been delegated by the earth" to call him back.[624] Although Jung presumed he was also in his primal form, he did not observe it directly.[625] The idea of a primal form as an intermediary between the body and the soul may help relate Jung's synchronicity theory to Susskind's string theory of holographic information conservation at the cosmic horizon. A comparison of Jung's concept of the primal form to the Hindu concept of a subtle material body is warranted by the fact that it was only after his encounter with the black Hindu that Jung realized how each box of three-dimensional space is hung up to and projected in from the horizon of the cosmos by a thread, which is the strongest of all the correlations between Jung's psychology and Susskind's holographic string theory.

As discussed above, the Vishnu-centric form of Hindu cosmology features a megaverse of bubble universes, each of which consists of a Vishnu Avatar in the center surrounded by eight concentric spherical shells of increasingly subtle material elements—earth, water, fire, air, ether, mind, intelligence, and false ego—which Krishna (the original Vishnu and archetypal Self) describes in the Bhagavad-gita.[626] The "primal form" Jung mentions in the context of his near-death experience is similar to what the Vaishnava philosophy describes as the subtle material body made of mind, intelligence, and false ego that carries the soul, or self, from one gross body made of earth, water, fire and air to the next after death.[627] The ether sphere serves as the intermediary realm from which the cosmic mind projects the grosser elements inward. Moreover, in the same series of verses in which Krishna describes the eight material elements, he also compares himself to a string on which everything is strung like pearls, and he furthermore identifies himself with the fundamental sound vibration of the ether element, the syllable "om." According to a related classic of Vaishnava philosophy, Srimad-Bhagavatam, each elemental sphere is ten times wider than the grosser element before it, which seems to correspond to the way the fabric of space-time is expanding at an exponential rate.[628] The wider the circumference of the sphere of space we perceive around us, the faster it is expanding away from Earth, which resembles the increasingly subtle material elements in the Vaishnava model: when the expansion of space-time reaches the speed of light at the cosmic horizon, the material universe ends and the eternal world begins.

Reinforcing the parallel between the Vaishnava concept of a subtle body and Susskind's string theory, we also saw earlier that in the Brihadaranyaka Upanishad Uddalaka Aruni asks: "Do you know the string on which this world and the next, as well as all beings, are strung together?"[629] Yajnavalkya later explains that the fundamental string that controls and unites everything is interwoven specifically at the ether element of the universe, or *akasha*, translated as space: "The things above the sky, the things below the earth, and the things between the earth and the sky, as well as all those things people here refer to as past, present, and future—on space, Gargi, are all these woven back and forth."[630] Within the cosmological context of the Vaishnava school of Vedanta philosophy, it is reasonable to suggest that meaningful coincidences are coordinated specifically by a thread that interweaves the past, present, and future at the outermost sphere encompassing the empirically observable universe, from which the illusory world of space-time is projected. In other words, meaningful coincidences between cosmos and psyche meet at the intermediary ether sphere, where the subtle material body made of mind, intelligence, and false ego interacts with the gross material body made of earth, water, fire, and air.

Synchronicity, the Axiom of Maria, and the Compassionate Love of a Suffering God

In *Synchronicity*, after saying that we cannot imagine a reduction of the distance between our present space and a space where future events can be objectively experienced, Jung goes on to write that, nevertheless, "since experience has shown that under certain conditions space and time can be reduced almost to zero, causality disappears along with them, because causality is bound up with the existence of space and time and physical changes, and consists essentially in the succession of cause and effect."[631] The relation of cause and effect consists of a linear, temporal succession of spatially connected events. Therefore, under conditions during which space and time are reduced to zero, causality must also be suspended. The singularity, which exists at each point of the horizon, is a point of zero volume in which time stops in such a way that the past, present, and future are fused together within it. Synchronicities imply the existence of such a realm because they reveal an organizing force that is outside of the realm of cause and effect, and thus outside the realm of space and time upon which causal relations depend. In other words, according to Jung, there is no physical link between the temporal coincidence of symbolically similar events in space (like Jung's discussion with his patient about her scarab dream and the beetle buzzing at the window): "Hence the interconnection of meaningfully coincident factors must necessarily be thought of as acausal."[632] Any form of interconnection that is acausal is also necessarily outside of space and time because space, time, and causality are inextricably interwoven.

In our survey of the history of the philosophical concept of the Self above we saw David Hume argue that factual knowledge can only come through our five bodily sense organs. We do not see, touch, taste, hear, or smell a soul, so there is no soul that gives us a continuous identity from one moment to the next. Hume further points out that we do not perceive space, time, or the idea of a relation between cause and effect with any of our sense organs either, which means that these concepts, upon which Newton based his science, are purely imaginary. Responding to Hume, Immanuel Kant argues that though space, time, and causality are not empirically real, neither are they fictions humans create to help us organize the chaotic flux of sense impressions; rather, they are *a priori* categories of thought forced upon the human mind at birth. In other words, space, time, and causality are the inborn lenses of perception through which our bodily sense perceptions are unconsciously organized for our conscious comprehension. We can have no knowledge of what the world is like before it is digested by our conceptual categories, though we can have certain knowledge (Newtonian physics) of how the inherently unknowable world will appear to a human observer.

In the chapter on near-death experiences, we examined correlations between the accounts of tunnel vision typically experienced during a near-death experience and tunnel vision as described by the special and general theories of relativity. I argued that NDE tunnel-vision accounts indicate that the psyche *is* the fabric of space-time (which includes the *a priori* concept of causality), so that, when a psyche rises out of a material body, it experiences its own exponential expansion outward in space and backward in time, culminating at the speed of light at the cosmic horizon, which is often experienced as the original point of light at the end of a dark tunnel.

In *Synchronicity*, Jung posits that synchronicity is the "connecting principle" that combines the material cosmos with the psychic world of perceived meaning, and can be defined as a fourth *a priori* category: "Space, time, and causality, the triad of classical physics, would then be supplemented by the synchronicity factor and become a tetrad, a *quaternio* which makes possible a whole judgment."[633] The fourth *a priori* principle of synchronicity unites the three principles of space, time, and causality by providing a way of conceiving of the existence of a realm where the past, present, and future of space can be experienced simultaneously. Jung goes on to provide a diagram of the relation between these four principles:

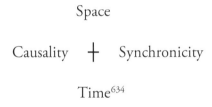

In *Synchronicity*, Jung explains that he changed his first diagram of the synchronicity *quaternio* cited above after conferring with Pauli:

> Pauli suggested replacing the opposition of space and time in the classical schema by (conservation of) energy and the space-time continuum. This suggestion led me to a closer definition of the other pair of opposites—causality and synchronicity—with a view to establishing some kind of connection between these two heterogeneous concepts. We finally agreed on the following *quaternio*:

Indestructible Energy

Constant		Inconstant
Connection		Connection
through		through
Effect	+	Contingence,
(Causality)		Equivalence,
		or "Meaning"
		(Synchronicity)

Space-Time Continuum

This schema satisfies on the one hand the postulates of modern physics, and on the other hand those of psychology.[635]

At the top of the revised *quaternio* mandala, Jung and Pauli place "Indestructible Energy," which refers to the principle of the conservation of energy. If we extend this principle to the more fundamental principle of information conservation, then we could identify "Indestructible Energy" with the omnicentric singularity and the holographic horizon of the cosmos (Pleroma), where Susskind says every bit of information is indestructibly conserved. By that reasoning, we could then identify the opposite pole, the space-time continuum, with the holographic illusion of three-dimensional space (creatura), projected from the cosmic horizon by vibrating threads. Regarding the horizontal polarity on the *quaternio* diagram above, although synchronicities seem to occur only occasionally in the three-dimensional world, where events are related by the "constant connection" of causality, at the cosmic horizon where past, present, and future occur simultaneously, synchronicity is the constant state of affairs. Moreover, even in the material realm of space-time, although synchronicities like Jung's scarab-beetle example only happen occasionally, Jung himself argues elsewhere that astrological synchronicities indicate a *constant* connection between the meaningful unfolding of history and the movements of the planets.[636]

The alteration to Jung's first *quaternio* diagram does not alter his original claim that, in fulfillment of the axiom of Maria, synchronicity is the fourth *a priori* category of thought that unites the other three principles of space, time, and causality: "Out of the Third comes the One as the Fourth."[637] A related manifestation of the axiom of Maria seems to be found in the four developmental phases of our inside-out black hole universe as described by Susskind's string theory. The first phase is the unexploded singularity in the quantum vacuum. The second phase is the continuous flaring forth of the universe from the singularity at the ongoing Big Bang, which manifests as the exponentially accelerating expansion of the fabric of space-time fueled by the anti-gravitational force (also known as dark energy and the cosmological constant) that erupts from the constant creation and destruction of virtual particle-antiparticle pairs at every point of the quantum vacuum. The third phase of universal development according to Susskind's string theory is the conservation of each bit of information describing the past, present, and future of each cubic volume of space on an infinitely hot holographic film at the cosmic horizon, where space is receding at the speed of light. Finally, the fourth developmental phase of the universe, according to Susskind, is the projection of each bit of information conserved at the cosmic horizon back into the volume of space by the fundamental threads that form the "cinematic hologram" we experience as everyday reality.[638]

If Susskind's theory is correct, then causally unrelated events that appear to be meaningfully united are indeed united at the horizon of the cosmos, each point of which contains the entire temporal sequence of the universe. Thus, Jung's suggestion that adding synchronicity as the fourth principle unites the other three *a priori* principles of space, time, and causality, and is therefore a manifestation of the axiom of Maria, finds a corresponding cosmological manifestation in the mandala shape of the inside-out black hole universe, and the four phases of its development, as described by Susskind's string theory. These four phases also seem to correlate with the four phases of universal creation described by mathematician and philosopher Alfred North Whitehead.

In *Process and Reality* Whitehead explains that "there are thus four creative phases in which the universe accomplishes its actuality. There is first the phase of conceptual origination, deficient in actuality, but infinite in its adjustment of valuation."[639] The first phase is equivalent to the infinite gravity of the singularity just prior to the Big Bang. "Secondly, there is the temporal phase of physical origination, with its multiplicity of actualities."[640] The second phase is equivalent to the ongoing Big Bang. "Thirdly, there is the phase of perfected actuality, in which the many are one everlastingly, without the qualification of any loss either of individual identity or of completeness of unity. In everlastingness, immediacy is reconciled with objective immortality."[641] This third phase is equivalent to holographic information conservation at the cosmic horizon, which Jung blissfully experienced during his near-death experience. Whitehead explains that "in the fourth phase, the creative action completes itself. For the perfected actuality passes back into the temporal world, and qualifies this world so that each temporal actuality includes it as an immediate fact of relevant experience."[642] The fourth phase is equivalent to what Susskind describes as the holographic illusion of three-dimensional space unfolding through linear time that is projected by fundamental strings from the eternal horizon of the cosmos.

The axiom of Maria states that "Out of the Third comes the One as the Fourth." Similarly, out of Whitehead's third phase of universal creation (which is equivalent to Susskind's concept of holographic information conservation at the cosmic horizon), comes the fourth phase that projects the harmonized universe back into three-dimensional space. Whitehead continues by summarizing the four phases:

> For the kingdom of heaven is with us today. The action of
> the fourth phase is the love of God for the world. It is the

particular providence for particular occasions. What is done in the world [Big Bang from the primordial singularity] is transformed into a reality in heaven [information conservation at the cosmic horizon], and the reality in heaven passes back into the world [cinematic hologram projected by strings from the cosmic horizon]. By reason of this reciprocal relation, the love in the world passes into the love in heaven, and floods back again into the world. In this sense, God is the great companion—the fellow-sufferer who understands.[643]

As a prelude to his description of the four phases of universal development, Whitehead writes that: "The ultimate evil in the temporal world is deeper than any specific evil. It lies in the fact that the past fades, that time is a 'perpetual perishing.'"[644] Whitehead overcame that ultimate evil with his theory that all of space-time is conserved at and projecting in from the kingdom of heaven, which seems very similar to the way Susskind battled and overcame Hawking's "evil" principle that information is destroyed in a black hole by explaining how it is simultaneously conserved by strings on the holographic event horizon, and, ultimately, at the cosmic horizon of the universe, from where it is projected back into the universe.

If we provisionally identify what Whitehead refers to as "God in his function as the kingdom of heaven" with the cosmic horizon (Pleroma) described by Susskind and Jung, then it is plausible to suggest that our experiences in the interior of the material universe (creatura), which are being projected back from the cosmic horizon by strings, have all been subtly adjusted by "the love of God" to communicate meaning to those with ears to hear. For example, by delaying the return of one event from the cosmic horizon by a moment, and hastening the projection of another event, the archetype of the Self could coordinate those two events in such a way that a human can easily interpret the odd coincidence as a meaningful message orchestrated specifically by an omniscient, omnipresent, omnipotent, and all-loving God. Such a theory is more plausible in the context of cosmologist Brian Swimme's maxim, Gravity is love. Tying Swimme's maxim together with Susskind's string theory, Jung's synchronicity theory, and Whitehead's concept of the kingdom of heaven, it is plausible to suggest that the infinite gravity of the singularity, which is present at each point of the cosmic horizon, manifests as the infinite love of the archetype of the Self. According to this hypothesis, an intentional agency would orchestrate the unfolding of the fundamental strings projected into the interior of the universe from the cosmic horizon, artistically coordinating the communication of a compensating message of unity to the suffering psyches imprisoned in our three-dimensional dream forms. But why does Whitehead call this hypothetical agent, this idea of God "the great companion—the fellow-sufferer who understands"? One possible answer is that the holographic illusion of space-time is the dream of God (as the Hindus claim), in which case we are God's subconscious projections, which indicates that God understands our suffering because we are the manifestation of God's repressed anxieties.

Perhaps the most famous historical example of a synchronicity that was interpreted as being sent by what Whitehead describes as a suffering God as an act of loving compassion for his suffering creatures is St. Augustine's conversion experience in the garden of Milan in 386 C.E. Augustine had been suffering terribly from the realization of his inability to overcome the lusty habits of his youth, which kept him from surrendering completely to Christ. He threw himself under a fig tree, and while still weeping bitterly he heard a child from a nearby house repeating a kind of sing-song phrase that he had never heard children utter before: "Take and read, take and read."[645] After carefully confirming in his own mind that there were no games in which children would repeat that phrase, he writes: "Damning the flood of my tears I arose, interpreting the incident as quite certainly a divine command to open my book of Scripture and read the passage at which I should open."[646] He opened his copy of St. Paul's Epistles, to Romans 13:13, where he read the following verse that cured him of his reluctance to embrace celibacy: "Not in rioting and drunkenness, not in chambering and impurities, not in contention and envy, but put ye on the Lord Jesus Christ and make not provision for the flesh in its concupiscences."[647] The moment he finished that sentence, Augustine says, "a light of utter confidence shone in my heart, and all the darkness of uncertainty vanished away."[648]

In *Cosmos and Psyche*, Richard Tarnas describes the link between Augustine's synchronicity and Petrarch's climbing of "Mont Ventoux in April 1336, an event that has long been regarded by scholars as representing the symbolic beginning of the Renaissance."[649] According to Tarnas, upon reaching the peak of Mont Ventoux, after much inner turmoil and reflection along the way, Petrarch pulled a copy of Augustine's *Confessions* out of his pack, and opened randomly to a passage in which Augustine describes practically the same panoramic view of fields and water that Petrarch was beholding, inspiring him to write later: "I could not believe that it was by a mere accident that I happened upon them. What I had there read I believed to be addressed to me and to no other, remembering that Saint Augustine had once suspected the same thing in his own case."[650] The same kind of synchronicity which inspired St. Augustine to inspire the birth of Western Christendom later inspired Petrarch to inspire the birth of the Renaissance.[651] Considering that all synchronicities indicate a meaningful connection between the ultimate pair of archetypal opposites, psyche and cosmos, they all point to the ultimate archetype of the union of all opposites, which Jung calls the Self, *unus mundus*, the One, and God. Thus, one implication of history-shaping synchronicities like Augustine's and Petrarch's is that the archetype of the Self has been pulling the evolution of the Western Mind toward itself all along.

Synchronicities in the History of Science Culminating with Susskind's String Theory

In *The Passion of the Western Mind*, Tarnas notes that the history of scientific advancement in the West is consistently marked by a series of fortunate coincidences: "As the inner gestalt changes in the cultural mind, new empirical evidence just happens to appear, pertinent writings from the past suddenly are unearthed, appropriate epistemological justifications are formulated, supportive sociological changes coincidentally take place, new technologies become available, the telescope is invented and just happens to fall into Galileo's hands." [652] He goes on to argue that synchronicities mark crucial junctures along each phase of the evolutionary path of the Western mind. A synthesis of Susskind's string theory and Jung's psychology may contribute to the emergence of a new paradigm within which it is scientifically reasonable to assume the existence of what Tarnas calls a "participatory consciousness reconnected to the universal."[653] That new paradigm, toward which the evolution of Western thought appears to be unfolding, is implied by the synchronicities that have occurred along the way, each of which inherently points to the archetype of wholeness through the union of opposites.

In *Number: The Language of Science*, Tobias Dantzig describes several independent but "nearly simultaneous" discoveries in the field of mathematics, "those twin-phenomena in which the history of mathematics is so abundant."[654] He lists these coincidental co-discoveries by connecting the names of the mathematicians who made them with a hyphen: Descartes-Fermat, Desargues-Pascal, Pascal-Fermat, Newton-Leibnitz, Wessel-Argand-Gauss, Lobatchevski-Bolyai-Gauss, and Cantor-Dedekind. After noting that other sciences reveal the same twin-phenomenon, Dantzig concludes that "it seems as if the accumulated experience of the race at times reaches a stage where an outlet is imperative, and it is merely a matter of chance whether it will fall to the lot of a single man, two men, or a whole throng of men to gather the rich overflow."[655]

In *Synchronicity: The Bridge Between Mind and Matter*, F. David Peat comments on this same cultural fact of nearly simultaneous discoveries of archetypally similar ideas being "in the air" like radio transmissions awaiting a proper receiver.[656] This imagery is very similar to Jung's claim that

> The collective unconscious surrounds us on all sides. . . . It is more like an atmosphere in which we live than something that is found *in* us. . . . Also, it does not by any means behave merely psychologically; in the case of so-called synchronicity it proves to be a universal substrate present in the environment rather than a psychological premise.[657]

Jung's description is consistent with the equation of the collective unconscious and the cosmic horizon, from which the infinite energy of the Big Bang is flooding back on all sides to form the holographic illusion of three-dimensional space. More specifically, Jung's claim that the collective unconscious is like a surrounding atmosphere correlates to Susskind's holographic principle in general, according to which all of the information in any three-dimensional volume of space is holographically stored on the two-dimensional surface area, so that the past, present, and future of the Earth, for example, are fused at each point of the planet's outermost atmosphere, which is exactly where Jung said his disembodied psyche saw the black rock temple with the black Hindu inside.

Jung and Pauli interpret the many instances of two or more unconnected people discovering the same revolutionary ideas at nearly the same time as evidence that those ideas are rooted in collective unconscious archetypes. Although the individual instances of synchronicity that mark each developmental stage of science, religion, and art point to different archetypes, all synchronicities indicate a union of the ultimate pair of opposites, mind and matter, and point, therefore, to the ultimate archetype of the Self, in which each conscious ego is rooted. For that reason, synchronicities can charge the ego that experiences them with a mystical sense of unity with the underlying ground of being. According to Peat: "Synchronicities are clearly of this very nature, for they open the floodgates of the deeper levels of consciousness and matter, which, for a creative instant, sweep over the mind and heal the division between the internal and the external."[658] Thus, it seems that just as individuals are guided toward the goal of individuation by mandala symbols of the Self in dreams, and by synchronicities while awake, the collective consciousness of the academic community is being unconsciously guided toward the archetype of the Self by Susskind's black hole cosmology and the synchronicities in the history of Western thought that have led to it. According to Peat, "such experiences release considerable meaning, energy, and creativity and give an intimation of the total transformation that is possible for both the individual and society."[659]

As Brain Greene explains in *The Elegant Universe*, the series of what can be recognized as synchronicities most directly related to Susskind's string theory began to emerge in 1968, when the Italian physicist Gabriele Veneziano, then working at CERN, fortuitously discovered that "an esoteric formula concocted for purely mathematical pursuits by the renowned Swiss mathematician Leonhard Euler some two hundred years earlier—the so-called Euler beta-function—seemed to describe numerous properties of strongly interacting particles in one fell swoop."[660] That Euler, in the late-eighteenth century, had no intention of mathematically mirroring the strong nuclear force (which was not discovered until 1932) powerfully supports Jung and Pauli's theory that the mirror-symmetries between the mathematical world of numbers and the physical world of things inevitably emerge from the underlying archetypes. Citing similar examples of mathematical formulas preceding the discovery of the physical processes they mirror, Dantzig writes that "the mathematician may be compared to a designer of garments, who is utterly oblivious of the creatures whom his garments may fit."[661]

Greene goes on to explain that, two years after Veneziano accidentally discovered the correlation between Euler's formula and the strong force, Yoichiro Nambu, Holger Nielson, and Leonard Susskind each independently "showed that if one modeled elementary particles as little, vibrating, one-dimensional strings, their nuclear interactions could be described exactly by Euler's function."[662] There is thus a threefold synchronicity related to the discovery of string theory: First, there is Euler's two-hundred-year-old formula, which just happens to describe the strong nuclear force. Second, there is Veneziano's unplanned discovery of that previously unsuspected mirror-symmetry. Finally, there is the nearly simultaneous, yet independent co-discovery by Nambu, Nielson, and Susskind that Euler's formula precisely describes the nuclear interactions of elementary particles if we model them as vibrating strings, as opposed to tiny points.

Not only does Susskind's holographic string theory provide a surprisingly plausible connecting mechanism to account for synchronicity (the strings that stretch out to and back from the holographic film at the cosmic horizon), but the entire history of string theory is evidence in favor of Jung's synchronicity theory. Indeed, according to Susskind himself, "the discovery of String Theory, which in a sense is still ongoing, was full of twists of fate, reversals of fortune, and serendipity."[663] It seems that the serendipitous correlation between Susskind's atheistically presented string theory and Jung's transpersonally oriented psychology is the ultimate reversal of fortune in the history of string theory; the inevitable "*enantiodramia*" before the final union of opposites.[664]

It is doubly ironic, then, that Susskind presents his string theory as the definitive alternative to the idea of God, because the cosmology he describes corroborates Jung's near-death experience account of the cosmic horizon and his related conception of the God archetype as the mandala-manifesting union of all opposites, while the series of synchronicities that led to Susskind's string theory indicate that the collective unconscious God archetype (the Self inside us all) has been orchestrating the emergence of Susskind's theory from the beginning, as if stringing him along.

An Archetypal Cosmology

In *Synchronicity*, Jung laments the difficulty of establishing empirical evidence for his theory. After citing the example of how Galileo's discovery of the moons of Jupiter met the prejudiced scorn of his age, Jung states that the sad fact that "man learns nothing from history . . . will present us with the greatest difficulties as soon as we set about collecting empirical material that would throw a little light on this dark subject [synchronicity], for we shall be quite certain to find it where all the authorities have assured us that nothing is to be found."[665] Though some types of synchronicity cannot generally be immediately experienced by more than a few people at a time (for example, Jung's "golden scarab" synchronicity, which only he and his patient witnessed), Jung believed that astrological synchronicities could provide collectively observable, regularly recurring evidence of meaningful coincidences between the archetypal quality of life on Earth and the positions of the planets, including the Sun and Moon.

In his 1930 memorial address for the translator of the *I Ching*, "Richard Wilhelm: In Memoriam," Jung says that "astrology would be an example of synchronicity on a grand scale if only there were enough thoroughly tested findings to support it."[666] Fulfilling Jung's hope, in *Cosmos and Psyche*, Richard Tarnas (who proved his world-class status as a cultural historian in *The Passion of the Western Mind*) provides thoroughly researched findings that clearly reveal symbolically significant coincidences between the positions of the planets (each of which is associated with a unique deity embodying a mythically defined combination of archetypes) and the historical evolution of cultural life in the West.[667] Susskind's empirically unsubstantiated string theory of holographic information conservation at the cosmic horizon provides a plausible connecting mechanism to account for the occurrences of synchronicities in general, and astrological synchronicities in particular. And conversely, astrological synchronicities provide the most widely accessible empirical evidence that indicates such a connecting mechanism must exist.

My purpose is not to explain the exact procedures of astrology, but to suggest that those procedures are adequately explained by Tarnas in a way that enables us competently to judge the evidence he presents for ourselves.[668] For the purpose of gathering empirical evidence to support the proposed synthesis of Susskind's string theory and Jung's psychology (especially his synchronicity theory), the main value of Tarnas' astrological study of the history of Western culture lies not so much in the fact that it enables us to predict the archetypal dynamics of the future unfolding of history (although it does do that); nor in the fact that it gives us nuanced insights into our own psychological development (which it also does); nor, for this purpose, does the chief value of Tarnas' book lay in the fact that it provides a cosmologically embedded understanding of the historical development of cultural world views. Rather, for the purpose of establishing empirical evidence that supports the synthesis of Susskind's and Jung's theories, the greatest benefit Tarnas' book provides is its potential to convince intelligent, skeptical people that astrological synchronicities simply occur at all, which automatically implies the existence of some cosmic coordinating mechanism to account for those meaningful coincidences. Susskind's string theory of holographic information conservation at the cosmic horizon and each concentric boundary of three-dimensional space appears to be the most plausible explanation for these astrological synchronicities. Thus, *Cosmos and Psyche* may be the most compelling compilation of empirical evidence for Jung's synchronicity theory *and* Susskind's holographic string theory available, while the Susskind-Jung synthesis provides an elaborate psycho-physical cosmology that explains how astrological correlations work.[669]

In resounding accord with Jung's theory that mandalas are the spontaneously emerging images of the archetype of wholeness through the union of opposites, it seems that as each field of thought approaches completeness, or wholeness, through the union of opposing principles, the mandala structure is often revealed as its fundamental ordering principle: in the field of psychology, Jung's mandala model of the Self, which unites the conscious and the unconscious; in the field of mathematics, the unit circle centered at point 0, which unites the "real" and "imaginary" number lines on the complex number plane (which extends to a point at infinity in the Riemann sphere); in the field of physics, Susskind's string theory of information conservation in the cosmic mandala of a black hole, including our inside-out black hole universe, which unites the opposing principles of general relativity and quantum mechanics. Given these historical precedents, it is reasonable to assume that as the field of cultural history approaches completeness, it too will reveal a mandala as the fundamental ordering principle through which it unites previously irreconcilable principles. It seems that the field of cultural history is nearing completeness in the method of archetypal history, which utilizes the astrological ordering principle of the horoscope mandala, an interpretive lens which unites the overarching opposition between the modes of thought associated with science and religion.[670]

As seen above, in *Mysterium Coniunctionis*, Jung writes that, "if mandala symbolism is the psychological equivalent of the *unus mundus*, then synchronicity is its parapsychological equivalent."[671] Therefore, if the empirically observable gravitational effects of black holes are the physical correlates of the psychic mandala images of the *unus mundus*, and if Susskind's quantum theory of gravity is correct, then synchronicity is the empirically observable, parapsychological equivalent of what Susskind calls the "cinematic hologram" projected by fundamental strings from the cosmic horizon of the universe.[672] The correlation between Jung's theory of the mandala images of the Self and his theory of astrological synchronicity becomes clear when he says that "the horoscope is itself a mandala (a clock) with a dark centre, and a leftward *circumambulatio* with 'houses' and planetary phases."[673] The horoscope mandala as a whole, representing the "real" positions of the planets and the "imaginary" archetypes (the planetary gods) with which they are associated, also seems archetypally similar to the mathematical mandala that gave birth to twentieth-century physics: the unit circle, which is one part "real," and one part "imaginary."

Another archetypal parallel is apparent in the way Susskind's mandala cosmology describes Earth in the center of the universe, and all of the information from the past, present, and future of three-dimensional space as being smeared out and recorded on a two-dimensional holographic film at the spherical horizon of the cosmos, while the geocentric horoscope mandala of archetypal astrology similarly describes the meaningful coincidences between the archetypal tenor of life on Earth (the central point) and the relative positions of the orbiting planets by superimposing all of them onto a single encompassing circle that also represents the twelve constellations of the zodiac. In other words, the fact that the circular perimeter of the horoscope mandala contains all of the information describing the qualitative dynamics of the three-dimensional volume of space (the solar system and surrounding constellations) is archetypally similar to Susskind's string theory, according to which all information from the volume of space is conserved ultimately on a two-dimensional film at the spherical border of the universe, where space is expanding away from Earth in every direction at the absolute speed of light.

In *On the Nature of the Psyche*, Jung describes the early sixteenth-century German alchemist and astrologer Paracelsus' equation of the planets and constellations with the archetypes embedded in our psyches, writing that Paracelsus

> beholds the darksome psyche as a star-strewn night sky, whose planets and fixed constellations represent the archetypes in all their luminosity and numinosity. The starry vault of heaven is in truth the open book of cosmic projection, in which are reflected the mythologems, i.e., the archetypes. In this vision, astrology and alchemy, the two classical functionaries of the psychology of the collective unconscious, join hands.[674]

From our perspective on Earth, the planets and fixed constellations all seem to be superimposed on a single two-dimensional sphere, known by astronomers as the celestial sphere. According to Susskind, our three-dimensional world is projected by one dimensional strings from the two-dimensional film at the cosmic horizon, in each point of which the past, present, and future are holographically interwoven, which means that the temporal forms of the material world radiate from the eternal forms of the ultimate celestial sphere. Plato called the eternal forms radiating in from the "mother substance" of the cosmic horizon *ideas*.[675] Referring to that word, Jung says: "It goes back to the *eidos* concept of Plato, and the eternal ideas are primordial images stored up . . . (in a supracelestial place) as eternal, transcendent forms."[676]

Jung equates his theory of the archetypes with Plato's theory of eternal forms, or *eidos*, of the supracelestial place, writing: "'Archetype' is an explanatory paraphrase of the Platonic *eidos*."[677] Thus, a synthesis of Susskind and Jung indicates that the holographic cosmic horizon is functionally equivalent to the collective unconscious container of the archetypes, which lends credence to Paracelsus' equation of the star-strewn celestial sphere with the archetypes from which the cosmos is projected.

It is reasonable to suggest that the planets and constellations on the celestial sphere reflect the archetypes of the collective unconscious if we assume that all of the planets and stars are interwoven with all of the archetypes in the holographic horizon of the cosmos. In that case, each archetype radiates its many material manifestations in the three-dimensional world by projecting fundamental threads from the cosmic horizon, which has two effects: first of all, it creates the celestial objects in the star-strewn night sky, in such a way, secondly, that the ceaselessly streaming cinematic strings are subsequently filtered through those planets and constellations on the celestial sphere on their way down to Earth. In other words, we receive the archetypes' numinous influence from the fundamental strings radiating from the collective unconscious cosmic horizon only after they pass through the filtering lens of the star-strewn night sky, which could account for why the planets and constellations seem to embody the meaning of certain archetypes.

For the purpose of establishing empirical evidence in support of Jung's synchronicity theory and Susskind's string theory, it can be demonstrated empirically that the positions of the celestial bodies on the celestial sphere at each moment are predictably synchronized with a psychological atmosphere of corresponding archetypal qualities on Earth. A particularly pertinent example is Tarnas' description of the Uranus-Neptune conjunction that peaked in 1992-1993, the latter of which was the same year Susskind and 't Hooft developed their holographic interpretation of string theory.[678] Uranus, according to Tarnas and many other astrologers, represents the Promethean archetype, the rebellious Titan who stole fire from the Olympian gods to give to humans, and is therefore associated, among other things, "with the heavens, the cosmic, the astronomical and astrological."[679] According to Tarnas, "Neptune is associated with the transcendent, spiritual, ideal, symbolic, and imaginative dimensions of life; with the subtle, formless, intangible, and invisible; with the unitive, timeless, immaterial, and infinite; with all that which transcends the limited literal temporal and material world of concretely empirical reality."[680]

In another passage, Tarnas explains how the emergence of string theory in the early 1990s is archetypally correlated with the conjunction (relative to Earth) of Uranus and Neptune:

> Many characteristic Uranus-Neptune themes were evident in the sciences during these same years. The rise of theories of hyperspace, alternative realities, virtual particles, invisible dark matter and dark energy, and multidimensional string theory (with the universe composed of strings "so small that a direct observation would be tantamount to reading the text on this page from a distance of 100 light-years") all suggest this archetypal gestalt. Similarly reflective of the Uranus-Neptune complex is the increasingly popular "multiverse" theory, with our universe seen as but one of countless other universes existing in other dimensions, with new self-reproducing inflationary universes being endlessly

produced out of black holes and big bangs like bubbles out of an infinite sea of bubbles.

Here we see the spontaneous rise in the scientific mind of Neptunian metaphors and qualities (sea, bubbles, infinity, invisible dimensions of reality, unfettered speculative imagination) combined with Uranian themes (astronomical science, surprising new realities, ceaseless cosmic creativity and new beginnings).[681]

Susskind's realization in the early 1990s that the universe we perceive is one of innumerable bubbles of holographic illusion floating in an infinite sea of parallel universes correlates beautifully with the archetypal qualities represented by the planets Uranus and Neptune, which were conjunct relative to Earth at the time. Even though Susskind would later present his holographic string theory as evidence against the need for an organizing psyche to fine tune the physical constants of nature required for life to exist in the universe, the historical fact that his theory coincidentally emerged when Uranus and Neptune were conjunct can be presented as an example of astrological synchronicity, which inherently points to the meaningful union of mind and matter in the mandala-manifesting archetype of the Self.

Susskind's theory furthermore provides a plausible cosmological mechanism to explain where synchronicities originate: at the cosmic horizon. Even without knowing how astrology works, one can see that it combines most of the symbolic components required for the synthesis of Susskind's string theory and Jung's psychology. First, astrology deals with the cosmic horizon from the geocentric perspective, which places each of us in the center of a cosmic mandala representing the Self. Second, it superimposes all of the planets and constellations on the circumference of the horoscope mandala, which is similar to the way that Susskind's string theory superimposes all of the information describing all of the planets in all of the galaxies in the universe at the cosmic horizon. Finally, astrology describes how the center of the cosmos (representing life on Earth) and the circumference are meaningfully related by synchronicities.

CONCLUSION
NDEs, String Theory, Cosmological
Synchronicities, and Plato's *Republic*

In a letter Jung wrote to A.D. Cornel on February 9, 1960, he lists two specific kinds of research that may provide empirical evidence for his synchronicity theory:

> Two roads for further investigation exist: 1 experiment, and 2 the study of case material.
> 1. Under certain conditions it is possible to experiment with archetypes, as my 'astrological experiment' has shown. . . .
> 2. This would require the observation of individual cases of death, severe illness, and serious accidents.[682]

Following Jung's advice, I have described correlations between Susskind's string theory and Jung's synchronicity theory by focusing especially on Jung's near-death experience and his endorsement of an archetypally informed approach to astrology.

However, to substantiate the claim that the mirror-symmetries between Susskind's string theory and Jung's psychology really are reflecting the same underlying archetype of the Self, it would also be helpful to demonstrate a similar combination of ideas in historical examples.[683] According to Whitehead, "the safest general characterization of the European philosophical tradition is that it consists of a series of footnotes to Plato."[684] It is therefore especially appropriate to seek corroborating historical examples of the Susskind-Jung synthesis from Plato, as we did above, and will do again now.

As described in several of Plato's Dialogues, knowledge is recollection of the eternal ideas we forget at birth, remember at death, and forget again at each new birth in a material body. More specifically, Plato describes death as a periodic return to the horizon of the cosmos, where souls can behold the eternal forms of knowledge.[685] Thus, it seems that the synthesis of Susskind's string theory and the four aspects of Jung's psychology discussed above (his Leap Day equation of 1952, translated as Psyche = Singularity; his near-death experience of the cosmic horizon; his theory of the psychic mandala images of the Self; and his theory of synchronicity) are prefigured in Plato's *Republic*. There is no historical material more central to the canon of Western philosophy than Plato's Dialogues, the most central of which is the *Republic*, rendering the parallels between Plato's cosmology in the *Republic* and the cosmology described by a synthesis of Susskind's string theory and Jung's psychology all the more arresting.

Recall the passage from Brian Greene, in which he compares Susskind's string theory to Plato's cave allegory from the *Republic*:

> Two millennia later, it seems that Plato's cave may be more than a metaphor. To turn his suggestion on its head, reality—not its mere shadow—may take place on a distant boundary surface, while everything we witness in the three common spatial dimensions is a projection of that faraway unfolding. Reality, that is, may be akin to a hologram. Or, really, a holographic movie.[686]

As discussed above, the two-dimensional cosmic horizon Susskind describes is perhaps more accurately described as a higher-dimensional region because it contains all of the information structuring the lower dimensions of space and the time dimension. Moreover, although, from our reference frame on Earth, the cosmic horizon is a one-sided, imaginary mathematical shell, the eye-witness accounts of near-death experience survivors indicate that, from the perspective of disembodied psyches who travel to it, the cosmic horizon is a higher-dimensional, hyper-realistic, ecstatic realm where the past, present, and future of three-dimensional space are experienced simultaneously. Thus, we can correlate Susskind's string theory of holographic information conservation at the cosmic horizon and Plato's cave allegory without turning the allegory on its head, as Greene suggests. Rather, Susskind's theory seems to fulfill the allegory by teaching us how to rotate the eye of our soul away from the three-dimensional world of material forms unfolding through time to the inner world of eternal forms, culminating with the idea of the Good, the archetype of the Sun. This spiritual Sun, of which the visible Sun is a reflection, can be correlated with Jung's archetype of the Self, which can be equated with the cosmic mandala formed by the gravitational singularity, the holographic horizon of the cosmos, and the psychoid string that connects them.

After the cave allegory Plato depicts Socrates developing a mathematical course of study that teaches students how to describe each successively higher dimension of nature: simple arithmetic that can be charted on a one-dimensional number line; two-dimensional plane geometry; three-dimensional solid geometry; and, finally, the four-dimensional study of time as measured by the periodic movements of solid bodies, especially the orbits of the planets and vibrations of musical strings. These four fields of mathematical study prepare the student to see how each of them is united in their common core, the brilliant idea of the Good. Unintentionally fulfilling the promise of this original academic curriculum, Susskind fused music and astronomy into a string theory that helps us rotate our understanding of ourselves away from our three-dimensional bodies by teaching us that they are holographic projections of our eternal selves interwoven with all knowledge at the cosmic horizon.

The corroborating parallels between Plato's cosmology and the synthesis of Susskind's and Jung's theories continue at the end of the *Republic*, in the myth of Er, in which Plato depicts Socrates recalling a tale he heard about a warrior named Er who woke up on his own funeral pyre twelve days after he died on the battlefield. According to Socrates, Er "said that when his soul [*psyche*] went forth from his body he journeyed with a great company and that they came to a mysterious region."[687] Er's perspective from that mysterious region enabled him to see the whole cosmos. Near the end of his vision, Er saw the spinning "spindle of Necessity," a rainbow-colored pillar of light piercing through the center of the geocentric cosmos, consisting of eight concentric "whorls" nested like bowls (upward facing hemispheres).[688] Allan Bloom nicely summarizes the passage in an endnote to his translation of the *Republic*:

> Er has reached the extremes of the cosmos, and he sees there the structure of the heavens. The whorls represent the spheres of the fixed stars, the planets, the sun, and the moon. The motions of these whorls account for the visible movements of those bodies; their color, brightness, and distance from each other are accounted for by the description of the lips of the whorls.[689]

The cosmos in the myth of Er resembles an upside-down umbrella (a set of concentric bowls with a spindle through the middle), though, above, we saw Plato depict the Pythagorean philosopher Timaeus describing the universe in a way that is more similar to Susskind's inside-out black hole model of the cosmos, with a central singularity and holographic horizon.[690] In the *Timaeus* the soul of the universe is described as the central point of a sphere that somehow permeates the volume and exterior boundary, the latter of which, furthermore, is compared to an eternal mother and receptacle of all being that mysteriously partakes of the intelligible.[691] It helps to keep the spherical mandala model of the universe from the *Timaeus* in mind when examining the myth of Er in the *Republic* because, it seems, in order to help us imagine the inner structure of the concentric spheres of the universe, and the way information is transmitted from the outermost sphere through the inner ones, Socrates presents the universe as if it is an upward facing set of nested hemispheres.

In a way that is especially similar to Susskind's string theory, in the myth of Er the information describing the past, present, and future of each soul's biography is encoded in the form of threads that are woven into the rim of the outermost hemisphere first, then through each concentric rim representing the planetary orbits around Earth. More specifically, according to Socrates, while in a disembodied state, Er perceived three sister goddesses, the Fates (representing past, present, and future), weaving the "threads of [the psyche's] destiny," first into the outermost perimeter of the spinning cosmos (Clotho), then with each concentric planetary orbit around Earth (Atropos).[692]

According to Er's account, lots are cast on the ground in front of the group of souls with whom he is traveling. The number each receives determines the order in which each soul gets to choose from the inventory of next lives, which are also cast before them. Er is commanded not to choose a lot, or a next life, so that he can tell people back on Earth what he saw when he returns to his body. After all the souls, influenced by the habits of their past lives, had chosen their next lives, the daemon (translated as "deity," a kind of guardian angel) associated with each life led its respective soul first to the outermost sphere of the cosmos, "to Clotho, to pass under her hand and under the revolving orbit of the spindle, and so to ratify the destiny the soul had chosen in the lottery. Then . . . the deity led the soul to Atropos and her spinning, to make the web woven by Clotho fixed and unalterable."[693]

In an endnote to this translation of the *Republic*, Robin Waterfield interprets this passage from the myth of Er astrologically:

Perhaps we are to imagine one of them spinning the warp, and the other the woof, of a person's life. There are clear astrological connotations to the passage: the word translated 'destiny' also means (or came to mean) 'degree on the zodiacal circle'; 'ratify' is cognate with the rulership of a planet. In short, as well as setting an individual's destiny in a more abstract sense, the Fates do so according to the positions of the planets (Atropos) and the zodiacal signs (Clotho). Note that, despite Plato's use of the word 'unalterable', it is only the broad framework which is fixed; the whole of Plato's philosophy leaves room for self-improvement within that framework.[694]

The three Fates, who represent past, present, and future, weave the thread of each soul's destiny first into the zodiacal signs at the cosmic horizon and then into the rim of each concentric orbit of the planets centering on Earth. It is therefore plausible to suggest, as Waterfield does, that, according to Plato's cosmological model, our fate is at least to some degree astrologically determined by—or as Jung and Tarnas would say, is synchronistically correlated with—the planetary archetypes. Those astrological synchronicities in Plato's model appear to be transmitted by the fundamental threads of destiny, which provides striking evidence for the suggestion that the synthesis of Susskind's and Jung's theories mirrors the same underlying archetype of wholeness that has inspired similar images and concepts among great thinkers in the past.

It is also plausible to suggest that the information describing the fate of each psyche in Plato's model is encoded on its thread of destiny by the combined sound vibrations of the singing Fates— "Lachesis singing the things that were, Clotho the things that are, and Atropos the things that are to be"—and the Sirens, whom Socrates describes as follows: "On each of the rims of the circles a Siren stood, borne around in its revolution and uttering one sound, one note, and from all the eight there was the concord of a single harmony."[695] The strings of destiny in the myth of Er contain the information required for each psyche's fate to unfold on Earth, and the Fates sing while weaving the information of each psyche's destiny into the rims of the concentric hemispheres of the cosmos—from the outermost sphere of fixed stars to the innermost sphere that carries the Moon—each of which further carries a singing Siren, thereby precisely connecting a near-death experience with the concepts of planetary archetypes, cosmic threads, musical vibrations, and information conservation at the cosmic horizon, and at each concentric boundary of three-dimensional space.

NOTES

[1] Carl Jung, *Memories, Dreams, Reflections*, Ed. Aniela Jaffe (New York: Vintage Books, 1989) 292.

[2] Carl Jung, *Encountering Jung: Jung on Synchronicity and the Paranormal*, Ed. Roderick Main (Princeton, New Jersey: Princeton University Press, 1997) 162.

[3] Plato, *The Collected Dialogues of Plato, Including the Letters*, eds. Edith Hamilton and Huntington Cairns (New Jersey: Princeton University Press, 1994), *Timaeus* 35a-37a, 51a-53a; *Republic* 514a-518c, 533d, 620e.

[4] According to Pauli,

> *The ordering and regulating factors must be placed beyond the distinction of "physical" and "psychic"*—as Plato's "ideas" share the notion of a concept and of a force of nature (they create actions out of themselves). I am very much in favor of referring to the "ordering" and "regulating" factors in terms of "archetypes"; but then it would be impermissible to *define* them as contents of the *psyche*. The mentioned inner images ("dominant features of the collective unconscious" after Jung) are rather *psychic* manifestations of the archetypes which, *however*, would *also* have to put forth, create, condition anything lawlike in the behavior of the corporeal world. The laws of this world would then be the *physical manifestations of the archetypes.* . . . Each law of nature should then have an inner correspondence and vice versa, even though this is not always directly visible today. (Harold Atmanspacher and Hans Primas, "Pauli's Ideas on Mind and Matter in the Context of Contemporary Science," *The Journal of Consciousness Studies* 13 [3]: 2006, 19)

Notice how Pauli equates Jung's concept of archetypes with Plato's concept of absolute ideas. According to Jung, "'Archetype' is an explanatory paraphrase of the Platonic *eidos*." (Carl Jung, *The Basic Writings of C.G. Jung*, Ed. Violet Staub de Laszlo [New York: Random House, 1993] 360). Elsewhere, again referring to the historical root of the word idea, Jung says "it goes back to the *eidos* concept of Plato, and the eternal ideas are primordial images stored up … (in a supracelestial place) as eternal, transcendent forms." (Carl Jung, *On the Nature of the Psyche* [New Jersey: Princeton University Press, 1969] 101)

[5] *Memories, Dreams, Reflections* 310; Carl Jung, *Two Essays on Analytical Psychology*, trans. R. F. C. Hull (Princeton, New Jersey: Princeton University Press, 1966) 237-238. While Jung and Pauli referred to the ultimate archetype as the *unus mundus* and archetype of the Self, in the famous cave allegory in the *Republic* Plato called it "the idea of the Good." (*Republic* 517c)

[6] According to Jung, "The mandala symbolizes, by its central point, the ultimate unity of all archetypes as well as of the multiplicity of the phenomenal world, and is therefore the empirical equivalent of the metaphysical concept of a *unus mundus*." (*Encountering Jung* 165)

[7] Leonard Susskind, *The Black Hole War: My Battle with Stephen Hawking to Make the World Safe for Quantum Mechanics* (New York: Little, Brown and Company, 2008) 438; *Memories, Dreams, Reflections* 334-335. Also, the phrase "cosmos and psyche" is the title of a book by Richard Tarnas, *Cosmos and Psyche: Intimations of a New World View* (New York: Penguin Group, 2006). The new world view described in this book is in line with, and partially inspired by the world view Tarnas describes.

[8] Leonard Susskind, *The Cosmic Landscape: String Theory and the Illusion of Intelligent Design* (New York: Back Bay Books, 2006) 204-207.

[9] Despite the overtly atheistic stance Susskind takes in his books, in an interview in 2011 he denied that he is either an atheist, an agnostic, or a believer. In a television interview about agnosticism Susskind explains that he is not interested in the "God hypothesis" because it raises more questions than it answers about the creation of the universe (Who made God? What is God made of? Does that material obey the laws of quantum mechanics?), and therefore fails to satisfy the scientific criteria for a valuable theory. When the interviewer, a self-described agnostic, points out that the same objection can be leveled at string theory, Susskind readily admits it. More than that, he softens his position about intelligent design:

I don't reject the possibility that there may have been an intelligence that in some way or another was involved with the creation of the universe. I don't reject it. Not at all. I simply ask, if it's true, how do you describe it? What are the rules? How did it get there? It just provokes more curiosity. . . . And until I can answer or at least attempt to get a hypothesis about that, I lose interest. . . . People ask me, am I an atheist? No. Am I a religious believer? No. Oh, that must make me an agnostic? No. I'm not even that! I just feel totally at sea. Totally at a loss for what to make out of the existence of the universe. (Leonard Susskind, in "Are Science and Religion at War?" *Closer to Truth*, written by Robert Lawrence Kuhn, directed by Peter Getzels, season 6, episode 11, PBS, first broadcast March 10, 2011, https://www.youtube.com/watch?v=0p-Sqo83GX0)

It seems blatantly contradictory for Susskind to say that he does not reject the theory of intelligent design, *not at all*, after he published a book entitled *The Cosmic Landscape: String Theory and the Illusion of Intelligent Design*. In that book, Susskind argues that the appearance of intelligent design is an illusion made possible by the tremendous plethora of universes in what he calls the megaverse: given enough alternative combinations of varying laws of physics and constants of nature presiding in each universe, some of them are bound to be perfectly fine-tuned for self-aware life to evolve. With that in mind, he argues that Charles Darwin and Alfred Wallace are the fathers of modern cosmology:

I'm not a historian, but I'll venture an opinion: modern cosmology really began with Darwin and Wallace. . . . They freed us from the supernatural by showing that complex and even intelligent life could arise from chance, competition, and natural causes. Cosmologists would have to do as well: the basis for cosmology would have to be impersonal rules that are the same throughout the universe and whose origin has nothing to do with our own existence. The only god permitted to cosmologists would be Richard Dawkins's "blind watchmaker." (*The Cosmic Landscape* 17-18)

Richard Dawkins is also popularly known as Darwin's Rottweiler for his over-the-top style of denigrating all forms of religious belief in the name of Darwinian science. By citing Dawkins as a prophet of modern cosmology's ideal god, Susskind clearly takes an atheistic stance. He portrays himself as an earnest atheist waging intellectual war against benighted belief in supernatural intelligence. It is to that atheistic persona that Susskind presents in his books that this book responds. Nevertheless, it is important to remember that in the interview cited above Susskind refuses to define himself as either an atheist or an agnostic, and says that he does not at all reject the possibility of intelligent design. Given the sincerity with which he seemed to be speaking in the interview, it seems to me that Susskind may have adopted the hardline atheistic pose in his books to dissociate himself as clearly as possible from the many religious interpretations of the holographic principle he applied to string theory, and thereby save his reputation in the largely atheistic, academic community, which determines who gets funded for research and who does not. Susskind even alludes to that scenario in a roundabout way by describing a hypothetical conversation between fish, some of whom are physicists (fyshicists) and some of whom are cosmologists (codmologists). They are discussing the Ickthropic principle, the equivalent of the Anthropic Principle for fish, which says that the water temperature is in the range that keeps water liquid

> because only in this case could fish exist to observe it!
>
> "Garbage!" said the fyshicists. "That's not science. It's religion. It's just giving up. And besides, if we agree with you, everyone will laugh at us and take away our funding." (*The Cosmic Landscape* 171)

Even if Susskind dismisses my proposed synthesis of his string theory with Jung's psychology, he should still be interested in this book because, in the same interview about agnosticism described above, he said "a strong need for faith-based, irrational beliefs, I am fascinated by it and *extremely* curious about it." (Are Science and Religion at War)

[10] To describe the relationship between archetypes and instincts, Jung uses the example of a Yucca moth which perceives a yucca flower, which opens each year "for one night only." (Carl Jung, *The Portable Jung*, ed. Joseph

Campbell [New York: Penguin Books, 1976] 51) The moths are born after their parents die, and die before their young are born, and they only see the yucca flower open for one night. After mating, the female moth instinctively gathers pollen from one flower, rolls it into a pellet, then visits another flower, cuts open the spindle, inserts her eggs, and finally seals the vase-like opening of the pistil with the pellet of pollen. No other moths could have taught her how to perform this complicated task, which indicates that her pattern of behavior is driven by some pre-programmed instinct that was triggered when the moth's sense perception of the yucca flower resonated with some inner archetype. According to Jung,

> Just as conscious apprehension gives our actions form and direction, so unconscious apprehension through the archetype determines the form and direction of instinct. If we call instinct "refined," then the "intuition" which brings the instinct into play, in other words the apprehension by means of the archetype, must be something incredibly precise. Thus the yucca moth must carry within it an image, as it were, of the situation that "triggers off" its instinct. This image enables it to "recognize" the yucca flower and its structure. (*The Portable Jung* 56)

[11] The following is a letter from Jung to Carl Seelig about Jung's association with Einstein and Pauli.

Dear Dr. Seelig, 25 February 1953

I got to know Albert Einstein through one of his pupils, a Dr. Hopf if I remember correctly. Professor Einstein was my guest on several occasions at dinner, when, as you have heard, Adolf Keller was present on one of them and on others Professor Eugen Bleuler, a psychiatrist and my former chief. These were very early days when Einstein was developing his first theory of relativity. He tried to instill into us the elements of it, more or less successfully. As non-mathematicians we psychiatrists had difficulty in following his argument. Even so, I understood enough to form a powerful impression of him. It was above all the simplicity and directness of his genius as a thinker that impressed me mightily and exerted a lasting influence on my own intellectual work. It was Einstein who first started me off thinking about a possible relativity of time as well as space, and their psychic conditionality. More than thirty years later this stimulus led to my relation with the physicist Professor W. Pauli and to my thesis of psychic synchronicity. With Einstein's departure from Zurich my relation with him ceased, and I hardly think he has any recollection of me. One can scarcely imagine a greater contrast than that between the mathematical and the psychological mentality. The one is extremely quantitative and the other just as extremely qualitative.

With kind regards,

Yours sincerely,

C.G. Jung ~Carl Jung, Letters Vol. II, Pages108-109. (*Encountering Jung*122)

[12] See David Lindorff, *Pauli and Jung: The Meeting of Two Great Minds* (Wheaton, Illinois: Quest Books, the Theosophical Publishing House, 2004).

[13] *Memories, Dreams, Reflections* 292.

[14] *Memories, Dreams, Reflections* 295-296.

[15] *Encountering Jung* 162.

[16] Robert Bruce Ware, *Hegel: The Logic of Self-Consciousness and the Legacy of Subjective Freedom*. (Edinburgh, England: Edinburgh University Press, 1999) 59-63.

[17] *The Cosmic Landscape* 180-181, 265-266, 269; *The Black Hole War* 339.

[18] *Pauli and Jung* 59.

[19] See Ken Wilber, ed., *Quantum Questions: Mystical Writings of the World's Greatest Physicists*. (Boston: Shambhala, 2001).

[20] *The Cosmic Landscape* 5-6.

[21] David Bohm, *Wholeness and the Implicate Order* (London: Routledge and Kegan Paul, 1980).

[22] *Wholeness and the Implicate Order* 188.

[23] Bohm's strategy was furthermore expanded to the field of neuroscience by the Stanford neuroscientist Karl Pribram, to the field of transpersonal psychology by Stanislav Grof, and to the field of political ecology by Al Gore. As Gore explains in his best seller, *Earth in the Balance: Ecology and the Human Spirit*: "My understanding of how God is manifest in the world can be best conveyed through the metaphor of the hologram." (Al Gore, *Earth in the Balance: Ecology and the Human Spirit* [Boston: Houghton Mifflin, 1992] 265)

[24] *Encountering Jung* 162.

[25] *The Black Hole War* 25.

[26] Norton M. Wise, ed., *The Values of Precision* (New Jersey: Princeton University Press, 1995) 147-148.

[27] Brain Greene, *The Fabric of the Cosmos: Space, Time, and the Texture of Reality* (New York: Vintage Books, 2005) 40-47.

[28] *The Fabric of the Cosmos* 42.

[29] *The Fabric of the Cosmos* 43.

[30] *The Fabric of the Cosmos* 43.

[31] To help clarify the epochal contrast between Einstein's theory of an elastic fabric of four-dimensional space-time, and Newton's theory of three, rigidly fixed dimensions of empty space and one dimension of forward flowing time, I turn to Newton's own definitions in his master work, *Philosophiæ Naturalis Principia Mathematica* (1687):

> I. Absolute, true, and mathematical time, of itself, and from its own nature, flows equably without relation to anything external, and by another name is called duration. . . .
> II. Absolute space, in its own nature, without relation to anything external, remains always similar and immovable. (Isaac Newton, in "Newton's Scholium on Time, Space, Place and Motion," *Stanford Encyclopedia of Philosophy*, para. 2-3, 2013,

http://plato.stanford.edu/entries/newton- stm/scholium.html)

Brian Greene comments on Newton's concepts of space and time as follows:

> Not everyone agreed. Some argued persuasively that it made little sense to ascribe existence to something you can't feel, grasp, or affect. But the explanatory and predictive power of Newton's equations quieted the critics. For the next two hundred years, his absolute conception of space and time was dogma. (*The Fabric of the Cosmos* 8)

[32] Brian Greene, *The Elegant Universe: Superstrings, Hidden Dimensions, and the Quest for the Ultimate Theory* (New York: W.W. Norton & Company, Inc., 2003) 25.

[33] *The Elegant Universe* 50.

[34] David Bohm, *The Essential David Bohm*, Ed. Lee Nichol (London: Routledge, 2003) 152.

[35] Albert Einstein, *Relativity. The Special and General Theory* (London: Routledge Classics, 2001) 29-31.

[36] Brian Greene, "The Fabric of the Cosmos: The Illusion of Time." *NOVA*, season 39, episode 6, directed by Randall MacLowry, PBS, November 9, 2011. Transcript: http://www.pbs.org/wgbh/nova/physics/fabric-of-cosmos.html#fabric-time.

[37] J. B. Kennedy, *Space, Time, and Einstein: An Introduction* (Montreal, Canada: McGill-Queen's University Press, 2003) 53.

[38] *Relativity. The Special and General Theory* 152.

[39] Roger Penrose seconds Einstein's claim: "The idea that the history of the universe should be viewed, physically, as a *four-*dimensional spacetime, rather than as a three-dimensional space evolving with time is indeed fundamental to modern physics." (Roger Penrose, "Introduction," in *Six Not-So-Easy Pieces: Einstein's Relativity, Symmetry, and Space-Time*, by Richard Feynman [New York: Basic Books, 1997] xiv) Susskind explains this concept:

There is a fourth direction to *space-time*: past-future. Ever since Einstein's discovery of the Special Theory of Relativity, physicists have been in the habit of picturing the world as a four-dimensional space-time that encompasses not only *the now*, but also all of the future and the past. A point in space-time—a where and a when—is called an event. (*The Cosmic Landscape* 38)

[40] According to Kennedy: "a few months after Einstein published his first paper on relativity in 1905, he sent in a sort of extended footnote to the same journal." (*Space, Time, and Einstein* 40)

[41] According to Susskind: "Mass and energy are really the same thing. They are just expressed in different units: to convert from mass to energy, you multiply by the square of the speed of light." (*The Cosmic Landscape* 73)

[42] *The Elegant Universe* 56.

[43] *The Elegant Universe* 67-72.

[44] *The Elegant Universe* 67.

[45] The gravitational waves Einstein predicted were detected for the first time on September 15, 2015, as reported on the LIGO Observatory website:

Gravitational Waves Detected 100 Years After Einstein's Prediction

News Release •n February 11, 2016

WASHINGTON, DC/Cascina, Italy (LIGO [Laser Interferometer Gravitational-Wave Observatory], "Gravitational Waves Detected 100 Years After Einstein's Prediction." *News*, February 11, 2016, https://www.ligo.caltech.edu/news/ligo20160211.)

While black hole mergers produce prodigious amounts of energy in the form of gravitational waves, they do not produce light. When two neutron stars merge, however, they produce both gravitational waves and light. This kind of event was first detected on August 17, 2017 (Physics.org, "Astronomers first to see source of gravitational waves in visible light,"

October 16, 2017, https://phys.org/news/2017-10-astronomers-source-gravitational-visible.html#jCp.)

[46] Michio Kaku, *Hyperspace: A Scientific Odyssey Through Parallel Universes, Time Warps, and the Tenth Dimension* (New York: Oxford University Press, 1994) 244.

[47] The National Center for Supercomputing Applications (NCSA) at the University of Illinois at Urbana-Champaign produced a website, *Wrinkles in Spacetime*, where they describe the history of relativity theory. The following is a description of Schwarzschild's two papers.

> For his first attempt, Schwarzschild simplified the problem by considering a perfectly spherical star at rest, ignoring the effects of the star's interior. He sent his preliminary solution of the star's spacetime curvature to Einstein, who reported the results on Schwarzschild's behalf at a physics meeting in January. The curvature of spacetime predicted by the solution became known as the Schwarzschild geometry and had profound implications on future research into gravitation and cosmology.
>
> A few weeks later, Schwarzschild sent a second paper, this time describing the spacetime curvature inside a star. Tragically, Schwarzschild died a few months later of an illness he contracted while at the Russian front.
>
> Schwarzschild was describing a **singularity**, a region of infinite spacetime curvature that is postulated to lie within what has more recently been termed a **black hole**. Einstein considered the "Schwarzschild singularity" and black holes as bizarre constructs, resisting the logic of his own theory right up to his death in 1955. (National Center for Supercomputing Applications [NCSA], *Wrinkles in Spacetime*, November 7, 1995, http://archive.ncsa.illinois.edu/Cyberia/NumRel/EinsteinEquatio ns.html#Spherical)

[48] *The Black Hole War* 455.

[49] I begin the review of the empirical evidence for the physical reality of black holes and the Big Bang with excerpts from the following online

overview entitled "Do Black Holes Really Exist?," which is presented on *The Universe Forum*, which was produced for the NASA Education Support Network by the Harvard Smithsonian Center for Astrophysics (2009), the Director of which is Roy Gould. The article explains that empirical evidence indicates that there are more than a million black holes in our galaxy, and a supermassive black hole weighing more than millions of stars in the center. It also indicates that the same basic pattern of black hole distribution is repeated in most, if not all other galaxies. It goes on to explain:

> Though we cannot see black holes directly, they are so powerful that we can see their unmistakable, dramatic effects on the matter around them. Here are three lines of evidence that black-hole hunters look for:
>
> **A blaze of X-rays...**
>
> **Super-powerful jets of matter...**
>
> **Rapidly moving stars...**
>
> The gravitational field of a black hole tugs on the stars in its vicinity. A super-massive black hole will make whole swarms of stars whip around as they fall under its influence. By following the motions of the orbiting stars, astronomers can deduce the location, and size, of the central black hole they cannot see.
>
> From these and other lines of evidence, astronomers are convinced that black holes are real, and that they play an important role in the universe. (Do Black Holes Really Exist?," which is presented on *The Universe Forum*, which was produced for the NASA Education Support Network by the Harvard Smithsonian Center for Astrophysics (2009), the Director of which is RoyGouldpara. 1-6)

As matter swirls into a rapidly spinning black hole, it creates what is known as an accretion disk: super-heated gas that emits X-ray radiation. That is one type of empirical evidence for black holes. Another type of evidence comes from powerful jets of matter traveling almost at the speed of light, which are sometimes seen spewing up and down from the center of accretion disks. The most dramatic confirmation of the third line of evidence for black holes—rapidly orbiting stars—came in 2008 from a team of astronomers led by Reinhard Genzel, which discovered a supermassive black hole in the center of our Milky Way galaxy. According to Genzel: "The stellar orbits in the galactic centre show that the central mass concentration of four million solar masses must be a black hole, beyond any reasonable doubt." (Reinhard Genzel, in "Proof that Albert Einstein's black holes do exist, claim scientists." *The Telegraph*, December 9, 2008, http://www.telegraph.co.uk/science/science-news/3690822/Proof-that-Albert-Einsteins-black-holes-do-exist-claim-scientists.html.)

Although black holes cannot be seen because light cannot escape from the event horizon, the indirect evidence for the existence of black holes is decisive enough to render it plausible to assume that there really is a singularity in each of their inscrutable centers, as the philosopher of science at Manchester University, J. B. Kennedy, explains: "If black holes are real and physical, then probably actual infinities are too." (*Space, Time, and Einstein* 190)

The empirical evidence for black holes is well established. Similarly, as we will see, the empirical evidence for the Big Bang began in 1929, with Hubble's discovery. In 1964, the two radio-astronomers, Penzias and Wilson, discovered the cosmic microwave background radiation of the Big Bang (*The Cosmic Landscape* 156). More recent and resounding evidence for the Big Bang comes from the WMAP satellite, which Kaku describes: "Today, it has finally been captured on film in exquisite detail by the WMAP satellite, yielding a map never seen before, a photo of the sky showing with breathtaking detail the microwave radiation created by the big bang itself, what has been called the 'echo of creation' by *Time* magazine." (Michio Kaku, *Parallel Worlds: A Journey through Creation, Higher Dimensions, and the Future of the Cosmos* [New York: Anchor Books, 2006] 6-7) According to Kaku, the precision of the WMAP pictures of the CMB radiation indicate that 4% of the mass in the universe comes from visible matter, 23% from dark matter, and 73% from the dark energy of the quantum vacuum (*Parallel Worlds* 11-12). The point for now is that empirical evidence indicates that the physical reality of both black holes and the Big Bang have been proven beyond a reasonable doubt, which indicates that the gravitational singularity is also real, although that idea is flatly rejected by many top physicists.

[50] Jean-Pierre Luminet, "Editorial note to: Georges Lemaître, The beginning of the world from the point of view of quantum theory," *General Relativity and Gravitation* 43 (2): 2011, 2911-2928, http://link.springer.com/article/10.1007%2Fs10714-011-1213-7#page-2. Luminet cites Lemaître's 1927 paper as the birth date of the Big Bang theory (Luminet 2913).

[51] Brian Greene, *The Hidden Reality: Parallel Universes and the Deep Laws of the Cosmos* (New York: Random House, 2011)12.

[52] *The Fabric of the Cosmos* 229.

[53] *The Hidden Reality* 23.

[54] *The Elegant Universe* 82; *Parallel Worlds* 12, 51, 104.

[55] *The Cosmic Landscape* 72.

[56] Physicist Heinz R. Pagels explains:

> Think of a wave moving through space. Sometimes the wave height is just higher than the average level and sometimes lower. The height of the wave is called its amplitude. What [Max] Born said was that the square of the wave amplitude at any point in space gave the probability for finding an individual electron there. For example, in regions of space where the wave amplitude is large, the probability of finding an electron there is also large; perhaps one out of two times an electron will be found there. Similarly, where the wave amplitude is small the probability of finding the electron is also small—say one in ten. The electron is always a true particle and its Schrodinger wave function only specifies the probability for finding it at some point in space. Born realized the waves are not material, as Schrodinger wrongly supposed; they are waves of probability, rather like actuarial statistics for the creation of individual particles that can change from point to point in space and time. (Heinz R. Pagels, *The Cosmic Code* [New York: Bantam Books, 1982] 62-64)

[57] According to Pagels,

> The probability for finding a particle at a point in space is not given by the height of the wave at that point but rather by the intensity of the wave—the height of the wave squared, gotten by multiplying the height at that point times itself. If you multiply any positive or negative number times itself, the result is always a positive number. Hence the intensity of a wave is always a positive number, and Born identified this with the probability for finding a particle—also always a positive quantity. (Pagels 115-117)

[58] According to Pagels,

> What Heisenberg showed was that if two matrices representing different physical properties of a particle, like the matrix q for the position of the particle and the matrix p for its momentum, had the property that p x q did not equal q x p, then one could not simultaneously measure both these properties of the particle with arbitrarily high precision. . . . A similar uncertainty relation is found for the uncertainty in the energy, ΔE of a particle and the uncertain in the elapsed time, Δt. . . .
>
> An important warning must be stated regarding Heisenberg's uncertainty relation: it does not apply to a single measurement on a single particle, although people often think of it that way. Heisenberg's relation is a statement about a statistical average over lots of measurements of position and momenta. (Pagels 69-73)

[59] Pagels 75.

[60] Pagels 69.

[61] Pierre Simon Laplace, *A Philosophical Essay on Probabilities*, trans. F.W. Truscott and F.L. Emory (New York: Dover Publications, 1951) 4, http://bayes.wustl.edu/Manual/laplace_A_philosophical_essay_on_probabilities.pdf.

[62] *The Black Hole War* 82.

[63] Pagels 145.

[64] Pagels 141-142.

[65] John Gribbin, *In Search of Schrödinger's Cat: Quantum Physics and Reality* (London: Black Swan, 1991) 225.

[66] Gribbin 227.

[67] Gribbin 228.

[68] Gribbin 230-231.

[69] *The Black Hole War* 169.

[70] Pagels 37.

[71] Pagels 53.

[72] Pagels 41.

[73] Pagels 43.

[74] Pagels 65.

[75] Pagels 268; Gribbin 257-259.

[76] Pagels 258-259.

[77] *The Cosmic Landscape* 75.

[78] Michio Kaku, in "Who's Afraid of a Big Black Hole?" *Horizon*, directed by Stephen Cooter, Episode no. 834, BBC, November 3, 2009.

[79] Gribbin 261.

[80] *The Cosmic Landscape* 88.

[81] Albert Einstein, "On a Stationary System With Spherical Symmetry Consisting of Many Gravitating Masses," *Annals of Mathematics* 40 (4): 1939, 92, http://www.jstor.org/stable/1968902.

[82] The following passage comes from a biography of Oppenheimer.

> On September 1, 1939, Oppenheimer and a different collaborator—yet another student, Hartland Snyder—published a

paper titled "On Continued Gravitational Contraction." Historically, of course, the date is best known for Hitler's invasion of Poland and the start of World War II. But in its quiet way, this publication was also a momentous event. The physicist and science historian Jeremy Bernstein calls it "one of the great papers in twentieth-century physics." At the time, it attracted little attention. Only decades later would physicists understand that in 1939 Oppenheimer and Snyder had opened the door to twenty-first-century physics. (Kai Bird and Martin J. Sherwin, *American Prometheus: The Triumph and Tragedy of J. Robert Oppenheimer* [New York: Alfred K. Knopf, 2005] 89)

The history of the concept of the gravitational singularity is intimately tied to the history of world war in the twentieth century. Karl Schwarzschild was a German artillery officer during World War I. In between calculating artillery trajectories (*The Elegant Universe* 78), he used Einstein's equations for general relativity to demonstrate that a star of sufficient density would create infinite curvature in the fabric of space-time. Oppenheimer published the first paper describing the physics of how a dying star could actually collapse into a singularity on the first day of World War II. As the chief scientist of the Manhattan Project, he then effectively ended that war with his famous quotes from Krishna's Bhagavad-gita at the first atomic test explosion at the Trinity site in New Mexico on July 16, 1945.

[83] *The Black Hole War* 30.

[84] *The Black Hole War* 30.

[85] There is much controversy over the theory of infinite gravity. In Episode 1 of a two-part Science Channel series, "Stephen Hawking: Master of the Universe," Kaku rejects the idea that the singularity could possibly have infinite gravity:

> We physicists say that a long time ago the universe was so small it was smaller than a basketball. You could put the universe in your pocket. It was smaller than an electron. Some people call it a *singularity of infinite gravity.* Now, that's silly. There's no such thing as *infinite* gravity. It just means we use the word singularity

to hide our ignorance. We don't know what the singularity is. (Michio Kaku, in *Stephen Hawking: Master of the Universe*. Directed by Gary Johnstone, Episode 1, Channel 4 (UK), March 2 2008, http://www.channel4.com/programmes/master-of-the-universe.)

If Kaku really believes we do not know what the singularity is, how can he be so sure it is *not* a point of infinite gravity? In the absence of a better answer, why not simply accept what the equations actually say? Susskind—who at least provisionally accepts the infinite gravity of the singularity in a black hole and in the quantum vacuum—quotes Pauli to respond to other physicists, such as Paul Dirac, who abhor the idea: "But as Dirac's contemporary Wolfgang Pauli quipped, 'just because something is infinite doesn't mean it's zero.'" (*The Cosmic Landscape* 75) However, although Pauli was against using mathematical tricks like renormalization to eliminate the infinities described by general relativity and quantum mechanics, he believed those infinities should nevertheless be eliminated, as he explains in the concluding remarks of his Nobel Prize acceptance speech of 1946:

> At the end of this lecture I may express my critical opinion, that a correct theory [of quantum gravity] should neither lead to infinite zero-point energies nor to infinite zero charges, that it should not use mathematical tricks to subtract infinities or singularities, nor should it invent a "hypothetical world" which is only a mathematical fiction before it is able to formulate the correct interpretation of the actual world of physics. (Wolfgang Pauli, "Exclusion Principle and Quantum Mechanics," *Nobel Lecture*, December 13, 1946, 42, http://www.nobelprize.org/nobel_prizes/physics/laureates/1945/pauli- lecture.pdf)

Pauli says that mathematical tricks—such as renormalization—should not be used to subtract infinities, either from the quantum vacuum or from inside black holes. As discussed earlier in this chapter, even renormalization fails to work when physicists combine quantum mechanics with general relativity to produce a quantum theory of gravity. Steven Weinberg, a physicist from the University of Texas at Austin, discusses the difficulties of trying to combine gravity (general relativity) with the other three forces of nature (described by quantum mechanics) as follows: "You get answers that the probabilities of the event you're looking at are infinite. Nonsense. It's not profound, it's just nonsense." (Steven Weinberg, in "The Elegant Universe: Einstein's Dream," *Nova,* hosted by Brian Greene, directed by Julia Cort and Joseph McMaster, episode no. 1, PBS, October 28 2003, transcript: http://www.pbs.org/wgbh/nova/physics/elegant-universe.html# elegant-universe-einstein) In fact, the probability of any event happening *is* infinite when we factor in the theory of infinite parallel universes, according to which every conceivable combination of atoms must necessarily take place in one universe or another. With that in mind I return to Kaku, who explains what happens when you combine general relativity with quantum mechanics: "In fact, you get an infinite sequence of infinities. Infinitely worse than the divergences of Einstein's original theory. This is a nightmare beyond comprehension." ("Who's Afraid of a Big Black Hole?")

Sean Carroll, Research Professor in Physics at the California Institute of Technology, aligns with other physicists who reject the singularity.

> General relativity says loud and clear, the universe had a first moment, which we call the Big Bang. The Big Bang is not a point in space, it's a moment in time. It's a moment when the density of the universe *was infinite*, when the expansion right *was infinite*. So a lot of cosmologists will say, there was a beginning. And the problem with this is that the prediction that there was a beginning, or the understanding that there was a beginning is based on general relativity and we know general relativity is not right. The reason we know it is not right is that for one thing it predicts a singularity, it predicts that things are infinite, and we don't think that that can be true. Also, general relativity is not compatible with quantum mechanics, which we do think is right. So basically, we have a prediction that the universe began based on a theory that we have no right to trust. So the right answer is, we don't know yet. (Sean Carroll, in "Did the Universe Have a Beginning?" *Closer to Truth,* written by Robert Lawrence Kuhn,

directed by Peter Getzels, season 12, episode 1, PBS, first broadcast March 3, 2014, https://www.closertotruth.com/series/did-the-universe-begin)

While general relativity and quantum mechanics do not mix without string theory, neither theory has ever been shown to be wrong. It would make just as much sense for Carroll to say that we have no right to trust quantum mechanics because it is not compatible with general relativity, which we do think is right. Therefore, that such a powerful and strict thinker would allow himself to use such an overtly illogical reason to reject the singularity makes me suspect that the main reason Carroll and other atheistic physicists like Kaku and Hawking reject the theory of a singularity at the Big Bang is that it has all of the characteristics of God. Stephen Hawking admits as much:

> Many people do not like the idea that time has a beginning, probably because it smacks of divine intervention. (The Catholic Church, on the other hand, seized on the big bang model and in 1951 officially pronounced it to be in accordance with the Bible.) There were therefore a number of attempts to avoid the conclusion that there had been a big bang. (*A Brief History of Time* 49)

We saw earlier that, despite his atheistic posture in his books, Susskind identifies himself as an agnostic in the television series *Closer to Truth*. In that same series, after rejecting the possibility that there is a personal God who can directly interfere in the workings of nature, Susskind says he is agnostic about the possibility of God at the origin of the universe, which, we should keep in mind, he equates with a singularity.

> If you were to ask me about the very beginnings of the universe, the origins of it, why it is there, does it have a purpose, could an intelligence have been involved in creating it and so forth. There I would have to say I am completely agnostic. I'm completely agnostic to the point that I just don't feel we are anywhere near understanding enough about the world to even address those questions. Not only not to answer them, but to even ask them properly, to make sense out of the questions. So I would say I am

almost beyond being an agnostic, that to say I'm not sure if there's a God or not a God. I have the feeling it's the wrong question. (Leonard Susskind, in "Arguing for Agnosticism?" *Closer to Truth*, written by Robert Lawrence Kuhn, directed by Peter Getzels, season 6, episode 10, PBS, first aired March 3, 2011, https://www.youtube.com/watch?v=WL38FGjV-u8)

To go beyond being an agnostic is to become an atheist, which is definitely how Susskind portrays himself in his books. Still, that Susskind refuses to reject the possibility of an actual singularity with infinite density supports his claim that he is completely agnostic about God's presence at the origin of the universe, for, as we saw above, many other overtly atheistic physicists bluntly reject the possibility of a gravitational singularity at the Big Bang because they reject the possibility of anything having infinite power.

[86] *The Black Hole War* 32.

[87] *The Fabric of the Cosmos* 331.

[88] *The Fabric of the Cosmos* 332.

[89] *Hyperspace* 225-226.

[90] *The Cosmic Landscape* 156.

[91] The following excerpt from a BBC television series "Stephen Hawking's Universe" begins with Hawking's and Penrose's graduate advisor at Oxford University, Dennis Sciama.

DENNIS SCIAMA: "Stephen said to me, 'In a certain sense that the universe is like a big star. Of course, the universe is expanding, but if in your mind you reverse the sense of time, then the universe is collapsing. It's a bit like a collapsing star, very large star. Should I work on that?'"

STEPHEN HAWKING: "I was awarded my doctorate for showing that the questions Penrose was raising about black holes would apply equally well to the early universe. Both the Big Bang and black holes would contain singularities, places where space and time come to an end, and the laws of physics break down."

("Black Holes and Beyond," *Stephen Hawking's Universe*, Episode no. 5, directed by Philip Martin, first broadcast September 21 1997. PBS) http://www.pbs.org/wnet/hawking/programs/html/5-1.html.

[92] *The Black Hole War* 146-147.

[93] Stephen Hawking, *A Brief History of Time: From the Big Bang to Black Holes* (New York: Bantam Books, 1996) 53.

[94] *A Brief History of Time* 120. As we saw above, in another passage from *A Brief History of Time*, Hawking explains that many physicists dislike the idea of the Big Bang because it implies the idea of a creator God:

> Many people do not like the idea that time has a beginning, probably because it smacks of divine intervention. (The Catholic Church, on the other hand, seized on the big bang model and in 1951 officially pronounced it to be in accordance with the Bible.) There were therefore a number of attempts to avoid the conclusion that there had been a big bang. (*A Brief History of Time* 49)

In Hawking's opinion, it is not the scientific implausibility of the idea, but, rather, a biased distaste for the theological implication of divine intervention that inspired a number of cosmologists to reject the idea of a gravitational singularity. The Catholic doctrine to which Hawking refers above comes from Pope Pius XII's speech "The Proofs for the Existence of God in the Light of Modern Natural Science: Address of Pope Pius XII to the Pontifical Academy of Sciences, November 22, 1951," in which he refers to the Big Bang theory as scientific evidence for the moment of God's creation:

> In fact, it would seem that present-day science, with one sweeping step back across millions of centuries, has succeeded in bearing witness to that primordial "Fiat lux" uttered at the moment when, along with matter, there burst forth from nothing a sea of light and radiation. . . .

Thus, with that concreteness which is characteristic of physical proofs, it has confirmed the contingency of the universe and also the well-founded deduction as to the epoch when the cosmos came forth from the hands of the Creator. (quoted in Papal Encyclicals Online, "The Proofs for the Existence of God in the Light of Modern Natural Science: Address of Pope Pius XII to the Pontifical Academy of Sciences, November 22, 1951," para. 44-50, http://www.papalencyclicals.net/Pius12/P12EXIST.HTM.)

In the context of the Big Bang theory, to say that the world came forth from the hands of the Creator is to equate the creator God with the singularity. It is important to note, however, that Lemaître himself was greatly displeased by the Pope's proclamation, as John Ferrell explains in his book, *The Day Without Yesterday: Lemaître, Einstein, and the Birth of Modern Cosmology* [New York: Thunder's Mouth Press, 2005] 197). Despite Lemaitre's disapproval of Pope Pius XII's correlation of the Big Bang with the divine moment of creation, as Hawking admits, that papal proclamation provoked a number of atheistic scientists to reject the theory. It is not implausible, therefore, to suspect that Hawking's own distaste for the idea of God eventually led him to reject the idea of a singularity which he formerly championed.

[95] "Who's Afraid of a Big Black Hole?"

[96] *Hyperspace* 263-264.

[97] *Hyperspace* 136.

[98] According to Ware:

On the one hand, the big bang is contained at every point within spacetime as the centre from which space is expanding outward. Yet, on the other hand, all of spacetime is contained within the big bang in the sense that we see the big bang surrounding us, as if it were the shell of an enclosing sphere. . . . Singularities represent fundamental indeterminacies in the sense that they are locations in the spacetime metric where spacetime (and indeed physics) comes to an end. . . . Leibnitz's principle of the identity of indiscernibles would suggest that we cannot separate one from another, or in simple terms, the interior of one black hole is the interior of all black holes. . . . Quantum physics has produced similar proposals. . . . Moreover, John Wheeler, writing in his classic text on *Gravitation*, has observed that because of quantum fluctuations, the same indeterminacy associated with the spacetime singularity that produced the universe as a whole must also recur in the form of a singularity at every point in spacetime. . . . Summarizing his own quantum approach to self-containment, David Bohm wrote that, "The totality of existence is enfolded within each region of space (and time). So, whatever part, element, or aspect we may abstract in thought, this still enfolds the whole and is therefore intrinsically related to the totality from which it has been abstracted. (Robert Bruce Ware, *Hegel: The Logic of Self-Consciousness and the Legacy of Subjective Freedom* [Edinburgh, England: Edinburgh University Press, 1999] 59-63)

[99] Jean Eisenstaedt, *The Curious History of Relativity: How Einstein's Theory of Gravity Was Lost and Found Again* (New Jersey: Princeton University Press, 2006) 303.

[100] *The Black Hole War* 180-181, 298-301.

[101] *The Cosmic Landscape* 261.

[102] *The Cosmic Landscape* 123. Susskind goes on to say: "I would say that this inevitability is beautiful." (*The Cosmic Landscape* 123)

[103] *The Cosmic Landscape* 237.

[104] Susskind repeatedly calls the fundamental strings "one-dimensional." (*The Cosmic Landscape* 229, 233, 278-279; *The Black Hole War* 293, 354, 455) However, he also says the strings have a width that is one Planck length long. In *The Cosmic Landscape* he explains: "Suppose we further reduce the size of the compact direction all the way down to the Planck length. Then no existing microscope would be able to resolve the second dimension. For all practical purposes the space would be one-dimensional." (*The Cosmic Landscape* 233)

[105] *The Cosmic Landscape* 220-221, 231-238, 280-281; *The Black Hole War* 293, 339-346.

[106] If the information in any volume of space is stored on the surface area, as Susskind's holographic principle says, then the three-dimensional information stored in the double-helix DNA molecules of a cell is actually a holographic movie projected from the inner surface of the cell wall.

[107] *The Cosmic Landscape* 341; *The Black Hole War* 440.

[108] *The Black Hole War* 87.

[109] *The Black Hole War* 91.

[110] *The Cosmic Landscape* 332, n2.

[111] Terrence Deacon, *Incomplete Nature* (New York: W. W. Norton & Company, Inc., 2010) 550.

[112] *The Cosmic Landscape* 332, n2.

[113] *Incomplete Nature* 4-8, 12-14. Deacon compares his concept of absential phenomena in the physical sciences to the number zero in mathematics. He explains that it was not until the details of how to use zero mathematically were finally tamed that the way was opened to modern physical science. He goes on to explain:

> That issues involving absential phenomena still mark uncrossable boundaries between disciplines, that the most enduring scientific mysteries appear to be centered around them, and that both academic and cultural upheavals still erupt over discussions of these issues, indicates that this is far from being an issue long ago settled and relegated to the dustbin of scientific history. Developing formal tools capable of integrating this missing cipher—absential influence—into the fabric of the natural sciences is an enterprise that should be at the center of scientific and philosophical debate. . . . If the example of zero is any hint, even just glimpsing the outlines of a systematic way to integrate these phenomena into the natural sciences could light the path to whole new fields of inquiry. And making scientific sense of these

most personal of nature's properties, without trashing them, has the potential to transform the way we personally see ourselves within the scheme of things. (*Incomplete Nature* 14)

Like the psyche, so can the singularity be categorized as absential phenomena, in the sense that it is outside space-time, and therefore cannot be empirically observed (though it has empirically observable effects on space-time). In the same way that the discovery of the number zero opened the door to modern physics, so does the discovery of the point of infinite density and zero volume open the door to a synthesis of modern physics and psychology. This book, centered on the equation Psyche = Singularity, provides at least a glimpse of the kind of outline "of a systematic way to integrate these [absential] phenomena into the natural sciences" that Deacon seeks.

[114] *Incomplete Nature* 73-79, 138, 289, 374, 551. Deacon explains that, despite its irrelevance to mainstream cognitive scientists, panpsychism "still attracts a wide following, mostly because of a serendipitous compatibility with certain interpretations of quantum physics." (*Incomplete Nature* 73) The first irony about Deacon's claim is that serendipity, which Jung and Pauli call synchronicity, is itself an indication of an underlying union of meaning-perceiving minds and the unfolding of matter through time, i.e., panpsychism. The second irony is that the founders of quantum theory, including Pauli, Heisenberg, Bohr, and Schrödinger—unanimously subscribed to and published papers in favor of panpsychism.

[115] This supposition is especially warranted by Deacon's particular choice of metaphors. For instance: "Ultimately, we need to identify the principles by which these unruly absential phenomena can be successfully woven into the exacting warp and weft of the natural sciences." (*Incomplete Nature* 12-13) Later he explains that he is providing "outlines of a future science that is subtle enough to include us, and our enigmatically incomplete nature, as legitimate forms of knotting in the fabric of the universe." (*Incomplete Nature* 17) I suggest that the future science subtle enough to include a definition of inherently meaningful information, and the psyches that perceive it, will partially consist in a fusion of Jung's psychology and Susskind's string theory.

[116] *The Black Hole War* 453.

[117] *The Black Hole War* 373.

[118] *The Black Hole War* 136.

[119] *The Black Hole War* 363.

[120] *The Black Hole War* 237.

[121] *The Black Hole War* 171.

[122] *The Black Hole War* 439-440, 407.

[123] *The Cosmic Landscape* 323.

[124] *The Cosmic Landscape* 316.

[125] *The Cosmic Landscape* 14.

[126] *The Cosmic Landscape* 21.

[127] "Arguing for Agnosticism?"

[128] *The Black Hole War* 439.

[129] *The Black Hole War* 74-75.

[130] *The Cosmic Landscape* 383.

[131] *The Hidden Reality* 147,162; *The Elegant Universe* 82; *Parallel Worlds* 12, 51, 104.

[132] *The Cosmic Landscape* 72.

[133] *The Cosmic Landscape* 72.

[134] Robert Sanders, "Saul Perlmutter awarded 2011 Nobel Prize in Physics." *Berkeley News*, October 4, 2011, http://news.berkeley.edu/2011/10/04/saul-perlmutter-awarded-2011-nobel-prize-in-physics/.

[135] NASA Science, "WMAP." *Missions*, June 28, 2012, http://science.nasa.gov/missions/wmap/.

[136] *The Cosmic Landscape* 75.

[137] *The Cosmic Landscape* 75.

[138] *The Cosmic Landscape* 78.

[139] *The Cosmic Landscape* 81.

[140] Lee Smolin, in "Smolin vs. Susskind: The Anthropic Principle." *Edge*, para. 1, August18, 2004, http://edge.org/3rd_culture/smolin_susskind04/smolin_susskind.html.

[141] *The Cosmic Landscape* 360- 361.

[142] *The Black Hole War* 4.

[143] For example, "It is sufficient to know that there is not a single important idea or view that does not possess historical antecedents. Ultimately they are all founded on primordial archetypal forms." (*On the Nature of the Psyche* 101)

[144] According to Graham Schweig,

> Vaishnavism is indeed a theistic tradition, but could be further characterized as a polymorphic monotheism, i.e., a theology that recognizes many forms (*ananta rupa*) of the one, single unitary divinity. The power of God is expressed in this Vaishnava metaphysics as the capacity to be in many places and appear in a variety of forms at the same time, without being diminished in any way. . . .
>
> Another aspect of this theology pushes our characterization closer to a polymorphic *bi*-monotheism, or many forms of the dual-gendered divinity. . . . The godhead is essentially androgynous, comprised of both supreme masculine and feminine aspects. (Graham M. Schweig, "The Intimate Deity," in *The Hare Krishna Movement*, eds. Edwin F. Bryant and Maria L. Ekstrand [New York: Columbia University Press, 2004] 18-19)

[145] According to A.C. Bhaktivedanta Swami Prabhupada:

> The Supreme Personality of Godhead is *sac-cid-ananda-vigraha*. Realization of impersonal Brahman is realization of His sat feature, or His aspect of eternity, and Paramatma realization is

realization of His sat and cit features, His aspects of eternity and knowledge. But realization of the Personality of Godhead is realization of all the transcendental features—sat, cit and ananda, bliss. When one realizes the Supreme Person, he realizes these aspects of the Absolute Truth in their completeness. Vigraha means "form." Thus the Complete Whole is not formless. If He were formless, or if He were less than His creation in any other way, He could not be complete. The Complete Whole must contain everything both within and beyond our experience; otherwise He cannot be complete. (*Bhagavad-gita As It Is,* Introduction.)

[146] *Bhagavad-gita As It Is* 7.24; Srimad-Bhagavatam 4.12.36. According to the Gaudiya Vaishnava school of Vedanta, the spiritual planet presided over by Radha and Krishna, known as Goloka Vrindavana, is the original source of all other spiritual and, by extension, material planets. Goloka Vrindavan, as we will see, is equivalent to Plato's ultimate idea of the Good.

[147] *Bhagavad-gita As It Is,* Introduction.

[148] For the concept of God's unconsciousness also see Jung's *Answer to Job*: "The fact of God's 'unconsciousness' throws a peculiar light on the doctrine of salvation." (*The Portable Jung* 585) The concept of God's unconscious mind also throws a peculiar light on that branch of theology known as theodicy, which studies how a good God can allow evil in the world. If we are living in God's dream, then it is as if we are the skeletons in God's closet, acting out his and her worst fears and repressions. Atheists, from this perspective, are the manifestations of God's self-doubt (see *The Portable Jung* 543).

[149] According to A.C. Bhaktivedanta Swami Prabhupada:

This material world is a product of the mahat-tattva, which is a state of the Lord's dreaming condition in His yoga-nidrā mystic slumber in the Causal Ocean, and yet the whole creation appears to be a factual presentation of His creation. This means that the Lord's dreaming conditions are also factual manifestations. He can therefore bring everything under His transcendental control, and thus whenever and wherever He does appear, He does so in His fullness." (Srimad-Bhagavatam 1.16.26-30, Purport)

[150] Srimad-Bhagavatam 1.3.1-2.

[151] "Practically speaking, there is no conflict between personalism and impersonalism. One who knows God knows that the impersonal conception and personal conception are simultaneously present in everything and that there is no contradiction. Therefore Lord Caitanya established His sublime doctrine: *acintya-bheda* and *abheda-tattvam*-simultaneously one and different." (*Bhagavad-gita As It Is* 7.8, Purport)

[152] "Brihadaranyaka Upanishad," *Upanishads, A New Translation by Patrick Olivelle* (Oxford, England: Oxford University Press, 1996), 4.4.5.

[153] For an expert comparison of quantum mechanics and the cosmology of the Gaudiya Vaishnava school of Vedanta, see quantum physicist Henry Stapp's *Report on the Gaudiya Vaishnava Vedanta Form of Vedic Ontology* (Berkley, California: The Bhaktivedanta Institute, 1994). It is also interesting to note that the Atman = Brahman equation seems similar to the particle-wave nature of the quantum world, which Jung and Pauli compared to the conscious-unconscious nature of the psyche. The following is physicist David Bohm's commentary on Atman = Brahman:

> Weber: It's dazzling and one can't help but draw the conclusion that you are saying: 'This is a universe that is alive (in its appropriate way) and somehow conscious at all the levels.'
>
> Bohm: Yes, in a way.
>
> Weber: That's what I take this to mean.
>
> Bohm: We don't know how far the self-awareness would go, but if you were religious, you would believe it is a sense of God, or as something that would be totally self-aware.
>
> Weber: You mean, as a whole. The question is: Is there a significance to the holomovement as a whole?

Bohm: Yes, that is a question of what proposal we want to explore. People have, in effect, been exploring notions of that kind in religions. One view is to say that the significance is similar to ourselves in a sense that Christians would say that God is a person.

Weber: Or, anyhow, a being.

Bohm: Well, they say three persons, the Trinity, which are one. Anyway, it is something like a human being, or rather the other way around; that man is the image of God. That implies that there is a total significance. If you say Atman, in Hinduism, something similar is implied.

Weber: Atman and Brahman, seen as identical; the micro- and the macrocosm.

Bohm: Yes, and Atman is from the side of meaning. You would say Atman is more like the meaning. But then what is meant would be Brahman, I suppose; the identity of consciousness and cosmos.

Weber: Looked at from the so-called subjective side it would be Atman. And what is meant is the objective.

Bohm: Meaning in this sense that somasignificant and signasomatic unite the two sides. This claims that the meaning and what is meant are ultimately one, which is the phrase 'Atman equals Brahman' of classical Hindu philosophy. (David Bohm, in *Quantum Implications: Essays In Honour of David Bohm*. Eds. Basil Hiley and F. David Peat [New York: Routledge, 1987] 445-446)

The co-discoverer of quantum mechanics, Erwin Schrödinger, also comments on this Vedic phrase:

From the early great Upanishads the recognition ATHMAN=BRAHMAN (the personal self equals the omnipresent, all-comprehending eternal self) was in Indian thought considered, far from being blasphemous, to represent the quintessence of deepest insight into the happenings of the world. The striving of all the scholars of Vedanta was, after having learnt to pronounce with their lips, really to assimilate in their minds this grandest of all thoughts. (Erwin Schrodinger, *What is Life? & Mind and Matter* [Cambridge, England: Cambridge University Press, 2012] 87)

This quote is from the Epilogue to *What is Life?*, which was first published in 1944. In his book Schrödinger chalks out his vision of applying quantum mechanics to the search for the self-replicating mechanism in a cell. It helped inspire the discovery of DNA nine years later. In his 1991 Foreword to this edition of Schrödinger's book, Sir Roger Penrose says, "Indeed, many scientists who have made fundamental contributions in biology, such as J. B. S. Haldane and Francis Crick, have admitted to being strongly influenced by (although not always in complete agreement with) the broad-ranging ideas put forward here by this highly original and profoundly thoughtful physicist." (Roger Penrose, "Foreword," in *What is Life? & Mind and Matter* [Cambridge, England: Cambridge University Press, 2012])

[154] *Bhagavad-gita As It Is,* Introduction.

[155] *Bhagavad-gita As It Is* 7.2-8; Srimad-Bhagavatam 3.11.41.

[156] Srimad-Bhagavatam 1.3.2.

[157] "There are five gross elements, namely earth, water, fire, air and ether. There are also five subtle elements: smell, taste, color, touch and sound." (Srimad-Bhagavatam 3.26.12)

[158] Srimad-Bhagavatam 3.11.40.

[159] As is explained in the Srimad-Bhagavatam: "The layers or elements covering the universes are each ten times thicker than the one before, and all the universes clustered together appear like atoms in a huge combination." (Srimad-Bhagavatam 3.11.41)

[160] *Bhagavad-gita As It Is* 7.2-8.

[161] *Bhagavad-gita As It Is* 10.20. We see this same terminology in the Apocalypse, the final book of the Bible, where Christ declares, "I am the

Alpha and Omega; the beginning and the end, saith the Lord God, who is, and who was, and who is to come, the Almighty." (Apocalypse, in The Holy Bible, *Douay-Rheims 1899 American Edition* (DRA) 1:8, http://www.drbo.org/)

[162] The most recent leap in astronomy is the detection of gravitational waves created by the collision of pairs of black holes and pairs of neutron stars. Astronomers contrast gravitational telescopes with optical telescopes by saying that gravity telescopes detect the sound created by the compression waves of space-time itself, just as a drum creates sound by creating compressions waves that travel through the air. According to the Vedic philosophy, ether cannot be seen, smelled, touched, or tasted, but it can be heard (as the syllable om), which seems similar to the way the fabric of space-time can only be heard by gravity telescopes.

[163] Brihadaranyaka Upanishad 3.7.3.

[164] Brihadaranyaka Upanishad 3:8:1-4.

[165] Brihadaranyaka Upanishad 3.8.5-8.

[166] Plato, *The Collected Dialogues of Plato, Including the Letters*, eds. Edith Hamilton and Huntington Cairns (New Jersey: Princeton University Press, 1994), *Apology* 24b.

[167] *Timaeus* 30b.

[168] *Timaeus* 35a-b.

[169] *Timaeus* 36d-37a.

[170] *Timaeus* 51a-51b. Later Timaeus reconfirms that the universe takes the shape of a sphere with a central point: "For as the universe is in the form of a sphere, all the extremities, being equidistant from the center, are equally extremities, and the center, which is equidistant from them, is equally to be regarded as the opposite of them all." (62d)

[171] *Timaeus* 51b.

[172] *Timaeus* 51c.

[173] *Timaeus* 51e-52b.

[174] *Timaeus* 52b-c.

[175] *Timaeus* 51b.

[176] *Timaeus* 53a.

[177] *Timaeus* 55c.

[178] Brihadaranyaka Upanishad 3:8:1-8.

[179] *The Cosmic Landscape 237.*

[180] *Timaeus* 55c.

[181] Yau explains the correlations between the Platonic solids and the elements in Plato's *Timaeus*:

> Earth would thus consist of tiny cubes, the air of octahedrons, fire of tetrahedrons, and water of icosahedrons. "One other construction, a fifth, still remained," Plato wrote in *Timaeus*, referring to the dodecahedron. "And this one god used for the whole universe, embroidering figures on it." (Shing-Tung Yau and Steve Nadis, *The Shape of Inner Space: String Theory and the Geometry of the Universe's Hidden Dimensions* [New York: Basic Books, A Member of the Perseus Books Group, 2010] xviii)

For the purpose of drawing parallels with string theory, it is important to note the image of *embroidering* figures on the horizon of space. Also, Plato describes the cosmic horizon as alternately non-existent, spherical, and dodecahedral, which was pointed out in the prestigious science journal, *Nature*, in 2003, when a team of French astronomers claimed that the cosmic microwave background radiation detected by the WMAP satellite indicates that the shape of the universe may be a Poincare´ dodecahedral space (Jean-Pierre Luminet, et al., "Dodecahedral space topology as an explanation for weak wide-angle temperature correlations in the cosmic microwave background," *Nature*, 425, 593-595, doi: 10.1038/nature01944, October 9, 2003). The correlation with Plato's *Timaeus* is summarized in the following article in *The Economist* magazine:

The shape of the universe
Platonic truths

Data from an American satellite suggest that the universe is a dodecahedron

Oct 9th 2003 | from the print edition

THERE are five Platonic solids of perfect symmetry. Three, the tetrahedron, octahedron and icosahedron, have triangular faces. A fourth, the cube, has square faces. The fifth, the dodecahedron, has pentagonal faces. Plato believed that the first four corresponded to the elements of which the Greeks thought the material world was composed: fire, air, water and earth. The dodecahedron, however, corresponded to quintessence, the element of the heavens. As Plato put it, "God used this solid for the whole universe, embroidering figures on it." [*Timaeus* 55c] And if the arguments of a paper in this week's *Nature* stand up, Plato will have been proved right. For Jean-Pierre Luminet, of the Paris Observatory, and his colleagues believe that the universe is, indeed, a dodecahedron.

They base their argument on data collected by the Wilkinson Microwave Anisotropy Probe (WMAP). This American satellite has been examining the microwave radiation generated shortly after the universe began. The wavelength of this radiation is remarkably pure, but like a musical note it has harmonics associated with it. These harmonics, like those of a note, reflect the shape of the object in which the waves were generated. In the case of the note, that object is a musical instrument. In the case of the microwave background, that object is the universe itself. (The Economist, "Platonic Truths," *The Economist* [London: The Economist Group Limited, October 9, 2003])

If we combine this observation-based theory of the dodecahedral topology of the CMB radiation with Susskind's holographic string theory of information radiating back from that cosmic horizon in the CMB radiation, and include Jung's NDE of the cosmic horizon, then we have a cosmology that matches Plato's *Timaeus* in two extremely important respects: (1) the cosmic horizon is a receiving vessel that is alternately described as formless, spherical, and dodecahedral; (2) it partakes mysteriously of the intelligible world of eternal forms.

[182] Yau xviii-xix. Susskind discusses Plato's *Timaeus* in *The Cosmic Landscape* (119-120).

[183] *The Cosmic Landscape* 5-6.

[184] *Timaeus* 30b.

[185] Yau 150. As he explains in endnote 29 to chapter 6, Yau's Susskind quote comes from an interview he had with Susskind on May 25, 2007.

[186] Yau 325-327. I left out the following passages from the quote above:

> As legend has it, Plato placed an inscription above the entryway to the school that read: *Let no one ignorant of geometry enter here. . . .*
>
> Plato regarded the truths of geometry as eternal and unchanging, whereas he regarded the knowledge derived from empirical science as more ephemeral in nature, unavoidably subject to revision. On these points, I heartily agree: Geometry can carry us far toward explaining the universe on scales both big and small (though perhaps not all the way down to the Planck scale), and when we prove something through rigorous mathematics, we can be sure it will stand the test of time. Geometrical proofs, like the diamonds advertised on TV, are forever. (Yau 325-326)

[187] Yau uses Donald Zeyl's translation of the *Timaeus*, and even quotes from Zeyl's Introduction. The following passage is also from Zeyl's Introduction to the *Timaeus*, where he summarizes the historical influence of the text, and how it was "eclipsed" by the *Republic* in the nineteenth century:

> From late antiquity onward, throughout the Middle Ages and well into modern times, the *Timaeus* enjoyed a position of preeminence among Plato's works. . . . The splendid vision of a mathematically ordered world modeled after the eternal, paradigmatic Forms—a work of art conceived and executed by a supremely wise and good deity—was received as the fitting climax

of Plato's transcendental philosophy and commended itself to generations of theologians of the early Christian era as a philosophical corroboration of their own creation theologies. Although Plato's influence as a whole declined during the later Middle Ages, the *Timaeus* retained its preeminence among Plato's dialogues well into the 19th century, when it was eclipsed by the *Republic*. (Donald J. Zeyl, "Introduction," in *Plato's Timaeus*, trans. Donald J. Zeyl [Indianapolis: Hacking Publishing Company, 2000] xiv)

[188] The cave allegory appears at the beginning of Book VII of the *Republic*.

[189] Plato, *The Collected Dialogues of Plato, Including the Letters*, eds. Edith Hamilton and Huntington Cairns (New Jersey: Princeton University Press, 1994), *Republic* 517c. Socrates goes on to explain that, after being educated by the state, the enlightened philosopher must be ordered to return to the affairs of worldly people.

> Down you must go then, each in his turn, to the habitation of the others and accustom yourselves to the observation of the obscure things there. For once habituated you will discern them infinitely better than the dwellers there, and you will know what each of the 'idols' is and whereof it is a semblance, because you have seen the reality of the beautiful, the just and the good. So our city will be governed by us and you with waking minds, and not, as most cities now … as in a dream by men who fight one another for shadows and wrangle for office as if that were a great good. (*Republic* 521c-d)

[190] *The Fabric of the Cosmos* 482.

[191] *The Fabric of the Cosmos* 485. In his next book, *The Hidden Reality*, Greene again compares Susskind's holographic principle to an inverted version of Plato's cave allegory (*The Hidden Reality* 272- 273), and furthermore recommends Susskind's most recent book: "If you're interested in the full story, I highly recommend Leonard Susskind's excellent book, *The Black Hole War*." (*The Hidden Reality* 255)

[192] *The Hidden Reality* 272-273.

[193] *The Hidden Reality* 272-273.

[194] Brihadaranyaka Upanishad 3.7.3.

[195] Stephen Hawking and Leonard Mlodinow, *The Grand Design* (New York: Random House, 2010) 44.

[196] Rudy Rucker, *The Fourth Dimension: A Guided Tour of the Higher Universes* (Boston: Houghton Mifflin Company, 1984) 88.

[197] *The Black Hole War* 299.

[198] *Republic* 518c.

[199] According to general relativity, if you were inside a black hole looking out you would see all of the light of the universe condensed into a single, infinitely bright point at the end of a dark tunnel. We will see this later in the book when we examine the light at the end of a tunnel often associated with near-death experiences.

[200] *Timaeus* 51b.

[201] Plato, *The Republic*, trans. H. D. P. Lee (London: Penguin Books, 2003) 620e.

[202] In the *Laws* Plato depicts the Athenian Stranger saying: "We may imagine that each of us living creatures is a puppet made by gods. . . . These interior states are, so to say, the cords, or strings, by which we are worked." (Plato, "Laws," in *The Collected Dialogues of Plato, Including the Letters*, eds. Edith Hamilton and Huntington Cairns [New Jersey: Princeton University Press, 1994] 644e)

[203] According to Susskind, consciousness is merely a biochemical by-product of a three-dimensional brain, which would seem to imply that consciousness does not exist in the two-dimensional holographic film at the cosmic horizon from where matter radiates inward. However, an interviewer once asked Susskind, "Are we the projection or is the outer surface the projection? Which one is reality?" Susskind replied, "That's your choice, you decide what you, ah, but the mathematics says they're equivalent." In response, another interviewer told Susskind that, "I feel like I'm here." Susskind countered, "Yeah, but so does your image on the boundary, it's

also saying 'I feel like I'm here.' . . . But the mathematics doesn't care which way you think about it. It says there's an equivalence. That's about all we can say." (Leonard Susskind, in "Is The Universe A Hologram?" *The Good Stuff*, PBS Digital Studios, August 4, 2015, https://www.youtube.com/watch?v=iNgIl-qIklU)

What Susskind does not seem to realize is that, according to his own holographic principle, if the images of us which are interwoven on the holographic boundary of space are self-aware, those versions of us would experience the past, present, and future of the entire universe simultaneously, because all space-time is interwoven into each point of the horizon. That universal omniscience is exactly what Jung said his disembodied psyche experienced at the cosmic horizon after his heart attack in 1944, and it is very similar to the near-death experience known as the myth of Er at the end of the *Republic*.

[204] Plato, "Phaedrus," in *The Collected Dialogues of Plato, Including the Letters*, eds. Edith Hamilton and Huntington Cairns, New Jersey: Princeton University Press, 1994, 247a-b.

[205] *Phaedrus* 247 b-c.

[206] *Pheadrus* 247 d-e.

[207] Plato does not mention the megaverse, but the Vedanta cosmology definitely does, which goes a long way toward supporting Jung's theory that all scientific discoveries are grounded in archetypal forms that have appeared earlier in religious and philosophical texts.

[208] In his *Lives of Eminent Philosophers*, Diogenes Laertius recounts another ancient Greek philosopher's recollection of Plato's disdain for Democritus' materialist philosophy:

> Aristoxenus in his *Historical Notes* affirms that Plato wished to burn all the writings of Democritus that he could collect, but that Amyclas and Clinias the Pythagoreans prevented him, saying that there was no advantage in doing so, for already the books were widely circulated. And there is clear evidence for this in the fact that Plato, who mentions almost all the early philosophers, never once alludes to Democritus, not even where it would be necessary

to controvert him, obviously because he knew that he would have to match himself against the prince of philosophers. (Diogenes Laertius, *Lives of Eminent Philosophers*, Ed. R. D. Hicks, Book 9, chapter 7, section 40, 1972,
http://www.perseus.tufts.edu/hopper/text?doc=Perseus:abo:tlg,00 04,001:9:7.)

In "The debate between Plato and Democritus," Werner Heisenberg weighed in on Plato's side:

> I think that on this point modern physics has definitely decided for Plato. For the smallest units of matter are, in fact, not physical objects in the ordinary sense of the word; they are forms, structures or—in Plato's sense—Ideas, which can be unambiguously spoken of only in the language of mathematics. (Heisenberg 52)

[209] *Republic* 522c-535a.

[210] In endnote 12 to Book VII of his translation of the *Republic* Allan Bloom explains: "In Greek mathematics the study of numbers and their attributes (*arithmetike*) is distinguished from that of calculation (*logistike*), which involves operations with numbers (addition, subtraction, etc.)." (Allan Bloom, *The Republic of Plato: Translated, with Notes, an Interpretive Essay, and a new Introduction by Allan Bloom* [New York: Basic Books, 1991] 465)

[211] Tarnas explains how the Greek thinkers in general, and Plato in particular, were disturbed by the "wandering" planets that appear occasionally to reverse direction and revolve around the Earth against the constantly revolving background of the outermost sphere of fixed stars. According to Tarnas,

> The planets were inexplicably defying the perfect symmetry and circular uniformity of the heavenly motions
>
> Because of his equation of divinity with order, of intelligence and soul with perfect mathematical regularity, the paradox of the planetary movements seems to have been felt most acutely by Plato, who first articulated the problem and gave directions for its solution. To Plato, proof of divinity in the universe was of the

utmost importance, for only with such certainty could human ethical and political activity have a firm foundation. . . .

But Plato not only isolated the problem and defined its significance. He also advanced, with remarkable confidence, a specific—and in the long run extremely fruitful—hypothesis: namely, that the planets, in apparent contradiction to the empirical evidence, actually move in single uniform orbits of perfect regularity. . . .

Astronomy and mathematics were to be mastered in order to penetrate the riddle of the heavens and comprehend their divine intelligence. Naive empiricism, which took the appearance of erratic and multiple planetary movements at face value, was to be overcome by critical mathematical reasoning, thereby revealing the simple, uniform, and transcendent essence of the celestial motions. (*The Passion of the Western Mind* 52-53)

[212] In the *Laws* (a less utopian version of the alternative city imagined in the *Republic*), Plato again has his leading literary character, in this case "the Athenian," lay out a step-by-step mathematical study of the four dimensions of space-time (*Laws* 8173-818b, 967d-e).

[213] *Republic* 530d.

[214] *Hyperspace* 154. Considering the importance Socrates places on understanding the synthesis of astronomy and music as a precursor to beholding the ultimate idea of the Good, it is helpful to hear Kaku reiterate the link between music and string theory:

The answer to the ancient question, "What is matter?" is simply that matter consists of particles that are different modes of vibration of the string, such as the note G or F. The "music" created by the string is matter itself. But the fundamental reason why the world's physicists are so excited by this new theory is that it appears to solve perhaps the most important scientific problem of the century, namely, how to unite the four forces of nature into one comprehensive theory. (Michio Kaku and Jennifer Thompson, *Beyond Einstein: The Cosmic Quest for the Theory of the Universe* [New York: Anchor/Doubleday, 1987] 5-6)

[215] The three forces united by quantum mechanics are described as the passing of a force-carrying particle, or boson (photons; gluons; Z, W+, W-particles), between two other quantum particles. String theory is a quantum theory of gravity because it provides a new type of boson to carry the force of gravity: the theoretical graviton (a closed loop of string).

[216] *Republic* 531d. The fifth step of knowledge—seeing the kinship between the mathematics that describe each of the four dimensions of nature—has to deal with the challenging fact that the units of measurement that apply to each of the four ascending dimensions of nature (meter, meter squared, meter cubed, and whatever unit we use to measure time) cannot be added and subtracted from each other. For example, we cannot add two meters and three cubic meters, nor can we add any spatial unit of measurement to a unit of time. In the *Laws*, the Athenian points out the "native and general, but ludicrous and shameful, ignorance of mankind" concerning the commensurability and incommensurability of the units of measurement with which we measure the different dimensions of nature (*Laws* 819d-820d). For more commentary on this issue, see Timothy Desmond, "Plato's Noble Lie and the Imaginary Number i: An Introduction to the Zero Zone System of Measurement in the Context of Plato's Republic and the Laws," *Journal of Futures Studies,* November 2009.

Continuing in the *Laws*, the Athenian later discusses the belief that the soul of the Sun somehow "infolds us"— a belief which was also central to the ideal city of the *Republic*.

> ATHENIAN: The sun, whose body can be seen by any man, but his soul by no man, any more than that of any other creature's body is to be seen, during life or at the time of death. We have every reason to believe that it infolds us in a fashion utterly imperceptible to all bodily senses, and is only to be discerned by the understanding. So here is a relevant consideration which we must apprehend by an act of pure understanding and thought. (*Laws* 898d-899c)

Recalling the cave allegory of the *Republic*, the visible Sun is the shadow of the intelligible Sun, or idea of the Good, which has all of the characteristics of the singularity, in which each of us and every atom that ever was or will be is mysteriously infolded. In the same way that the incommensurability of general relativity and quantum mechanics is at least mathematically resolved in Susskind's description of the gravitational singularity, so too is the apparent incommensurability of every pair of opposites overcome in the all-infolding idea of the Good.

[217] *Fabric of the Cosmos* 266.

[218] *Timaeus* 35a-b, 36d-37a, 51b.

[219] *Republic* 517c.

[220] *Republic* 533c-d. In his critique of the translation of the *Republic* which I have been using all along, philosophy professor Robert McGahey says that the phrase "Orphic myth" is "Paul Shorey's overzealous gloss." (Robert McGahey, *The Orphic Moment: Shaman to Poet-Thinker in Plato, Nietzsche, and Mallarme* [Albany: State University of New York Press, 1994] 40)

[221] McGahey 40.

[222] Plato, "Plato's Phaedo," trans. R. Hackforth (Cambridge: Cambridge University Press, 1972), 69c-d.

[223] *Timaeus* 53a.

[224] "This simple agricultural instrument figured in the mystic rites of Dionysus; indeed: in art he is represented as an infant so cradled; and from these traditions and representations he derived the epithet of *Liknites*, that is, 'He of the Winnowing-fan.'" (James George Frazer, *The Golden Bough* [New York: Macmillan Publishing Company, 1922] 450)

[225] Friedrich Nietzsche, *The Birth of Tragedy Out of the Spirit of Music*, in *The Basic Writings of Nietzsche,* ed. & trans. Walter Kauffman (New York: Random House, 1968) 73.

[226] *The Basic Writings of C.G. Jung* 327-328. Carl Jung, *The Basic Writings of C.G. Jung,* Ed. Violet Staub de Laszlo (New York: Random House, 1993) 327-328.

[227] Euripides, "The Bacchae," *The Complete Greek Tragedies*, ed. David Greene and Richard Lattimore, trans. William Arrowsmith (Chicago: University of Chicago Press, 1959) 73-75.

228 *Laws* 654a. Regarding Plato's reference to the Pythagorean claim that astronomy and music are kindred sciences (*Republic* 530d), the Pythagorean science of music involved studying the relation between mathematical ratios of vibrating strings and the harmonic or dissonant sounds they made. J. B. Kennedy attracted world-wide attention in the summer of 2010 when he published an article entitled "Plato's Forms, Pythagorean Mathematics, and Stichometry," with *Aperion* (43 [1]:1-32, 2010). Stichometry is the ancient practice of counting the number of regularly spaced letters forming regularly spaced lines arranged into columns (typically on a scroll of standard size), then correlating the content of the words with the numbers of the lines in which they appear, thereby adding an unannounced, mathematical dimension of meaning to the surface reading of the text. Using rigorous academic research methods, and computerized letter-counting algorithms, Kennedy discovered that Plato used stichometry to correlate the surface content of *all* of his dialogues (written on scrolls) with a 12-note Pythagorean musical scale. According to Kennedy, who went on to publish a book on his theory: "Musicologists prefer to call the 'scale' in the dialogues a 'division of the canon', where 'canon' is the common, ancient term for a monochord" (J. B. Kennedy, *The Musical Structure of Plato's Dialogues* [Durham, UK: Acumen, 2011] 255)

The notes of the Pythagorean "scale" are determined by dividing a monochord, or *canon*, into 12 equal parts, and measuring the way each vibrating fraction sounds in relation to the vibration of another whole string of equal length. Briefly stated, according to Kennedy, each of Plato's dialogues is stichometrically divided into 12 equal parts, in such a way that conventionally moral themes such as God, the idea of the Good, and immortal souls, regularly appear near those 12ths of the dialogue that correspond to the consonant notes of the underlying musical scale, while conventionally immoral themes such as denial of the gods and praise of tyranny appear near the dissonant notes. Although Kennedy acknowledges that none of the characters in Plato's dramatic Dialogues can necessarily be said to speak for Plato himself, he argues that we *can* detect Plato's personal beliefs by observing how he chose to align the surface content of the conversations with the underlying musical scale. If we assume that consonant notes denote a positive valuation and dissonant notes a negative one, then Plato comes across as a Pythagorean moralist, and not as a Nietzschean nihilist, as, for example, Leo Strauss is supposed to have supposed.

A year after his revolutionary article appeared, Kennedy published a book in which he states:

> The structures, in particular, related to core Pythagorean doctrines such as the "harmony of the spheres", to the theory of relative harmony, and to constructions of the pentagon and regular polyhedral. The general fact that the dialogues have a musico-mathematical substructure seems to conform with the Pythagorean tenet, reported already in Aristotle, that the fabric of reality, beneath appearances, is somehow mathematical. In short, the structures tend to confirm the picture of a tradition with secret doctrines about the musico-mathematical structure of the cosmos. (*The Musical Structure of Plato's Dialogues* 249)

[229] T. Z. Lavine, *From Socrates to Sartre: the Philosophic Quest* (New York: Bantam Books,1984) 42.

[230] *The Passion of the Western Mind* 100.

[231] *The Passion of the Western Mind* 103.

[232] Augustine, *Confessions*, trans. F. J. Sheed (Indianapolis: Hackett Publishing Company, Inc., 1993) 7:9, 116. According to Tarnas:

> That supreme Light, the true source of reality shining forth outside Plato's cave of shadows, was now recognized as the light of Christ. . . . Thus Augustine held that the Platonic Forms existed within the creative mind of God and that the ground of reality lay beyond the world of the senses, available only through a radical inward-turning of the soul. (*The Passion of the Western Mind* 103)

[233] *The Passion of the Western Mind* 103.

[234] The Gospel According to St. John, in The Holy Bible, *Douay-Rheims 1899 American Edition (DRA)*, 1:1, http://www.drbo.org/.

[235] *Confessions* 12:13, 241. Earlier, in Book 7 of *Confessions*, Augustine cites the Bible verse about the *heaven of heavens*:

> And since from the heavens, O our God, *all Thy angels praise Thee in the high places, and all Thy hosts, sun and moon, all the stars and the lights, the heavens of heavens, and the waters that are above the heavens, praise thy name*—I no longer desired better, because I had thought upon them all and with clear judgement I realized that while certain higher things are better than lower things, yet all things together are better than the higher alone. (*Confessions* 7:13, 120)

[236] *Confessions* 12:9, 239.

[237] *Timaeus* 51a-51b. Augustine's description of the love of the outermost sphere for God is also very similar to Aristotle's theory that the original movement of the universe is caused by the love of the sphere of fixed stars for God, the infinitely powerful, spatially unextended, unmoved Mover outside each point of the cosmic horizon (*Passion of the Western Mind* 63-64).

[238] *Confessions* 12:15, 243.

[239] *Confessions* 12:11, 240.

[240] *Confessions* 13:15, 269.

[241] *Confessions* 13:15, 269-270.

[242] *The Passion of the Western Mind* 194-195.

[243] Robert Osserman, *Poetry of the Universe: A Mathematical Exploration of the Cosmos* (New York: Anchor Books, 1996) 118. Dan Stober, "Robert Osserman, noted Stanford mathematician, dies at 84," *Stanford News*, December 16, 2011, http://news.stanford.edu/news/2011/december/robert-osserman-obit- 121611.html.

[244] Quoted in *Cosmos and Psyche* 369.

[245] Dante writes:

O abounding grace, by which I dared to fix my look on the Eternal Light so long that I spent all my sight upon it! In its depths I saw that it contained, bound by love in one volume, that which is scattered in leaves through the universe, substances and accidents and their relations as it were fused together in such a way that what I tell of is a simple light. I think I saw the universal form of this complex, because in telling of it I feel my joy expand. Thus my mind, all rapt, was gazing, fixed, still and intent, and ever enkindled with gazing. At that light one becomes such that it is impossible for him ever to consent that he should turn from it to another sight; for the good which is the object of the will is all gathered in it. (quoted in *Cosmos and Psyche* 369)

[246] According to Tarnas, "Newton's joyful exclamation, 'O God, I think thy thoughts after thee!' was only the culmination of a long series of such epiphanies marking the milestones of modern science's birth." (*The Passion of the Western Mind* 300) Newton was echoing Copernicus' own opinion, while Kepler, who found the precise mathematical descriptions for Copernicus' heliocentric theory, nevertheless maintained the basic model of Augustine's Platonic cosmos, "taking the center for the Father, the spherical surface for the Son, and the intermediate space . . . for the Holy Spirit." (Stanford Encyclopedia of Philosophy, *Johannes Kepler*, May 21, 2015, https://plato.stanford.edu/entries/kepler/)

[247] By Descartes' own definition, the gravitational singularity must be a mental substance, because it exists without being extended in space.

[248] Rene Descartes, *The Mediations*, in *Discourse on Method and the Meditations*, trans. F. E. Sutcliffe (London: Penguin Books, 1968), 123-134. The quote above is from the *Third Meditation*. Importantly for my proposed identification of the psyche with the gravitational singularity, it meets most of the criteria of Descartes' idea of God: it is infinitely powerful, it is not extended in space, it contains every bit of information from the past, present, and future, and it created everything that exists at the Big Bang. But how can a point that is not extended in space nevertheless be omnipresent? Descartes' contemporary Catholic theologian Blaise Pascal says it is possible if we think of God as "a point moving everywhere at an

infinite speed." (Blaise Pascal, *Penses*, trans. A. J. Krailscheimer [London: Penguin Books, 1966] 153)

[249] Tarnas explains the ironic history of the emergence of the atheistic enlightenment out of the mathematical-mystical philosophy of Pythagoras and Plato (which Copernicus, Kepler, Galileo, and Newton all accepted to varying degrees):

> Mathematical patterning was simply "in the nature of things," or in the nature of the human mind, and was not interpreted in a Platonic light as giving evidence of an eternal changeless world of pure spirit. . . . Paradoxically, the Platonic philosophy had served as the sine qua non for a world view that seemed directly to controvert the Platonic assumptions. (*The Passion of the Western Mind* 292-293)

[250] According to Lavine: "He opposed Descartes's causal mechanism by destroying Descartes's idea of cause and effect. We may say that Hume dealt with Descartes by destroying him. In turning to David Hume we are about to encounter the excitement of the most destructive force in the history of Western philosophy." (Levine 130)

[251] David Hume, *An Enquiry Concerning Human Understanding*, in *Four Fundamental Questions: An Introduction to Philosophy*, ed. Richard Bilsker (Iowa: Kendall Hunt Publishing Company, 2011) 309.

[252] According to Hume: "If any impression gives rise to the idea of the self, that impression must continue invariably the same, through the whole course of our lives; since self is supposed to exist after that manner. But there is no impression constant and invariable." (David Hume, *A Treatise of Human Nature*, in *Four Fundamental Questions: An Introduction to Philosophy*, ed. Richard Bilsker (Iowa: Kendall Hunt Publishing Company, 2011) 99-100.

[253] *A Treatise on Human Nature* 100. Hume's comment on the rapid succession of sense impressions giving the illusion of continuity gains support from David Bohm's interpretation of the quantum vacuum. As discussed earlier, the quantum vacuum is created by the constant creation and annihilation of virtual particle-antiparticle pairs. Bohm, who pioneered

Susskind's own attempt to combine quantum mechanics and general relativity in a holographic model, called the quantum vacuum the implicate order, from which the explicate order of empirically observable objects is projected, and back into which it enfolds at an enormously rapid rate. According to Bohm, "a 'particle' is to be understood as a recurrent stable order of unfoldment in which a certain form undergoing regular changes manifests again and again, but so rapidly that it appears to be in continuous existence." (*Wholeness and the Implicate Order* 246) How rapidly do particles fold in and out of the quantum vacuum? According to Shelli Joye the entire universe unfolds from and folds back into the vacuum "10^{44} times per second." (Shelli Renee Joye, "The Pribram-Bohm Holoflux Theory of Consciousness: An Integral Interpretation of the Theories of Karl Pribram, David Bohm, and Pierre Teilhard de Chardin," Ph.D. diss., California Institute of Integral Studies, 2016, 160)

[254] *A Treatise on Human Nature* 105-106.

[255] Immanuel Kant, *Kant's Prolegomena to Any Future Metaphysics: Edited in English by Paul Carus; With an Essay on Kant's Philosophy, and Other Supplementary Material for the Study of Kant (1912)* (Ithaca, New York: Cornell University Library, 2009) 4.

[256] *The Passion of the Western Mind* 343-346. Kant made an important distinction between pure *a priori* categories of thought and synthetic *a priori* categories of thought. Synthetic *a priori* categories are only discovered *after* humans make empirical observations; once the empirical observation is made, the human realizes that the truth thereby discovered must necessarily hold true everywhere in the universe. He uses the example of 5 + 7 = 12. There is nothing in the definition of 12 that reveals 5 and 7 within it, so we must make an empirical observation (such as counting on our fingers or imagining some similar scene), after which we realize that it is impossible to imagine 5 + 7 equaling any number other than 12. In other words, by using empirical observations (including images in our minds) we can arrive at eternal truths.

[257] Immanuel Kant, *Critique of Pure Reason*, in *Four Fundamental Questions: An Introduction to Philosophy*, ed. Richard Bilsker (Iowa: Kendall Hunt Publishing Company, 2011) 324.

[258] *Critique of Pure Reason* 325.

[259] *Critique of Pure Reason* 324. According to Tarnas, "Thus the cosmological estrangement of modern consciousness initiated by Copernicus and the ontological estrangement initiated by Descartes were completed by the epistemological estrangement initiated by Kant: a threefold mutually enforced prison of modern alienation." (*The Passion of the Western Mind* 419)

[260] *Timaeus* 51a-51b; *Confessions* 2:13, 241.

[261] *The Cosmic Landscape* 265-266, 269; 2008, 339.

[262] Atmanspacher and Primas 19.

[263] *The Basic Writings of C. G. Jung* 360. The farther out in expanding space we look, the farther back in time we see, so that "the remotest times" of the Big Bang are conserved at and echoing back from the outermost sphere of the universe, at each point of which, according to Susskind's theory, the past, present, and future of all three-dimensional space is interwoven. I argue that the universal images of the archetypes are also interwoven there.

[264] *On the Nature of the Psyche* 101.

[265] *The Republic* 530d.

[266] *The Black Hole War* 4.

[267] *The Black Hole War* 5. In *Memories, Dreams, Reflections*, Jung partially agrees with Susskind's reasoning: "We cannot visualize another world ruled by quite other laws, the reason being that we live in a specific world which has helped to shape our minds and establish our basic psychic conditions." (*Memories, Dreams, Reflections* 300) However, Jung goes on to say that, though we cannot *visualize* the other world of the afterlife, we can experience images of it that rise into consciousness from the archetypes of the collective unconscious during dreams, which are the same images that inspired ancient mythology. Jung says he experienced the eternal world directly at the cosmic horizon when his psyche was no longer confined in his material body, but he admits that it is impossible to translate those subjective experiences into words that we can visualize on Earth.

Nevertheless, twentieth-century physics has exactly the same problem of translating its findings into everyday language that conforms to the physical world as it is revealed by our five bodily sense organs. The simple fact that we cannot adequately imagine the afterlife does not mean it is not real; if that were the case, then our inability to visualize the past, present, and future coexisting in the space-time continuum would render general relativity false as well. The forces of nature help form the psychic structure through which we are aware of nature, but if the collective unconscious archetypes are interwoven at the holographic horizon of the cosmos, then it is more reasonable to say that our psychic structure is formed by the eternal archetypes, from which the illusion of three-dimensional space is projected by fundamental strings. The eternal archetypes form the natural world that forms our psychic structure.

[268] *Memories, Dreams, Reflections* 300.

[269] See, for example, Ken Wilber's *Quantum Questions*.

[270] *The Black Hole War* 5. On this point, see especially Jung, *Memories, Dreams, Reflections* 300-301.

[271] *Relativity* 152.

[272] "Introduction," *Six Not-So-Easy Pieces* ix-xvi. According to Susskind, "Ever since Einstein's discovery of the Special Theory of Relativity, physicists have been in the habit of picturing the world as a four-dimensional space-time that encompasses not only *the now*, but also all of the future and the past." (*The Cosmic Landscape* 38)

[273] *The Portable Jung* 51-52.

[274] As Richard Tarnas explains:

> In his later work, however, and particularly in his relation to the study of synchronicities, Jung began to move toward a conception of archetypes as autonomous patterns of meaning that appear to structure and inhere in both psyche and matter, thereby in effect dissolving the modern subject-object dichotomy. Archetypes in this view were more mysterious than a priori categories—more ambiguous in their ontological status, less easily restricted to

a specific dimension, more like the original Platonic and Neoplatonic conception of archetypes. (*The Passion of the Western Mind* 425)

[275] *The Basic Writings of C. G. Jung* 310. Jung's concept of enantiodrama is reminiscent of aphorism 289 from Nietzsche's *The Gay Science*.

> *Embark!*— . . . What is needful is a new justice! And a new watchword. And new philosophers. The moral earth, too, is round. The moral earth, too, has its antipodes. The antipodes, too, have the right to exist. There is yet another world to be discovered—and more than one. Embark, philosophers! (Friedrich Nietzsche, *The Gay Science*, trans. Walter Kaufmann [New York: Vintage Books, a division of Random House, 1974] 232)

[276] *The Black Hole War* 305. If all of the archetypes are folded into one another in the ultimate archetype of the Self, as Jung and Pauli theorized, and if the Self is the universal mandala formed by the central singularity and surrounding horizon of the cosmos as described above, then it seems that the material events historically unfolding through the holographic movie of three-dimensional space (including each emotional moment of our individual biographies) are simultaneously being projected out from the conscious mind (singularity) and in from the unconscious mind (cosmic horizon) of the Self. In other words, the holographic motion picture of universal history is formed by a union of the outgoing conscious mind and incoming unconscious mind of the Self archetype. It seems plausible to suggest that the intersection of these outgoing and incoming waves of radiation may result in the apparently solid forms we inhabit, like standing waves. In any event, the parallels between Jung's psychology and Susskind's cosmology indicate that each bit of information describing the past, present, and future of three-dimensional space is woven into each archetype, all of which are interwoven in the central singularity and at each point of the outermost sphere of the universe, from where every bit of information constituting the entire movie of space-time is projected inward by rapidly vibrating, elastic strings that transform the eternal knowledge of the archetypal forms into empirically observable holograms.

[277] Fritjof Capra, *The Tao of Physics: An Exploration of the Parallels between Modern Physics and Eastern Mysticism* (Boston: Shambhala Publications, Inc., 1999) 23.

[278] Rene Descartes, *The Mediations*, in *Discourse on Method and the Meditations*, trans. F. E. Sutcliffe (London: Penguin Books, 1968), 123-134. The quote above is from the *Third Meditation*. Importantly for my proposed identification of the psyche with the gravitational singularity, it meets most of the criteria of Descartes' idea of God: it is infinitely powerful, it is not extended in space, it contains every bit of information from the past, present, and future, and it created everything that exists at the Big Bang. But how can a point that is not extended in space nevertheless be omnipresent? Descartes' contemporary Catholic theologian Blaise Pascal says it is possible if we think of God as "a point moving everywhere at an infinite speed." (Pascal 153) A point moving everywhere infinitely fast would return to each point of space an infinitely increasing number of times at each instant. If we analyze that idea in terms of general relativity, the infinitely fast point would be a gravitational singularity.

[279] *Encountering Jung* 162.

[280] *The Elegant Universe* 78-79; *Parallel Worlds* 114; *The Black Hole War* 32.

[281] *Encountering Jung* 122.

[282] *Encountering Jung* 162.

[283] *Memories, Dreams, Reflections* 295.

[284] Schrödinger introduces Jung's quote as follows:

> I maintain that it amounts to a certain simplification which we adopt in order to master the infinitely intricate problem of nature. Without being aware of it and without being rigorously systematic about it, we exclude the Subject of Cognizance from the domain of nature that we endeavour to understand. We step with our own person back into the part of an onlooker who does not belong to the world, which by this very procedure becomes an objective world. . . . I wish to go into more detail about some of the points I have made. First let me quote a passage from a

paper of C. G. Jung which has gratified me because it stresses the same point in quite a different context, albeit in a strongly vituperative fashion. While I continue to regard the removal of the Subject of Cognizance from the objective world picture as the high price paid for a fairly satisfactory picture, for the time being, Jung goes further and blames us for paying this ransom from an inextricably difficult situation. (Schrödinger 118-119)

Schrödinger, Heisenberg, and Pauli all took Jung seriously.

[285] *On the Nature of the Psyche* 79. This quote is from Jung's 1946 version of the essay, which remained the same in the final draft of 1954 in *On the Nature of the Psyche*, which I cite in this book.

[286] It is important to note that Jung recognizes that much of ancient and medieval, especially esoteric (alchemical and astrological), Western thought agrees with the East in being panpsychic, or at least enchanted.

[287] Schrödinger 121.

[288] *On the Nature of the Psyche* 125.

[289] *On the Nature of the Psyche* 127.

[290] *On the Nature of the Psyche* 138. In *Psychology and Religion* Jung says there is no Archimedean point:

> There is no Archimedean point from which to judge, since the psyche is indistinguishable from its manifestations. The psyche is the object of psychology, and—fatally enough—also its subject. There is no getting away from this fact. (*Psychology and Religion* 43)

In *Four Archetypes* Jung says again that there is no Archimedean point outside the psyche:

> To inquire into the substance of what has been observed is possible in natural science only where there is an Archimedean point outside. For the psyche, no such outside standpoint exists— only the psyche can observe the psyche. (Carl Jung, *Four Archetypes: Mother/Rebirth/Spirit/Trickster*,

trans. R.F.C. Hull [New Jersey: Princeton University Press] 85.

[291] *On the Nature of the Psyche* 86.

[292] *On the Nature of the Psyche* 143.

[293] *Encountering Jung* 160-161.

[294] The existence of subtle matter could also potentially explain the nature of dark matter and dark energy.

[295] *The Cosmic Landscape* 73.

[296] *Encountering Jung* 161-162.

[297] In his *Penses*, Blaise Pascal explains that it is possible to imagine God as being omnipresent and yet undivided if we think of "a point moving everywhere at an infinite speed." (Pascal 153)

[298] Equivalently, accelerating any piece of matter to light speed (as happens at the event horizon and cosmic horizon) would compact that material into an infinitely dense point.

[299] *Memories, Dreams, Reflections* 324.

[300] *The Black Hole War* 331.

[301] The following comments about the singularity come from the BBC 2 television series, *Horizon*, from an episode in the 2009-2010 season entitled "Who's Afraid of a Big Black Hole?" The scene opens with Michio Kaku standing in front of a black board with a piece of chalk, writing out the Schwarzschild solution to Einstein's general relativity equations, which describes a black hole, ending with the radius equal to 0, followed by an infinity symbol describing the mass:

> Michio Kaku: To a mathematician, infinity is simply a number without limit. To a physicist, it's a *monstrosity*. It means that, first of all, gravity is *infinite* at the center of a black hole, that time *stops*, and what does that mean? Space makes no sense; it means the collapse of everything we know about the physical universe [he draws a rectangle around the infinity symbol on the black board, then laughs]. In the real world, there's no such thing as

infinity. Therefore, there is a fundamental flaw in the formulation of Einstein's theory [he nods his head with conviction].

Samuel West (Narrator): According to Einstein, then, all the mass of a black hole is contained within an infinitely small point that takes up precisely no space at all. This impossible object of infinite density and infinite gravity is called the singularity.

Andrew Strominger (Harvard University): We know what a singularity is. A singularity is when we don't know what to do.

Max Tegmark (MIT): To me what's so embarrassing about a singularity is that we can't predict anything about what's going to come out of it. Now I could have a singularity here and then, *boom*, out comes a pink elephant with purple stripes. And that's consistent with what the laws of physics predict, because they don't predict anything.

Andrew Strominger: The singularity is when our understanding of nature breaks down, that's what a singularity is.

Michio Kaku: [Points to the infinity symbol in the general relativity equation for a black hole on the black board.] Einstein realized there was a problem when he was shown this infinity. But he thought that black holes could never physically form. Therefore, it was an academic question. Sure, there was a problem in these equations [points to the infinity symbol again], but it didn't matter because Mother Nature could never create a black hole. ("Who's Afraid of a Big Black Hole?")

[302] *The Cosmic Landscape* 75.

[303] Wolfgang Pauli, "Exclusion Principle and Quantum Mechanics," Nobel Lecture, December 13, 1946, 42. http://www.nobelprize.org/nobel_prizes/physics/laureates/1945/pauli-lecture.pdf.

[304] "Who's Afraid of a Big Black Hole?"

[305] "Stephen Hawking's Universe"

[306] According to Hawking:

The universe would be completely self-contained and not affected by anything outside itself. It would neither be created nor destroyed. It would just BE.

It was at the conference in the Vatican mentioned earlier that I first put forward the suggestion that maybe time and space formed a surface that was finite in size but did not have any boundary or edge. My paper was rather mathematical, however, so its implications for the role of God in the creation of the universe were not generally recognized at the time (just as well for me). (*A Brief History of Time* 141)

[307] *Two Essays on Analytical Psychology* 237-238.

[308] Gottfried Wilhelm Leibnitz, who independently discovered calculus at the same time as Newton, made this same argument in *The Monadology*. In that essay he calls souls monads and argues that they come into existence all at once because they have no parts, and no extension in space, and therefore require no assembly time. Neither is there any way to discern any outward difference between one monad and another. In fact, according to Leibnitz, because monads have no extension in space, they have "no windows" through which to observe other monads, nor do they have any way of affecting other monads, at least externally: "It follows from what has just been said, that the natural changes of the Monads come from an internal principle, since an external cause can have no influence upon their inner being." (Gottfried Wilhelm Leibnitz, *Monadology*, in *Four Fundamental Questions: An Introduction to Philosophy*, ed. Richard Bilsker [Iowa: Kendall Hunt Publishing Company, 2011] 192) If no monad can contact another, why does it seem as if each of us is constantly responding to the promptings of others in a meaningful way? Leibnitz argues that the reason monads (including the apparently material atoms which are actually made of monads) can meaningfully communicate with each other is that God, the supreme monad, has synchronized the isolated utterances and actions of each monad with every other through an infinitely complex, "pre-established harmony," which is similar to Jung's synchronicity theory.

[309] Sean Kelly, *Coming Home: The Birth and Transformation of the Planetary Era* (Bearington, Massachusetts: Lindisfarne Press, 2010) 136.

[310] Kelly 136.

[311] The following recollections of Jung's near-death experience come from *Memories, Dreams, Reflections*, an auto-biographical summary of his life's work, compiled at the behest and with the help of his student, Aniela Jaffe.

[312] *Memories, Dreams, Reflections* 290.

[313] *Memories, Dreams, Reflections* 290-291.

[314] The most famous black Hindu worshipped along the coast of the Gulf of Bengal is the ultimate "Hindu," the form of Vishnu named Krishna (which means "black"). Evangeline Rand traces out the places Jung actually visited in India, among which include the most famous temple dedicated to Krishna, the Jagannath temple in the district of Puri, in the state of Orissa (now known as Odisha), near the Gulf of Bengal (Evangeline Rand, *A Jasmine Journey: Carl Jung's travel to India and Ceylon 1937-1938 and Jung's Vision During Illness "Something New" Emerging from Orissa, 1944* [North Vancouver, B.C.: Living Infinity, Ltd., 2013] 76).

[315] *Memories, Dreams, Reflections* 290-291.

[316] *Memories, Dreams, Reflections* 291.

[317] *Memories, Dreams, Reflections* 291.

[318] *Memories, Dreams, Reflections* 292.

[319] *Memories, Dreams, Reflections* 292.

[320] *Memories, Dreams, Reflections* 295-296.

[321] *The Black Hole War* 293-294.

[322] *The Black Hole War* 434.

[323] *Memories, Dreams, Reflections* 292, 295.

[324] *The Black Hole War* 299.

[325] *The Black Hole War* 300-301.

[326] *Memories, Dreams, Reflections* 291.

[327] In a way that supports Jung's claim to have become one with his entire biography at the outermost limit of Earth's atmosphere, and Susskind's theory that information is stored holographically at every concentric boundary of space, in 1995 Michael Persinger, a physical neuroscientist and professor at Laurentian University in Ontario, published a paper entitled "On the Possibility of Directly Accessing Every Human Brain by Electromagnetic Induction of Fundamental Algorithms." Persinger is an atheist who tries to discount religious experiences as the effect of electromagnetic stimulation of the brain. He is most famous for his so-called "God helmet" experiments which induce in some people experiences of the presence of disembodied entities. Nevertheless, Persinger argues that the information of every human brain on Earth is holographically stored in Earth's magnetic field and is furthermore accessible to each of us. He explains the detail of his theory in "No More Secrets," a lecture given at Laurentian University in Ontario, Canada, on March 3, 2011 https://www.youtube.com/watch?v=9l6VPpDublg&t=2270s.

[328] *The Passion of the Western Mind* 425. Considering the greater extent of his research into the field of parapsychology in general, and NDEs in particular, I analyze Grof's work much more closely than either van Lommel's or Alexander's.

[329] Stanislav Groff, *Psychology of the Future: Lessons from Modern Consciousness Research* (New York: State University of New York Press, 2000) ix.

[330] *Psychology of the Future* 314. In his book *Brighter Than a Thousand Suns: A Personal History of the Atomic Scientists* Robert Jungk reports Oppenheimer recalling two quotes from the Bhagavad-gita. The other, less frequently cited quote is the one to which Grof was evidently referring when he compared his first LSD trip to the mystical literature about light that is like millions of suns:

> If the radiance of a thousand suns
>
> Were to be burst into the sky,
>
> That would be like

The splendor of the Mighty One— (Robert Jungk, *Brighter Than a Thousand Suns: A Personal History of the Atomic Scientists* [Orlando, Florida: Harcourt, Inc., 1986] 201)

[331] *Bhagavad-gita As It Is* 11.12, 11.32.

[332] Grof goes on to say, "There were experiences that I didn't have names for but later, when I read about the black hole, white holes, I mean it was something in that category, pulsars. Amazing, amazing cosmic experience. So I came down very, very impressed, and it just generated this life time interest in this non-ordinary states. . . . This became my, my vocation, my profession, my passion." (Stanislav Grof, "Stan Grof about his LSD experience," *Youtube*, March 29, 2008, http://www.youtube.com/watch?v=5ig3eU_oDS0.)

[333] *The Cosmic Landscape* 154-155.

[334] *The Cosmic Landscape* 312-313.

[335] Gribbin 190-91.

[336] *The Essential David Bohm* 152. This quote is part of Bohm's response to Rene Weber's question about a possible correlation between modern physics and the ancient Greek and eastern metaphors equating light with the divine. Directly pertinent to this chapter, she specifically asks Bohm to comment on why light is "the central metaphor in near-death experiences." (*The Essential David Bohm* 152)

[337] *Psychology of the Future* ix.

[338] *Psychology of the Future* 2.

[339] *The Cosmic Landscape* 80-81.

[340] Michio Kaku, "Cosmic Holes," *The Universe,* directed by Laura Verklan, episode no. 16, History, December 4, 2007.

[341] *Psychology of the Future* 64.

[342] *The Essential David Bohm* 85.

[343] *The Essential David Bohm* 105.

[344] *The Black Hole War* 294-295.

[345] *The Black Hole War* 296.

[346] *The Black Hole War* 298.

[347] Brihadaranyaka Upanishad *3.7.3, 3.8.1-8; Bhagavad-gita As It Is 7.4-8*.

[348] Stanislav Grof, *The Ultimate Journey: Consciousness and the Mystery of Death* (Santa Cruz: The Multidisciplinary Association for Psychedelic Studies, 2006) 143-144.

[349] Erwin Lazlo, *Science and the Akashic Field: An Integral Theory of Everything* (Rochester, VT: Inner Traditions, 2007) 20.

[350] Lazlo 22.

[351] *The Cosmic Landscape* 332; *The Black Hole War* 373.

[352] *The Cosmic Landscape* 380.

[353] *The Black Hole War* 439.

[354] Sri Isopanishad, The Bhaktivedanta Book Trust (BBT): The Pre-1978 Books by His Divine Grace A. C. Bhaktivedanta Swami Prabhupada, http://causelessmercy.com/?P=Iso., 15.

[355] *Psychology of the Future* 300.

[356] *Psychology of the Future* 20.

[357] *Psychology of the Future* 20.

[358] *Psychology of the Future* 33.

[359] *The Ultimate Journey* 174.

[360] *The Ultimate Journey* 171.

[361] Apocalypse 1:8, 21:6.

[362] *Bhagavad-gita As It Is 7.6*.

[363] Carl Jung, *Synchronicity: An Acausal Connecting Principle* (New York: Bollinger Press, 1973) 93.

[364] *The Black Hole War* 299.

[365] *The Ultimate Journey* 167-168.

[366] Pim Van Lommel, *Consciousness Beyond Life: The Science of the Near-Death Experience* (New York: HarpersCollins Publishers, 2010) 167.

[367] Van Lommel 167.

[368] Van Lommel 171.

[369] Van Lommel 172-173.

[370] Van Lommel 205.

[371] Van Lommel 205.

[372] Van Lommel 209.

[373] Van Lommel 210-212.

[374] Van Lommel 244-245. Van Lommel goes on to say:

> Dutch Nobel Laureate Gerard 't Hooft believes that the entire universe might be based on the holographic principle, a view he sees as compatible with string theory. In this theory the strings are one-dimensional oscillating lines (wave functions) floating in space-time. The idea of a holographic universe is based on an as-yet-unknown medium, believed to be strings or branes (this medium used to be known as the ether); in a nonlocal universe everything is encoded as wave functions in nonlocal space. Scientists now know that a vacuum is not empty; at absolute zero, -273.15 degrees Celsius, it is full of energy (a "plenum"), and at the subatomic level it undergoes constant quantum fluctuations that create new quanta "from nothing," which then immediately disappear again. . . . In two recent and accessible books, *The Connectivity Hypothesis* and *Science and the Akashic Field*, Systems theorist Ervin Laszlo uses holographic field theory to argue that the entire universe is a fully interconnected holographic information field. His ideas are based on the theory of a zero-point field in the quantum vacuum or "cosmic plenum." (Van Lommel 246-247)

[375] Susskind describes the quantum vacuum as consisting of miniature black holes tightly packed at the Planck scale. The energy produced by the constant creation and annihilation of virtual particle-antiparticle pairs creates "virtual black holes" that rapidly pop into and out of existence (*The Cosmic Landscape* 88). If there is a singularity in the center of each of the virtual black holes of which the quantum vacuum is made, then the quantum vacuum is a bubbling sea of psyches, which furthermore supports van Lommel's significant claim that the quantum vacuum is equivalent to "the collective unconscious as defined by psychiatrist and psychologist Carl G. Jung." (Van Lommel 304) Although I equate the collective unconscious with the cosmic horizon, according to Leibnitz's principle of the identity of indiscernibles the cosmic horizon and the quantum vacuum are the same thing, in as much as both of them consist of singularities that are outside of space-time by virtue of being its source and boundary.

Van Lommel points out that Jung sometimes referred to the collective unconscious as "the transpersonal aspect of consciousness." (Van Lommel 305) He explains that the "psychologist Jorge Ferrer takes stock of the many different versions of transpersonal theory," and notes that Ferrer describes the transpersonal aspect of consciousness as "the spiritual dimension of humanity." (Van Lommel 305) Informed by Ferrer, he goes on to explain that "the term *transpersonal psychology* originated in the work of the clinical psychologist and founder of humanistic psychology Abraham H. Maslow and the work of psychologist Stanislav Grof, who is often described as the founder of transpersonal psychology." (Van Lommel 305; see also *Cosmos and Psyche* 305)

The point for this book is that van Lommel places his research into NDEs directly in the line of transpersonal psychology as developed by Jung and Grof, who is furthermore a colleague of Ferrer's, Tarnas', Kelly's, and Swimme's at the California Institute of Integral Studies, where I earned a Ph.D. in Philosophy and Religion, with a concentration in Philosophy, Cosmology, and Consciousness.

[376] In 1975 Dr. Raymond Moody published *Life After Life*, in which he coined the term "near-death experience." (Raymond Moody, *Life After Life* [New York: Harper Collins Publishers, (1975) 2015], xv)

Pim van Lommel summarizes Moody's list of the twelve most typical aspects of an NDE. Numbers 8-11 relate to the experience of a light at the end of a dark tunnel:

> 8. Seeing a brilliant light or a being of light; experiencing complete acceptance and unconditional love and gaining access to a deep knowledge and wisdom.
>
> 9. The panoramic life review, or review of life from birth: people see their entire life flash before them; there appears to be no time or distance, everything happens at once. . . .
>
> 10. The preview or flash forward. . . .
>
> 11. The perception of a border: people are aware that if they cross this border or limit they will never be able to return to their body. (Van Lommel 11-12)

[377] *The Ultimate Journey* 163-165.

[378] *The Ultimate Journey* 171.

[379] Considering my intention is to draw only the most basic parallels between the tunnel vision of an NDE and the tunnel vision described by general relativity (and, later, special relativity), the following excerpt from an article about gravitational lensing from Wikipedia is sufficient to make my case.

> A **gravitational lens** refers to a distribution of matter (such as a cluster of galaxies) between a distant source (a background galaxy) and an observer, that is capable of bending (lensing) the light from the source, as it travels towards the observer. This effect is known as gravitational lensing and is one of the predictions of Albert Einstein's general theory of relativity.
>
> Although Orest Chwolson (1924) or Frantisek Klin (1936) are sometimes credited as being the first ones to discuss the effect in print, the effect is more commonly associated with Einstein, who published a more famous article on the subject in 1936. . . .
>
> It is usually referred to in the literature as an **Einstein ring**, since Chwolson did not concern himself with the flux or radius of

the ring image. (Wikipedia, "Gravitational Lens," 2013, http://en.wikipedia.org/wiki/Gravitational_lens.)

[380] *The Black Hole War* 36.

[381] *The Black Hole War* 455.

[382] Karen Masters, "What Would You See from Inside a Black Hole?" *Curious About Astronomy? Ask an Astronomer*, October 2002, para. 1-5, http://curious.astro.cornell.edu/question.php?number=348.

[383] Masters para. 1-5.

[384] *The Cosmic Landscape* 384.

[385] Van Lommel 26.

[386] Van Lommel 27.

[387] Sara Slater, "What Happens to Spacetime Inside a Black Hole?" *Curious About Astronomy? Ask an Astronomer*, January 2005, para. 1-4, http://curious.astro.cornell.edu/question.php?number=652.

[388] Clifford Pickover, *Black Holes: A Traveler's Guide* (New York: John Wiley & Sons, Inc. 1996) 26-27.

[389] Pickover 42.

[390] Alexis Brandeker, "What Would a Relativistic Interstellar Traveler See?" *The Original Usenet Physics FAQ*, eds. Scott Chase, Michael Weiss, Philip Gibbs, Chris Hillman, and Nathan Urban, May 2002, para. 1-9, http://math.ucr.edu/home/baez/physics/Relativity/SR/Spaceship/spaceship.html.)

[391] Atmanspacher and Primas 19.

[392] Plato, *The Republic of Plato: Translated, with Notes, an Interpretive Essay, and a new Introduction by Allan Bloom* (New York: Basic Books, 1991) 614c-e.

[393] *The Republic of Plato* 614d.

³⁹⁴ Van Lommel 27-29.

³⁹⁵ According to van Lommel:

> A little pinpoint of light appears in this dark space, and people are often pulled toward it at an incredible speed. They describe it as a tunnel experience.
>
> People move through this dark, occasionally multicolored or spiral-shaped narrow space, sometimes accompanied by visible or invisible beings or by music. They approach the light, which slowly intensifies to become an exceptionally bright but nonblinding light. Eventually people are wholly enveloped by this light and feel completely absorbed by it. This process is coupled with an indescribable feeling of bliss, a sense of unconditional love and acceptance. The journey through the tunnel appears to be a passing from our physical world to another dimension where time and distance no longer play a role. This sensation of moving through a tunnel toward the light has become almost synonymous with near-death experience. (Van Lommel 27. See also *The Ultimate Journey* 164, 168, 171; and *Psychology of the Future* 165)

³⁹⁶ Ursala Goodenough, "Gravity Is Love, And Other Astounding Metaphors," *13.7 Cosmos and Culture: Commentary on Science and Society*, NPR blog, 2010,
http://www.npr.org/blogs/13.7/2010/10/21/130724690/gravity-is- love.

³⁹⁷ In agreement with Swimme's equation of gravity and love, St. Augustine also said: "My love is my weight: wherever I go my love is what brings me there." He explains that things move because they are seeking their natural resting place: oil floats on water, and water falls through oil, because their respective weights incline them to those places. Similarly, says Augustine, "It is by Your fire, Your beneficent fire, that we burn and we rise, rise towards the peace of Jerusalem, since I have rejoiced in those who said to me: *We shall go to the house of the Lord.*" (*Confessions* 13:9, 266). As we saw earlier, Jerusalem and the house of the Lord are Biblical terms Augustine

uses in his *Confessions* to refer to the cosmic horizon, also known as the *heaven of heaven.*

[398] Eben Alexander, "Heaven is Real: A Doctor's Experience with the Afterlife," *Newsweek*, October 8, 2012, 29, http://mag.newsweek.com/2012/10/07/proof-of-heaven-a-doctor-s-experience-with-the-afterlife.html.

[399] Eben Alexander, *Proof of Heaven: A Neurosurgeon's Journey into the After Life* (New York: Simon and Schuster, 2012) 48.

[400] *Proof of Heaven* 9.

[401] *Proof of Heaven* 9.

[402] *Proof of Heaven* 9.

[403] *Proof of Heaven* 154.

[404] *Proof of Heaven* 150.

[405] *Proof of Heaven* 151.

[406] *Psychology of the Future* 20.

[407] *Proof of Heaven* 47-48.

[408] *Proof of Heaven* 47-48.

[409] *Proof of Heaven* 47-48.

[410] *Proof of Heaven* 47.

[411] *Bhagavad-gita As It Is* 10.21.

[412] *Bhagavad-gita As It Is* 10.25.

[413] *Bhagavad-gita As It Is* 7.4, 7.7, 7.8.

[414] *Proof of Heaven* 30-31.

[415] *Proof of Heaven* 70.

[416] *Proof of Heaven* 160.

[417] *Proof of Heaven* 70.

[418] *Proof of Heaven* 72.

[419] *Proof of Heaven* 45-46.

[420] *Proof of Heaven* 45-46.

[421] *Proof of Heaven* 46.

[422] *Bhagavad-gita As It Is* 7.8, 10.25.

[423] *Proof of Heaven* 160.

[424] *Proof of Heaven* 160.

[425] *Proof of Heaven* 9.

[426] Van Lommel 22.

[427] *Memories, Dreams, Reflections* 289-290.

[428] *Memories, Dreams, Reflections* 290.

[429] *Memories, Dreams, Reflections* 290-291.

[430] *Memories, Dreams, Reflections* 291.

[431] Earlier we saw Michael Persinger, a physical neuroscientist and professor at Laurentian University in Ontario, explain a similar theory about a layer of holographic information conservation in the outer-edge of Earth's atmosphere, which he described in a paper entitled "On the Possibility of Directly Accessing Every Human Brain by Electromagnetic Induction of Fundamental Algorithms," and in a lecture entitled "No More Secrets." Raymond Kurzweil describes a similar theory in his book *The Singularity is Near: When Humans Transcend Biology* (New York: The Penguin Group, 2005). The self-described "singulatarian" and well-respected futurist, Kurzweil claims that the historical Singularity is a culminating point of exponential technological progress that enables humans to utilize the computing power of singularities inside black holes to download our intelligence into technologically enhanced "smart matter" which will infuse itself throughout and transform the very substance of space-time in all the universes of the megaverse, granting us omnipresent immortality (Kurzweil 364). Importantly for my paper, Kurzweil explicitly grounds his vision of the historical Singularity on Leonard Susskind's principle of holographic

information conservation in black holes and the cosmic horizon (Kurzweil 361-366). What is especially interesting for my purposes is that Kurzweil, coming from an atheistic, materialist starting point, concludes with the same idea of the historical Singularity as many Christian mystics: at a specific point in time on Earth, humans will collectively gain an immortal, blissful life of godlike intelligence and power by merging with an all-pervasive cosmic consciousness.

Rupert Sheldrake—who earned his Ph.D. in biochemistry from Cambridge University, where he subsequently conducted research projects—rejects Plato's idea of eternal Laws of Nature, but he also rejects the neo-Darwinian, mechanistic theory of life.

> I suggest a new possibility. The regularities of nature are not imposed on nature from a transcendent realm, but evolve within the universe. What happens depends on what has happened before. Memory is inherent in nature. It is transmitted by a process called morphic resonance, and works through fields called morphic fields.
>
> In this book, I discuss the hypothesis of formative causation primarily in the context of biology and chemistry. (Rupert Sheldrake, *Morphic Resonance: The Nature of Formative Causation* [Rochester, Vermont: Park Street Press, (1981) 2009] xiv)

In the preface Sheldrake goes on to explain that his theory of morphic fields and morphic resonance is consistent with Bohm's idea of the implicate order, which is related to the theory of the quantum vacuum. He also points out a possible link with the extra-dimensions of space implied by string theory: "Theories of these kinds may help to relate morphic fields and morphic resonance to the physics of the future. But at present no one knows how the phenomena of morphogenesis are related to physics, whether conventional or unconventional." (Sheldrake xxv)

[432] *Memories, Dreams, Reflections* 291.

[433] *Memories, Dreams, Reflections* 292.

[434] *Memories, Dreams, Reflections* 292.

[435] *Memories, Dreams, Reflections* 293.

[436] According to Alexander, the cosmic horizon is an "immense void, completely dark, infinite in size, yet also infinitely comforting. . . . It was as if I were being born into a larger world, and the universe itself was like a giant cosmic womb." (*Proof of Heaven* 47)

[437] *Memories, Dreams, Reflections* 294-295.

[438] *Memories, Dreams, Reflections* 293.

[439] *Memories, Dreams, Reflections* 310.

[440] Bird and Sherwin 89.

[441] e.g. *Encountering Jung* 165; *Memories, Dreams, Reflections* 197.

[442] Apocalypse 1:8.

[443] *Bhagavad-gita As It Is* 10.20.

[444] *On the Nature of the Psyche* 116-117; *Four Archetypes* 43; *Encountering Jung* 156.

[445] *Encountering Jung* 165; *Memories, Dreams, Reflections* 197.

[446] *Memories, Dreams, Reflections* 197.

[447] Carl Jung, *The Archetypes and the Collective Unconscious* (New Jersey: Princeton University Press, 1990) 355.

[448] *The Archetypes and the Collective Unconscious* 356-357.

[449] According to Jung:

> It might be that psyche should be understood as unextended intensity and not as a body moving with time. One might assume the psyche gradually rising from minute extensity to infinite intensity, transcending for instance the velocity of light and thus irrealizing the body. . . . Psyche=highest intensity in the smallest space. (*Encountering Jung* 161-162)

[450] *The Archetypes and the Collective Unconscious* 357.

[451] Earlier I made this same argument in relation to Grof's cartography of the three progressively deeper layers of the unconscious: the personal, the perinatal, and the collective.

[452] *The Basic Writings of C.G. Jung* 558.

[453] *On the Nature of the Psyche* 116-117; *Four Archetypes* 43; *Encountering Jung* 156.

[454] *The Portable Jung* 442.

[455] *On the Nature of the Psyche* 139.

[456] *The Black Hole War* 363, 440.

[457] *The Black Hole War* 439.

[458] This comparison of the holographic horizon to the archetypes of the collective unconscious also agrees with Kant's observation that space and time, which are not empirically observable with any of our five sense organs, are a priori categories of the mind.

[459] *The Portable Jung* 324.

[460] *The Portable Jung* 324.

[461] *The Portable Jung* 324.

[462] *The Basic Writings of C.G. Jung* 327-328.

[463] *The Basic Writings of C.G. Jung* 325-327, 568-570; *Two Essays on Analytical Psychology* 173-174, 221; *The Portable Jung* 91, 450.

[464] *The Basic Writings of C.G. Jung* 309, 625-626; *On the Nature of the Psyche* 116- 117; *Two Essays on Analytical Psychology* 221.

[465] *Memories, Dreams, Reflections* 324.

[466] *The Portable Jung* 442.

[467] The spherical perimeter of the universe for someone standing a few feet to the East of me will be a few feet farther to the East than it is for me, and the same distance closer from the West. In the most extreme case, people I

see inhabiting a planet at the perimeter of the universe will see Earth at the perimeter and themselves in the center.

[468] *The Black Hole War* 438.

[469] *The Black Hole War* 438.

[470] *Synchronicity* 114. In the same passage Jung argues that astrology is a collectively observable, empirically verifiable form of synchronicity.

[471] *Memories, Dreams, Reflections* 197.

[472] *The Cosmic Landscape* 269.

[473] *The Portable Jung* 325.

[474] *The Curious History of Relativity* 307-308.

[475] *The Curious History of Relativity* 258-259.

[476] Slater para. 3.

[477] Slater para. 4.

[478] *Memories, Dreams, Reflections* 193.

[479] *Memories, Dreams, Reflections* 193-195.

[480] *Memories, Dreams, Reflections* 378.

[481] In *Encountering Jung*, Roderick Main writes: "*Septem Sermones* express in germinal form almost all of Jung's developed ideas: the nature of the unconscious, individuation, the problem of opposites, the archetypes, and the self." (*Encountering Jung* 6)

[482] Carl Jung, in *The Gnostic Jung and the Seven Sermons to the Dead*, ed. Stephen Hoeller (Wheaton, Illinois: Theosophical Publishing House, 1982) 44-45; see also *Memories, Dreams, Reflections* 379.

[483] *On the Nature of the Psyche* 116-117; *Four Archetypes* 43.

[484] According to Jung,

> We must be able to distinguish the qualities of the Pleroma. Its qualities are the PAIRS OF OPPOSITES, such as:

the effective and the ineffective

fullness and emptiness

the living and the dead

light and dark

hot and cold

energy and matter

time and space

good and evil

the beautiful and the ugly

the one and the many and so forth.

(*The Gnostic Jung and the Seven Sermons to the Dead* 47)

[485] *The Cosmic Landscape* 88.

[486] According to Peat, "the key to Jung's cosmogony was the pleroma, an ancient term that has its origin in Gnostic creation myths and signifies a ground or 'godhead' out of which all reality is born." (David F. Peat, *Synchronicity: The Bridge Between Matter and Mind* [New York: Bantam New Age Books, 1988] 196) Several pages earlier, Peat compares the Pleroma to quantum theory (Peat 191-192).

[487] Peat 197.

[488] Van Lommel 304.

[489] Brian Swimme and Joel Pitney, "Brian Swimme on Emptiness and the Quantum Vacuum," *EnlightenNext Magazine*, July 21, 2009, para. 5, http://magazine.enlightennext.org/2009/07/21/brian-swimme-on-emptiness-and-the-quantum-vacuum/.

[490] According to Jung:

Negative electricity is as good as positive electricity: first and foremost it is electricity. The psychological opposites, too, must be regarded from a scientific standpoint. True opposites are never incommensurables; if they were they could never unite. All contrariety notwithstanding, they do show a constant propensity to union, and Nicholas of Cusa defined God himself as a *complexio oppositorum*.

Opposites are extreme qualities in any state, by virtue of which that state is perceived to be real, for they form a potential. The psyche is made up of processes whose energy springs from the equilibration of all kinds of opposites. (*On the Nature of the Psyche* 116-117)

[491] *On the Nature of the Psyche* 116-117.

[492] *Four Archetypes* 43; see also *On the Nature of the Psyche* 125-126.

[493] *The Essential Jung: Selected and Introduced by Anthony Storr* (New Jersey: Princeton University Press, 1983) 343-344.

[494] *The Essential Jung* 343.

[495] *The Essential Jung* 343.

[496] *The Essential Jung* 343.

[497] *The Essential Jung* 343.

[498] *The Essential Jung* 343-344.

[499] Referring to the implications of the megaverse theory, Susskind asks, for example, "What if Germany had won World War II?" (*The Cosmic Landscape* 316)

[500] *Encountering Jung* 162.

[501] *Memories, Dreams, Reflections* 197, see also 335.

[502] *Memories, Dreams, Reflections* 196.

[503] *The Portable Jung* 450; *The Archetypes and the Collective Unconscious* 568-570.

[504] *Memories, Dreams, Reflections* 200.

[505] According to Jung:

My method and whole outlook therefore begin with individual psychic facts which not I alone have established, but other observers as well. The material brought forward—folkloristic, mythological, or historical—serves in the first place to demonstrate the uniformity of psychic events in time and space. . . . If for instance we study the mandala structures that are always cropping up in dreams and fantasies, ill-considered criticism might raise, and indeed has raised, the objection that we are reading Indian or Chinese philosophy into the psyche. But in reality all we have done is to compare individual psychic occurrences with obviously related collective phenomena. The introspective trend of Eastern philosophy has brought to light material which all introspective attitudes bring to light all over the world, at all times and places. (*On the Nature of the Psyche* 137)

[506] Confucius, *The Doctrine of the Mean*, in *Four Fundamental Questions: An Introduction to Philosophy*, ed. Richard Bilsker (Iowa: Kendall Hunt Publishing Company, 2011) 406-407.

[507] *Memories, Dreams, Reflections* 389.

[508] The very first line of the Tao Te Ching reads: "The Tao that can be told of is not the Absolute Tao." (Lao Tzu, *The Tao Te Ching*, in *Four Fundamental Questions: An Introduction to Philosophy*, ed. Richard Bilsker (Iowa: Kendall Hunt Publishing Company, 2011, 1:1, 161)

[509] Lau Tzu 25.3, 166.

[510] Lau Tzu 65.4, 173.

[511] The Tao is the eternal source and boundary of everything; it is the cosmic root of all archetypal pairs of opposites, most famously symbolized by the Yin-Yang mandala.

Available from
https://upload.wikimedia.org/wikipedia/commons/thumb/1/17/Yin_yang.s vg/260px-%20Yin_yang.svg.png260px-Yin_yang.svg.png

[512] Chuang Tzu, *The Writings of Chuang Tzu,* in *Four Fundamental Questions: An Introduction to Philosophy,* ed. Richard Bilsker (Iowa: Kendall Hunt Publishing Company, 2011) Book II, Part I, Section 3, 256.

[513] Georg Wilhelm Friedrich Hegel, *The Hegel Reader,* ed. Stephen Houlgate (Malden, Massachusettes: Blackwell Publishing Ltd., 1998) 401, see also 270-271.

[514] These correlations furthermore imply a possible equivalence of freedom and dark energy, the mysterious, anti-gravitational force suspected of causing the accelerating expansion of space-time, which is believed to radiate from each point of the quantum vacuum, which is suspected of being a boiling sea of miniature black holes created by the constant creation and annihilation of virtual particle-antiparticle pairs. If the omnicentric singularity and its horizon form the archetype of the union of all opposites, it is fitting that they are the source and container of both gravity and dark energy.

[515] *Encountering Jung* 162.

[516] Carl Jung, *Mysterium Coniunctionis: An Inquiry Into the Separation and Synthesis of Psychic Opposites in Alchemy* [New Jersey: Princeton University Press, 1977] 463. In the same way that all of our conscious thoughts are rooted in the central point of our awareness of our own consciousness (our ego), so is the significance of each archetype of the collective unconscious

concentrated on the central-most archetype of archetypes, the mandala-manifesting Self, in which they are rooted. Jung goes on to say:

> The analogy is so striking that a layman unfamiliar with this symbolism is easily misled into thinking that the mandala is an artificial product of the conscious mind. Naturally mandalas can be imitated, but this does not prove that all mandalas are imitations. They are produced spontaneously, without external influence, even by children and adults who have never come into contact with any such ideas. (*Mysterium Coniunctionis* 463)

[517] Hegel 28.

[518] Ware 59-63.

[519] To state this crucial concept another way, as the source of space-time that stands outside of the four forces of nature, the only thing that can force the singularity to do anything is itself, which is the same as being absolutely free.

[520] "Black Holes and Beyond." According to Kant, space and time are inborn, *a priori* categories of thought through which our perception of the material universe is filtered. In Jungian terms, they are archetypes of the collective unconscious mind. Therefore, if the Self consists of the complementary union of the central singularity (individual conscious mind) and surrounding horizon of the cosmos (collective unconscious mind), then to say that space and time come to end at the horizon is equivalent to saying that space and time come to an end at their source in the minds of each of us.

[521] *Memories, Dreams, Reflections* 292-293. For comparisons of Hegel and Jung, see Sean Kelly's *Individuation and the Absolute: Hegel, Jung, and the Path Toward Wholeness* (Mahwah, New Jersey: Paulist Press, 1993).

[522] *The Portable Jung* 470.

[523] Lindorff explains that Jung

> believed from his dreams and from a myriad of sources that the common ground between psyche and matter rested in the

mystery of whole numbers, particularly one through four. He saw them as the simplest and most fundamental of the archetypes, in that they are directly related to both matter and psyche—to the former mathematically, to the latter symbolically.

Jung noted that the integers are related qualitatively to the very structure of the psyche, as well as to stages of consciousness (consider the Axiom of Maria). But rather than speak of the need to infuse physics with psychology, Jung believed it was more rewarding to investigate the commonality upon which the two fields were founded, the archetype of number. (Lindorff 160-161)

[524] *Synchronicity* 96-98.

[525] *The Basic Writings of C.G. Jung* 325-327, 568-570; *Two Essays on Analytical Psychology* 173-174, 221; *The Portable Jung* 91, 450.

[526] Tobias Dantzig, *Number: The Language of Science: A Critical Survey Written for the Cultured Non-Mathematician* (New York: Plume, 2007) 31, 84.

[527] Dantzig 190.

[528] Dantzig 190.

[529] Dantzig 190.

[530] Wikipedia, https://en.wikipedia.org/wiki/Imaginary_unit.

[531] *Synchronicity* 98.

[532] *The Archetypes and the Collective Unconscious* 357.

[533] *The Portable Jung* 379. On the same note, Jung says,

"As experience shows, symbols of a reconciling and unitive nature do in fact turn up in dreams, the most frequent being the motif of the child-hero and the squaring of the circle, signifying the union of opposites." (*The Portable Jung* 630)

[534] *Timaeus* 51a-51b. Later Timaeus reconfirms that the universe takes the shape of a sphere with a central point: "For as the universe is in the form of a sphere, all the extremities, being equidistant from the center, are equally

extremities, and the center, which is equidistant from them, is equally to be regarded as the opposite of them all." (*Timaeus* 62d)

[535] *Psychology and Religion* 53.

[536] Carl Jung, *Civilization in Transition: The Collected Works of C. G. Jung Volume 10* (London: Routledge and Kegan Paul, 1964) 423-424.

[537] Wikipedia, http://en.wikipedia.org/wiki/Riemann_sphere.

[538] Osserman 91-92.

[539] Osserman 91-92.

[540] *Hyperspace* 30.

[541] *Hyperspace* 93.

[542] *Hyperspace* 93.

[543] Hegel 28.

[544] *Memories, Dreams, Reflections* 310.

[545] *The Archetypes and the Collective Unconscious* 533; *Four Archetypes* 121; *Synchronicity* 39.

[546] *Two Essays on Analytical Psychology* 110.

[547] *The Portable Jung* 470.

[548] *Two Essays on Analytical Psychology* 80.

[549] *Two Essays on Analytical Psychology* 80.

[550] *Two Essays on Analytical Psychology* 167.

[551] Fred Alan Wolf, *The Dreaming Universe: A Mind-Expanding Journey into the Realm Where Psyche and Physics Meet* (New York: Simon & Schuster, 1994) 294-295.)

[552] See Lindorff 166-176.

[553] *The Cosmic Landscape* 269-270.

[554] This is similar to the complementarity between Atman and Brahman in Vedanta philosophy.

[555] Wolf 163.

[556] *A Brief History of Time* 133-134.

[557] Dantzig 208-212.

[558] According to Jung:

> But they knew in those days that the circle signified the Deity: "God is an intellectual figure whose center is everywhere and the circumference nowhere," as one of these philosophers [Nicholas of Cusa] said, repeating St. Augustine. A man as introverted and introspective as Emerson could hardly fail to touch on the same idea and likewise quote St. Augustine. The image of the circle— regarded as the most perfect form since Plato's *Timaeus*, the prime authority for Hermetic philosophy—was assigned to the most perfect substance, to the gold, also to the *anima mundi* or *anima media natura*, and to the first created light. And because the macrocosm, the Great World, was made by the creator "in a form round and globose," the smallest part of the whole, the point, also possesses this perfect nature. As the philosopher [Plato] says: "Of all shapes the simplest and most perfect is the sphere, which rests in a point." This image of the Deity dormant and concealed in matter was what the alchemists called the original chaos, or the earth of paradise, or the round fish in the sea, or the egg, or simply the *rotundum*. That round thing was in possession of the magical key which unlocked the closed doors of matter. (*Psychology and Religion* 53-54)

[559] Similarly, though eye-witnesses such as Jung and Grof say that the circumference of the cosmos can be directly encountered during an out-of-body experience, it could still be said that the circumference is nowhere in the sense that it is perceived as transcending all points of space and time by virtue of containing all of them.

[560] In a footnote to the passage above, Jung quotes a late-seventeenth-century alchemical book where the central point of the mandala is described in terms very similar to the singularity of the Big Bang: "'For there is in every body a centre, the seeding-place or spermatic point.' This point is a

'point born of God.' (59) Here we encounter the doctrine of the 'panspermia'." (*The Basic Writings of C.G. Jung* 642)

[561] *Psychology and Religion* 53-54.

[562] *Timaeus* 51a-51b.

[563] *Psychology and Religion* 53-54

[564] *Psychology and Religion* 53-54.

[565] "Who's Afraid of a Big Black Hole?" 2009.

[566] According to Campbell:

> It might be said, in fact, that the principle of relativity had been defined already in mythopoetic, moral, and metaphysical terms in that sentence from the twelfth-century hermetic *Book of the Twenty-four Philosophers*, "God is an intelligible sphere, whose center is everywhere and circumference nowhere," which has been quoted with relish through the centuries by a significant number of influential European thinkers; among others, Alan of Lille (1128-1202), Nicholas Cusanus (1401-1464), Rebelais (1490?-1553), Giordano Bruno (1548-1600), Pascal (1623-1662), and Voltaire (1694-1778).
>
> In a sense, then, our recent mathematicians, physicists, and astronomers have only validated for their own fields a general principle long recognized in European thought and feeling. (Joseph Campbell, *The Masks of God: Creative Mythology* [New York: Viking Penguin Inc.,1968] 31.

[567] Pascal 89.

[568] *Memories, Dreams, Reflections* 197.

[569] According to Pascal:

> I want to show him [the skeptic] a new abyss. I want to depict to him not only the visible universe, but all the conceivable immensity of nature enclosed in this miniature atom. Let him see there an infinity of universes, each with its firmament, its planets, its earth, in the same proportions as in the visible world, and on

that earth animals, and finally mites, in which he will find again the same results as in the first. . . . Anyone who considers himself in this way will be terrified at himself, and, seeing his mass, as given by nature, supporting him between these two abysses of infinity and nothingness, will tremble at these marvels. . . . These extremes touch and join by going in opposite directions, and they meet in God and God alone. (Pascal 89-91)

[570] *Two Essays on Analytical Psychology* 153.

[571] Pascal 1, as A. J. Krailsheimer explains in his Introduction to his translation of *Pensées* cited above.

[572] Dantzig 279. Dantzig explains the pioneering role of those mathematicians in modern physics:

By clearing away the débris of ancient mathematics, the genius of these men prepared the ground for the new. The essential characteristics of modern mathematical thought are *the permanence of formal laws* and the *principle of correspondence.* The first led to the generalized number concept, the second permitted the establishment of the kinship between seemingly remote and dissimilar concepts. (Dantzig 205)

Jung and Pauli extended these mathematical principles to the theory that the formal laws of physics correspond to the formal laws of psychology because both emerge from the permanent forms—the psychoid archetypes.

[573] In his essay about Pauli's anonymous mandala dreams, Jung cites the Upanishads and other historical sources, including the Gnostic concept of the Pleroma, to help explain how each individual self can be simultaneously one with and different from the archetypal Self:

This totality is ego plus non-ego. Therefore the centre of the circle which expresses such a totality would correspond not to the ego but to the self as the summation of the total personality. (The centre with a circle is a very well-known allegory of the nature of God.) In the philosophy of the Upanishads the Self is in one aspect the *personal* atman, but at the same time it has a cosmic and metaphysical quality as the *suprapersonal* Atman.

> We meet with similar ideas in Gnosticism: I would mention the idea of the Anthropos, the Pleroma, the Monad, and the spark of light (Spinther) in a treatise of the Codex Brucianus. (*The Portable Jung* 367)

Of all the mandala images of God preserved from history, the one that most succinctly parallels Susskind's cosmology of a megaverse of inside-out black hole universes is the Vaishnava cosmology featuring the three nested Purusha Avatars of Vishnu, as we saw above. Jung mentions Purusha in *On the Nature of the Psyche* while developing the theme of God as the omnicentric point and the personified universe with "many eyes":

> Multiple eyes are also a characteristic of Purusha, the Hindu cosmic man. . . . Monoimos the Arabian, according to Hippolytus, taught that the First Man was a single Monad. . . . This Monad is the iota or dot, and this tiniest of units, which corresponds to Khunrath's one *scintilla*, has "many faces" and "many eyes." Monoimos bases himself here mainly on the prologue to the Gospel of St. John! Like Purusha, his First Man is the universe (*anthropos einai to pan*). . . . If the luminosity appears in monadic form as a single star, sun, or eye, it readily assumes the shape of a mandala and must then be interpreted as the self. (*On the Nature of the Psyche* 108-109)

Regarding Jung's comments about Monoimos, the prologue to the Gospel of St. John states: "In the beginning was the Word, and the Word was with God, and the Word was God." (John 1:1) Here we see a direct link between the Logos, or Word, who is Christ, and the idea of a central point that is the entire universe.

[574] Rucker 17.

[575] Rucker compares the geometry of the hypersphere to Dante's description of God as an all-encompassing point at the cosmic horizon.

> To see why this is so, consider the fact that if space is hyperspherical, then one can cover all of space by starting at any

point and letting a sphere expand outwards from that point. The curious thing is that if one lets a sphere expand in hyperspherical space, there comes a time when the circumference of the sphere turns into a point and disappears.

This fact can be grasped by considering the analogous situation of the sequence of circular latitude lines on the spherical surface of the earth. This line of thought appears in Dante's *Paradisio* (1300). . . .

Beyond the nine spheres of angels lies a *point* called the Empyrean, which is the abode of God.

The puzzling thing about Dante's cosmos . . . is that here the Empyrean appears not to be a point, but rather to be all of space (except for the interior of the last sphere of angels). But this can be remedied if we take space to be hyperspherical! (Rucker 17)

[576] Rucker 17.

[577] Osserman 118. Regarding Susskind's claim that hard-nosed scientific types disregard theories about a divine intelligence overseeing the universe, Osserman, who is sympathetic to Dante's Platonic cosmology, earned his Ph.D. in mathematics from Harvard, formerly served as chair of the Department of Mathematics at Susskind's own Stanford University in the 1970s, and was furthermore born and raised in the Bronx, just like Susskind (Stober). Dante's notion of traveling through concentric spheres toward the cosmic horizon, arriving at which results in a vision of God as a supernaturally brilliant point of light, is also similar to many near-death experience descriptions, as Pim van Lommel points out (Van Lommel 83-84).

[578] *Civilization in Transition* 414.

[579] *Civilization in Transition* 414. Jung goes on to say:

The psychic situation of mankind and the Ufo phenomenon as a physical reality bear no recognizable causal relationship to one another, but they seem to coincide in a meaningful manner. The meaningful connection is the product on the one hand of projection and on the other of round and cylindrical forms which embody the projected meaning and have always symbolized the union of opposites. (*Civilization in Transition* 417)

[580] *Memories, Dreams, Reflections* 291.

[581] *Memories, Dreams, Reflections* 323.

[582] *Memories, Dreams, Reflections* 323.

[583] *Memories, Dreams, Reflections* 323.

[584] *Memories, Dreams, Reflections* 324.

[585] *Memories, Dreams, Reflections* 323.

[586] *Memories, Dreams, Reflections* 1989, 323; see also *The Portable Jung* 423; *Four Archetypes* 64.

[587] In his analysis of Nietzsche's *The Birth of Tragedy*, Joseph Campbell explains:

Also accepted is the recognition, which Schopenhauer seems to have been the first to have realized, of this Kantian concept of the *a priori* forms of sensibility and categories of logic as practically identical with the Hindu-Buddhist philosophy of *maya*. And accordingly, as Vishnu is the lord of *maya*, the god whose dream is the universe and in whom (as all figures in a dream are actually but functions of the energy of the dreamer) all things, all beings, of this *maya*-world are but refractions of the one substance, so also, in Hellenic mythology, is Apollo. (*Creative Mythology* 338)

Actually, in *The Birth of Tragedy*, Nietzsche directly equates Apollo with *maya*, which implies that Apollo's counter-part and half-brother, Dionysus, is more aptly equated with Vishnu (or possibly Shiva, who is Vishnu's shadow). Nietzsche also mentions the god Herakles, who has similarities with Vishnu.

[588] *Memories, Dreams, Reflections* 324.

[589] According to Kaku:

Even *Science* magazine, always careful not to exaggerate the claims of scientists, compared the birth of the superstring theory to the discovery of the Holy Grail. This revolution, *Science* magazine claimed, may be "no less profound than the transition from real numbers to complex numbers in mathematics." (Kaku and Thompson 3-4)

590 *The Cosmic Landscape* 348.

591 *Memories, Dreams, Reflections* 334.

592 *Memories, Dreams, Reflections* 334.

593 *Memories, Dreams, Reflections* 335.

594 *Memories, Dreams, Reflections* 335.

595 *Memories, Dreams, Reflections* 335.

596 Augustine describes the "*heaven of heaven*, the intellectual heaven, where it is given to the intellect to know in one act, and not part by part, but wholly, in full sight, *face to face*: not to know now one thing, now another but, as has been said, to know in one act without any succession of time." (*Confessions* 12:13, 241) Later Augustine again describes the cosmic horizon as God's face when he explains that the angels who live beyond the universal spheres of matter do not have to read the Bible because God is present to them face to face: "For they ever see Your face, and in Your face they read without syllables spoken in time what is willed by Your eternal will." (*Confessions* 13:15, 269-270)

597 *The Black Hole War* 209.

598 *The Black Hole War* 210.

599 *The Black Hole War* 210.

600 *The Black Hole War* 210.

601 *The Black Hole War* 210.

602 *The Basic Writings of C. G. Jung* 368.

[603] In an earlier section of this chapter I cited the final part of the following excerpt from the episode entitled, "Who's Afraid of a Big Black Hole?" of the BBC television series, *Horizon*, in which Michio Kaku and Andrew Strominger discuss the crisis in physics caused by the inability of quantum mechanics and general relativity to describe the singularity of a black hole.

> Samuel West (Narrator): The failure of these two great theories to understand black holes means they are at best an approximation to the laws governing the universe.
>
> Andrew Strominger (Harvard University): The equations no longer make any sense, and nobody knows exactly what we're supposed to do about that.
>
> Michio Kaku (City College of New York): Well it's awful. It means that physics is having a nervous breakdown. It means the collapse of physics as we know it, you know, something is fundamentally wrong. Nature is smarter than we are.
>
> Andrew Strominger: Black holes are the key to taking the next step, they're the doorway to our next step in understanding the basic laws of the universe around us. ("Who's Afraid of a Big Black Hole?")

[604] "The Elegant Universe: Einstein's Dream." According to Einstein, "The important point for us to observe is that all these constructions and the laws connecting them can be arrived at by the principle of looking for the mathematically simplest concepts and the link between them." (Albert Einstein, "On the Method of Theoretical Physics," *The Herbert Spencer lecture, delivered at Oxford, June 10, 1933* [Mein Weltbild, Amsterdam: Querida Verlag, 1934, Copyright 1954, by Crown Publishers. Inc. Fifth Printing. February, 1960] 275, https://namnews.files.wordpress.com/2012/04/29289146-ideas-and-opinions-by-albert-einstein.pdf) According to Chopin: "Simplicity is the final achievement. After one has played a vast quantity of notes and more notes, it is simplicity that emerges as the crowning reward of art." (Frederic Chopin, in *If Not God, Then What? Neuroscience, Aesthetics, and the Origins*

of the Transcendent, by Joshua Fost [Portland, Oregon: Clearhead Studies, Inc, 2007] 93)

[605] *Hyperspace* 139.

[606] *Parallel Worlds* 79.

[607] *The Elegant Universe* 211. In the various medieval legends of the Holy Grail, this most-prized object referred to several things, from a magical tray to the cup in which Jesus Christ transubstantiated wine into his own divine blood at the Last Supper before his Crucifixion, the same cup in which the blood from the spear wound in the crucified Christ's side is said to have been caught. The Holy Grail is the ultimate goal of the mythic quest of the chivalrous knights of the round table, and seems to symbolize the crucible in which opposites are united with their common source, the God archetype, or Self. In *Memories, Dreams, Reflections*, Jung says that the stories of the "Holy Grail" had been "of the greatest importance to me" since he first read them at the age of fifteen. He goes on to say that the world of the Chivalrous knights is "in the deepest sense, my own world." (*Memories, Dreams, Reflections* 165). He did not elaborate on the symbolic significance of the Grail because his wife, Emma Jung, had made Grail studies her specialty, and he did not want to "intrude upon my wife's field." (*Memories, Dreams, Reflections* 215) Nevertheless, we can infer that Jung considered the Grail to be a symbol of the Self because it was the object which held "the greatest importance" to Jung since he was fifteen, and because it represented the deepest reality of his own world, which is the archetype of the Self, the ultimate archetype of the union of all opposites.

[608] In *Pauli and Jung*, Paul Lindorff explains,

> Just as it was physics' destiny to seek completeness in relationship to the psychology of the unconscious, it was the destiny of Jung's psychology to explore its relationship to an established field like physics. This, Pauli claimed, would recreate the wholeness that [early-seventeenth-century alchemist] Fludd had feared would be lost with the development of science. . . . Physics was in need of expansion (completeness) by assimilating the unconscious, and

Jung's psychology needed the academic status that physics enjoys in spite of its incompleteness.

Pauli anticipated this archetype of wholeness: "I don't know whether and when this *coniunctio* will be realized, but I have no doubt that this would be the most beautiful destiny that could befall psychology and physics." (Lindorff 156-157)

[609] In *Encountering Jung*, Roderick Main summarizes the relationship between Jung's theory of synchronicity and his theory of the *unus mundus*:

The synchronistic principle 'suggests that there is an inter-connection or unity of causally unrelated events, and thus postulates a unitary aspect of being which can very well be described as the *unus mundus*' (Jung 1954- 5: 464-65). This postulated unitary background to existence, in which the concepts of psyche and matter and space and time merge into a psychophysical space-time continuum, was where Jung considered the archetypes themselves, as opposed to their phenomenal manifestations, ultimately to be located. To express this ambivalent nature—at once psychic and physical yet neither because beyond both—he was led to coin the term 'psychoid'. The ability of the archetype to manifest synchronistically in independent psychic and physical contexts is itself an indicator of its fundamentally psychoid nature. (*Encountering Jung* 36)

[610] *On the Nature of the Psyche* 86, 93; Atmanspacher and Primas 19.

[611] *Mysterium Coniunctionis* 464.

[612] *Encountering Jung* 122.

[613] According to R. F. C. Hull,

Jung used the term "synchronicity" only in 1930, in his memorial address for Richard Wilhelm, the translator of the *I Ching*, or *Book of Changes*. . . . He referred to synchronicity again in his "Travistock Lectures" in London, 1935. . . . Again in the Lectures he equated it with the Chinese concept of Tao. . . . Years later, in his forward (written before 1950) to the Wilhelm/Baynes translation of the *I Ching*, Jung gave an exposition of the principle of synchronicity. He was already preparing an extended monograph, but his first formal presentation of the theory was a brief lecture—his last—at the Eranos Conference of 1951 at Ascona, Switzerland. The monograph was published the following year, together with a monograph by Pauli on "The Influence of Archetypal Ideas on the Scientific Theories of Johannes Kepler." (*Synchronicity*, translator's introduction, vi-vii)

[614] *The Cosmic Landscape* 269.

[615] *The Portable Jung* 510.

[616] *The Portable Jung* 511.

[617] *The Portable Jung* 23.

[618] *Memories, Dreams, Reflections* 292.

[619] *Synchronicity* 29-30.

[620] *The Essential David Bohm* 152.

[621] *Memories, Dreams, Reflections* 295-296.

[622] *Memories, Dreams, Reflections* 294-295.

[623] *Memories, Dreams, Reflections* 296.

[624] *Memories, Dreams, Reflections* 292.

[625] *Memories, Dreams, Reflections* 292.

[626] (*Bhagavad-gita As It Is* 7.4-8)

[627] This is described in a verse from Srimad-Bhagavatam, with a purport (explanatory remark) from Swami Prabhupada:

> The great sage Nārada continued: The living entity acts in a gross body in this life. This body is forced to act by the subtle body, composed of mind, intelligence and ego. After the gross body is lost, the subtle body is still there to enjoy or suffer. Thus there is no change.

PURPORT:

The living entity has two kinds of body—the subtle body and the gross body. . . . The subtle body's activities, be they pious or impious, create another situation for the living entity to enjoy or suffer in the next gross body.

Thus the subtle body continues, whereas the gross bodies change one after another. (Srimad-Bhagavatam 4.29.60)

[628] Srimad-Bhagavatam 3.11.41.

[629] Brihadaranyaka Upanishad 3.7.3.

[630] Brihadaranyaka Upanishad 3:8:1-4.

[631] *Synchronicity* 29-30.

[632] *Synchronicity* 29-30.

[633] *Synchronicity* 96.

[634] According to Jung:

Here synchronicity is to the three other principles as the one-dimensionality of time is to the three-dimensionality of space, or as the recalcitrant "Fourth" in the *Timaeus*, which, Plato says, can only be added "by force" to the other three. Just as the introduction of time as the fourth dimension in modern physics postulates an irrepresentable space-time continuum, so the idea of synchronicity with its inherent quality of meaning produces a picture of the world so irrepresentable as to be completely baffling. The advantage, however, of adding this concept is that it makes possible a view which includes the psychoid factor in our description and knowledge of nature—that is, an a priori meaning or "equivalence." The problem that runs like a red thread through the speculations of alchemists for fifteen hundred years thus repeats and solves itself, the so-called axiom of Maria the Jewess (or Copt): "Out of the Third comes the One as the Fourth." (*Synchronicity* 96-98)

[635] *Synchronicity* 98-99.

[636] *Encountering Jung* 84.

[637] *Synchronicity* 98.

[638] *The Black Hole War* 305.

[639] Alfred North Whitehead, *Process and Reality, Corrected Edition*, Eds. David Ray Griffin and Donald W. Sherburne (New York: The Free Press, 1978), 350.

[640] *Process and Reality* 350.

[641] *Process and Reality* 350.

[642] *Process and Reality* 350.

[643] *Process and Reality* 350-351.

[644] *Process and Reality* 340. Similarly, in the *Republic* Socrates says "that which destroys and corrupts in every case is the evil; that which preserves and benefits is the good." (*The Republic* 608e) By this definition, the highest good is that which preserves the most information, which points to the cosmic horizon. The theory that Plato valued cosmic information conservation at the cosmic horizon as the highest idea of the Good is supported by the fact that he concluded the *Republic* with the myth of Er, the last paragraph of which reads as follows: "And so, Glaucon, the tale was saved, as the saying is, and was not lost. And it will save us if we believe it, and we shall safely cross the River of Lethe, and keep our soul unspotted from the world." (*Republic* 621b-c)

[645] *Confessions* 8:12, 146.

[646] *Confessions* 8:12, 146.

[647] *Confessions* 8:12, 146.

[648] *Confessions* 8:12, 146.

[649] *Cosmos and Psyche* 52.

[650] According to Tarnas:

> He at once recognized the coincidence as part of a larger pattern
> of such transformative moments that had happened to others in

the history of spiritual conversions: "I could not believe that it was by a mere accident that I happened upon them. What I had there read I believed to be addressed to me and to no other, remembering that Saint Augustine had once suspected the same thing in his own case." For indeed Augustine had undergone a nearly identical experience at his own momentous spiritual turning point: In the garden of Milan in 386, in a frenzy of spiritual crisis, he heard a child's voice from a nearby house mysteriously repeating the words, "*Tolle, lege*" ("Pick up and read"). Uncertain of their significance, he finally opened at random a copy of Saint Paul's epistles and there read words that spoke with uncanny precision to the nature of his lifelong conflict and its resolution, immediately after reading which "the light of certainty flooded my heart and all dark shadows of doubt fled away." (Confessions, VIII, 29) (*Cosmos and Psyche* 52-53)

[651] *The Passion of the Western Mind* 90.

[652] *The Passion of the Western Mind* 439. Tarnas goes on to say:

As new psychological predispositions and metaphysical assumptions emerge from within the collective mind, from within many individual minds simultaneously, they are matched and encouraged by the synchronistic arrival of new data, new social contexts, new methodologies, new tools that fulfill the emerging archetypical gestalt. (*The Passion of the Western Mind* 439)

[653] *The Passion of the Western Mind* 439.

[654] Dantzig 203-204.

[655] Dantzig 203-204.

[656] According to Peat:

An obvious example of such synchronicities are the simultaneous discoveries made by scientists who are not in direct communication with each other. Scientists often speak of ideas as "being in the air," almost as if new concepts take the form of radio transmissions, complete in themselves but waiting for a competent receiver to pick them up. . . . Of equal importance was the independent discovery of calculus by both Newton and Leibnitz.

Even more striking synchronicities can be found when such parallel evolutions of thought take place in totally different fields. . . . The many examples of coincidental movements of thought, feeling, and ideas between unconnected groups and across disciplines suggests that a deeper meaning lies beyond these coincidences and synchronicities. (Peat 30-32)

[657] Carl Jung, *Letters of C. G. Jung: Volume I, 1906-1950*. Ed. Gerhard Adler in collaboration with Aniela Jaffe. Translated by R. F. C. Hull (New York: Routledge, 2015) 433.

[658] *Synchronicity: The Bridge Between Matter and Mind* 235.

[659] *Synchronicity: The Bridge Between Matter and Mind* 235.

[660] *The Elegant Universe* 137.

[661] Dantzig 240.

[662] *The Elegant Universe* 137. In *The Fabric of the Cosmos*, Greene again addresses that grand mathematical coincidence:

These physicists showed that if the strong force between two particles were due to a tiny, extremely thin, almost rubber-band-like strand that connected the particles, then the quantum process that Veneziano and others had been pouring over would be mathematically described using Euler's formula. The little elastic strings were christened *strings* and now, with the horse properly before the cart, string theory was officially born. (*The Fabric of the Cosmos* 339-340)

[663] *The Cosmic Landscape* 204.

[664] *The Basic Writings of C.G. Jung* 310.

[665] Jung says,

Let us return to the problem of the empirical basis of synchronicity. The main difficulty here is to procure empirical material from which we can draw reasonably certain conclusions, and unfortunately this difficulty is not an easy one to solve. The experiences in question are not ready to hand. We must therefore look in the obscurest corners and summon up courage to shock the prejudice of our age if we want to broaden the basis of our understanding of nature. When Galileo discovered the moons of Jupiter with his telescope he immediately came into head-on collision with the prejudices of his learned contemporaries. . . . It is sad but unfortunately true that man learns nothing from history. This melancholy fact will present us with the greatest difficulties as soon as we set about collecting empirical material that would throw a little light on this dark subject, for we shall be quite certain to find it where all the authorities have assured us that nothing is to be found. (*Synchronicity* 33)

[666] *Encountering Jung* 84.

[667] According to Jung:

Not unlike the anomalous situation that confronted Newtonian physics in the late nineteenth century with the Michelson-Morley experiment that measured the speed of light, synchronicity represented a phenomenon that, simply put, should not have been occurring, at least not in a random, purposeless universe. Yet the problem has remained ambiguous, for although coincidences are often personally significant, they tend to resist objective assessment. Only if such phenomena were in some sense public and pervasive rather than private and exceptional—only if the archetypal patterns were more universally discernible and associated more widely with collective experience and the world at large rather than sporadically with isolated special cases—could the suggestion of a deeper order be effectively substantiated in a way that could influence the cultural world view.

One special, highly controversial class of synchronicities, however, did appear to resemble this description. In the course of his career Jung's attention was increasingly drawn to the ancient cosmological perspective of astrology, which posits a systematic symbolic correspondence between planetary positions and the events of human existence. (*Cosmos and Psyche* 61)

[668] According to Tarnas:

Every reader with a modest degree of preparation can take the principles set forth in this book, focus on those experiences and events that are most personally significant in his or her life, and determine whether the archetypal astrological understanding offers a larger perspective, sheds new light, brings deeper meaning, provides greater intelligibility.

To help the reader make an informed judgment on these matters is one of the principal purposes of this book. In the following chapters, therefore, I present both the basic technical knowledge necessary to begin the exploration and illustrative examples of correlations in history and in the lives of significant cultural figures. (*Cosmos and Psyche* 69)

[669] To describe Tarnas' method of astrologically analyzing cultural history, Rod O'Neal, a founding editor of *Archai: The Journal of Archetypal Cosmology*, coined the term "archetypal historiography." The purpose of the *Archai* journal is summarized in the Background section of the journal website as follows: "*Archai* is dedicated to furthering the research orientation and methodology established by Richard Tarnas in *Cosmos and Psyche: Intimations of a New World View* (New York: Viking, 2006)" (Archai 2012).

[670] Another way to express this same idea is based on Jung and Pauli's theory that mirror-symmetries between the field of physics and the field of psychology emerge from the same underlying archetypes. According to this theory, it is plausible to suspect that when the ratio of the number of bits of information to the radius of the mental space (the ruling paradigm) of any field of knowledge approaches the psychological equivalent of the Schwarzschild radius, we should expect those disparate bits of knowledge to collapse into the mental equivalent of a black hole. For this analogy to work, one would have to look for a parallel between the collapse of a star into a black hole and the collapse of a field of knowledge into a new paradigm governed by some mandalic ordering principle. There is also the

question: how would you measure the Schwarzschild radius of mental space?

671 *Mysterium Coniunctionis* 464.

672 *The Black Hole War* 305.

673 *The Portable Jung* 445.

674 *On the Nature of the Psyche* 105.

675 *Timaeus* 51b.

676 *On the Nature of the Psyche* 101.

677 *The Basic Writings of C.G. Jung* 360.

678 *The Black Hole War* 210.

679 *The Cosmic Landscape* 94.

680 *The Cosmic Landscape* 96.

681 *Cosmos and Psyche* 422.

682 *Encountering Jung* 107.

683 *On the Nature of the Psyche* 137

684 Whitehead 39.

685 In addition to the myth of Er in the *Republic*, see also the *Phaedrus* (247a–250c), the *Meno* (81b–d), and the *Phaedo* (107d–114c). In *Myth and Reality*, historian of religions Mircea Eliade summarizes the link between Plato's theories of reincarnation and knowledge:

> For Plato, in the last analysis, knowing amounts to recollecting. Between two terrestrial existences the soul contemplates the Ideas: it enjoys pure and perfect knowledge. . . . Death is therefore the return to a primordial and perfect state, periodically lost during the soul's reincarnation. (Mircea Eliade, *Myth and Reality* [New York: Harper and Row, 1963] 124)

686 *The Hidden Reality* 272-273; see also *The Fabric of the Cosmos* 482.

687 *Republic* 614 b-c.

688 *Republic* 616 b-d.

689 Bloom 471-472.

690 According to Socrates,

> In four days they arrived at a place from which they could see a straight light, like a column, stretched from above through all of heaven and earth, most of all resembling the rainbow but brighter and purer. . . . And there, at the middle of the light, they saw the extremities of its bonds stretched from heaven; for this light is that which binds heaven, like the undergirders of triremes, thus holding the entire revolution together. From the extremities stretched the spindle of Necessity, by which all the revolutions are turned. . . . For there are eight whorls in all, lying in one another with their rims showing as circles from above, while from the back they form one continuous whorl around the stem, which is driven right through the middle of the eighth. (*The Republic of Plato* 616b-e)

Notice how the rainbow pillar that runs vertically through the center of the universe is also compared to a trireme: the rope that runs around the hull of a ship and can be tightened by a mechanism to keep the ship's frame together under the stress of the sea. How can the vertical axis of the universe, the spindle of Necessity, be simultaneously a rope surrounding the circumference, the cosmic horizon? In the following passage Luminet describes a similar optical effect in the way extreme gravity causes the accretion disk around the equator of black hole to appear to be wrapped around the entire sphere of the horizon.

> Let us take a black hole and a thin disk of gas viewed from the side, either by a distant observer or a photographic plate, if one wants to immortalize the setup. In an ordinary situation, meaning in Euclidean space, the curvature is weak. This is the case for the solar system when one observers the planet Saturn surrounded by its magnificent rings, with a viewpoint situated slightly above the planet, but one can mentally reconstruct their elliptic outlines

quite easily. Around a black hole, everything behaves differently, because of the optical deformations due to the curvature of space-time. Strikingly, we see the top of the disk in its totality, whatever the angle from which we view it may be. The back part of the disk is not hidden by the black hole, since the images that come from it are lifted to some extent by the spatial curvature and reach the distant observer. Much more astonishing, one also sees the bottom of the gaseous disk. In fact, the light rays that normally propagate downwards, in a direction opposite to that of the observer, climb back to the top and provide a secondary image, a highly deformed picture of the bottom of the disk. In theory, there is a tertiary image that gives an extremely distorted view of the top after the light rays have completed three half-turns, then an image of order four that gives a view of the bottom that is even more squashed, and so on to infinity.

To describe this final image, no caption fits better than these verses by Gerard de Nerval, written a century and a half ago:

In seeking the eye of God, I saw nought but an orbit

Vast, black, and bottomless, from which the night which there lives

Shines on the world and continually thickens.

A strange rainbow surrounds this somber well,

Threshold of the ancient chaos whose offspring is shadow,

A spiral engulfing Worlds and Days!

(Gerard de Nerval, "Le Christ aux Oliviers")

(Jean-Pierre Luminet, *The Wraparound Universe*, trans. Eric Novak [Wellesley, Mass.: A. K. Peters, 2008] 31-32)

The most notable parallel between Luminet's description of the optical deformation of an accretion disk surrounding a black hole and the Myth of Er is the way the rainbow-pillar of light that pierces the center of the cosmos also encompasses its circumference like the rope that binds the boards that make the hull of a ship together.

[691] "And in the center he put the soul, which he diffused throughout the body, making it also to be the exterior environment of it." (Timaeus 35a-b) After describing the central point of the spherical universe as the location of its soul, which permeates the volume of space, and becomes the spherical horizon, Timaeus later says that the outermost sphere actually has no shape at all, this "mother and receptacle of all created and visible and in any way sensible things … an invisible and formless being which receives all things and in some mysterious way partakes of the intelligible, and is most incomprehensible." (*Timaeus* 51a-51b)

[692] *The Republic* 620e.

[693] Plato, *Oxford World's Classics, Plato, Republic: Translated with an Introduction and Notes by Robin Waterfield* (New York: Oxford University Press, 1993) 620e.

[694] Robin Waterfield, *Oxford World's Classics, Plato, Republic*: *Translated with an Introduction and Notes by Robin Waterfield* (New York: Oxford University Press, 1993) 458.

[695] *The Republic of Plato* 617b-c.

BIBLIOGRAPHY

"About *Archai.*" *Archai: The Journal of Archetypal Cosmology*, http://www.archaijournal.org/about.html.

Alexander, Eben. "Heaven is Real: A Doctor's Experience with the Afterlife." *Newsweek*, October 8, 2012, http://mag.newsweek.com/2012/10/07/proof-of-heaven-a-doctor-s-experience-with-the-afterlife.html.

———. *Proof of Heaven: A Neurosurgeon's Journey into the After Life.* New York: Simon and Schuster, 2012.

Atmanspacher, Harald, and Hans Primas. "Pauli's Ideas on Mind and Matter in the Context of Contemporary Science." *The Journal of Consciousness Studies* 13 (3): 5-50, 2006.

Augustine. "City of God," in *Nicene and Post-Nicene Fathers.* First Series, Vol. 2., Trans. Marcus Dods, Ed. Philip Schaff (Buffalo, NY: Christian Literature Publishing Co., 1887), accessed from Wikisource, March 24, 2018, https://en.wikisource.org/wiki/Nicene_and_Post-Nicene_Fathers:_Series_I/Volume_II/City_of_God/Book_XX/Chapter_14

———. *Confessions.* Trans. F. J. Sheed. Indianapolis: Hackett Publishing Company, Inc., 1993.

Bhagavad-gita. *Bhagavad-gita As It Is, with Roman transliteration, English equivalents, translation and elaborate purports.* The Bhaktivedanta Book Trust (BBT): The Pre-1978 Books by His Divine Grace A. C. Bhaktivedanta Swami Prabhupada. http://causelessmercy.com/?P=Bg.

Bird, Kai, and Martin J. Sherwin. *American Prometheus: The Triumph and Tragedy of J.Robert Oppenheimer.* New York: Alfred K. Knopf, 2005.

Bohm, David. *The Essential David Bohm*. Ed. Lee Nichol. London: Routledge, 2003.

———. *Quantum Implications: Essays In Honour of David Bohm*. Eds. Basil Hiley and F. David Peat. New York: Routledge, 1987.

———.*Wholeness and the Implicate Order*. London: Routledge and Kegan Paul, 1980.

Brandeker, Alexis. "What Would a Relativistic Interstellar Traveler See?" *The Original Usenet Physics FAQ*. Eds. Scott Chase, Michael Weiss, Philip Gibbs, Chris Hillman, and Nathan Urban, May, 2002, http://math.ucr.edu/home/baez/physics/ Relativity/SR/Spaceship/spaceship. Html, 2002.

Brihadaranyaka Upanishad. *Upanishads, A New Translation by Patrick Olivelle*. Oxford, England: Oxford University Press, 1996.

Campbell, Joseph. *The Masks of God: Creative Mythology*. New York: Viking Penguin Inc, 1968.

———. *The Masks of God: Occidental Mythology*. New York: The Viking Press, 1964.

Capra, Fritjof. *The Tao of Physics: An Exploration of the Parallels between Modern Physics and Eastern Mysticism*. Boston: Shambhala Publications, Inc., 1999.

Carroll, Sean. In "Did the Universe Have a Beginning?" *Closer to Truth*. Written by Robert Lawrence Kuhn. Directed by Peter Getzels. Season 12. Episode 1. PBS. March 3, 2014, https://www.closertotruth.com/series/did-the-universe-begin.

Chopin, Frederic. In *If Not God, Then What? Neuroscience, Aesthetics, and the Origins of the Transcendent*, by Joshua Fost. Portland, Oregon: Clearhead Studies, Inc, 2007.

Chuang Tzu. *The Writings of Chuang Tzu*. In *Four Fundamental Questions: An Introduction to Philosophy*, ed. Richard Bilsker. Iowa: Kendall Hunt Publishing Company, 2011.

Confucius. *Doctrine of the Mean.* In *Four Fundamental Questions: An Introduction to Philosophy*, ed. Richard Bilsker. Iowa: Kendall Hunt Publishing Company, 2011.

Dantzig, Tobias. *Number: The Language of Science: A Critical Survey Written for the Cultured Non-Mathematician.* New York: Plume, 2007.

Dawkins, Richard. "Queerer Than We Can Suppose" Douglas Adams Memorial Lecture, the Royal Institution in London, March 11, 2003, http://dotsub.com/view/2e6446ef-42c7-483a-bbda-df65b1cc4c84/viewTranscript/eng.

———. *The Selfish Gene.* Oxford, England: Oxford University Press, 1976.

Deacon, Terrence. *Incomplete Nature.* New York: W. W. Norton & Company, Inc., 2012.

Descartes, Rene. *The Mediations.* In *Discourse on Method and the Meditations.* Trans. F. E. Sutcliffe. London: Penguin Books, 1968.

———. *The Passions of the Soul.* In *Four Fundamental Questions: An Introduction to Philosophy*, ed. Richard Bilsker. Iowa: Kendall Hunt Publishing Company, 2011.

Desmond, Timothy. "Plato's Noble Lie and the Imaginary Number i: An Introduction to the Zero Zone System of Measurement in the Context of Plato's Republic and the Laws." *Journal of Futures Studies.* November 2009.

———. "Raising Plato's Curriculum from the Dead: the Myth of Er in Light of Susskind's String Theory, Tarnas's Archetypal Astrology, and Jung's Near-death Experience of the Cosmic Horizon." *Archai: The Journal of Archetypal Cosmology* (4: 61-97). 2012.

Diogenes Laertius, *Lives of Eminent Philosophers*. Ed. R.D. Hicks. Book 9, chapter 7, section 40, 1972. http://www.perseus.tufts. edu/hopper/text?doc=Perseus:abo:tlg,0004,001:9:7.

"Do Black Holes Really Exist?" *The Universe Forum*. Produced for NASA by the Harvard Smithsonian Center for Astrophysics. Last modified September 2009, http://www.cfa.harvard.edu/ seuforum/bh_reallyexist.htm

Edmunds, Radcliffe. "Tearing apart the Zagreus Myth: A Few Disparaging Remarks on Orphism and Original Sin." *Classical Antiquity*, Volume 18, No. 1, April, 1999, 40. http://www.brynmawr.edu/classics/redmonds/zagreus.pdf.

Einstein, Albert. "On a Stationary System With Spherical Symmetry Consisting of Many Gravitating Masses." *Annals of Mathematics* 40 (4): 922-936, 1939. http://www.jstor.org/stable/1968902.

————. "On the Method of Theoretical Physics." *The Herbert Spencer lecture*. Delivered at Oxford, June 10, 1933. Published in Mein Weltbild, Amsterdam: Querida Verlag, 1934. Copyright. 1954, by Crown Publishers. Inc. Fifth Printing. February, 1960. https://namnews.files.wordpress.com/2012/04/29289146-ideas-and-opinions-by-albert-einstein.pdf

————. *Relativity: The Special and General Theory*. London: Routledge Classics, 2001.

Eisenstaedt, Jean. *The Curious History of Relativity: How Einstein's Theory of Gravity Was Lost and Found Again*. New Jersey: Princeton University Press, 2006.

Eliade, Mircea. *Myth and Reality*. New York: Harper and Row, 1963.

Euripides. "The Bacchae." *The Complete Greek Tragedies, Vol. V*. Eds. David Greene and Richard Lattimore, trans. William Arrowsmith. Chicago: University of Chicago Press, 1959.

Ferrell, John. *The Day Without Yesterday: Lemaître, Einstein, and the Birth of Modern Cosmology*. New York: Thunder's Mouth Press, 2005.

"The First Douglas Adams Memorial Lecture." April 14, 2003. https://h2g2.com/entry/A1023256

Frazer, James George. *The Golden Bough*. New York: Macmillan Publishing Company, 1922.

Genzel, Reinhard. In "Proof that Albert Einstein's black holes do exist, claim scientists." *The Telegraph*, December 9, 2008, http://www.telegraph.co.uk/science/science-news/3690822/ Proof-that-Albert-Einsteins-black-holes-do-exist-claim-scientists.html.)

Goodenough, Ursala. "Gravity Is Love, And Other Astounding Metaphors." *13.7 Cosmos and Culture: Commentary on Science and Society*. NPR blog, July 13, 2010, http://www.npr.org/blogs/ 13.7/2010/10/21/130724690/gravity-is- love.

Gore, Al. *Earth in the Balance: Ecology and the Human Spirit*. Boston: Houghton Mifflin, 1992.

"Gravitational Lens." *Wikipedia*. 2013. http://en.wikipedia.org/ wiki/Gravitational_lens.

Greene, Brian. *The Elegant Universe: Superstrings, Hidden Dimensions, and the Quest for the Ultimate Theory*. New York: W.W. Norton & Company, Inc., 2003.

———. "The Fabric of the Cosmos: The Illusion of Time." *Nova*. Directed by Randall MacLowry. Episode no. 713. PBS. November 9, 2011. Transcript: http://www.pbs.org/wgbh/ nova/physics/fabric-of-cosmos.html#fabric- time.

———. *The Fabric of the Cosmos: Space, Time, and the Texture of Reality*. New York: Vintage Books, 2005.

———. *The Hidden Reality: Parallel Universes and the Deep Laws of the Cosmos*. New York: Random House, 2011.

Gribbin, John. *In Search of Schrödinger's Cat: Quantum Physics and Reality*. London: Black Swan, 1991.

Grof, Stanislav. *Psychology of the Future: Lessons from Modern Consciousness Research*. Albany, New York: State University of New York Press, 2000.

———. "Stan Grof about his LSD experience." Youtube. March 29 2008, http://www.youtube.com/watch?v=5ig3eU_oDS0.

———. *The Ultimate Journey: Consciousness and the Mystery of Death*. Santa Cruz: The Multidisciplinary Association for Psychedelic Studies, 2006.

Hawking, Stephen. *A Brief History of Time: From the Big Bang to Black Holes*. New York: Bantam Books, 1996.

———. In "Black Holes and Beyond." *Stephen Hawking's Universe*. Directed by Philip Martin. Episode no. 5. PBS. September 21,1997, http://www.pbs.org/wnet/hawking/ programs/html/5-1.html.

———. *Stephen Hawking: Master of the Universe*. Directed by Gary Johnstone. Episode 1. Channel 4 (UK). March 2, 2008, http://www.channel4.com/programmes/master-of-the-universe.

———. *The Universe in a Nutshell*. New York: Bantam Books, 2001.

Hawking, Stephen, and Leonard Mlodinow. *The Grand Design*. New York: Random House, 2010.

Hegel, Georg Wilhelm Friedrich. *The Hegel Reader*. Ed. Stephen Houlgate. Malden, Massachusettes: Blackwell Publishing Ltd., 1998.

Heisenberg, Werner. "The Debate between Plato and Democritus." In *Quantum Questions*. Ed. Ken Wilber. Boston: Shambhala, 2001.

The Holy Bible, *Douay-Rheims 1899 American Edition (DRA)*. http://www.drbo.org/.

Hume, David. *An Enquiry Concerning Human Understanding.* In *Four Fundamental Questions: An Introduction to Philosophy.* Ed. Richard Bilsker. Iowa: Kendall Hunt Publishing Company, 2011.

————. *A Treatise on Human Nature.* In *Four Fundamental Questions: An Introduction to Philosophy.* Ed. Richard Bilsker. Iowa: Kendall Hunt Publishing Company, 2011.

"Johannes Kepler." *Stanford Encyclopedia of Philosophy.* May 21, 2015. https://plato.stanford.edu/entries/kepler/

Joye, Shelli Renee. "The Pribram-Bohm Holoflux Theory of Consciousness: An Integral Interpretation of the Theories of Karl Pribram, David Bohm, and Pierre Teilhard de Chardin." Ph.D. dissertation. California Institute of Integral Studies, 2016.

Jung, C. G.. *The Archetypes and the Collective Unconscious.* Translated by R.F.C. Hull. New Jersey: Princeton University Press, (1959) 1990.

————. *The Basic Writings of C.G. Jung.* Edited by Violet Staub de Laszlo. New York: Random House, 1993.

————. *Civilization in Transition: The Collected Works of C. G. Jung Volume 10.* London: Routledge and Kegan Paul, 1964.

————. *Encountering Jung: Jung on Synchronicity and the Paranormal.* Edited by Roderick Main. Princeton, New Jersey: Princeton University Press, 1997.

————. *The Essential Jung: Selected and Introduced by Anthony Storr.* New Jersey, Princeton University Press, 1983.

————. *Four Archetypes: Mother/Rebirth/Spirit/Trickster.* Trans. R.F.C. Hull. New Jersey: Princeton University Press, (1959) 1992.

————. In *The Gnostic Jung and the Seven Sermons to the Dead.* Ed. Stephan Hoeller. Wheaton, Illinois: Theosophical Publishing House, 1982.

———. *Letters of C. G. Jung: Volume I, 1906-1950.* Selected and edited by Gerhard Adler in collaboration with Aniela Jaffe. Translated by R. F. C. Hull. New York: Routledge, 2015.

———. *Memories, Dreams, Reflections.* Edited by Aniela Jaffe. New York: Vintage Books, (1961) 1989.

———. *Mysterium Coniunctionis: An Inquiry Into the Separation and Synthesis of Psychic Opposites in Alchemy.* New Jersey: Princeton University Press, 1977.

———. *On the Nature of the Psyche.* New Jersey: Princeton University Press, 1969.

———. *The Portable Jung.* Edited by Joseph Campbell. New York: Penguin Books, 1976.

———. *Psychology and Religion: West and East: The Collected Works of C. G. Jung Volume 11.* London: Routledge and Kegan Paul, 1953.

———. *Synchronicity: An Acausal Connecting Principle.* Translated by R. F. C. Hull. New York: Bollinger Press, (1960) 1973.

———. *Two Essays on Analytical Psychology.* Translated by R. F. C. Hull. Princeton, New Jersey: Princeton University Press, (1953) 1966.

Jungk, Robert. *Brighter Than a Thousand Suns: A Personal History of the Atomic Scientists.* Orlando, Florida: Harcourt, Inc., (1956) 1986.

Kaku, Michio, and Jennifer Thompson. *Beyond Einstein: The Cosmic Quest for the Theory of the Universe.* New York: Anchor/Doubleday, 1987.

———. "Cosmic Holes." *The Universe.* Directed by Laura Verklan. Episode no. 16. History. December 4, 2007.

———. *Hyperspace: A Scientific Odyssey Through Parallel Universes, Time Warps, and the Tenth Dimension.* New York: Oxford University Press, 1994.

———. *Parallel Worlds: A Journey through Creation, Higher Dimensions, and the Future of the Cosmos.* New York: Anchor Books, 2006.

———. *Visions.* New York: Anchor Books, 1997.

———. In "Who's Afraid of a Big Black Hole?" *Horizon.* Directed by Stephen Cooter. Episode no. 834. BBC. November 3, 2009.

Kant, Immanuel. *Critique of Pure Reason.* In *Four Fundamental Questions: An Introduction to Philosophy.* Ed. Richard Bilsker. Iowa: Kendall Hunt Publishing Company, 2011.

———. *Kant's Prolegomena to Any Future Metaphysics: Edited in English by Paul Carus ; With an Essay on Kant's Philosophy, and Other Supplementary Material for the Study of Kant (1912).* Ithaca, New York: Cornell University Library, 2009.

"Karl Schwarzschild." *Wikisource.* Last modified December 7, 2015, https://de.wikisource.org/wiki/Karl_Schwarzschild.

Kelly, Sean. *Coming Home: The Birth and Transformation of the Planetary Era.* Bearington, Massachusetts: Lindisfarne Press, 2010.

———. *Individuation and the Absolute: Hegel, Jung, and the Path Toward Wholeness. Mahwah, New Jersey: Paulist Press, 1993.*

Kennedy, J. B. *The Musical Structure of Plato's Dialogues.* Durham, UK: Acumen, 2011.

———. "Plato's Forms, Pythagorean Mathematics, and Stichometry," *Aperion.* 43 (1):1-32, 2010, http://personalpages.manchester.ac.uk/staff/jay.kennedy/Kennedy_Apeiron_proofs.pdf.

———. *Space, Time, and Einstein: An Introduction.* Montreal, Canada: McGill-Queen's University Press, 2003.

Kurzweil, Ray. *The Singularity is Near: When Humans Transcend Biology.* New York: The Penguin Group, 2005.

Lao Tzu. *The Tao Te Ching.* In *Four Fundamental Questions: An Introduction to Philosophy.* Ed. Richard Bilsker. Iowa: Kendall Hunt Publishing Company, 2011.

Laplace, Pierre Simon. *A Philosophical Essay on Probabilities,* translated into English from the original French 6th ed. by Truscott, F.W. and Emory, F.L. New York: Dover Publications, 1951, http://bayes.wustl.edu/Manual/laplace_A_philosophical _essay_on_probabilities.pdf

Laszlo, Ervin. *Science and the Akashic Field: An Integral Theory of Everything.* Rochester, VT: Inner Traditions, 2007.

Lavine, T. Z. *From Socrates to Sartre: the Philosophic Quest.* New York: Bantam Books,1984.

Leibnitz, Gottfried Wilhelm. *Monadology.* In *Four Fundamental Questions: An Introduction to Philosophy.* Ed. Richard Bilsker. Iowa: Kendall Hunt Publishing Company, 2011.

LIGO (Laser Interferometer Gravitational-Wave Observatory). "Gravitational Waves Detected 100 Years After Einstein's Prediction." *News.* February 11, 2016. https://www.ligo.caltech. edu/news/ligo20160211

Lindorff, David. *Pauli and Jung: The Meeting of Two Great Minds.* Wheaton, Illinois: Quest Books, the Theosophical Publishing House, 2004.

Luminet, Jean-Pierre. "Editorial note to: Georges Lemaître, The beginning of the world from the point of view of quantum theory." *General Relativity and Gravitation* 43 (2): 2911-2928, 2011, http://link.springer.com/article/10.1007%2Fs10714-011-1213-7#page-2.

———. *The Wraparound Universe.* Trans. Eric Novak. Wellesley, Mass.: A. K. Peters, 2008.

Luminet, Jean-Pierre, et al. "Dodecahedral space topology as an explanation for weak wide-angle temperature correlations in the cosmic microwave background." *Nature*. 425, 593-595, doi: 10.1038/nature01944, October 9, 2003

Masters, Karen. "What Would You See from Inside a Black Hole?" *Curious About Astronomy? Ask an Astronomer*. October 2002, http://curious.astro.cornell.edu/question.php?number=348.

McGahey, Robert. *The Orphic Moment: Shaman to Poet-Thinker in Plato, Nietzsche, and Mallarme*. Albany: State University of New York Press, 1994.

Montgomery, Colin, Wayne Orchiston, and Ian Whittingham. "Michell, LaPlace, and the Origin of the Black Hole Concept." *Journal of Astronomical History and Heritage* 12 (2): 90-96, 2009, http://adsabs.harvard.edu/abs/2009JAHH...12...90M.

Moody, Raymond. *Life After Life*. New York: Harper Collins Publishers, (1975) 2015.

NCSA (National Center for Supercomputing Applications). *Archive*. November 7, 1995, http://archive.ncsa.illinois.edu/Cyberia/ NumRel/EinsteinEquations.html#Spherical.

Newton, Isaac. In "Newton's Scholium on Time, Space, Place and Motion." *Stanford Encyclopedia of Philosophy*. August 22, 2011. http://plato.stanford.edu/entries/newton- stm/scholium.html.

Nietzsche, Friedrich. *The Birth of Tragedy Out of the Spirit of Music*. In *Basic Writings of Nietzsche*. Translated and edited with commentaries by Walter Kaufmann. New York: Random House, 1968.

————. *The Gay Science*. Translated by Walter Kaufmann. New York: Vintage Books, a division of Random House, 1974.

Osserman, Robert. *Poetry of the Universe: A Mathematical Exploration of the Cosmos*. New York: Anchor Books, 1996.

Pagels, Heinz. *The Cosmic Code*. New York: Bantam Books, 1982.

Papal Encyclicals Online. "The Proofs for the Existence of God in the Light of

Pascal, Blaise. *Penses*. Translated with an Introduction by A. J. Krailscheimer. London: Penguine Books, 1966.

Pauli, Wolfgang. "Exclusion Principle and Quantum Mechanics." Nobel Lecture, December 13, 1946, http://www.nobelprize.org/ nobel_prizes/physics/laureates/1945/pauli- lecture.pdf.

Peat, David F. *Synchronicity: The Bridge Between Matter and Mind*. New York: Bantam New Age Books, 1988.

Penrose, Roger. Introduction. In *Six Not-So-Easy Pieces: Einstein's Relativity, Symmetry, and Space-Time*, by Richard Feynman, ix-xvi. New York: Basic Books, 1997.

———. Foreword. In *What is Life?: The Physical Aspect of the Living Cell; With, Mind and Matter; & Autobiographical Sketches*. Cambridge: Cambridge University Press, 2012.

Persinger, Michael. "No More Secrets." Lecture given at Laurentian University in Ontario, Canada, on March 3, 2011, https://www.youtube.com/watch?v=9l6VPpDublg&t=2270s.

———. "On the Possibility of Directly Accessing Every Human Brain by Electromagnetic Induction of Fundamental Algorithms." *Perceptual and Motor Skills*, 80, 791-799. ISSN 0031-5125. June 1995, http://www.livingplanet.be/ persinger.pdf.

Pickover, Clifford A. *Black Holes: A Traveler's Guide*. New York: John Wiley & Sons, Inc., 1996.

Plato. "Laws." In *The Collected Dialogues of Plato, Including the Letters*. Edited by Edith Hamilton and Huntington Cairns. New Jersey: Princeton University Press, 1994.

———. "Phaedrus." In *The Collected Dialogues of Plato, Including the Letters*. Edited by Edith Hamilton and Huntington Cairns. New Jersey: Princeton University Press, 1994.

———. "Plato's Phaedo." Trans. R. Hackforth. Cambridge: Cambridge University Press, 1972.

———. *Plato, Republic: Translated with an Introduction and Notes by Robin Waterfield*. New York: Oxford University Press, 1993.

———. *The Republic of Plato: Translated, with Notes, an Interpretive Essay, and a new Introduction by Allan Bloom*. New York: Basic Books, 1991.

———. "Republic." In *The Collected Dialogues of Plato, Including the Letters*. Edited by Edith Hamilton and Huntington Cairns. New Jersey: Princeton University Press, 1994.

———. *The Republic*. Trans. H.D.P. Lee. London: Penguin Books, 2003.

———. "Timaeus." In *The Collected Dialogues of Plato, Including the Letters*. Edited by Edith Hamilton and Huntington Cairns. New Jersey: Princeton University Press, 1994.

"Platonic Truths." *The Economist*. London: The Economist Group Limited, October 9, 2003.

Pope Pius XII, "Modern Natural Science: Address of Pope Pius XII to the Pontifical Academy of Sciences, November 22, 1951." http://www.papalencyclicals.net/Pius12/P12EXIST.HTM. 2014.

"Proof that Albert Einstein's black holes do exist, claim scientists." *The Telegraph*, December 9, 2008. http://www.telegraph.co.uk/science/science-news/3690822/Proof-that-   Albert-Einsteins-black-holes-do-exist-claim-scientists.html.

Rand, Evangeline. *A Jasmine Journey: Carl Jung's travel to India and Ceylon 1937-1938 and Jung's Vision During Illness "Something New" Emerging from Orissa, 1944*. North Vancouver, B.C.: Living Infinity, Ltd., 2013.

Rucker, Rudy. *The Fourth Dimension: A Guided Tour of the Higher Universes*. Boston: Houghton Mifflin Company, 1984.

————. *Infinity and the Mind: The Science and Philosophy of the Infinite*. New Jersey: Princeton University Press, 2005.

Sanders, Robert. "Saul Perlmutter awarded 2011 Nobel Prize in Physics." *Berkeley News*. October 4, 2011. http://news.berkeley. edu/2011/10/04/saul-perlmutter-awarded-2011-nobel-prize-in-physics/

Schrödinger, Erwin. *What is Life?: The Physical Aspect of the Living Cell; With, Mind and Matter; & Autobiographical Sketches.* Cambridge: Cambridge University Press, 2012.

Schweig, Graham M. "The Intimate Deity." In *The Hare Krishna Movement*. Eds. Edwin F. Bryant and Maria L. Ekstrand. New York: Columbia University Press, 2004.

Sheldrake, Rupert. *Morphic Resonance: The Nature of Formative Causation*. Rochester, Vermont: Park Street Press, (1981) 2009.

Slater, Sara. "What Happens to Spacetime Inside a Black Hole?" *Curious About Astronomy? Ask an Astronomer.* January 2005, http://curious.astro.cornell.edu/question.php?number=652.

Smolin, Lee. In "Smolin vs. Susskind: The Anthropic Principle." *Edge*. August18, 2004, http://edge.org/3rd_culture/ smolin_susskind04/smolin_susskind.html.

Sri Isopanisad. The Bhaktivedanta Book Trust (BBT): The Pre-1978 Books by His Divine Grace A. C. Bhaktivedanta Swami Prabhupada. http://causelessmercy.com/?P=Iso.

Srimad-Bhagavatam. The Bhaktivedanta Book Trust (BBT): The Pre-1978 Books by His Divine Grace A. C. Bhaktivedanta Swami Prabhupada. http://causelessmercy.com/?P=SB1.

Stapp, Henry. *Report on the Gaudiya Vaishnava Vedanta Form of Vedic Ontology*. Berkley, California: The Bhaktivedanta Institute, 1994.

Stober, Dan. "Robert Osserman, noted Stanford mathematician, dies at 84." *Stanford News*. December 16, 2011, http://news.stanford.

edu/news/2011/december/robert-osserman-obit- 121611.html.

Susskind, Leonard. In "Arguing for Agnosticism?" *Closer to Truth*. Written by Robert Lawrence Kuhn. Directed by Peter Getzels. Season 6. Episode 10. PBS. March 3, 2011, https://www.youtube.com/watch?v=WL38FGjV-u8.

————. *The Black Hole War: My Battle with Stephen Hawking to Make the World Safe for Quantum Mechanics*. New York: Little, Brown and Company, 2008.

————. *The Cosmic Landscape: String Theory and the Illusion of Intelligent Design*. New York: Back Bay Books, 2006.

————. In "Is The Universe A Hologram?" *The Good Stuff*. PBS Digital Studios. August 4, 2015, https://www.youtube.com/watch?v=iNgIl-qIklU.

Swimme, Brian, and Joel Pitney. "Brian Swimme on Emptiness and the Quantum Vacuum." *EnlightenNext Magazine*. July 21, 2009, http://magazine.enlightennext.org/2009/07/21/brian-swimme-on-emptiness-and-the-quantum-vacuum/.

Tarnas, Richard. *Cosmos and Psyche: Intimations of a New World View*. New York: Penguin Group, 2006.

————. *The Passion of the Western Mind: Understanding the Ideas That Have Shaped our World View*. New York: Ballantine Book, 1991.

Tegmark, Max. In "Who's Afraid of a Big Black Hole?" *Horizon*. Directed by Stephen Cooter. Episode no. 834. BBC. November 3, 2009.

Van Lommel, Pim. *Consciousness Beyond Life: The Science of the Near-Death Experience*. New York: HarpersCollins Publishers, 2010.

Ware, Robert Bruce. *Hegel: The Logic of Self-Consciousness and the Legacy of Subjective Freedom*. Edinburgh, England: Edinburgh University Press, 1999.

Waterfield, Robin. *Oxford World's Classics, Plato, Republic: Translated with an Introduction and Notes by Robin Waterfield.* New York: Oxford University Press., 1993.

Weinberg, Steven. In "The Elegant Universe: Einstein's Dream." *Nova.* Hosted by Brian Greene, directed by Julia Cort and Joseph McMaster. PBS. October 28, 2003. Transcript: http://www.pbs.org/wgbh/nova/physics/elegant-universe.html#elegant-universe-einstein.

Whitehead, Alfred North. *Process and Reality, Corrected Edition.* Eds. David Ray Griffin and Donald W. Sherburne. New York: The Free Press, 1978.

Wilber, Ken, ed. *Quantum Questions: Mystical Writings of the World's Greatest Physicists.* Boston: Shambhala, 2001.

Wise, M. Norton, ed. *The Values of Precision.* New Jersey: Princeton University Press, 1995.

"WMAP." *Missions.* NASA Science. June 28, 2012, http://science.nasa.gov/missions/wmap/.

Wolf, Fred Alan. *The Dreaming Universe: A Mind-Expanding Journey into the Realm Where Psyche and Physics Meet.* New York: Simon & Schuster, 1994.

Yau, Shing-Tung and Steve Nadis. *The Shape of Inner Space: String Theory and the Geometry of the Universe's Hidden Dimensions.* New York: Basic Books, A Member of the Perseus Books Group, 2010.

Zeyl, Donald J. "Introduction." In *Plato's Timaeus.* Trans. Donald J. Zeyl. Indianapolis: Hacking Publishing Company, 2000.

ACKNOWLEDGMENTS

I would like to start by thanking my parents, James and Cecilia Desmond, without whose loving support this book would have been impossible. My special thanks also go to Sean Kelly, who chaired the dissertation committee overseeing the development of these ideas at the California Institute of Integral Studies (CIIS), along with Brian Swimme. Their enthusiastic encouragement gave me the faith I needed to invest the time and effort required to write this book. Thanks also to F. David Peat for agreeing to be the third member of my dissertation committee, and for supplying his first-hand knowledge of David Bohm. Acknowledgments also go to Richard Tarnas, who founded the Philosophy, Cosmology, and Consciousness (PCC) program at CIIS. His books, *The Passion of the Western Mind* and *Cosmos and Psyche*, led me to that program, which led to this book. I also want to thank Grant Maxwell, my editor and publisher, for recognizing something worthwhile in my ideas, and for motivating me to shape them into this book. I am also very grateful to the Honorable Thomas P. Grumbly for hiring me to work at the Supporters of Agricultural Research (SoAR) Foundation while I was writing *Psyche and Singularity*. My friends and co-workers there, Andrea Putman, Tim Fink, and A., also deserve my thanks. Thanks also to Pablo Carlos Budassi for allowing me to use his iconic picture for the cover of this book. Finally, I want to thank the physicists whose books and interviews I cite throughout the book, especially Leonard Susskind, Brian Greene, and Michio Kaku.

INDEX

Printed in Poland
by Amazon Fulfillment
Poland Sp. z o.o., Wrocław

31748346R00219